REFRAMING SOCIAL FOUNDATIONS
OF EDUCATION FOR A NEW ERA

REFRAMING SOCIAL FOUNDATIONS OF EDUCATION FOR A NEW ERA

AN ANTHOLOGY OF SELECTED WORKS FOR UNDERGRADUATE STUDENTS

FIRST EDITION

Edited by Sarah Militz-Frielink

Northern Illinois University

cognella®

SAN DIEGO

Bassim Hamadeh, CEO and Publisher
Angela Schultz, Senior Field Acquisitions Editor
Susana Christie, Senior Developmental Editor
Jeanine Rees, Production Editor
Emely Villavicencio, Senior Graphic Designer
Greg Isales, Licensing Coordinator
Stephanie Adams, Senior Marketing Program Manager
Natalie Piccotti, Director of Marketing
Kassie Graves, Senior Vice President, Editorial
Jamie Giganti, Director of Academic Publishing

cognella®
SAN DIEGO

CONTENTS

INTRODUCTION

It is with great joy that I introduce *Reframing Social Foundations of Education for a New Era: An Anthology for Undergraduate Students*, a collection of carefully chosen pieces that is designed to introduce students to this exciting and interdisciplinary field of inquiry. I feel that I can personally identify with the material in this text. In 2009, I graduated with my master's degree in Social Foundations of Education from Northern Illinois University (NIU) and have taught foundations of education classes to undergraduates ever since. A few years after I graduated, and much to the dismay of myself and many others, NIU unfortunately eliminated the Social Foundations of Education master's degree program—due to budget cuts and an apparent "neoliberal" need to slash humanities-based curricular traditions. At the time, I was working on my PhD at the University of Illinois at Chicago and immediately felt the sting and sadness of the program's disappearance. This volume, as a partial compensation for such misguided policy decisions, is intended to highlight the significance of the field for preparing teachers to teach in rapidly changing historical and social environments.

Overview of Social Foundations as a Field

Social Foundations of Education is an interdisciplinary field that draws upon history of education, philosophy of education, educational policy, sociology of education, and comparative education. Students who study the Social Foundations of Education are immersed in coursework rich in the humanities. The field of Social Foundations was founded in 1934 when George Counts published his informative volume titled *The Social Foundations of Education*. According to Counts, "teachers and school leaders need to study the Social Foundations of Education if they are to understand the consequences of their actions as educators, and to be able to make informed and ethical choices within their educational practice" (Tozer et al., 2011, p. 1). The ultimate aim of Social Foundations as a discipline is summarized best by the Council for Social Foundations in Education (1996): "The purpose of Foundations study is to bring these disciplinary resources to bear in developing interpretive, normative, and critical perspectives on education, both inside and outside of schools" (as cited in Petrovic et al., 2011, p. 71). These perspectives encourage students to examine cultural and social topics as well as educational dilemmas that impact curriculum, educational policy, and society.

Social Foundations as an official program initially appeared at Colombia Teachers College. During the 1920s, faculty at Teachers College in the Kilpatrick discussion group discussed the need for "a new approach to teacher education." In highlighting the interdisciplinary nature of Social Foundations, students fulfilled the foundations of education master's degree with eight credit hours of work completed in six separate departments at Teacher's College: History of Education, Philosophy of Education, Psychology, Educational Sociology, Educational Economics, and Comparative Education (Gottlieb, 1994). "In 1934 the first integrated course in social foundations, Education 200F was created and largely developed by Kilpatrick, Rugg, Childs, Cottrell and Counts, among others" (Gottlieb, 1994, pp. 3–4). "The founders of foundations of education at Columbia Teachers College were not as concerned with teacher education as an academic/professional field as they were with the conditions of society at large and their belief that teachers could affect those conditions" (Gottlieb, 1994, pp. 4–5).

As Greenberg (1965) observes:

> The content of study in social foundations of education endeavors to interpret the issues that are influencing and have influenced society. Critical inquiry is developed through analysis, interpretation, and evaluation which stresses the significant aspects of our open-society. Personal introspection becomes more and more necessary. The need for understanding the socio-cultural complexities with its impact upon the educational scene seems imperative in the training of our future teachers and administrators. (p. 283)

In October of 1934, the Social Foundations faculty and students at Teachers College launched a new educational journal, *The Social Frontier* (Provenzo, 2011, p. 1). "Largely under the intellectual leadership of George S., Counts and William Heard Kilpatrick, the journal represented a conscious act of educational criticism and social and political reconstruction" (Provenzo, 2011, p. 1). "Counts and his followers believed that education, the schools, and the teachers who worked in them could play a critical role in the process of social reconstruction that had to be undertaken in order to emerge from the Depression" (Provenzo, 2011, p. 1). Despite early enthusiasm for the journal, the journal, along with many other Social Foundations faculty, had to weather constant attacks from the larger anti-left and conservative movement in education.

The tension in teacher preparation programs between vocational education and humanities-based education in the curriculum has resulted in great debates over the priorities in course offerings. Scholars who favor the Social Foundations approach argue for the inclusion of humanities-rich curriculum that foundations of education programs offer, whereas other scholars, more focused on practical matters in education, emphasize the importance of teachers learning on the vocational track.

Reframing the Field for a New Era

Since the 1930s, the field of Social Foundations has evolved over the decades to reflect the needs of scholars and educators in the field. Two critical areas have emerged over the past four decades in response to fulfilling new needs that have developed in schools and society, which are crucial for educators interested in Social Foundations: ecological literacy and contemplative studies. This section will examine ecological literacy and contemplative studies and their new role in the field of Social Foundations of Education.

Teachers and administrators who study the Social Foundations of Education delve into often overlooked dimensions not only of education but of the human condition itself. The opportunity for personal reflection on the various dimensions of their practice, which is paramount to the discipline, helps educators generate fresh ideas and innovative methodologies. Personal reflection lends itself to types of spiritual practices such as engaging in contemplative studies—an umbrella of spiritual practices that reframe Social Foundations of Education as a discipline. The idea of spirituality—especially the nonreligious kind—in schools is not a new concept to the sphere of education (Dewey, 1929/1999; Hill, 1989; hooks, 1994; Lewis, 2000; Mayes, 2005; Palmer, 1983; Tisdell, 2006; White, 1996). For example, in 1993 the National Curriculum Council (NCC) published a document on spiritual and moral development that emphasizes the applicability of the word spiritual to all pupils within the domain of public education. Although this document originated in the United Kingdom, the thrust of the document legitimizes the nonreligious spiritual aims of education and applies to the reframed field of foundations of education:

> The term "spiritual" applies to all pupils. The potential for spiritual development is open to everyone and is not confined to the development of religious beliefs or conversion to a particular faith. To limit spiritual development in this way would be to exclude from its scope the majority of pupils in our schools who do not come from overtly religious backgrounds. The terms needs to be seen as applying to something fundamental in the human condition ... it has to do with the universal search for human identity ... with the search for meaning and purpose in life and for values by which to live by. (White, 1996, p. 34)

The search for human identity is a worthy endeavor for students studying Social Foundations of Education. One way to engage in this search for meaning and purpose in life is through contemplative practices, which have evolved over the years to "cultivate deeper awareness into the nature of the mind, facilitate empathy and compassion, support wisdom and the active realization of the inter-connectivity of life" (Eppert, 2013, p. 338). Eppert (2013) writes about how the historical, philosophical, social, and aesthetic contents and contexts of contemplative practice point to holistic ways of living, knowing, and being within the world. What do contemplative practices look like in the classroom? Eppert (2013) describes contemplative practices as varied as the soma arts, such as yoga or tai chi; visual arts; dance, music, rituals, and ceremonies; nonviolent activism; meditation; storytelling and other relational modes of dialogue; and deep listening (p. 338). For example, Ramdas Lamb (2013), who argues for the inclusion of yoga and transcendental meditation in higher education programs, states that "yoga could play a pivotal role. The system evolved as a means to gain control over one's physical, mental, and emotional being in order to develop an ego-transcending self-awareness, to realize a deeper meaning of life, and to experience true happiness" (p. 190). Lamb (2013) points out how yoga alleviates physical, mental, and emotional maladies: "Among those ailments that the practice of yoga helps include arthritis and stiff joints, chronic pain, digestive problems, fatigue, high blood pressure, headaches, and a weakened immune system" (p. 189).

Besides physical benefits, yoga delivers democratic aims for educators studying Social Foundations. According to Hyde (2012), "School yoga curriculum and instruction represent mindfulness pedagogies that are critical in the Freirean sense of involving *conscientization*—social consciousness raising starting with liberating the self from oppressive beliefs; and *praxis*—reflection and action upon the world in order to transform it" (p. 121). Both conscientization and praxis are critical for educators in the field of Social Foundations. Both represent education as a practice of freedom in the Freirean sense.

In addition, given the environmental catastrophes now unfolding throughout the world, there is a growing need for our curricular purposes to be transformed in a way to meet these challenges. For many in the field of Social Foundations of Education (Khan, 2004), the moral ideal of ecological literacy must emerge as a core part of an ongoing effort to transform educational purpose. David Orr (2004) outlines the environmental urgency we face in today's world:

> If today is a typical day on planet earth, we will lose 116 square miles of rain forest, or about an acre a second. We will lose another 72 miles to encroaching deserts, the results of human mismanagement and overpopulation. We will lose 40 to 250 species and no one knows whether that number is 40 or 250. Today the human population will increase by 250,000. And today

we will add 2,700 tons of chlorofluoro-carbons and 15 million tons of carbon dioxide to the atmosphere. Tonight, the earth will be a little hotter, its waters more acidic, and the fabric of life a little more threadbare. (p. 7)

The need for educators to promote the development of ecological literacy among the current and next generation of young Americans can no longer be plausibly denied. In recognizing these trends, Social Foundations as an interdisciplinary field has begun to integrate ecological literacy as part of its critical approach for addressing this pressing social problem.

Conclusion

The field of Social Foundations of Education has proven itself to be flexible enough to incorporate into its interdisciplinary breadth the emergent fields of ecological literacy and spirituality in education. This anthology is organized on the basis of several cutting-edge themes to reflect the reframing of Social Foundations for a new era. The text includes pieces that address important questions and initiate conversations about race and racism, gender and LGBTQ+ issues, spirituality in education, environmental justice, the history of the education of marginalized groups, as well as democratic theory. It is my hope that students who encounter the many authors contained in this volume will discover an abundance of fascinating educational conundrums and critical questions that are articulated from a wide range of disciplinary perspectives. To encounter these perspectives critically will go a long distance in exercising our moral and civic imaginations.

References

Dewey, J. (1929/1999). *Individualism old and new*. Prometheus Books.

Eppert, C. (2013). Awakening education: Toward a rich tapestry of mindful and contemplative engagement for social/environmental transformation. In J. Lin, R. L. Oxford, & E. J. Brantmeier (Eds.), *Re-envisioning higher education: Embodied pathways to wisdom and social transformation (pp. 337–352)*. Information Age Publishing.

Gottlieb, E. (1994). Foundations of education: Texts and the canon [Paper presentation]. AERA Annual Meeting New Orleans.

Greenberg, N. (1965). Social Foundations of Education. *Peabody Journal of Education*, *42*(5), 281–284. https://www.jstor.org/stable/1490982

Hill, B. (1989). "Spiritual development" in the Education Reform Act: A source of acrimony, apathy, or accord? *British Journal of Educational Studies*, *37*(2), 169–182.

hooks, b. (1994). *Teaching to transgress*. Routledge.

Hyde, A. (2012). The Yoga in Schools Movement: Using standards for educating the whole child and making space for teacher self-care. *Counterpoints*, 425, 109–126. https://www.jstor.org/stable/42981793

Kahn, R. (2010). *Critical Pedagogy, ecoliteracy, and planetary crisis: The ecopedagogy movement*. Peter Lang.

Lamb, R. (2013). Yoga and higher education: Adding concentration, clarity, and compassion to learning. In J. Lin, R. L. Oxford, & E. J. Brantmeier (Eds.), *Re-envisioning higher education: Embodied pathways to wisdom and social transformation (pp. 177–192)*. Information Age Publishing.

Lewis, J. (2000). Spiritual education as the cultivation of qualities of the heart and mind. *Oxford Review of Education, 26*(3), 266.

Mayes, C. (2005). *Jung and education.* Rowman & Littlefield Education.

Orr, D. W. (2004). *Earth in mind: On education, environment, and the human prospect.* Island Press.

Palmer, P. (1983). *To know as we are known: Education as a spiritual journey.* Harper.

Petrovic, J., Kuntz, A., & Kunz, A. (2011). (Re)placing foundations in education: Politics of survival in conservative times. *Counterpoints, 352,* 69–86. https://www.jstor.org/stable/42980809

Provenzo, E. F. (2011). *The social frontier: A critical reader.* Peter Lang.

Tisdell, E. J. (2006). Spirituality, cultural identity, and epistemology in culturally responsive teaching in higher education. *Multicultural Perspectives, 8*(3), 19–25.

Tozer, S., Gallegos, B., Henry, A., Bushnell Greiner, M., Groves Price, P. (Eds.). (2011). *Handbook of research in the social foundations of education.* Routledge. https://doi.org/10.4324/9780203874837

White, J. (1996). Education, spirituality and the whole child: A humanist perspective. In R. Best (Ed.), *Education, spirituality and the whole child* (pp. 30–42). Cassell.

UNIT 1. CURRENT ISSUES INVOLVING RACE AND RACISM

A Primer on Critical Race Theory (CRT)

Critical race theory, often referred to as CRT, views race as a social construct; characteristics like skin tone are assigned different meanings in particular social and historical contexts (Chapman et al., 2013). Omi and Winant (1994) interpret the concept of race from a sociohistorical perspective, which is given "expression by the specific social relations and historical context in which they are embedded" (p. 4). They argue that "racial meanings have varied tremendously over time and between different societies" (Omi & Winant, 1994, p. 4). They posit that "in the United States, the black/white color line has historically been rigidly defined and enforced. Any racial intermixture makes one 'nonwhite'" (Omi & Winant, 1994, pp. 4–5). According to Chapman and colleagues (2013):

In the United States, for example, any physical marker of African American ancestry is usually taken as sufficient to identify a person as "Black"—that same person could board a flight to Brazil and on disembarking, would find that he was viewed very differently by most Brazilians because the conventional race categories in that society are markedly different to the common-sense assumptions in North America. (p. 1019)

CRT is a relatively new approach for understanding and resisting inequalities in education. This approach has its "roots in centuries old diasporic experiences and struggles of people of color especially (but not exclusively) enslaved Africans and their descendants in the United States" (Chapman et al., 2013, p. 1019). CRT is based on five basic tenets. First, "racism and racial inequality are endemic to American society" (Delgado, 1995, as cited in Quaynor & Litner, 2014, p. 53). Second, "CRT challenges notions of neutrality, objectivity, and color blindness"

(Quaynor & Litner, 2014, p. 53). Third, "CRT is historically based" (Quaynor & Litner, 2014, p. 54). Fourth, "the experiential knowledge of people of color is both recognized and prized" (Quaynor & Litner, 2014, p. 53). Lastly, "CRT challenges the tenets of liberalism which often viewed racial equality as 'a long slow, but always upward pull'" (Crenshaw, 1988, as cited in Quaynor & Litner, 2014, p. 54).

The Origins of Critical Race Theory

CRT originated in the field of legal studies. The legal scholar Derrick Bell is generally credited for creating this theory in the 1970s and 1980s. CRT was based on the idea that gains made during the civil rights movement were being compromised. CRT began to take shape when "individual legal scholars and small groups of students met to conceive ways of challenging the dominant institutional and societal ideologies that perpetrated racial inequalities with the goal of dislodging racial discrimination" (Bell, 1995; Delgado, 1995; Matsuda et al., 1993, as cited in Quaynor & Litner, 2014, p. 54). One of the goals of the CRT movement was to increase the number of tenure track professors of color at Harvard University. Students organized protests calling for a course called "Race, Racism, and American Law." When the Harvard administration refused, students created an alternative course for which they invited guest lecturers to lead discussions on Derrick Bell's 1987 landmark book, *We are not saved: The elusive quest for racial justice* (Quaynor & Litner, 2014).

White Supremacy

Under the lens of CRT, white supremacy and its common meaning—individuals or small groups who commit the most obvious acts of racial hatred toward non-White people—is viewed differently in the sense that "White Supremacy lies in the operation of forces that saturate the everyday mundane actions and policies that shape the world in the interests of White people" (Chapman et al., 2013, p. 1021).

Racism

When White people think of the word racism, they think about conscious and deliberate individual acts of racial hatred; discrimination is viewed as abnormal in the educational setting. CRT views racism as an institutional facet of normal life that occurs widely through routine activities and procedures that are unquestioned by policymakers and people in power. For example, racism is present in curricular and policy decisions in a school: policies related to hiring practices that make it harder for minority teachers to teach advanced classes or have secure jobs; some curricular decisions exclude people of color from being present in history or social studies lessons. CRT is not only concerned with race, but also with the intersection of other categories of oppression such as gender, social class, and disability.

Critical Race Theory in Education

Although CRT came from the field of legal studies, the theory started appearing in educational literature in the mid-1980s. "Specifically, Gloria Ladson-Billings and William Tate introduced critical race theory of education, originating from an analysis of the failure of the implementation of *Brown v. Board of Education* to provide for educational equality" (Quaynor & Litner, 2014, p. 55). CRT has evolved over time and now appears in a plethora of educational domains, including mathematics, literacy, policy, qualitative educational research, curriculum inquiry, and teacher education.

Conclusion

CRT is a dynamic theory that parts ways with other racial theories placing White racism at the center of its work. Scholars who utilize CRT in their work are known for their activist work, because CRT values educational activism. Although CRT has faced criticism from both sides of the political spectrum, many new scholars and graduate students are building bodies of work using CRT.

References

Chapman, T. K., Dixson, A. D., Gillborn, D., & Ladson-Billings, G. (2013). Critical race theory. In B. J. Irby, G. H. Brown, R. Lara-Alecio, & S. Jackson (Eds.), *The handbook of educational theories* (pp. 1019–1026). Information Age Publishing.

Omi, M., & Winant, H. (1994). *Racial formation in the United States* (2nd ed.). Routledge.

Quaynor, L., & Litner, T. (2014). Critical race theory in education. In S. Totten & J. Pedersen (Eds.), *Educating about social issues in the 20th and 21st centuries, volume 4: Critical pedagogues and their pedagogical theories* (pp. 53–70). Information Age Publishing.

Reflections on the Racial Web of Discipline

Crystal T. Laura

"I'd rather be a bum than go back," my baby brother told me when I asked about what was happening at school. That was back in 2008. The U.S. economy was slipping deeper into a recessionary sinkhole, and a steady flow of reports surfaced about a fourteen-year-high unemployment rate, hiring freezes, layoffs, and cuts in wages and working hours. At a time when many people began staying in or going back to school, my brother seemed to be looking for a way out.

"As a teacher, a student of education policy and curriculum, and your big sister," I said to him, "I have got to keep it real with you." I told my brother that high school dropouts are far more likely than graduates to be unemployed and underemployed, to earn less when they get a job than those with a high school diploma, and to get caught up in the criminal justice system than those who complete high school.[1] "Research tells us," I went on, "that high school dropouts are overwhelmingly black and male—just like you—and disproportionately represented in our state and federal prisons."[2] My brother admitted that he had been flunking almost all of his classes, serving more and more time on school punishment, and getting in trouble with the law.

Within days, I practically moved back in with my parents to be near my brother in the midst of his daily life as it unfolded. Almost intuitively, I documented much of what occurred in

1. Erica R. Meiners, *Right to Be Hostile: Schools, Prisons, and the Making of Public Enemies* (New York: Routledge), 60.
2. Becky Petit and Bruce Western, "Mass Imprisonment and the Life Course: Race and Class Inequality in U.S. Incarceration," *American Sociological Review 69*, no. 2 (2004): 151–69.

and around my family home, as we shared meals and watched television together, gossiped and conversed, drove each other around town, and otherwise hung out. I catalogued the details of critical incidents, the settings in which they took place, the conversations that occurred within and about them, and my own interpretations of it all. I kept two journals—one to keep track of what I was seeing, what I understood my brother and others to be seeing, and what I deemed particularly important to reflect upon with the family; the other to chronicle this process. I certainly wanted him to stay, excel, and be emotionally and spiritually well in school. But I was also deeply invested in better understanding why leaving school made sense to him, what was going on with him in that moment, how he had come to that point, and where the places of conflict and change might have been.

The truth was that long before, and better than anyone else, my brother knew he would drop out of school—as soon as he could figure out what else someone his age might do with himself. He was a boy of five or six when he learned that he was "different"; at ten he was a "problem child"; at fifteen he was "disabled." To him, "dropout" seemed like a natural progression. It took several months of sustained attention and digging for me to figure this out. By then, he had discovered the Job Corps. He left home and high school in October 2008.

I think of my brother each time the subject of "bad kids" emerges in my teacher education courses. The last semester I taught a class on urban educational policy, that topic was a particular favorite among students; almost everyone wanted to know how to run a tight ship, stay sane, and keep safe with so many "troublemakers" and "class clowns" in contemporary public schools. Whenever I pushed people to unpack the beliefs embedded within this kind of teaching philosophy and everyday language, things always got ugly. Public schools were equated with city schools, city kids with cultural poverty and dysfunction. The stock stories commodified by the mainstream media—the news, Hollywood films, cable and network television, and the music industry—about pathological and dangerous youth poured. And the grapevine, with its salacious tales from the field, was tugged as proof positive that some children—mostly poor kids and kids of color—will inevitably fall through the cracks.

As lively as these discussions were, no one ever seemed to want to talk about the connections between how we think and talk about children and how we treat them in social and academic contexts. A hush usually fell over the class of twenty-five future teachers when I suggested that demonizing ideology and discourse enables a whole social web of discipline—a web of relationships, conditions, and social processes—that works on and through the youth who rub against our understanding of "good" students. Part of this silence was certainly rooted in the fact that challenging and unlearning what we assume we know is uncomfortable, and that finagling around contradictions and tensions is easier than diving into and grappling with them. But I found that profound ignorance also accounted for the group's resistance to a structural examination of the conversation around "bad kids." Herein lay the teachable moment, and I tended to lean on critical education research for support and perspective.

One of the most powerful metaphors in critical education literature is "the school to prison pipeline." The phrase conjures a vivid, unambiguous image, the meaning of which few would debate: poor and black and brown children being sucked into a vortex from mainstream educational environments and heaved onto a conveyor belt carrying them onto a one-way path toward privatized prisons, where the economic outcome of under-education and discipline is most evident.

Each year, Civic Enterprises reported in *The Silent Epidemic,* almost one-third of public school students and nearly one-half of youth of color do not graduate high school with their class.[3] The problem is particularly acute for African-Americans, who represent about 15 percent of those below the age eighteen but make up 14 percent of all school dropouts, 26 percent of all youths arrested, 46 percent of those detained in juvenile jails, and 58 percent of all juveniles sent to adult prisons.[4] The school to prison pipeline is not an ideological claim; the numbers speak for themselves.

Stacks of research reports convey the magnitude of the plight facing, in particular, black adolescent males in our public schools. At all levels of the K-12 trajectory—elementary, middle, and high school, black boys lag behind their peers academically. Pedro Noguera put it this way: on every indicator associated with progress and achievement—enrollment in gifted programs, advanced placement classes, and otherwise enriched courses—black males are vastly underrepresented. Conversely, in every category associated with failure and distress—discipline referrals, grade retention, and dropout rates—black males are overrepresented.[5] Black boys have the lowest graduation rates in most states; nearly half of all black adolescent males in the United States quit high school before earning a diploma.[6]

My teacher education students typically sat up a little straighter when I told them about my brother's schooling experiences. Eyebrows raised when I pointed to the published material about the ways in which contemporary educational policies and practices, such as school punishment and the application of special education categories, work together to move young people like him from schools to jails.

It surprised them to learn that in 1994, federal legislation mandated a one-year expulsion for any public school student in possession of a firearm on school grounds.[7] Shortly thereafter, the Safe School Act revised and broadened the law to prohibit any student from bringing a "dangerous weapon"—just about anything that looks harmful—to school. Predictably, the number of school expulsions exploded, and disproportionately affected black youth.

Zero Tolerance: Resisting the Drive for Punishment in Our Schools, a book that I assigned to the class, was written in response to this reality.[8] Contributing authors to the anthology examine the dangers of zero tolerance policies and explore alternatives; they tell stories from the ground floor of schools and classrooms; they examine the legal precedents that zero tolerance policies bring in; they look at how the media enables and promotes zero tolerance, and what it means for students with disabilities; they

3. Civic Enterprises, *"The Silent Epidemic: Perspectives of High School Dropouts."* Civic Enterprises, retrieved September 24, 2010, http://civicenterprises.net/pdfs/thesilentepidemic3-06.pdf.

4. Coalition for Juvenile Justice (2006), "African American Youth and the Juvenile Court System," retrieved September 25, 2010, hltp://juyjustice.org/factsheets.html.

5. Pedro A. Noguera, *The Trouble with Black Boys: And Other Reflections on Race, Equity, and the Future of Public Education* (San Francisco: Jossey-Bass, 2008), xvii.

6. Schott Foundation for Public Education, "Public Education and Black Male Students." 2004, retrieved September 24, 2010 from http://schottfoundation.org.

7. Advancement Project, Padres and Jovenes Unidos, Southwest Youth Collaborative, & Children & Family Justice Center of Northwestern University Law School, *Education on Lockdown: The Schoolhouse to Jailhouse Track,* retrieved September 24, 2010, http://advancementproject.org.

8. William Ayers, Bernardine Dohrn, and Rick Ayers, eds., *Zero tolerance: Resisting the Drive for Punishment in Schools,* (New York: The New Press, 2001).

deal with broad issues of race and racism in education, and the political economy that supports zero tolerance; and they provide the statistical landscape of the problem. In the closing chapter, Michelle Fine and Kersha Smith synthesize the research to assess the impact of zero tolerance policies, given their intended purposes and "unintended" consequences. They argue that zero tolerance policies are neither effective nor worth their salt, neither equitable nor educational: "They do not make schools safer; they produce perverse consequences for academics, school/community relations, and the development of citizens; they dramatically and disproportionately target youth of color; and they inhibit educational opportunities."[9]

In response to a flurry of books and reports by academics, organizers, and journalists that effectively show how zero tolerance punishes students by depriving them of an education, some school districts have scrapped these policies. In Chicago, where I live and work, zero tolerance policies in the district's schools were abolished in 2006 in favor of restorative justice approaches to harm and healing. Nevertheless, the number of suspensions has nearly doubled since then. Black boys in elementary school in my hometown are five times more likely to be suspended than white boys in the city's public school system.[10]

Black boys comprise 23 percent of the district's student population, but amount to 61 percent of those who are expelled. One in four black boys was suspended at least once in 2008. In suburban Cook County, where my brother went to school, the racial disparity is also apparent: black boys accounted for just 11 percent of students, but 35 percent of those suspended at least once, and 44 percent of those expelled. At mixed-race schools, where black male students comprise just 12 percent of enrollment, they make up 30 percent of those suspended and 54 percent of those expelled. The risk is great, even at all-black and predominantly black schools, where the overall rate of suspensions and expulsions is highest.

But the problem is much bigger than Chicago. Black youth, particularly males, are more likely than any other group in the United States to be punished in schools, typically through some form of exclusion. Black students are disciplined more frequently and more harshly than their peers for less serious and more subjective reasons, such as disrespect, disruption, excessive noise, threats, loitering, among others.[11] As unbelievable as the over-disciplining of black students may seem to well-intentioned adults, it is all too real for the youth who experience it. Young people are sharp and extraordinarily attentive to their own thinking and the thinking of others. They know intuitively what we have spent more than thirty years documenting; they are well aware of these disciplinary discrepancies.[12]

More than ten years ago, Ann Ferguson conducted a study of "Rosa Parks Elementary School" on the West Coast—where black boys made up one-quarter of the student body, but accounted for nearly half the number of students referred for discipline; where three-quarters of those suspended were boys, four-fifths of those were black; and where black males of ten and eleven were routinely described as "at-risk" of failing,

9. Michelle Fine and K. Smith, "Zero Tolerance: Reflections on a Failed Policy that Won't Die," in Ayers, et al., eds., *Zero tolerance: Resisting the Drive for Punishment in Schools,* 256–63.
10. "Reaching Black Boys" *Catalyst Chicago XX* no. 5 (2009).
11. Russell J. Skiba, "When Is Disproportionality Discrimination?: The Overrepresentation of Black Students in School Suspension," in Ayers, et al., eds., *Zero Tolerance,* 176–87.
12. Rosa Hernández. Sheets, "Urban Classroom Conflict: Student-Teacher Perception," *The Urban Review* 28, (1996):165–183, and Frances Vavrus and K. Cole, "'I Didn't Do Nothin': The Discursive Construction of School Suspension," *The Urban Review* 34 no. 2 (2002) 87–111.

"unsalvageable," or "bound for jail." She tried to understand how school labeling practices and the exercise of rules worked as part of a hidden curriculum to marginalize and isolate black boys in disciplinary spaces and brand them as criminally inclined. To explore these processes, Ferguson had to pay attention to everyday life at the school, observing all of the sites where she was given access and talking to kids and adults about their beliefs, relationships, and the common practices that give rise to a practice in which the children who are sent to disciplinary spaces in school systems across the United States are disproportionately black and male.

In *Bad Boys: Public Schools in the Making of Black Masculinity* Ferguson described what she found. Presuming that schooling is a system for sorting and ranking students to take a particular place in the existing social hierarchy, Ferguson perceived that the politics of "misbehavior" played out in the labeling of black students as substandard or deficient in the application of school rules. She learned that what counts as "proper" behavior was filtered through stereotypical representations, beliefs, and expectations that school adults held about their children. Black boys, in particular, were refracted through cultural images of black males as both dangerous and endangered, and their transgressions were framed as different from those of other children.

Black boys were doubly displaced. As black children, they were not seen as childlike, but adultified; their misdeeds were "made to take on a sinister, intentional, fully conscious tone that is stripped of any element of childish naivete."[13] As black males, they were denied the masculine dispensation that casts white males as "naturally naughty"; they were discerned as willfully bad.[14] Perhaps Ferguson's greatest insight was that the youth themselves were acutely "aware not only of the institution's ranking and labeling system, but of their own and other children's position within that system," a perceptivity that shaped some of the boys' processes of disengaging from school.[15]

The research is clear: those who are absent from school—physically or mentally—perform poorly, and they are at risk of dropping out. A 2001 report by the Coalition for Juvenile Justice, a national nonprofit organization representing state juvenile justice advisory groups, found that a student who is suspended just once is three times more likely to leave school without a diploma: "Suspension is a moderate to strong predictor of a student dropping out of school; more than 30% of sophomores who drop out have been suspended. Beyond dropping out, children shut out from the education system are more likely to engage in conduct detrimental to the safety of their families and communities."[16]

Excessive discipline is often a critical first step out of schools for select youth—black boys, in this case—who disproportionately find themselves in prison. Being designated as disabled nudges the other foot out of the schoolhouse door. We have known for decades that black kids, especially young black males, end up in subjective disability categories more often than other children. Critiques of the disproportional placement of black youth in special education began circulating, at least among academics, as early as the

---

13. Ann Arnett Ferguson, *Bad Boys: Public Schools in the Making of Black Masculinity* (Ann Arbor, University of Michigan Press, 2001), 83.

14. Ann Arnett Ferguson, *Bad Boys,* 80.

15. Ibid., 97.

16. Coalition for Juvenile Justice, (2006), 13.

1960s, when people began noticing that schools had devised new ways to subvert the Supreme Court's 1954 desegregation decree.[17]

The story of the overrepresentation of youth of color in special education is a familiar one, but the numbers are no less unsettling. Black children constitute about 17 percent of all students enrolled in school, but they account for 33 percent of those identified as cognitively disabled. Black students are nearly two times as likely to be labeled learning disabled as white students, almost two times as likely to be labeled emotionally disturbed, and three to four times as likely to be labeled mentally retarded. Among all disability categories, mental retardation is the most likely to be assigned to black youth, particularly black males.[18] And, contrary to the expected trend, black boys who attend school in wealthier communities are actually more likely to be labeled mentally retarded than those attending predominantly black, low-income schools.[19]

The implications for black youth of these three classifications in particular—Learning Disability (LD), Emotional Disturbance (ED), and Mental Retardation (MR)—are far reaching. Students labeled ED and MR have the lowest graduation rates and the highest dropout rates.[20] More than half of all black students with emotional and behavior problems leave school, and the majority of all students with emotional and behavior problems who do not finish high school are arrested within three to five years of quitting school.[21] Young people without a high school diploma are more likely to be unemployed and underemployed, to earn less when they get a job than those with a high school diploma, and to be incarcerated.[22]

The data is consistent and robust, and many smart people agree that disagreement about the interpretation and application of these "judgment" categories is part of the problem. "Neither 'rationality' nor 'science'" control the process by which a child is assessed for these disabilities and referred for special education." Beth Harry and Janette Klingner wrote in their book, *Why Are So Many Minority Students in Special Education?*[23] Rather, the authors noted six perspective-based factors that shaped the outcomes of conferences on eligibility and placement: (1) school personnel's impressions of the family, (2) a focus on intrinsic deficit rather than classroom environment, (3) teacher's informal diagnoses, (4) dilemmas of disability definitions and criteria, (5) psychologists' philosophical positions, and (6) pressure from high stakes testing to place a student in special education.[24]

17. L.M. Dunn, "Special Education for the Mildly Retarded-Is Much of It Justifiable?" *Exceptional Children* 35 no. 1 (1968): 5–22.

18. DJ. Losen and G. Orfield, eds., *Racial Inequity in Special Education* (Cambridge, MA: Harvard Education Press, 2002).

19. D.P. Oswald, M.J. Coutinho, and A.M. Best, "Community and School Predictor of Overrepresentation of Minority Children in Special Education," in Losen and Orfield, eds., *Racial inequity in Special Education,* 1–13.

20. U.S. Department of Education, 2002; T. Hehir, *New Directions in Special Education: Eliminating Ableism in Policy and Practice* (Boston: Harvard Educational Publishing Group, 2005).

21. J. McNally, "A Ghetto within a Ghetto: African-American Students Are Over-represented in Special Education Programs," *Rethinking Schools Online 17, no.* 3 (2003), retrieved September 24, 2010, http://rethinkingschools.org/archive/17_03/ghet173.shtml.

22. Becky Petit and Bruce *Western,* "Mass Imprisonment and the Life Course: Race and Class Inequality in U.S. Incarceration," *American Sociological* Review 69 (2004): 151–69.

23. B. Harry and J.K. Klingner, "Why Are So Many Minority Students in Special Education?" *Understanding Race and Disability in Schools* (New York: Teachers College Press, 2005), 103.

24. Ibid.

The meaning of each "judgment" category has been understood differently across states, applied inconsistently within schools and districts, and shifted through time. As the category of MR became overpopulated with black students in the early years after *Brown* v. *Board of Education,* the new label of LD gave well-resourced families of white children a different and purportedly less stigmatizing way to explain their children's difficulties, to gain access to special services, and to set apart their children's disabilities from those of their peers of color.[25] With increasing legal pressure during the 1970s and throughout the 1980s to minimize the number of youth of color diagnosed as mentally retarded, the same effects of racial bias that had once produced high rates of mental retardation among this group were expressed through an LD diagnosis.[26] This contextualizes Harry and Klingner's report that the number of students labeled MR between 1974 and 1998 declined from 1.58 percent to 1.37 percent, while ED increased from 1 percent to more than 5 percent, and LD increased from 1.21 percent to 6.02 percent.[27]

Certainly, some students do benefit from the resources and accommodations that a disability label provides, but research shows that many do not.[28] More specifically, it suggests that special education is often a dumping ground for youth of color, and that black boys are especially susceptible to being under-educated—labeled, shunned, and treated in ways that create and reinforce an inevitable cycle of failure.[29]

When my students were sufficiently inundated with the kinds of material discussed above, they urged me to help them sift through and make sense of it all. I broke it down like this: What I gather from some of the research on school discipline and special education is that these policies are panoptic systems of surveillance, exercises of power used continuously and purposely to monitor poor youth and youth of color.[30] Black boys in particular are unevenly punished and tracked into educational disability categories in their early years, practices that tend to reinforce the very problems they intend to correct. And although this is enough to make reasonable people want to holler, even more insidious is the internalization by those under surveillance of the experiences and labels assigned to them, when they believe that exclusion and isolation is acceptable, when they learn to condition themselves. Finally, black boys who have been sorted, contained, and then pushed out of schools become black men—men whose patterns of hardship are pronounced and deeply entrenched—men who comprise nearly 50 percent of the adult males in prison—men who have been well primed neither for college, career, nor full participation in our democracy, but instead for punitive institutionalization.

The weight of my day job hit me hard when I stood behind a glass partition in a Chicago jail and watched my baby brother approach from the other side. He was barely eighteen; lanky, big brown eyes swollen, bruised, and uncharacteristically dim. He cupped his hands around the grate covering a hole in the

25. B.A. Ferri and D.J. Connor, *Reading Resistance: Discourses of Exclusion in Desegregation and Inclusion Debates,* (New York: Peter Lang, 2006).
26. C. Ong-Dean, *Distinguishing Disability: Parents, Privilege, and Special Education,* (Chicago: University of Chicago Press, 2009).
27. Harry and Klingner, "Why Are So Many Minority Students in Special Education?", 4.
28. D. Fuchs and L.S. Fuchs, "What's *'Special' about Special Education?" Phi Delta Kappan* 76 (1995): 522–30; R.E. Slavin, "Students at Risk of School Failure: The Problem and Its Dimensions," in R.E. Slavin, N.L. Karweit, and N.A. Madden, eds., *Effective programs for students at risk* (Needham Heights, MA: Allyn & Bacon, 1989) 3–17.
29. Pedro Noguera, *The Trouble with Black Boys,* xxi.
30. Michel Foucault, *Discipline and Punish: The Birth of the Prison* (New York: Vintage Books, 1995).

divide between us. My mind raced—anger, fear, helplessness, and despair swirled in circuitous loops. My feet softened and as I pressed toward the glass. I listened intently to the sound of his self-chastisement, and I heard the synchronized chorus of our country's power structures—the media, the law, the economy, the public mind, and the field of education—egging him on.

***

A vigorous defense of public education is directly connected with the struggle for black community empowerment. Despite the many arguments now circulating in favor of privatization and "school choice' in many African-American neighborhoods, only a strong public schools system will produce real results for our children....

It makes absolutely no sense to divert billions of dollars away from struggling public institutions to finance privately owned corporations that consider education merely as a profit-making venture. The fight to preserve and enhance public education is inseparable from the struggle for black empowerment and black freedom.

—Manning Marable, "Public Education and Black Empowerment,"
Z Magazine, April 4, 2001

A Note on the Politics of Place and Public Pedagogy

Critical Race Theory, Schools, Community, and Social Justice

David Stovall

A comrade often reminds me to understand urban public education as "contested space." When I first heard this concept, I felt that I had an idea of what he was talking about, but I wasn't quite sure. After further conversation and reflection, I began to understand what he really meant. For him, the contested space of urban public education is the sum total of all parties vying for power and perceived control of schools or policies that impact said institutions. Expanding his description of education in a broader sense, the spaces that stand outside of the traditional school setting (community centers, board meetings, school design team collaboration, community organization, etc.) should also be included in this discussion.

All of the aforementioned spaces should be considered political—not political in terms of partisan politics but "political" meaning relating to power, influence, and function. Integrated throughout the spaces of students, parents, teachers, and administrators, this political landscape can determine the "status" of a school and its place on the ladder of political will. Additionally complicated by issues of race, class, gender, sexual orientation, and ability, this specific pecking order can determine the way schools receive monies needed for daily operations or additional resources for additional programming to address site-specific needs (e.g., specialized curriculum, support for non-traditional scheduling, community liaisons, etc.). In addition to understanding the people who make the school a reality, naming the various systems of power at play is critical for developing holistic praxis in addressing issues of justice in public education.

Noting the various levels of power in the political landscape of urban public schools, this chapter speaks to the struggles of a community-engaged researcher at one site amidst political struggles for power and control. In these spaces it becomes critically important for engaged researchers who work in schools and communities to utilize perspectives centered in a practice that has the issues and concerns of students, parents, and community members at its center. Such commitment to praxis (action and reflection on the world in order to change it) challenges us to maintain balance between theoretical understandings and practical certainties. Sometimes referenced as "making the philosophical practical," I share Tozer's (2003) challenges in that

> I am troubled...by my own uncertainty about the relationship between my educational activism and philosophy of education, and I am seeking a way to make that uncertainty constructive instead of paralyzing. (p. 9)

By recording and theorizing an instance where educational researchers have made the conscious decision to actively involve themselves in developing social justice initiatives in urban schools and community spaces, we are able to document the contradictions and synergy between theory and practice.

From a pedagogical perspective, community-engaged researchers find themselves in a Freirean moment. As liberatory practice, our work calls for us to balance the constraints placed on us by oppressive forces (in this case the bureaucracy of urban central school offices) and our educational philosophies of co-creating spaces for young people to critically analyze the world while working to change it. Such practice is "public" in the sense that it does not take place behind closed doors. Instead, it is "out in the open" to be challenged and critiqued. Where critical accounts exist in relation to the political economy of schooling (i.e., Apple, 1995; Freire, 2003; Lipman, 2004; Spring, 1980), site-specific examples provide researchers with additional tools with which to address such concerns. Continuing such work requires us to speak candidly about what we experience in educational research with communities amidst struggles for power.

For the purposes of this chapter, I refer to the work mentioned in the previous paragraph as the "politics of place," which captures many of the problems of urban education (e.g., lack of resources, irrelevant curriculum, schools existing in isolation to communities, etc.). In relation to education broadly speaking, the politics of place includes the site-specific effects of policies created by political entities that have the potential to negatively impact the work we do with young people, teachers, community members, and administrators inside and outside of traditional school spaces. For my purposes here, place refers to the spaces we occupy as educators (broadly speaking) with regard to larger political structures that impact communities and school systems. Recognition of the "places" in which we operate allows us to assess and navigate our situations, enabling us to work closer with those concerned with social justice in education. Borrowing from the discipline of critical geography, investigating the politics of place includes substantive analysis of the diverse and rapidly changing set of ideas and practices linked by a shared commitment to emancipatory politics (Johnson, Gregory, Pratt, & Watts, 2000). Expanding this definition, Gieryn (2000) states that place "is not just a setting or backdrop, but an agentic player in the game—a force with detectable and independent effects on social life" (p. 466). In later sections, such effects are analyzed through the convergence of housing and educational policy with relation to a community-based education project. Place is discussed beyond physical location to reveal the deep, interwoven connections between displacement and business models disguised as education plans. I also draw in my analysis upon Critical Race Theory

(CRT), which seeks to address these relationships through the blending of research and practice. Through these exercises I am attempting to make my pedagogy accessible and transparent in spaces external to the traditional school setting.

Narrative, Critical Race Theory, and the Politics of Place

As a theoretical construct, CRT reminds us of the centrality of narrative when investigating issues of power and privilege. As a method, CRT uses "storytelling" to analyze myths, presuppositions, and conventional wisdoms about race to construct a different reality—one that reveals oppression and how it works. Positioned as "counterstories," the purpose of such narratives is to "document the persistence of racism from those injured by its legacy" (Yosso, 2006, p. 10). Through these narratives we are able to locate the detectable effects of racism on social life, as people begin to locate themselves in larger historical understandings of the myths and assumptions that fuel popular discourses on race. As an interdisciplinary concept, CRT draws from a broad base of literature in the humanities, social sciences, legal theory, and education, which enables us to discuss the subtleties and overarching premises in the investigation of race. For the purpose of this chapter, I incorporate Solorzano's (1997) education-centered explanation of CRT and its aims as an analytical tool.

CRT consists of the basic insights, perspectives, methods, and pedagogies that seek to identify, analyze, and transform those structural and cultural aspects of education that maintain subordinate and dominant racial positions in and out of the classroom. CRT in education includes the following five elements that form the basic model: (a) the centrality of race and racism, and their intersectionality with other forms of subordination in education, (b) the challenge to dominant ideology around school failure, (c) the commitment to social justice in education, (d) the centrality of experiential knowledge, and (e) the transdisciplinary perspective (Solorzano, 1997, p. 3). Separating overt bigotry from the subtleties of institutional racism, CRT reminds us that the complexities of racism, no matter the form, are endemic to daily life in the United States (Delgado & Stefancic, 2001).

Coupled with the realities of class, the politics of race were highly visible in my brief tenure as a board member for the City as Classroom School (CAC), a project I will describe below. Through the following narratives and reflection, I will try to unpack the various layers of school creation within a politically contested moment in Chicago school reform. The story I tell speaks to a politics of place—it is a winding tale of political maneuvering, community inclusion, and educational justice. By providing specific details of my participation as a board member, my hope is to help readers understand the subtleties of the interplay between political, social, economic, and racial realities in a specific Chicago context. The subtle forms of the aforementioned realities are visible through the language and outcomes of the systems that governed our process on the board.

Locating "Social Justice"

The term "social justice" also deserves some attention. For the purposes of this account, social justice in urban education refers to the ability to create places where young people, families, community members, teachers, and administrators can critically analyze their experiences, conditions, and contexts while participating in a process to change oppressive conditions that may limit their ability to work in solidarity with each other. I propose this working definition to fend off critics who would malign "social justice" work as empty radical leftist rhetoric. If we are intentional in the language describing our work, it becomes easier to share our ideas and concepts with individuals and groups who are working to change the processes and conditions that shape urban schools. Discussed in detail throughout the account, intentionality becomes a key concept in my attempt at developing praxis.

The Site: City and Social Justice

Several scholars have described their work in communities as "activist scholarship," "engaged research," or "participatory action research" (PAR) (Cammarota & Fine, 2008; Ginwright, Cammarota, & Noguera, 2006). Although I align my work with many of these scholars, the concept "community-engaged researcher" best speaks to my attempt to integrate the day-to-day community work I do, with research to address the issues and concerns expressed by those communities in relationship to education. I try to streamline my work as professor at an urban public university with community initiatives aimed at securing useful, relevant, community-controlled schools.

This disposition has led me to do my work in a number of ways. Before I became involved with the City as Classroom School, I taught a high school social studies class in a city-wide program in Chicago called City as Classroom. This program sought to bring together a group of high school seniors from different high schools throughout the city to take courses in traditional and non-traditional educational settings, all of which collectively addressed issues pertaining to inequality, community, and social justice. Because I teach a college course on educational foundations from a critical perspective, I was contacted to create a unit for the program. For 10 weeks, 28 high school seniors from three Chicago high schools took my course on race and the media (Stovall, 2004). Teaching in a cohort of six other instructors, students attended classes on community organizing, language arts, law, and graphic design in addition to my class. Instead of traditional classroom settings, classes took place in spaces ranging from community centers to beauty salons. These spaces were believed to be just as valuable as traditional educational spaces in that they provided relevance to the students. The program's creator felt that taking classes in "real world" settings would allow students to grasp the broader concept of education as the process of making informed decisions. Additionally, if students were interested in the classes and the people who taught or worked in the places where they were held, there was also the potential to identify a career path. In the same vein, the interests of the students would be the site to develop academic rigor in the form of community presentations, academic reports, and a semester-end culminating project detailing each student's experience in the program.

After 3 years of operating the program, the director decided to use the format of the program to develop a high school with the same premise. The original concept for the high school was that it would operate from a central location, while the rest of the city would serve as the classroom, allowing students to process their experiences while engaging a curriculum centered in unpacking concepts of community and self-empowerment. Similar to the model used by Metropolitan Regional Career and Technical Center in Providence, Rhode Island, traditional classroom space would be reduced, with the majority of learning experiences taking place in spaces identified by young people as their places of interest (Levine, 2002). Supporting the work of the director, I was asked to serve on the advisory board of the City as Classroom High School (CAC), while agreeing to continue to teach an on-site social studies course during the spring semester.

In reference to the politics of place, the director of the initiative was able to connect her efforts to a larger political struggle of a community to address issues of equitable education. Community members expressed a desire to explore educational options to provide opportunities for young people in their neighborhood. Because many of the schools in the neighborhood were suffering from severe overcrowding and lack of resources, CAC sought to address these issues through a curriculum centered in self-empowerment and cultural relevance. The life of the school, albeit short (the school only lasted 3 months), is important to those who are intentional in making their pedagogy public. Operating in this contested space, the following account provides insight into the struggle to push for innovations despite the ripe contradictions of urban public education.

Board Formation: Naming the Intersections of Power and Privilege

Because the school was new, CAC board members were asked to perform numerous tasks. From cleaning the halls to developing fundraisers, each board member was expected to participate on committees constructed to advise the director on issues of curriculum development, community engagement, and budget. Because of the concept of the school and the numerous responsibilities involved, board members represented a broad spectrum of interests, and a broad spectrum of employment and social backgrounds. I sat on the board with parents, community organizers, neighborhood residents, lawyers, bankers, former school principals, high school teachers, university administrators, real estate developers, and other university faculty. The diversity of the board was originally conceptualized as a strength from which the development of the school could benefit, as each member could contribute various resources, knowledges, and talents. Instead, the background and experiences of board members created a chasm of sorts. My point is not to stereotype or malign those who share the "privileged" occupations of many of the board members. Rather, the particular instance discussed in this account requires a deconstruction of the dynamics of the board's decision-making process. Remaining accountable to issues of race, class, gender, sexual orientation, and ability, the nature of my position as university professor complicates matters, placing me in the "privileged" group to some degree.

Such contradictions are important to note as I have openly sided with members of the "unprivileged" group on the board, arguing against the influences of those who side with the mainstream establishment. The politics of place remain complex in that I am making the biased claim that I do not share the same vision of social justice as some board members. Doubly problematic to the situation, my occupation in name (university professor) would place me in the mainstream establishment, despite my personal involvement with educational justice efforts. As an African American male occupying the position of university professor, the contradictions on the surface required me to constantly revisit my position on the board. Where the university title holds privilege on paper, my lived reality as an African American male in an urban setting reveals glaring contradictions. Coupled with a disproportionate racial and class dynamic (most of the board members who held affluent occupations were White, while the majority of people of color were employed in middle- to working-class occupations), the complexities are important to note in unpacking the board's commitment to the school's vision.

Upon first sight, the formation of the board would appear problematic. A common question asked of the school's director was "if the school has a social justice agenda centered in the issues and concerns of low-income students, parents, and community members of color, why all the representation from the establishment on its board?" Although accepted as valid critique from people external to the board, the response (from some board members and the school's director) was that the board members were selected based on previous relationships, access to resources (leverage), and support of the CAC program before it became a school. Because we were all hand-selected as board members and were brought into the fold with a deadline looming, there was little effort placed in mapping out the possibilities of conflicting views of board members. Nevertheless, our rushed formation cannot be used as an excuse. Instead, my reflection notes this reality as key to making my practice transparent and "public." With regard to this public school that was granted flexibility in terms of structure and curriculum, many of the board members sided with policies that justified a substandard, status-quo education for students who would be attending the school. While the idea for the school was noble and progressive, many board members felt that an education for "these" students (read African American, Latino/a and poor) should focus on rudimentary issues to get students "up to speed." Coupled with insights from Critical Race Theory, the following example is a description of an instance that reveals the tug-of-war between social justice and mainstream views on education.

First Meeting: Convening the Board

The first board meeting was held at the home of two prominent business people in the city. Upon entering the home, I was quite surprised to notice the house had live-in housekeepers and an au pair. Noting its palatial size (five floors, three car garage, carriage house/servant quarters, half-acre front lawn), we were directed upstairs to the main dining hall to a table that sat approximately 35 people. Upon viewing the room, I hesitated to sit down due to the fact that I was extremely uncomfortable in this setting. Viewing African American and Latino/a "house servants" in 2004 was a disturbing experience and signaled an age where rights for these groups were even more limited than they are today. Despite my personal struggles with the environment, I saw a few familiar faces trickle into the meeting. As we engaged in small talk, we all stated how flabbergasted we were with the space and began to ask each other questions around how big the place *really* was.

The director of the proposed school was present, and she directed everyone to be seated so the program could begin. Again, I was startled with the idea of a "program" before an initial board meeting. Many times I feel as if these programs have an unnecessary performative element to them, assuring the "gracious benefactors" that the people of color they are about to support will not do them bodily harm. Despite my comparison to the glee clubs from Historically Black Colleges and Universities that performed Negro Spirituals for the pleasure of White benefactors in the 19th century, I reminded myself that I was here for something bigger and should be respectful of the space. Since I knew and worked with about a third of the people seated at the table, I decided to calm down and take on my role as active listener.

After everyone was seated, the director introduced one of the homeowners, thanking her for the use of her space. Following the introduction, an African American woman stood up and welcomed the group. At this moment, I thought *damn...this is a real CRT moment here: the politics of race and class are completely in overdrive. Here's a rich Black woman with servants, nannys, and a dining hall in her house!* Then, again to my surprise, her husband stood up and he was Black too! From this moment I felt as if I were locked into some type of terrible Oprah Winfrey nightmare that I would never be able to recover from. In my mind I thought, *shit... these are the moments that the purveyors of White supremacy live for...the perfect opportunity to tell Black folks to shut the hell up...this rich Black couple proves the point that the rest of y'all are making excuses!* The positionality of the homeowners was rife with contradictions. Even though I didn't know them and had no right to judge, I still had to contend with the space they occupied among their White peers, also seated at the dining table. They represented *the* success story—the idea that all the "poor, underprivileged" students we would serve at the school should aspire to. Absent from the discussion would be the fact that despite their positions, many African Americans and Latino/as continue to occupy spaces of subservience in comparison to the wealthy. This was the exception that can be positioned as the norm. Because I didn't want to kill the meeting before it begun, I made it my business to concentrate and make sense of the moment.

The program began with one of my comrades and his student. In addition to being a teacher, he's a poet whose works have been distributed locally and nationally. His student was also a singer with an amazing voice. He began with a poem about Chicago and the numerous contradictions within our city. I thought this to be a nice jab to the establishment who are often in the game of selling the city's positive attributes without grappling with the facts of what Chicago can mean to different groups. His student sang a song and recited a poem seconding the contradictions of love and hate for the city. Following the poem, the director had us introduce ourselves. During the introductions, I noticed that the majority of people did not affiliate themselves with K-12 institutions or community organizations. Instead, they were employees of established business or legal firms. In fact, while looking around the room, besides the owners of the home and the director, I was one of the few people of color seated at the table. As people began to introduce themselves as lawyers, bankers, and real estate developers, the most notable realization was that there were only two parents on the board and no students. Again, and similar to the boards of many well-resourced schools that serve students of color, a board that has very little stake in the community controls the majority of decision-making. Similar to the development of many Historically Black Colleges and Universities, the White and privileged are situated in positions of power, creating a system of indirect rule (Watkins, 2001). While the faces visible to the world are those of color (in this case the students), the "movers and shakers," despite their perceived good will, remain White.

Upon reflection, I understood (but didn't agree with) the director's position that these people could be important to the process. The positions they held could possibly allow the director to broker leverage with Chicago Public Schools (CPS). On the other hand, the operative word is *could*. Over the last 10 years, an approach by entities interested in establishing schools is to develop a board filled with people of "influence." Most times these "influential" people are from the business or legal community, and often have proximal relationships with central school offices. As a tactic, recruiting people from the business and legal community can demonstrate to central educational offices that the director of the institution is in line with current policies to "ramp up" historically underperforming schools by demonstrating their value to free market economies. Referenced as the new "neoliberal" tradition in urban education, this process can become critically dangerous to communities interested in community input in education (Arrastia, 2007, p. 2).

Returning to the meeting, the goals and objectives of the school were explained to the group. To my surprise, there were very few questions or objections. Instead, the group decided on a meeting time for the next meeting. I went home a bit conflicted, but because I knew the director well and trusted her work, at minimum I committed to attend the next board meeting.

Meeting #2

On a late summer evening, board members were gathered to discuss the school's structure and committee assignments. Because the board was large (it had 20-plus members), we were assembled in a space that served as an office and classroom. Compounding the situation, the community representative (soon to become chair of the executive committee) was a real estate developer in the neighborhood where the school is located. When a colleague noticed who the person was, he leaned over to me and asked "what's he doing here?" Because the developer was viewed in a negative light by many community members (due to his participation in the redevelopment/gentrification of a section of the neighborhood), my colleague was startled at his attendance at the meeting. Throughout the course of the meeting, it was revealed to the rest of the board that he was responsible for securing the school's newest location (the first school site was rejected by the school director due to scheduling conflicts). From informal conversations with other board members, it was also revealed that the developer was vilified in the community as a shrewd businessman with a penchant for making business decisions that were in opposition to the needs of community members. Many of his commercial developments were responsible for the rising property taxes in the neighborhood, which have prevented many residents from affording rent or making mortgage and property tax payments on their homes. Discussed at length later in the following section, the effects of gentrification on schooling are paramount in halting the ability of low-income families to remain in their communities and attend schools in gentrifying areas. Revisiting Gieryn's (2000) notion of place, the physical backdrop and setting are as critical as the idea of who will be deemed valuable or disposable in the larger context of the city. As the meeting reached its end, I still wanted to support the work of the director, but it was becoming increasingly difficult as contradictions in the process became increasingly apparent.

A Tale of Converging Policies: The Plan for Transformation and Renaissance 2010

It is important to note that my interactions with the board took place during a pivotal historical moment in Chicago. The politics of place are critical to this discussion in order to understand the context of public schools in Chicago and the current intersection of housing and education reforms that continue to negatively impact many African American and Latino/a poor and working-class communities throughout the city. These policies were central to the school's formation, as they heavily influenced the board's decision-making process.

Documented extensively by Lipman (2003, 2004, 2006), the current wave of "reform" in Chicago is deeply rooted in a neoliberal agenda, centered in making Chicago a global city, attracting business, retail, and other commercial entities. Central to this neoliberal agenda is the positioning of the free-market economy as supreme, rationalizing the idea that people who are able to access opportunities afforded by the market are deserving of its benefits. In the realm of education, neoliberalism as policy is masked in the rhetoric of "choice," "competition," "educational opportunities." As families supposedly "choose" their educational options, missing from the equation is the fact that many will not be able to select those opportunities because rising housing costs will prevent them from living within the city limits. "Choice" in this sense is a false one, because choice is only afforded to the few that are able to remain.

Of course, there is a deeper story here. Despite the positive spin portrayed in media outlets or official city documents, the mayor's attempt to frame Chicago as a global city has resulted in aligning the needs of the business community with his own to create a development plan. Missing from this "development" rhetoric is the critical analysis revealing the realities of forced displacement. Positioned as early as 1971 (and argued as coming to fruition in the summers of 2000 and 2004), Chicago has been involved in a housing redevelopment and school reform project, respectively known as the "Plan for Transformation" and Renaissance 2010. They are intimately connected with each other in that access to quality schools directly affects a family's choice of where to live.

As a result of converging policies, many educational initiatives operate in concert with redevelopment efforts to foster displacement among the city's working-class African American and Latino/a populations (Lipman, 2004). Since 2000, the Chicago Housing Authority (CHA), under its Plan for Transformation, has demolished over 50% of its public housing units. First calling for the demolition of all high-rise buildings (those over eight stories) by 2010, the plan has also supported the demolition of row house and medium-sized buildings. While many of the razed public housing complexes have been replaced with "mixed-income" developments, thousands of former CHA residents are unable to access the new construction. In order to live in the new mixed-income developments, residents have to meet a set of requirements. Most notably are the stipulations that require former CHA residents to work at least 30 hours per week, and have no history of drug abuse (Lipman, 2006). Additionally, and possibly most damning, no applicant to the new developments can have a felony conviction. On the surface, this would appear promising. But to the contrary, as we often know in issues concerning race and class, a counterstory exists.

To supplement the Plan for Transformation, the mayor, with Chicago Public Schools (CPS), in conjunction with the Civic Committee of The Commercial Club of Chicago (a conglomerate of the main business interests in Metropolitan Chicago), produced Renaissance 2010, an overarching policy proposing to close 70 existing underperforming schools and re-open them as 100 new schools under the rubric of charter, contract, or performance school. Beginning with the Civic Committee's 2003 report *Left Behind*, (Commercial Club of Chicago, 2003) school problems (e.g., high dropout rates, low test scores, low rates of literacy, etc.) are constructed to be directly related to a failing system. A section from the introduction reads as follows:

> The problem lies in the system, which lacks competitive pressures pushing it to achieve desired results. It responds more to politics and pressures from the school unions than to community or parental demands for quality. Schools, principals and teachers are largely insulated from accountability or responsibility for results...The constraints of the citywide teachers' union contract, including the tenure system and the difficulty of removing teachers for cause, make management of the system's human resources difficult. State achievement tests are not given in every grade every year, so it is impossible to see exactly where gains are made—or where students consistently fail to advance. Success is not rewarded; and failure is not—or infrequently—penalized. (Commercial Club of Chicago, 2003, p. 3)

The rhetoric of the previous excerpt is loaded for several reasons. "Accountability" and "responsibility" serve as coded proxies, marking test scores as the de facto marker of academic achievement. Neoliberal rhetoric of "constraints," "management," and "gains" speak to a desired emphasis on the primacy of market economies and the centrality of individual self-interest in all spheres of economic and social life (Lipman, 2004, p. 48). In short, Renaissance 2010 is not an education plan as much as it is a business strategy. Utilizing free market, neoliberal rhetoric, schools become the conduit through which to attract affluent families to the city.

Returning to the creation of CAC, the potential realities presented by Renaissance 2010 and the Plan for Transformation were critical to the creation of the school. While some members of the board thought it was a benign policy, others understood its deeper connotations and what it could potentially mean for the school's creation. CPS, in an attempt to aggressively roll out its policy through school closings and new school openings, offered CAC an opening as a Renaissance 2010 school. For those of us who viewed our efforts to be in solidarity with efforts around the city in revealing the "truths" of these policies, this invitation made the school's creation even more contentious.

Phone Conference and Final Decision

Because opening day was looming, CPS required the director to decide whether or not the school would be part of Renaissance 2010. Because she was an astute observer of the dissent of some board members, she called a meeting of the board to decide which direction to go. Where I was not able to physically attend the meeting due to travel, they agreed to link me into a conference call so I could relay my opinions about the recent CPS invitation.

The ensuing conversation was not civil. Some of the board members thought the meeting to be unnecessary as opening day was getting closer. Continuing their sentiment, some felt that we needed to understand the "imperfectness" of CPS and should just "go along" with whatever proposal was placed forward. In explaining the policy's under-explained rhetoric of choice, I shared the particulars of the reality of the policy and what it was doing to communities across the city. I felt this was of particular importance to the group because one of the proposed sites for the school was in a neighborhood that was experiencing significant gentrification. One of the board members who was key in spearheading the gentrification process took offense to my comments that connected gentrification to public education. In response, I reiterated that CAC should caution itself in agreeing to a policy that could further isolate students in other parts of the city. He continued that my comments were negative and unsupportive of the effort to create the school. In response, I reminded him that there were other options we should explore before hastily "jumping into bed with CPS," increasing our chances of further demise.

At the end of the conversation, the group decided to go with Renaissance 2010 because it was viewed as the only option. While I was upset with the decision, I knew there were other concerns as opening-day loomed near.

Conclusion: Honesty, Truth, and the Consequences of Public Pedagogy

As we prepared for opening day, it was clear that CPS never wanted the school to prosper. The director and teachers had to scramble to find necessities (chairs, tables, desks, school supplies, etc.) until the night before opening day. Additionally, the budget allocation formula for a school of this size (the freshman class had

60 students) did not allow the director to hire the recommended number of instructors for the program (her proposal requested 5 but she received 3). Some board members spent day and night calling neighboring schools and private donors to provide desks, tables, and chairs for the students. The lone two computers in the building were the director's own.

In the end, leverage and influence from members of the board allowed for the school's approval, but it did not go far enough to secure the essentials needed to ensure a quality educational institution. In the end, due to lack of resources (inability to hire instructors, minimal budget for supplies, no front office staff, no custodial staff) coupled with low-morale and frustration on all levels, the school was forced to close its doors 3 months after opening day. The director realized the constraints of CPS would not allow her vision of young people being able to interrogate their realities through academic and non-academic settings, and she called a meeting of her staff. Beginning with three instructors, the staff had been reduced to two, as one of the teachers left due to his displeasure with CPS's lack of support of the initiative. The staff decided that the school could not function in its current state, and made the collective decision to close the school's doors before the Christmas break. The last month of school was spent brokering transfers for students to neighboring public schools.

In reflection, it was a sad, but illuminating experience for those of us involved in the process. As I attempted to make my pedagogy public by participating in an educational model geared at centering itself in the needs of students, I was painfully reminded that our inability to effectively resist the barrage of converging education and urban development policies proved deadly to our process. The board process existed outside of traditional classroom spaces, and represented an attempt to support an alternative model to challenge traditional high stakes testing and irrelevant curriculum. Nevertheless, some of the former board members remain comrades and we continue to work with each other on educational projects inside and external to traditional educational outlets. This experience, although maddening at times, equipped us with the tools to strengthen our work as educators who are concerned with issues of social justice. The places we occupy continue to operate as contested spaces, but our ability to reflect, resist, plan, and persist will stand as testament to our support of education as the process by which we can change how we think, talk, and act.

References

Apple, M. (1995). *Education and power* (2nd ed.). New York: Routledge.

Arrastia, L. (2007). Capital's daisy chain: Exposing Chicago's corporate coalition. *Journal of Critical Education Policy Studies, 5*(1). Retrieved August 15, 2008, from www.jceps.com/?pageID=article&articleID=86

Cammarota, J., & Fine, M. (Eds.). (2008) *Revolutionizing education: Youth participatory action research in motion*. New York: Routledge.

Commercial Club of Chicago. (2003). *Left behind: Student achievement in Chicago's public schools*. Chicago: Civic Committee, The Commercial Club of Chicago. Retrieved August 15, 2008, from http://www.commercialclubchicago.org/civiccommittee/initiatives/education/left_behind.pdf

Delgado, R., & Stefancic, J. (2001). *Critical race theory: An introduction*. New York: New York University Press.

Freire, P. (2003). *Education for critical consciousness*. New York: Continuum Books.

Gieryn, T. E. (2000). A space for place in sociology. *Annual Review of Sociology, 26*(1), 463–496.

Ginwright, S., Cammarota. J., & Noguera P. (2006). *Beyond resistance: Youth activism and community change—New democratic possibilities for practice and policy for America's youth*. New York: Routledge.

Johnson, R. J., Gregory, D., Pratt, G., & Watts, M. (Eds.). (2000). *The dictionary of human geography*. Oxford, UK: Blackwell.

Levine, E. (2002). *One kid at a time: Big lessons from a small school*. New York: Teachers College Press.

Lipman, P. (2003). Chicago school policy: Regulating Black and Latino youth in the global city. *Race, Ethnicity, and Education, 6*(4), 331–355.

Lipman, P. (2004). *High stakes education: Inequality, globalization, and urban school reform*. New York: Routledge.

Lipman, P. (2006). Chicago school reform: Advancing the global city agenda. In J. P. Koval, L. Bennett, M. I. J. Bennett, F. Demissie, R. Garner, & K. Kim (Eds.), *The new Chicago: A social and cultural analysis* (pp. 248–258). Philadelphia: Temple University Press.

Solorzano D. (1997). Images and words that wound: Critical race theory, racial stereotyping, and teacher education. *Teacher Education Quarterly, 24*(3), 186–215.

Spring, J. (1980). *Educating the worker-citizen: The social, economic, and political foundations of educational reform.* New York: Longman.

Stovall, D. O. (2004). Take two on media and race. In F. Ibanez-Carrasco & E. Meiners (Eds.), *Public acts: Disruptive readings on making curriculum public* (pp. 117–134). New York: Routledge.

Tozer, S. (2003). Making the philosophical practical. In G. Noblit & B. Hutt-Echeverria (Eds.), *The future of education studies* (pp. 8–38). New York: Peter Lang.

Watkins, W. (2001). *The white architects of black education: Ideology and power in America, 1865–1954.* New York: Teachers College Press.

Yosso, T. (2006). *Critical race counterstories along the Chicana/Chicano educational pipeline.* New York: Routledge.

Narratives of Racism and Education

Richard A. Quantz

On May 1, 1992, Rodney King, a man whose beating by police after a routine traffic stop was captured on video and whose attackers were exonerated by a jury, sparking several nights of violence in the streets of Los Angeles, pleaded with the American people at a press conference, "I just want to say, you know, can we, can we all get along, can we, can we get along?"[1] King's plea tapped a desire that nearly all Americans have, and yet experience shows us that, as a nation and as a people, we have still not yet figured out how to "get along." There are an unlimited number of experts who are willing to tell us why we fail in this, but, in truth, there are a limited number of cultural narratives that these experts tap and formulate into their unique specific narrative. This chapter will begin by clarifying some language about racism and then will explore a few of the cultural narratives that Americans often draw upon when discussing educational issues. In this chapter, I focus on the issue of affirmative action in college admissions to provide a concrete example.

Exploring Some Terms

As defined in the last chapter, *race* is a term used to refer to a category of our language and our social institutions that purports to classify people based on physiological groupings. Hopefully this definition makes clear that when I talk about race, I am talking about something that exists in our language and in our society and culture, *not* in our biological constructions. In other

---

1. Rodney King, "Can We All Just Get Along?" YouTube video, May 1, 1992, at www.youtube.com/watch?v=1sONfxPCTU0.

words, as I use the term, race does not exist in biology. It is not a category of nature. However, race does exist; it exists in society.

Racism, Not Prejudice

I also wish to make a distinction between the terms *prejudice* and *racism*. These terms do not refer to the same thing. *Prejudice* refers to a belief or an attitude about a group of people based on an insufficient knowledge of the group. While we usually use the term as a negative attitude, people can also be prejudiced about a group of people in a positive way. Notice that, as an attitude or belief, prejudice exists *in the minds* of people. Prejudice is, then, a category of our minds, a psychological construct of individuals.

I will use the term *racism* to refer to any act or program that results in the creation or maintenance of inequality or domination of a people based on race. Notice that racism exists *in the world*; it does not exist in people's minds. It is an act that occurs in the social world, or it is a set of rules or codes that governs the way people act (i.e., a program). Racism is a sociological construct, located in the sociocultural aspects of societies.

This reading addresses the sociocultural parts of our society. It is not a psychology reading. For that reason, in this reading, I am interested in racism, not prejudice. It is not that I do not think prejudice is important. Rather, I think the way in which racism is realized in our sociocultural world is also important and is something that needs to be studied directly, not through the lens of a psychological construct such as prejudice. In other words, I will be discussing racism. Hopefully you will have the opportunity to consider prejudice from other texts.

Let me try to clarify this. If prejudice exists in individual minds and racism exists in actions and codes that govern actions, then we can create four theoretically possible categories of interaction between prejudice and racism (see Table 15.1) as outlined in four types: W can be prejudiced and engage in racist acts, X can be prejudiced and not engage in racist acts, Y can be unprejudiced and engage in racist acts, or Z can be unprejudiced and not engage in racist acts.

Table 1 Four Theoretically Possible Categories of Interaction Between Prejudice and Race

	Racist	Not Racist
Prejudiced	W	X
Unprejudiced	Y	Z

Most Americans equate prejudice with racism. The assumption is that if a person is prejudiced, then that person is racist and if a person is racist, then that person must be prejudiced. In this way, the discussion of racism is typically limited to Type W in the Table 1. In this reading, however, I am interested in both Type W and Type Y.

Type W: Prejudicial Racism

Prejudicial racism occurs when a person commits a racist act because of their prejudiced attitudes or beliefs. Just because a person is prejudiced does not mean that s/he has to act on those prejudices. In fact, it is nearly impossible for anyone to grow up in America without some prejudices. Consider again how we define prejudice as a belief or an attitude about a group of people based on an insufficient knowledge of the group. Do you have a belief or attitude of a group of people that you will acknowledge results from an insufficient knowledge of that group? How could you not? I certainly do. Don't we all? The problem for us here is not which one of us is prejudiced, but what the nature of those prejudices might be and, more importantly, do we act on our prejudices? Or, perhaps it is better to ask, *when* do we act on our prejudices? Because all of us have them and undoubtedly, at one time or another, act on our prejudices, what we really want to know is does that act caused by prejudice result in the creation or maintenance of inequality or domination of a people based on race and, if so, how pernicious is the racist act that results from that prejudice?

Given that racism requires action that creates or maintains inequality or domination, we need to know whether or not the action that we take because of our prejudice results in the creation or maintenance of inequality or domination based on race. If it does, then it moves beyond the psychological category of attitude and into the social world of action, and it is Type W racism. Prejudicial racism is pernicious. In its worst forms, it is more than ugly; it is destructive; it is murderous.

For example, on June 7, 1998, Lawrence Russell Brewer and two of his friends brutally beat James Byrd Jr., then chained his ankles and attached the chain to the back of their pickup truck and dragged him for three miles along a country road in East Texas. Byrd's crime? He was black, and the three white men took offense. Prejudicial racism must be addressed and stopped long before it gets to the point that resulted in James Byrd's death. Schools cannot tolerate such racism. But for all the damage done by prejudicial racism, I am more concerned about institutional racism because the incidents of prejudicial racism, even if frequent, are always located in the acts of individuals, whereas the effects of institutional racism are pervasive, continuous, and ultimately more damaging.

Type Y: Institutional Racism

Institutional racism occurs when a person acts in a manner that follows the rules or codes, either explicit or covert, that are institutionalized within the organizations and the structures of society when those codes lead to the creation or maintenance of inequality or domination of a people based on race. Because most Americans reduce racism to prejudice, they presume that if we could just get rid of prejudice, we would get rid of racism. But when racism refers to any act or program that results in the creation or maintenance of inequality or domination of a people based on race, then it should become clear that racism is being conducted on a daily basis by people who do not even realize they are engaged in racist acts. Racist acts are carried out by people who may not be acting on their prejudices at all, but may just be following the rules of their job. They may even be antiracists. They may even be members of the group that is the target of the racism.

For example, any teacher who taught American history in an American high school in 1993 and used any of the five best-selling textbooks would have taught that the history of America is the history of people of European descent in the Americas. At least one of those texts did have an introductory chapter on the pre-Columbian Americas. And one of the texts inserted alternative voices from different class and ethnic perspectives around several topics. But, overwhelmingly, the books explored not only the history of Americans of European descent as if their history is the history of the nation, but also told that history from the point of view of European-Americans. People of African, Asian, and Latin American descent and those descended from the First People of the Americas were not seen as integral to our history.[2] The effect of teaching a history that equates the history of the nation with the history of people descended from Europeans is necessarily to construct an inequality between Americans based on race. It is, therefore, by definition, a racist curriculum. Simply doing one's job as defined, simply following the textbook, simply teaching the curriculum, simply teaching to the AP test necessarily required the 1993 American history teacher to engage in racist action, to act as a racist. It makes no difference if the teacher had not been prejudiced against African Americans, Asian Americans, Latinos/as, and Indigenous Americans; in fact, it didn't even make a difference if the teacher had been an African American, an Asian American, a Latino/a, or a Native American, they were engaging in racist acts simply by teaching the curriculum.

The same is true of the teaching of language, literature, science, and even math. Just by doing their job, most teachers are required to engage in racist acts. That does not mean that they are prejudiced. That does not mean that they are bad people or immoral people. It means that they live in a nation whose institutions were constructed at a time in which the country was overtly racist. Is there anyone who would deny that in the middle of the nineteenth century when the American public school system began, and at the beginning of the twentieth century when it became bureaucratized and institutionalized, that this nation was overtly a racist nation? Of course we were. So why are we surprised to learn that the structures upon which these institutions were built were riddled with racist codes? Given that today's institutions carry forth those same basic structures, why are we surprised that racism has been institutionalized into the very practices of our organizational life? Why are we surprised to find that our schools have built right into them codes that create or maintain inequality or domination based on race?

When we emphasize prejudicial racism and minimize institutional racism, we may begin to mistakenly think that if we could only get people to stop being prejudiced, we would end racism. But when we realize that once racism is built into the rules and codes of our institutions, one need not be prejudiced to produce racism, then we realize the necessity for examining and uncovering those racist codes. To do so, of course, requires us to look at race in a conscious way. To figure out what it is and where it does and does not influence practices, results in the creation or maintenance of inequality or domination of a people based on race. In order to successfully focus on race, we must engage in racialization.

Racialization

Racialization has two different, but related, usages. One is *racialization*, defined as the sociocultural processes that create races. The other is *racialization*: the recognition that race is a relevant category in understanding a particular social event or condition. Many people equate this kind of racialization with racism, but if we think carefully about it, we will realize that the act of racialization (recognizing that race is relevant) can be racist, but the failure to racialize can also be racist. This kind of racialization is racist whenever the racialization

2. Michael Romanowski, "The Ethical Treatment of Japanese American Internment Camps: A Content Analysis of Secondary American History Textbooks," PhD diss., Miami University, Oxford, OH, 1993.

results in the creation or maintenance of inequality or domination of a people based on race. And the failure to racialize is racist whenever the refusal to recognize race as a relevant category results in the creation or maintenance of inequality or domination of a people based on race. In other words, in order to understand whether the act of racialization is or is not racist, we must decide whether or not the recognition of race as a relevant category maintains the inequalities of our legacy as a racist society or whether it works to transform that legacy. This idea will be developed further in a discussion of the narratives of racism that follows.

Privilege

Privilege is a term that we hear about more and more whenever someone addresses any of our social inequalities, such as race, gender, social class, sexuality, or ability. But the idea of privilege is often misunderstood both by those who wield the term as a sledgehammer against others as well as by those who deny its attribution to themselves.

For most people, privilege could be summed up by this quip from the commentator and columnist and then Texas commissioner of agriculture, Jim Hightower, who at the 1988 Democratic Convention said that the presumed Republican nominee for president, George H. W. Bush, had been "born on third base and thinks he hit a triple." To many Democrats, the line seemed to apply even more appropriately to his son, George W. Bush, and has become a common dismissal of those born of privilege. But while the quip might be good for a laugh, does it really help us understand privilege?

We all know that a large number of college students are privileged. For example, Su Jin Jez shows that in the United States, students from the top 10 percent income group are more than four times more likely to attend a four-year college than students from the bottom 10 percent. And I know that male students have heard that they benefit from gender privilege and that white students have heard that they benefit from white privilege. In fact, my experience is that most white students and male students have heard it so many times that they are tired of hearing about it—particularly when most of them do not feel that they enjoy any privilege whatsoever.

On the other hand, students from low-income groups and from racial and ethnic minority groups are likely to agree that a large number of their classmates are privileged. Many of them may think we have not talked about it enough. And finally, what of the realization that regardless of the class status of their family or their own race or gender or sexuality, any graduate of an American university possesses a kind of privilege when compared to the nearly 72 percent of Americans older than twenty-five without a college diploma?[3]

Let's get one thing straight from the start: to be privileged does *not* mean a person does not deserve their achievements. It does *not* mean that a person has not worked hard to accomplish what they have achieved. It does *not* mean that he is a bad, immoral, undeserving person. Take me as an example. I am a white, straight male from an upper-middle-class Protestant family who attended nothing but highly rated schools (private school through eighth grade, one of the "Top 10" public high schools in the country, and the University of Virginia). I have enjoyed enormous privilege throughout my life. Does that mean that I have not had to work to get where I am? Does it mean I can stop working now? Does it mean everything has been

---

3. "Bachelor's Degree or Higher, Percent of Persons Age 25+, 2008–2012," in *State and County Quick Facts* (Washington, DC: US Census Bureau, 2013), http://quickfacts.census.gov/qfd/states/00000.html.

handed to me? Absolutely not. But what it does mean is that my whole life I have been able to believe that *if* I were to work hard that the system would pay off for me and, therefore, I had a lot of incentive to work hard. Furthermore, it has given me extra chances (retakes, if you will—yes, believe it or not, I have had to take advantage of several "retakes" in my life). It means that I "know people." Or if I don't, my father did or my mother or my uncles or my friends' parents or my headmaster. And we all know how much it is "who you know, not what you know" that greases the chain of success.

People who live without the kind of privileges that I have had have often had to act on faith, on the hope that if they work hard enough the system will pay off for them. They also have to walk a straight and narrow path. Mistakes are not permitted—party too much one semester, get pregnant, get caught smoking weed one time, get sick and get behind in your coursework, and suddenly you find yourself in a ditch. Those without privilege may not be permitted back onto the path. Who do they know? Who is going to be able to work the school system to put the pressure on to get them into that honors class or to find the lawyer who can actually get their potential felony dropped to a misdemeanor? And even if they do everything right, who do they know who is going to find them that summer internship that will lead to the career that they are hoping for or get them that initial interview with that television station or bank or nonprofit that they hope to land?

Too many people (both those without much privilege as they lay that label on others as well as those who refuse to believe that the label is a legitimate description of their lives) think that privilege is like being born on third base and thinking you hit a triple. If I were to think that my privilege denigrated my own achievements, made me less moral, uncaring, or undeserving, well, I'd reject that label as well. But that is not what privilege gives most of us. Perhaps for some it does, but for most of us, privilege just opens doors; it doesn't wheel us across the threshold. It only throws the mattress under us when we fall; it doesn't keep us from falling. It only provides us a ladder to get back up; it doesn't climb it for us. No, those of us with class, race, gender, sexuality, able-bodied privileges still have to earn our own way. But, we have to admit, our path may not be quite the same path as those born without our privileges.

Another mistaken idea about privilege is that it is something we created for ourselves. This, of course, is the problem that Hightower's quip is zeroing in on. Too many of us with privilege actually do believe we did it all on our own, and anyone could do what we have done if they only had our talents and worked as hard as we did. But that misunderstands how privilege works. Here is the thing about privilege: those with privilege did not create their own privilege, nor can they give it away. I was born white in a nation that privileges whiteness. I was born in a nation that privileges males. I was born in a nation that privileges heterosexuality and middle-class values and Protestantism. I did not ask to be born into those categories. My privileges have been thrust upon me. They were given to me without my asking for them. And there is little I can do to give them away because they are not mine to give but belong to the others who place them upon me. I can pretend that I do not have those privileges, but at any time I can reclaim them and so, acting as if I am not privileged fools only me.

For those of us who have been anointed with these privileges, we are not to be blamed, nor are we to blame ourselves or feel guilty for what others have laid upon us. We are not to be held accountable for the fact that we have privileges. But, we can be held accountable, and we should be held accountable, for how we use the privileges that we have been granted. In whose interests do we use our privilege? Do we use these privileges to gain more privilege for ourselves and for those who already have plenty of privilege and the rewards of privilege, or do we use the privileges given to us to work with and for those with less privilege than we have? For those of us with race privilege, do we use our privilege to create or maintain inequality or domination of a people based on race? Or do we use our privilege to seek out, illuminate, and eradicate inequality or domination of a people based on race?

The truth is that every student at an American university has some privileges. Some have more than others, but every student has them. The students' task is to decide whether to deny their privilege, or whether to acknowledge it. And then, the students' task is to decide in whose interest they are going to use these privileges. Will they use their privilege to leverage more resources for themselves exclusively, or will they use it to work on behalf of the interests of other people? Luckily, for those who are in teacher education, speech and hearing, or social services, they have chosen a profession that will make it easy for them to use their privilege for others' benefits. But, they still must choose to do so. They still must decide to acknowledge their own privilege and to use it in others' interests. And if after coming to recognize their own privilege, they continue to deny it or continue to use their privilege for their own benefit alone, then others have a right to point out that they may not be living up to the moral obligations that come along with such social privileges.

Two Narratives About Affirmative Action

On March 6, 1961, when President John F. Kennedy issued Executive Order 10925 ordering all federal contractors to "not discriminate against any employee or applicant for employment because of race, creed, color, or national origin" and ordering contractors "to take *affirmative action* to ensure that applicants are employed, and that employees are treated during employment, without regard to their race, creed, color, or national origin," affirmative action was seen as an important mechanism for fighting racism.[4] But in 1996, when the voters of the state of California passed the California Civil Rights Initiative, known as Proposition 209, essentially ending affirmative action in the state of California; and in 1998, when the voters of the state of Washington passed the Washington State Initiative, known as Initiative 200, accomplishing much the same thing in Washington; and again in 2006, when the voters of Michigan passed the Michigan Civil Rights Initiative, known as Proposition 2, all but eliminating affirmative action in Michigan, affirmative action had come to be understood by many as a mechanism that did not fight racism but one that advanced a form of racism referred to as "reverse racism"—that is, racism against whites. How could this be? What changed between Kennedy's Executive Order and Proposition 2 in Michigan? And just as important, which is it? Is affirmative action racist or antiracist? Or is it both? Or, perhaps, neither? An examination of the cultural narratives that underpin this debate might help us answer those questions and bring clarity to an important educational issue that is typically blanketed in fog.

---

4. "Executive Order 10925: Establishing the President's Committee on Equal Employment Opportunity" (Washington, DC: US Equal Employment Opportunity Commission, March 6, 1961), www.eeoc.gov/eeoc/history/35th/thelaw/eo-10925.html (emphasis added).

The Affirmative Action as Antiracism Narrative

The cultural narrative that is Affirmative Action as Antiracism includes many different themes, ideas, heroes, tropes, and ideographs. Any one person's use of it in the telling of a specific narrative will almost certainly not include everything that I am going to lay out in this section, but they will draw on some of it, and they would probably find themselves in agreement with much of it. The basic plot of the cultural narrative Affirmative Action as Antiracism might be stated this way: In our nation's past, we practiced and enforced explicit racism, but following World War II, a movement began demanding the civil rights of all regardless of race, which required not only that everyone begin to be treated equally, but that positive steps be taken to overcome the legacy that our earlier history of racism had created. Although it is understood to be a temporary transitional practice, until our racist legacy has been countered and dissipated, affirmative action must be continued.

Let us admit it plainly and openly and without rancor or guilt: the United States of America was, at least partly, founded on racism, and that unfortunate legacy still affects our lives today. Think about it. Following the invasion of the Americas by the Europeans, the indigenous people were nearly eradicated. Some have estimated that the population was reduced by as much as 95 percent as a result of disease, war, and enslavement. We might argue about the percentage of decline, about the cause of the decline, about whether it is evidence of genocide or not, but we cannot deny that following the arrival on the American continents by the Europeans, the indigenous people were nearly eradicated.

As the Affirmative Action as Antiracism narrative describes it, the interactions between the Europeans and the native population quickly became hostile with war and mutually murderous attacks—each side against the other. But it is a mistake to see these mutual acts of war as "both sides were to blame" because one side was a group of invaders attempting to steal others' land, and the others were trying to protect themselves and their land from these thieves. And also, from the beginning, the native people were treated as racially inferior, which the Europeans used to justify their thievery of the land and their slaughter of women and children. It was used to justify the trading of blankets treated with small pox in order to kill a whole tribe through disease.[5] (Might this be seen as an early case of a weapon of mass destruction?) Such racism was used to justify the practice of signing a treaty and then breaking it when the European population grew large enough to want to expand. This practice of the use of violence to steal people's land, to massacre villages, to enslave, and to force the survivors onto reservations in the most hostile and unproductive land on the continent can only be explained by the belief that the indigenous people were somehow racially inferior to the Europeans and their descendants and, therefore, not deserving of the normal protections of a "white people."

Furthermore, according to the Affirmative Action as Antiracism narrative, after the practice of enslavement of indigenous people proved to be difficult because too many of them died or escaped, the new Europeans in America turned to enslaved people who had been kidnapped from Africa and shipped across the ocean to work for them without pay and without the right to quit or, in fact, any rights at all. While Europeans and North African people around the Mediterranean and along the Atlantic coast had a long history of kidnapping and enslaving captives after raiding villages, the slave trade to the Americas took a

---

5. Peter d'Errico, "Jeffrey Amherst and Smallpox Blankets," Peter d'Errico's Law Page, http://people.umass.edu/derrico/amherst/lord_jeff.html.

much more violent and pernicious form than the traditional form of slavery—if for no other reason than in the early forms of European and Middle Eastern and North African slavery, enslaved people had some rights and they were still considered human beings and not mere chattel. But once slavery became justified by race, rather than the spoils of war, it ended any thought that slaves were fully human with the claim to any rights at all.

In fact, while the so-called Indian problem died out by the end of the nineteenth century (due to the near extinction of the people) and the Civil War had put an end to overt slavery, American racism did not come to an end. The latter part of the nineteenth century and the first half of the twentieth century witnessed a combination of covert and overt forms of racism that today we often refer to under the umbrella Jim Crow. Legal segregation; legal discrimination in schooling and employment; law enforcement that protected the white while attacking the black, the indigenous, the Latino/a, and the Asian created a de facto inequality where some gained and others lost based on their so-called race.

According to the Affirmative Action as Antiracism narrative, it was only after World War II that the dominant European-descended people began to question the validity of such practices. Perhaps the change in mind of the American people of European descent was largely influenced by the horror of the Jewish Holocaust (especially when it became clear that the Germans' attempt to exterminate the Jews was justified by the American experience and practices of racism), or perhaps it was connected to the need of the United States to woo the people of Africa in the struggle against the Soviet Union in the Cold War.[6] Whatever the cause, the 1950s are often seen as the beginning of the American rejection of racism as a legitimate practice. By the 1960s, this movement had grown significantly strong to write into law that racism would no longer be tolerated and to demand the enforcement of those laws.

Most Americans, whichever narrative they use to describe affirmative action, will accept much of the narrative that was just told about America's racist history. They might argue about specifics, but the general story is agreed upon; the key differences come next. According to the Affirmative Action as Antiracism narrative, nearly 500 years of racism has left a legacy that cannot be undone by merely pretending everyone is white—which is what being "color blind" actually does. The racism has been built into our society and into our culture, where it languishes still, creating a very different life experience for people defined as white and everybody else. This racist legacy is built into what passes for our history and our language and our laws and our education. Its effects have created an unequal distribution of wealth and of rights that continues to affect everyone's lives. One does not have to go back to slavery to see evidence of this institutional racism.

For example, the Affirmative Action as Antiracism narrative reminds us that one of the important interventions of the federal government during the Great Depression of the 1930s was the creation of the Home Owners Loan Corporation (HOLC) to help financially stressed homeowners to refinance mortgages to escape foreclosure. In order to protect their own investment, the HOLC developed a formula for determining the "mortgage risk," which in turn was used by the banks to determine the requirements of the refinancing. An important part of determining the risk was whether or not the home was located in a segregated neighborhood or not. A completely segregated "native white" neighborhood (meaning no recent European immigrants such as Italians or Irish or Jews) received higher support than any mixed neighborhood, and a

6. Derrik Bell, "*Brown v. Board of Education* and the Interest-Convergence Dilemma," *Harvard Law Review* 93 (1980): 518–533.

completely segregated black neighborhood was rated as too risky for any refinancing. This practice, called *redlining* for the maps that were created to show the various risk of neighborhoods, which used red for the "too risky for investment" category, favored investment in the suburbs and helped create the segregation between the white suburb and black city.[7]

Following World War II, the federal government created the Servicemen's Readjustment Act, better known as the G. I. Bill, which attempted to help our nation adjust to a peacetime economy and to reward our soldiers by creating new opportunities for them. Everyone knows that the G. I. Bill made it possible for hundreds of thousands of soldiers, children of Southern and Eastern European immigrants and their Irish brethren, to attend college—something that had been nearly impossible for the largely working-class so-called ethnic whites to accomplish in large numbers before the war. Fewer, however, are aware that it also created a system that made it possible for these same people to purchase homes. One section of the G. I. Bill created a system whereby the federal government would guarantee loans from private banks to American veterans to purchase a home as long as the buyer and the home met certain criteria. Before this law, a prospective homebuyer had to put down as much as 60 percent of the cost of a home before a bank would loan them money for the purchase. Following the passage, banks could offer much better deals with lower down payments and lower interest rates. Using the new technology developed during the war for the civil engineering of barracks, roads, bridges, airbases, and other mass construction projects, the suburbs exploded. However, the regulations that made all of this possible did not treat all property the same. Using the same "risk assessment" practices as the HOLC maps of the 1930s, the federally guaranteed loans for veterans favored white neighborhoods, but by now children of European descent had been born in America and were, therefore, "native-born." They were now considered white enough to take advantage of the federally guaranteed mortgages and buy into the all-white suburban neighborhoods. On the other hand, the returning black servicemen and -women were restricted to buying in heavily black neighborhoods, which drove up the conditions and interest of their loans.

Understand that the practice of redlining made it all but impossible for blacks to even buy into an all-white neighborhood because even one black owner increased the so-called risk factor, reducing the worth of everyone's property in the neighborhood. Realtors refused to show such property to blacks since if it were sold, the reduction in worth of the other properties in the neighborhood would reduce their future commissions and even if they did show the property, the owners would not sell to a black family, since they did not want to hurt their friends and former neighbors financially. The practice of redlining combined with the G. I. Bill moved even more white families (now that the Irish and Southern and Eastern Europeans were considered white) out of the cities, and created even more segregation between the suburbs and the cities.

The practice of redlining was finally outlawed in the late 1960s, and by the middle 1970s the more blatant continuation of these practices was minimized. Today, informal and illegal redlining still occurs, and when caught, violators are punished, but (and this is key for understanding today's situation) the legacy of the practice of redlining still lives with us, not only in the segregation between heavily black inner-city neighborhoods, but with the discrepancy of family wealth based on race. Some scholars suggest that today's

7. For a short explanation of redlining and the HOLC, see Lloyd Wynn, "The Birth of Redlining: The Real History of the Homeowners Loan Corporation," *The Black Commentator* 273, April 17, 2008, www.blackcommentator.com/273/273_sm_birth_of_redlining.html.

discrepancy in wealth between white and black America (the median wealth of white Americans may be as much as twenty times greater than black Americans) results from the snowball effect that accrued to whites through their ability to acquire homes in the suburbs during this period while relegating blacks to being renters living in the inner city.[8] This, of course, continues to affect us as a result not only of the discrepancy of wealth, but of the quality of the schools that children living in the suburbs have when compared to the average student living in the inner city.

Those who tell the Affirmative Action as Antiracism narrative might point out that this reflects the present-day situation, in which many students of color find themselves living in pockets of high poverty and unemployment and low levels of nutrition and health care, which are the direct result of our nation's history of racism. Notice that no one today need be prejudiced. In fact, most of the players in the above narrative did not need to be prejudiced either. Once the HOLC created the racist maps[9] based on a "risk assessment," which racialized risk by assuming that risk was related to race, and once the G. I. Bill based their mortgage policies on these same maps, the actors did not themselves need to hold any racial prejudices at all. We can probably assume that many, perhaps even most, maybe even overwhelmingly most, were racially prejudiced, but *they did not need to be* in order to engage in racist acts. All they needed to do is to act to protect their own and their neighbors' economic well-being based on the rules built into the system. This is classic institutional racism.

And the racism that created the segregation between urban and suburban districts also created the favored suburbs with their higher real estate worth, which in turn resulted in white and wealthy schools educating mostly children who live in economic privilege. And it also created the non-white and less wealthy school districts that must struggle to educate a high number of children who live in poverty. Our nation's racist legacy has been built right into our present educational system. It does not require parents or legislatures to be prejudiced to maintain this racism. It only requires that they now ignore race, that they act "color-blind," and continue to work to make sure their own and their neighbors' and their constituents' children get the best education possible and let the parents and legislators in the neighboring districts do the same. The result is the maintenance of inequality based on race, creating white privilege for whites in the suburbs and victimization from racism for those students of color who live in the poorer urban districts with inadequate schools. Given the inequality that continues to appear in wealth, in influence, in status, and in the quality of schools, racism is institutionalized in the system as it is. According to those who tell it, the Affirmative Action as Antiracism narrative racializes the situation—that is, it recognizes that race still plays a role in the inequality of our housing and educational systems. The only way to overcome this heritage of racism is to take positive steps to counter racism's continued legacy and to continue, again in the words of

---

8. For a brief and clear explanation of the snowball effect in wealth accumulation, see "Interview with Dalton Conley, Background Readings for *Race: The Power of an Illusion*," PBS, www.pbs.org/race/000_About/002_04-background-03-03.htm. For a discussion of the wealth gap between whites, blacks, and Hispanics, see Rakesh Kochhar, Richard Fry, and Paul Taylor, "Wealth Gaps Rise to Record Highs between Whites, Blacks, Hispanics," *Pew Research: Social and Demographic Trends* (Washington, DC: Pew Research Center, 2011), www.pewsocialtrends.org/2011/07/26/wealth-gaps-rise-to-record-highs-between-whites-blacks-hispanics/.

9. Remember that "racism" only requires the creation or maintenance of inequality or domination of a people based on race.

President Kennedy, "to take *affirmative action*" to ensure that all children regardless of their race have the opportunity to take advantage of our public education system in order to achieve all they are capable of despite that legacy.

And this legacy, the Affirmative Action as Antiracism narrative tells us, is found in admissions policies at universities when those admissions policies forbid the consideration of factors of race. So-called objective measures, such as standardized test scores, have this racist legacy built right into them, not because the tests ask bad questions, but because the tests measure only a limited aspect of what it takes to succeed in the university. The SAT tests can only explain about 20–30 percent of success in the first, second, third, or fourth year of college.[10] Furthermore, these tests appear to overestimate the success of some groups (primarily white males and Asian Americans) and underestimate the success of other groups (such as women, non-whites, and non-Asians).[11] A 2011 report based on results in Ohio claims that two of the four subsections of the ACT exam have no predictive value at all, though the other two do show some ability to predict students' college success.[12] Given the latent institutionalized racism in the education and economic situation of students of color, there continues to be the necessity for some kind of consideration to be given to attract and retain students who themselves still suffer from the racism institutionalized into our system. Once again, those who tell this particular narrative want to make sure that we understand that it does not require any present-day descendant of Europeans to be racially prejudiced. It does not suggest that children of the white middle class are racists themselves, but it does suppose that privilege bestowed upon them due to their race and class position and the privilege resulting from the high quality of their schools has influenced their high test scores.

If, as a nation, we wish to correct the half a millennium of racism upon which the present society still rests, we who may not have done the wrong, but who have certainly benefited from privileges without any fault of our own nor any merit either, will have to take positive measures, affirmative action, to right a wrong we did not create but from which today we still benefit.

The Affirmative Action as Racism Narrative

The Affirmative Action as Racism narrative does not have much disagreement with the first part of the story just told. Perhaps it would tell our early history with less stress on the racist part, but it certainly

10. Jennifer L. Kobrin et al., "Validity of the SAT for Predicting First-Year College Grade Point Average," Research Report No. 2008-5 (New York: College Board, 2008); Krista D. Mattern and Brian F. Patterson, "Validity of the SAT for Predicting Second-Year Grades: 2006 SAT Validity Sample," Statistical Report No. 2011-1 (New York: College Board, 2011); Krista D. Mattern and Brian F. Patterson, "Validity of the SAT for Predicting Third-Year Grades: 2006 SAT Validity Sample," Statistical Report No. 2011-3 (New York: College Board, 2011); Krista D. Mattern and Brian F. Patterson, "Validity of the SAT for Predicting Fourth-Year Grades: 2006 SAT Validity Sample," Statistical Report No. 2011-7 (New York: College Board, 2011).

11. Leonard Ramist, Charles Lewis, and Laura McCamley-Jenkins, "Student Group Differences in Predicting College Grades: Sex, Language, and Ethnic Groups," Report No. 93-1 (New York: College Board, 1994).

12. Eric P. Bettinger, Brent J. Evans, and Devin G. Pope, *Improving College Performance and Retention the Easy Way: Unpacking the ACT Exam* (Washington, DC: National Bureau of Economic Research, 2011), http://faculty.chicagobooth.edu/devin.pope/research/pdf/Final%20AEJ%20Paper.pdf.

acknowledges that the early history of the United States was racist. It also acknowledges that while the Civil War ended slavery, Jim Crow laws and other such practices continued an overt and immoral racism for decades afterwards. Where the tellers of this narrative veer off is in the aftermath of the civil rights movement of the 1950s and 1960s. According to this cultural narrative, the civil rights movement rightfully argued that a person's race should have no place in their treatment. It should not matter if a person is white, black, Asian, Latino/a, or a member of an Indigenous Nation, only her/his abilities and accomplishments as an individual should be taken into account.

Those who ascribe to this narrative argue that the problem with the Affirmative Action as Antiracist narrative is that in America, a person should be treated as an individual and not as a member of a group. A person should not benefit from who their father might be, but neither should he or she be punished for what their grandfather or great-grandfather might have done. He or she should be treated only on their own individual merit. It is true, they suggest, that in the past America was racist, but following a series of court cases and legislative actions in the 1950s and 1960s, those practices, thankfully, they might add, are in our past.

And they should stay in our past. What was wrong with the past practice was that an African American or a Mexican American or a Chinese American was denied entry to the nation's best colleges and universities due to their race. But, they ask, isn't taking into consideration an individual's race in affirmative action doing exactly the same thing? Isn't one person's being favored and another's being disfavored because of their race wrong, whether it is to advantage the advantaged or to advantage the disadvantaged? Let a person stand before the admissions committee as an individual with his or her own record, and not have to carry the burden of their ancestors' deeds as well.

But what about the point made in the Affirmative Action as Antiracist narrative that without affirmative action, the present-day African American and Latino/a and Native American is burdened by the very same legacy of racism that the European American now benefits from? Isn't the rejection of affirmative action merely institutionalizing the racist past in the present inequalities? Isn't it kind of like a relay race where one team is required to carry a weight of a hundred pounds on each leg and then, on the last lap, this admittedly unfair practice is removed, so that for the rest of the race no one is required to carry any extra weight? True, the last leg may be equal, but by then the team whose early legs carried the extra weight are far behind. How could we ever expect them to catch up to make the race fair unless we act in some way to overcome the past wrong?

The Affirmative Action as Racism narrative counters by suggesting that the moment we begin to take into consideration factors that are beyond the control of the individual, it is wrong. True, in the relay-race metaphor, the advantaged team may be far ahead at the time the weight is removed, but there is no last lap in the relay of life. Given enough time, those whose early runners were disadvantaged will catch up if they are worthy. They may have to make up ground a little at a time, but now they have an incentive to do so. Simply bringing them up to the front or adding hundred-pound weights to the legs of those in the lead removes such incentives. Besides, this isn't a relay race. Every race is a race among individuals. No, they counter, the best remedy to past wrongs is simply to stop the wrong practice.

Besides, they add, whenever you substitute the thinking of government bureaucrats for that of ordinary people, you get wrong thinking. The best adjudicator of quality is the marketplace. Let competition and the market determine who gets admitted to colleges and universities. "Playing the race card," many add, is not the solution. The only way to overcome racism is to stop racializing. Anytime you racialize, you introduce racism, they argue. So, take race out of it. Remember, race does not exist. It is not real, so why keep practices such as affirmative action to maintain the illusion that it is real? We need a color-blind policy in which everyone is treated as raceless.

The Model Minority Narrative

In 1960, Asian and Pacific Islanders constituted only one-half percent of the American population.[13] Since the 1920s, immigration laws made it very difficult for Asians to immigrate to the United States. This was not by accident but by design. In the 1920s, racial prejudice against Asians created an immigration policy calculated to keep Asians out. By 1965, however, the United States was deeply involved in a war in Southeast Asia, and combined with the successful domestic civil rights movements, and perhaps attempting to overcome the shameful internment of Japanese Americans during World War II, a new law opened up immigration to Asians. The result is that in the years since, Asian Americans have become the fastest-growing minority group by percentage, having a rate of growth of between 43 percent (people who identify as only of Asian descent) and 60 percent (people who identify as of mixed descent, including some Asian) from 2000 to 2010.[14] But whereas the overall growth rate may be quite high, Asian Americans still constitute a small percentage of the overall American population. The 2010 US Census data for Asian Americans and Pacific Islanders show 5 percent.[15] During this time, "Asian" as a racial category has been renarrated from the pre-WWII myth of Asians as the "Yellow Peril" (a story that told of Asians flooding the Americas, stealing their jobs, and taking over America with an incomprehensible culture) to the "Model Minority," which has come to be as much a burden for many Asian Americans as a boon.

The Model Minority narrative suggests that Asian Americans have succeeded in America as a result of a strong work ethic and a commitment to education. It points to statistics of high test scores and high rates of college and graduate school enrollment. For example, nationally, close to 43 percent of Asian Americans graduate from college compared with 25 percent of white Americans. Such statistics are often used to support the idea that other minority groups need to do only as the Asians have done and develop good morals and a strong work ethic; then they too can succeed as the Asian Americans have done.

One of the primary problems with this narrative is that it essentializes the category of Asian American, erasing distinctions among the subpopulations as well as ignoring their history. As mentioned in the last chapter, the category "Asian American" includes a wide range of people who often do not see much in common with each other until they find themselves in the racialized American society. Consider that this

13. "Table 1: United States—Race and Hispanic Origin—1790 to 1990," *People and Households* (Washington, DC: US Census Bureau, 2002), www.census.gov/population/www/documentation/twps0056/tab01.pdf.

14. Padmananda Rama, "U.S. Census Show Asians Are Fastest Growing Racial Group," The Two-Way: Breaking News from NPR (Washington, DC: National Public Radio, 2012), www.npr.org/blogs/thetwo-way/2012/03/23/149244806/u-s-census-show-asians-are-fastest-growing-racial-group.

15. Karen R. Humes, Nicholas A. Jones, and Roberto R. Ramirez, "Table 2: Population by Hispanic or Latino Origin and Race for the United States: 2010" (Washington, DC: US Census Bureau, 2011), www.census.gov/prod/cen2010/briefs/c2010br-02.pdf.

category, according to the US Census, includes the following different ethnic and national identities: Asian Indian, Bangladeshi, Bhutanese, Burmese, Cambodian, Chinese, Filipino, Hmong, Indo-Chinese, Indonesian, Iwo Jiman, Japanese, Korean, Laotian, Malaysian, Maldivian, Nepalese, Okinawan, Pakistani, Singaporean, Sri Lankan, Taiwanese, Thai, and Vietnamese.[16] Do we really expect all of these communities to experience the world in the same way?

In fact, the high success rates in education are not uniformly spread throughout these populations. Though a high percentage of Asian Indians, Chinese, Japanese, Koreans, and Pakistanis have high test scores and educational attainment, other Asians do not perform as well. For example, Vietnamese have a graduation rate closer to white Americans (about 20 percent), while Laotians, Cambodians, and Hmong have a graduation rate closer to Latinos/as, of 10 percent.[17]

Besides the difference in ethnic/national identity, the Model Minority narrative ignores the history of immigration and the structures that the 1965 immigration law created. For example, the 1965 law favors immigrants from the Eastern Hemisphere, including Asia, who already have high educational attainment, while there is no such bias for immigrants from the Western hemisphere. This means that the overwhelming percentage of Asian immigrants come to this country having already attained a high education in their home country. As we all know, because the best predictor of success in school is the social class of the parents, and that is, in turn, partly determined by parent educational attainment, we should not be surprised that the children of these highly educated Asians themselves succeed in school. What distinguishes the Vietnamese, Laotians, and Hmong from other Asians who immigrated to this country is that as a group, they have a much higher percentage of immigrants with low education attainment in their home country before immigration because of the large number who immigrated during the Vietnam War as refugees.

But even within those groups that have a high success rate, such as the Chinese, individual success is largely determined by social class and educational attainment of the student's parents. For example, those Chinese who immigrate to the United States largely to work in restaurants are not highly educated and their children do not, as a group, succeed particularly well in American schools. Effects of social class also can be seen in Korean Americans, where those of lower income do not perform well in school either.[18] In other words, the Model Minority narrative is only supported when we use selective data that erase national and ethnic identities and ignore social class.

Finally, the myth of the model minority places a burden on many Asian American youth who do not identify with this narrative. They find themselves trying to live up to a narrative that is unrealistic; the narrative is, in fact, a lie. For too many Asian American youth, this discrepancy between their own sense of self and educational success leads to a high degree of stress and depression, which in turn leads to

16. Jessica S. Barnes and Claudette E. Bennett, "The Asian Population: 2000," Census Brief (Washington, DC: US Census Bureau, 2002), www.census.gov/prod/2002pubs/c2kbr01-16.pdf.

17. C. N. Le, "Socioeconomic Statistics & Demographics," *Asian-Nation: The Landscape of Asian America*, 2011, www.asian-nation.org/model-minority.shtml.

18. Jamie Lew, "Burden of Acting Neither White nor Black: Asian American Identities and Achievement in Urban Schools," *The Urban Review* 38, no. 5 (2006): 335–352.

high suicide rates.[19] While some Asian Americans benefit from this myth, others are punished by it, and other minority groups such as Latinos/as and African Americans are stigmatized by it. If the Model Minority narrative is a myth even for Asian Americans, then how can it serve as a beacon of hope for Latinos/as and African Americans? It is a false story, one that provides false evidence for the Rags to Riches and the Individualism (Stand on Your Own Two Feet) narratives. As a result, the Model Minority narrative can be considered an example of institutional racism. An individual need not be prejudiced against Asians to believe in the narrative. Simply by the use of selective data that seem to support a widely held, but false, narrative, people may act in ways that work to maintain the racial oppression that many members of minority racial groups experience.

Conclusion

In the above telling of the two narratives of affirmative action, we see the rhetorical strategies of two sides as they tell their stories. We see tropes and ideographs called upon in order to make their narrative more persuasive. Hopefully, as we listen to these two narratives, we are able to see other commonly accepted narratives embedded in them. This is especially true of the latter narrative (Affirmative Action as Racist), which is why it requires so much less explanation or evidence for so many people to accept it. Because it uses many other narratives that people already accept, there is little need to make the argument. Notice, for example, how the Affirmative Action as Racist narrative takes up versions of the cultural narratives that I present in Chapter 4. We see elements of the narratives we called Stand on Your Own Two Feet and Market Fundamentalism. We also see oblique appeals through ideographs and tropes to the Melting Pot, the Balkanization, and the Minority as Problem narratives. On the other hand, we also find, at least some easily recognized cultural narratives in the Affirmative Action as Antiracist narrative. For example, we find this narrative to be fully compatible with, perhaps even a variation of, the narrative we called Cultural Pluralism. But it also obliquely suggests the Minority as Victim and the Radical Promise of Democracy narratives, and perhaps even a kind of variation on the American Jeremiad narrative (although in this case our origins were not completely pure—along with much good, we embedded wrong, and now it is necessary for us to get back onto the track of pursuing good).

The Model Minority narrative also depends heavily on widely accepted cultural narratives, including Rags to Riches and Individualism. Though analysis of the full set of facts refutes the implicit argument of the Model Minority narrative, it is rhetorically supported by cultural narratives, which lead people to assume its truth. When a specific narrative is supported rhetorically by widely accepted cultural narratives, it is easier to convince people to accept it. How many of you reading this chapter right now are still convinced the Model Minority narrative is essentially true? To refute myths based on widely accepted cultural narratives requires much more work than to advance them, making it much more difficult for opponents of institutional racism to convince people of its reality.

---

19. Elizabeth Cohen, "Push to Achieve Tied to Suicide in Asian-American Women," CNN.com, 2007, www.cnn.com/2007/HEALTH/05/16/asian.suicides/.

Of course, the use of rhetoric to make your argument more persuasive does not mean that the argument is not a strong one. Good rhetoric is a wise strategy for strong or weak arguments. I am not suggesting that we should eliminate rhetorical strategies from our public discussions. Rather, we relate these narratives because they are frequently called upon by our policy-makers, our politicians, and our news commentators to try to persuade Americans toward certain interests, and when we can spot them and separate them out from the basic arguments, we are in a better position to understand the fundamental issues and more wisely support one or the other side. Our task as readers of their texts is to be able to see what they are doing so that we can make our decisions based on the strength of their argument, rather than merely the persuasiveness of their rhetoric.

We also present these narratives so that we can come to recognize our own biases built into the narrative that we accept as "commonsense." If you accept one of these narratives as the obvious truth, then you will be more easily persuaded by a text that appeals to that narrative, even if the text's argument is weak. When a text's creator throws a narrative that we already accept into our face, we may often be blind to the text's argument. We may find ourselves accepting and agreeing with a text that, in reality, works against our beliefs and against our commitments simply because we did not unpack the text's rhetoric to examine its argument. Of course, the opposite is true as well. When we listen to an argument that seems to challenge cultural narratives that we hold to be true, we demand more evidence from the speaker than we do from those who support our narratives. Knowing this, we should learn to be more reflective of our own positions and demand just as much evidence from those who support our narratives as we do from those who challenge them.

When it comes to racism in this country, no one should be surprised that the rules and codes of our institutions are embedded with racism, nor should he or she be surprised that many of our narratives are equally infused with racism. How could it be otherwise? How could many of our cultural narratives with their origins in the nineteenth and early twentieth centuries not have hidden within them racist elements? Even if we ourselves are not racist, even if we are antiracist, even if we identify as members of a minority race, just by accepting and using these narratives without having carefully examined them, we can act in the interest of racism and continue to act in ways that result in the creation or maintenance of inequality or domination of a people based on race.

This reading has examined at length a few cultural narratives, but there are plenty of other topics in education in which race and racism play parts. Consider the arguments around testing and the accountability system, around a common curriculum, around charter schools, around language instruction, around discipline, and around school funding, to name just a few. Each of these issues has proponents of one position or another whose texts appeal to cultural narratives with embedded racial narratives—some of these cultural narratives racialize in a way that works to maintain inequality or domination of racial minorities, while others racialize in a way to work against such domination and to transform our system of inequality. A smart, educated, and wise person will be able to recognize many of them. Pull the texts out and reconsider the value of the argument put forth in them. Hopefully, this section of the book will serve as a start in figuring out how to do this, but I acknowledge that it can only be a start. It requires all of us to reconsider our own beliefs to decide to what extent our beliefs have any real truth to them or are merely versions of a cultural narrative that we learned when we were young and now accept as true, as commonsense.

Critical Race Theory

Thandeka K. Chapman, Adrienne Dixson, David Gillborn, and Gloria Ladson-Billings

Thandeka K. Chapman, et al., "Critical Race Theory," *Handbook of Educational Theories*, ed. Beverly Irby, Genevieve H. Brown and Rafael Lara-Aiecio, pp. 1019–1026. Copyright © 2013 by Information Age Publishing. Reprinted with permission.

"Race" is a social construct; the characteristics that are usually taken to denote "racial" phenomena (especially physical markers such as skin tone) are assigned different meanings in particular historical and social contexts. Far from being a fixed and natural system of genetic difference, race is a system of socially constructed and enforced categories that are constantly recreated and modified through human interaction. In the United States, for example, any physical marker of African American ancestry is usually taken as sufficient to identify a person as "Black"—that same person, however, could board a flight to Brazil and, on disembarking, would find that he was viewed very differently by most Brazilians because the conventional race categories in that society are markedly different to the "common-sense" assumptions in North America. Despite its contested, changing, and ultimately deceitful character, however, race remains one of the most important characteristics in relation to how people experience education and the kinds of outcome that they are likely to achieve. Critical race theory (CRT) is a relatively new, fast growing, and radical perspective that places an understanding of race and racism at the very heart of its approach but also seeks to understand how racism intersects with other forms of oppression such as class, gender, and disability. In this chapter we outline the tenets of CRT in education and discuss recent developments as CRT scholars seek to establish the approach and offer support to colleagues within a hostile and discriminatory system. We begin by describing the origins of the approach, as a radical activist perspective that has had to fight for recognition from its very inception to the present day.

The Origins of Critical Race Theory

CRT is a relative newcomer as a discrete approach to understanding and opposing inequalities in education, but the approach has its roots in the centuries old diasporic experiences and struggles of people of color, especially (but not exclusively) enslaved Africans and their descendents in the United States. The perspective builds on this tradition in numerous ways, including the central role it devotes to political struggle, its concern for storytelling, and the significant position accorded to key Black intellectual figures of the nineteenth and twentieth centuries such as Frederick Douglass and W. E. B. Du Bois (Baszile, 2008; Mills, 2003).

As a self-consciously new and oppositional form of antioppressive theory, CRT began in the 1970s and 1980s in the work of legal scholars. Derrick Bell is frequently "credited as the originator and force behind the movement" (Lee, 1995, p. 390): not only through his ground-breaking scholarship on the law's role in protecting and legitimating race inequality (Bell, 1980a) but also through his personal campaigns and sacrifices as he challenged the raced and gendered status quo of the academy in general and his then employer, Harvard Law School, in particular (see Crenshaw, 2002; Ladson-Billings, 2011; Lee, 1995; Tate, 1997) "Having been the first black professor tenured by Harvard Law School," Bell wrote, "I became one of the few of any race to be fired" (as cited in Lee, 1995, p. 387).

CRT emerged as an alternative to dominant perspectives, not only the conservative mainstream but also the ostensibly radical tradition of *critical legal studies* (CLS) which, in the words of Cornel West (1995) deconstructed liberalism, yet seldom addressed the role of deep-seated racism in American life. Frustration with the silence on racism prompted CRT scholars to foreground race and to challenge not only the foci of existing analyses, but also the methods and forms of argumentation that were considered legitimate. Their attempts to position race/racism as a central feature were met with a visceral reaction, especially by "some of the White male heavies of CLS who portrayed the "race turn" as a threat to the movement's very existence" (Crenshaw, 2002, p. 1355).

In addition to Derrick Bell, the foundational critical race theorists in law include Kimberlé Crenshaw, Richard Delgado, Alan Freeman, Angela Harris, Charles Lawrence, Mari Matsuda, and Patricia Williams. These writers represent a range of racial/ethnic heritages (including people of African American, Latina/o, Asian American, and White backgrounds) but share a commitment to analyses and oppose the workings of race inequality in legal culture and, more generally, in U.S. society as a whole.

There is no single canonical statement of CRT; the perspective is built upon a series of key insights which are constantly refined through their application analytically and practically. In this sense, critical race theorists view social theory as a work in progress. But this does not mean that CRT is any less serious about the importance of theory—quite the contrary. From its first iteration as a new approach, critical race scholars have staked a claim to the conceptual importance of their work. Kimberlé Crenshaw, for example, describes how she and colleagues sought to find a form of words that could be used to describe (and provide a rallying point for) the new ideas they were developing as they began to organize what was to become the first ever CRT workshop (held at the University of Wisconsin, Madison in July 1989):

> Turning this question over, I began to scribble down words associated with our objectives, identities, and perspectives, drawing arrows and boxes around them to capture various aspects of who "we" were and what we were doing ... we settled on what seemed to be the most telling marker for this peculiar subject. We would signify the specific political and intellectual location of the project through "critical," the substantive focus through "race," and the desire to develop a coherent account of race and law through the term "theory." (Crenshaw, 2002, pp. 1360–1361)

This practical and strategic orientation reflects a perspective that Derrick Bell (1992) terms "racial realism," that is, a determination to continually interrogate the workings of race and racism in the real world rather than as hypotheticals in an abstract analytic context. The real world focus of CRT should not be seen as in any way lessening its claim to be taken seriously as a major innovation in social theory. From its inception CRT has encountered patronizing and dismissive responses from academics who find its focus on racism distasteful and/or threatening (Crenshaw, 2002); unfortunately this same response was encountered when CRT moved into education (Gillborn, 2009; Ladson-Billings, 2011).

CRT quickly began to move beyond law schools and was introduced into educational studies in the mid-1990s by Gloria Ladson-Billings and William Tate IV (1995). Subsequently the approach has been adopted by numerous scholars, especially people of color working with qualitative methods, most notably Thandeka Chapman, Adrienne Dixon, Marvin Lynn, Laurence Parker, Celia Rousseau, Daniel Solórzano, David Stovall, Edward Taylor, and Tara Yosso. CRT is also building an international presence, and has begun to grow especially quickly in the United Kingdom (Gill-born, 2005, 2008; Hylton, 2008; Preston, 2007).

Tenets of Critical Race Theory

There is no single dogmatic statement of CRT but the approach is broadly characterized by a focus on the central importance of White racism and the need for active struggle towards greater equity:

> Although Critical Race scholarship differs in object, argument, accent, and emphasis, it is nevertheless unified by two common interests. The first is to understand how a regime of white supremacy and its subordination of people of color have been created and maintained.... The second is a desire not merely to understand the vexed bond between law and racial power but to change it. (Crenshaw, Gotando, Peller, & Thomas, 1995, p. xiii)

White Supremacy

In CRT the phrase "White supremacy" is used very differently to its common meaning—the term usually refers to individuals and groups who engage in the crudest, most obvious acts of race hatred. But for critical race theorists the more important, hidden, and pervasive form of White supremacy lies in the operation of forces that saturate the everyday mundane actions and policies that shape the world in the interests of White people:

> a political, economic, and cultural system in which whites overwhelmingly control power and material resources, conscious and unconscious ideas of white superiority and entitlement are widespread, and relations of white dominance and non-white subordination are daily reenacted across a broad array of institutions and social settings. (Ansley, 1997, p. 592)

White supremacy, understood in this way, is as central to CRT as the notion of capitalism is to Marxist theory and patriarchy to feminism (Mills, 2003; Stovall, 2006). This perspective on the nature and extent of contemporary racism is one of the key defining elements of critical race theory. CRT views racism as more than just the most obvious and crude acts of race hatred; it focuses on the subtle and hidden processes which have the effect of discriminating, regardless of their stated intent:

> CRT begins with a number of basic insights. One is that racism is normal, not aberrant, in American society. Because racism is an ingrained feature of our landscape, it looks ordinary and natural to persons in the culture. (Delgado & Stefancic, 2000, p. xvi)

Racism

When White people hear the word racism, they tend to imagine acts of conscious and deliberate race-hatred—discrimination is assumed to be an abnormal and relatively unusual facet of the education system. In contrast, CRT suggests that racism operates much more widely, through the routine, mundane activities and assumptions that are unquestioned by most practitioners and policymakers: what Delgado and Stefancic (2000) call "business-as-usual forms of racism" (p. xvi). For example, racism is figured in the selection and training of teachers (where minoritized teachers tend to have less secure jobs and to teach less advanced classes); in the identification of ability in school (where both formal and informal forms of assessment encode the assumptions and experiences of White people, thereby disadvantaging minoritized students); and through the selection of curricula (that celebrate a false notion of society as color-blind, where anyone can succeed on the basis of their individual merit and where racist violence is presented as an historical aberration committed by bad men disconnected from wider structures and institutions of White racial domination): see Brown and Brown (2010); Gillborn (2008); Tate (1997). This is part of what is sometimes called CRT's *critique of liberalism*.

CRT portrays dominant legal claims of neutrality, objectivity, color blindness, and meritocracy as camouflages for the self-interest of powerful entities of society (Tate, 1997).

CRT is not critical of the *idea* of a meritocracy (a place where people rise according solely to their efforts and talents) but rather it attacks the *ideology* of meritocracy, that is, the false belief that such a state actually exists in places like the United States and the United Kingdom. In these systems, characterized by deep and recurring race inequity, the pretence of a meritocracy disguises the continued benefit that White people draw from racism and allows race inequities to be presented as just and necessary, as a mere reflection of the deficiencies of the people who suffer racism (Delgado & Stafancic, 2001).

In addition to a focus on racism, CRT is also distinguished by certain other themes. For example, there is a *call to context* which challenges researchers to pay close attention to the historical location of particular events and, in particular, to recognise *the experiential knowledge of people of color*. CRT does not assume that any group of people can simply read off one "true" view of reality but there is a belief that people who experience racism are uniquely positioned to understand certain elements of its operation and power (Tate, 1997). This belief finds powerful expression in the use of *storytelling*.

Richard Delgado (1989) is one of the leading advocates of the need to "name one's own reality." Inspired by the scholarship of Derrick Bell, and the centuries old traditions of storytelling in minoritized communities, Delgado has argued forcefully for the use of narrative and counterstorytelling as a means of presenting a different reading of the world; one that questions taken for granted assumptions and destabilizes the framework that currently sustains, and masks, racial injustice. Both Bell and Delgado have produced rich narratives that span numerous publications, where their invented characters explore and challenge the operation of racism in society.

One of the greatest contributions of CRT is its emphasis on narratives and counterstories told from the vantage point of the oppressed. In doing so, CRT exposes the contradictions inherent in the dominant storyline that, among other things, blames people of color for their own condition of inequality. Critical race theorists understand that narratives are not neutral, but rather political expressions of power relationships. (Zamudio, Russell, Rios, & Bridgeman, 2011).

This approach makes CRT an easy target for those who are willing to oversimplify and seize the opportunity to accuse the approach of merely inventing its data (see Taylor, Gillborn, & Ladson-Billings, 2009). Mainstream critics frequently misunderstand the nature of counterstorytelling and ignore the fact that most CRT "chronicles" are tightly footnoted so that detailed evidence is marshalled to back up each substantive part of the argument. CRT scholars are not making up stories—they are constructing narratives out of the historical, sociocultural and political realities of their lives and those of people of color (Ladson-Billings, 2006, p. xi).

Another distinctive CRT theme is its *revisionist critique of civil rights laws* as fundamentally limited as a means of addressing inequality. Detractors have sought to present CRT as disrespectful of civil rights campaigns and victories but this is a misrepresentation. CRT is not critical of the campaigns, nor the people who sacrificed so much to advance race equality (see Crenshaw et al., 1995). Rather, CRT exposes the limits to law and policymaking, and shows how even apparently radical changes are reclaimed and often turned back over time. A key element here is the concept of *interest convergence* (Bell, 1980b). Put simply, this view argues that advances in race equality come about only when White elites see the changes as in their own interest. Derrick Bell (2004), the leading African American legal scholar, coined the idea of interest convergence and has summarized the notion like this: Justice for blacks versus racism = racism. Racism versus obvious perceptions of White self-interest = justice for Blacks (p. 59)

It is important to note that interest convergence does not envisage a rational negotiation, between minoritized groups and White power holders, where change is achieved through the mere force of reason and logic. Rather, history suggests that advances in racial justice must be won, through protest and mobilization, so that taking action against racism becomes the lesser of two evils for White interests.

Bell (2004) argued that a study of the civil rights movement reveals that time and again the "perceived self-interest by whites rather than the racial injustices suffered by blacks has been the major motivation in racial-remediation policies" (p. 59). For example, the moves to outlaw segregation in the 1960s are usually presented as a sign of growing enlightenment, but they have to be understood within the context of the "cold war" and the fact that the United States was having difficulty recruiting friendly African states when Soviet interests could point to the forms of apartheid that operated in the Southern United States. As W. E. B. Du Bois noted of the famous *Brown vs Board of Education* desegregation case: "No such decision would have been possible without the world pressure of communism" which made it "simply impossible for the United States to continue to lead a 'Free World' with race segregation kept legal over a third of its territory" (as cited in Bell, 2004, p. 67). The obvious signs of segregation have gone—such as separate toilets and lunch counters—but the reality continues in economic, residential, and educational terms.

Similarly, in the United Kingdom, the racist murder of Stephen Lawrence (a Black teenager stabbed by a White gang as he waited for a London bus) is widely hailed as a landmark case that changed race relations forever. An official inquiry into the police's failure to prosecute Stephen's killers revealed gross incompetence, disregard and deep-rooted racism. Much of the inquiry was held in public and the nightly coverage in the news media meant that the catalogue of police errors and racism was broadcast nationally, initially to a sceptical public but eventually to a growing sense of outrage. When the inquiry report was published, in 1999, the revelations about the police's arrogance, incompetence and racism were such that inaction by policymakers was inconceivable (Macpherson, 1999). The Prime Minister, Tony Blair, promised changes in the law and said that the report signaled "a new era in race relations ... a new more tolerant and more inclusive Britain" ("Prime Minister's Questions," 1999, column 380–381). Radical changes were made to race relations legislation; more than 45,000 public bodies faced a new legal duty to pro-actively ensure race equality. All state-funded schools had to design a race equality policy, monitor achievements for signs of bias, and publicly plan to eradicate any signs of race inequity. On paper these are some of the most far reaching equality duties anywhere on Earth but in practice they have been largely ineffective because most schools have ignored their duties while the national education department has paid lip-service to race equality but continued to press ahead with key reforms (such as expanding the use of hierarchical teaching groups and promoting a national "gifted and talented" scheme) that have *increased* the institutional barriers to success facing most Black students in school (Gillborn, 2005, 2008; Gillborn & Youdell, 2000; Tomlinson, 2008).

The Stephen Lawrence case in the United Kingdom, like the *Brown* decision in the United States, exemplifies the way in which apparently radical civil rights breakthroughs have uncertain consequences in practice. Delgado and Stefancic (2001) argue that such events can be seen as *contradiction closing cases* which heal the gulf between the reality of racism in practice and the public rhetoric of equal opportunities and social justice: "after the celebration dies down, the great victory is quietly cut back by narrow interpretation, administrative obstruction, or delay. In the end, the minority group is left little better than it was before, if not worse" (p. 24).

CRT is not only concerned with race/racism, but with the intersection of race with other categories of oppression and exclusion, including social class, gender and disability. This concern with *intersectionality* is especially strong in critical race feminism (Wing, 1997). Indeed, building on Crenshaw's work, United Kingdom scholars Avtar Brah and Ann Phoenix (2004) argue that intersectionality itself can provide a useful focus that offers numerous advances on current single-issue thinking (see, also, Loutzenheiser & MacIntosh, 2004). As Crenshaw (1995) indicated, rather than viewing intersectionality as a kind of problem to be solved, the best way ahead may be to use intersectionality as a key means of understanding how White supremacy operates and how to mount effective resistance (see African American Policy Forum, n.d.).

New Developments and Continuing Struggles

> Then he said to them all: "If anyone would come after me, he must deny himself and take
> up his cross daily and follow me." (Luke 9:23)

The Gospel of Luke is considered one of the most complete accounts of the life of Jesus Christ (Knight, 2003). In this instance, informing followers that they must be willing to view Christianity as the central aspect of their lives, not merely an add-on. Similarly, *race work,* especially race work done through the lens of CRT, requires that scholars be mindful of, and willing to accept, the important responsibility of directly challenging racism and White supremacy, especially as it manifests in the daily realities of education and education policy. CRT calls for embracing interdisciplinary scholarship and applying a more specific set of concepts and tenets that separate CRT from the commonly used critical theories and sociocultural theories in education. The charge to "take up your cross daily" is important for CRT scholars in that it reminds them that serious race work is always already activist in nature; that they must commit and recommit to it daily, fully cognizant of the possible costs to their relationships with peers and, indeed, their professional trajectories.

In the years that have elapsed since the publication of Ladson-Billings and Tate's (1995) groundbreaking article, CRT in education has established itself as an important theoretical framework for scholars who are concerned with race and educational equality. Many edited books with social justice frameworks host one or two chapters that utilize CRT and an increasing number of books have been published, both edited and sole authored, with an overarching focus informed by critical race theory (e.g., Dixson & Rousseau, 2006; Epstein, 2006; Ladson-Billings, 2003; Ladson-Billings & Tate, 2006; Lopez & Parker, 2003; Parker, Deyhle, & Villenas, 1999; Prendergast, 2003; Taylor et al., 2009; Yosso, 2006; Zamudio et al. 2011). CRT scholars have also used special issues of numerous well established peer-reviewed journals to explore and develop the approach (including *Cultural Politics of Education* 2007; *Educational Administration Quarterly* 2007; *Educational Philosophy and Theory* 2004; *Educational Studies* 2003; *Equity and Excellence* 2002; *Qualitative Inquiry* 2002; *Qualitative Studies in Education* 1998; *Race Ethnicity and Education* 2005, 2009; and *Teachers College Record* 2011). Special issues have proven to be particularly significant in offering CRT scholars a supportive and extended context within which to develop a diverse set of articles focused on different articulations of CRT. While the status of the journals has helped to bolster the standing of CRT, the special issues have also provided a way forward free from the conservative (sometimes reactionary) attitudes of the academic *mainstream* which still tends to view CRT as at best *specialist* and at worst as a threat to established standards.

Scholars in the millennium have employed various tenets of CRT to highlight past and present educational conditions and events. Some have used the interest convergence principle to examine how marginalized groups have struggled with the political power bloc to gain greater, more equitable access to education (Alemán & Alemán, 2010; Irvine & Irvine, 2007; Milner & Howard, 2004). These struggles often yield some measure of access for minority groups but simultaneously create larger gains for White majority political stakeholders. White scholars have increasingly contributed to CRT analyses of the centrality of race/racism, especially around questions of Whiteness, to unpack issues of White supremacy and colorblind ideologies among teachers and, indeed, within the academy (Allen, 2009; Marx, 2004; Pennington, 2007; Preston, 2007; Rogers & Mosley, 2006).

Nontraditional Moves and CRT Scholarship

As noted above, critical race theorists do not define themselves solely through their academic scholarship measured in publications, presentations, and organizational leadership in academic spaces. Critical race scholars typically view activism as a key part of their role (Stovall, 2006; Stovall, Lynn, Danley, & Martin, 2009) and, in education, they have increasingly moved to collectivist forms of activism and support that mirror the initial workshops and conferences that gave birth to the approach. The U.S. has seen the greatest number of such innovations, including an annual CRT conference, the development of the Critical Race Studies in Education Association (CRSEA) and a dedicated professional development course on CRT in education at the annual meeting of the American Educational Research Association (AERA)—the largest scholarly association for educational researchers in North America. In this way, CRT scholars have heeded the charge to "take up thy cross" within the often hostile and fraught arena of the academy. In the UK similar moves have taken place with the aim of establishing CRT as a distinctive approach to social theory (Pilkington, Housee, & Hylton, 2009 and to offer dedicated spaces for support, e.g., through a national network of CRT practitioners and the first ever U.K.-wide conference on CRT in education (held in London in 2009). These developments have proven vital as a means of offering support to colleagues who face academic persecution in the forms of emotional and institutional isolation and ideological marginalization: for example, we have worked with published scholars who have been warned that community activism might jeopardize their tenure applications (by detracting from their standing as "serious" academics) and graduate students who have been told that they *cannot* use CRT because it's not a real theory.

In 2009 Dixson and Chapman facilitated the first CRT professional development workshop for educational researchers at the AERA annual meeting in San Diego, CA. In addition to offering support to beginning researchers, the workshop was designed to address the growing misuse of CRT in education research where researchers sometimes claim to be following the path of CRT (and examining racialized educational inequity) but are often carving their own personalized path without understanding, or applying, key elements of the theory. Returning to our original metaphor, the call to use CRT should not be taken up in discreet parts and presented as acontextual, undertheorized, and underanalyzed in a way that disregards the multifaceted theoretical framework developed by CRT scholars to date. Many graduate students and new scholars hail from colleges and universities with few seasoned scholars who have built a body of work using CRT. This means that new scholars are not receiving the close professional mentoring they need to move their work, and the field, forward with new instantiations of CRT. In order to help educational researchers who were interested in CRT to develop a more substantive understanding, Dixson and Chapman invited senior and midcareer scholars who have published significant CRT work in education to serve as mentors to graduate students and new scholars seeking to use CRT. The response to the seminar was extremely positive: the course was oversubscribed and participants' reactions were so positive that a second course was invited the following year.

The need to mentor new scholars has been extended into the annual conference held by the CRSEA. Looking towards its fifth conference in May 2011, the conference has integrated sessions on the dissertation process, cultivating an area of scholarship, publications, and building coalitions which have gained in popularity each year. The CRSEA is working toward institutionalizing forms of mentoring to support new and existing CRT scholars. Sharing these experiences, making the information available to a wider breadth of scholars, and creating transparent pathways are ways in which CRT scholars are seeking to promote the tenet of social justice located in CRT.

Despite the increasing intensification and marketization of higher education, CRT scholars continue to push the boundaries of traditional academic forms of work by asserting the value of their work with local education agencies, community organizations, families, and children. Scholars have documented their social justice efforts in various publication formats, helped influence district and local policies, worked alongside legal challenges to educational inequity, and changed programs and practices in teacher education. Although the path is often difficult, as new scholars insist on a more balanced integration of service, teaching, and research in the field of education, CRT holds the promise of serving children and families of color in multiple ways that we have yet to envision and cannot wait to behold.

Conclusion

CRT represents a dramatic break with previous approaches to studying racism in education and is being taken up by a growing array of scholars internationally. The approach goes a good deal further than previous perspectives (such as multicultural and anti-racist education) by developing a coherent body of conceptual tools that draws on an interdisciplinary perspective, values educational activism alongside groundbreaking analyses, and places White racism at the very centre of its work. Perhaps predictably, the approach has faced criticism from both sides of the political spectrum. CRT's usefulness will be limited not by the weakness of its constructs but by the degree that many Whites will not accept its assumptions; I anticipate critique from both left and right (Taylor, 1998, p. 124). CRT is a dynamic and changing field that offers a framework for critical analysis of educational inequality that is both insightful and inclusive; it remains to be seen whether the field of education is capable of sustaining, and even embracing, such a radical challenge.

References

African American Policy Forum. (n.d.). *Primer on intersectionality*. Retrieved from http://aapf.org/wp/uploads/2009/03/aapf_intersectionality_primer.pdf

Alemán E., Jr., & Alemán, S. M. (2010). "Do Latin@ interests always have to 'converge' with White interests?": (Re)claiming racial realism and interest-convergence in critical race theory praxis. *Race Ethnicity & Education, 13*(1), 1–21.

Allen, R. L. (2009). "What about poor White people?" In W. Ayers, T. Quinn, & D. Stovall (Eds.), *Handbook of social justice in education* (pp. 209–230). New York, NY: Routledge.

Ansley, F. L. (1997). White supremacy (and what we should do about it). In R. Delgado & J. Stefancic (Eds.), *Critical White studies: Looking behind the mirror* (pp. 592–595). Philadelphia, PA: Temple University Press.

Baszile, D. T. (2008). Beyond all reason indeed: The pedagogical promise of critical race testimony. *Race Ethnicity & Education, 11*(3), 251–265.

Bell, D. (1980a). *Race, racism and American Law*. Boston, MA: Little Brown.

Bell, D. (1980b). Brown v. Board of Education and the interest convergence dilemma. *Harvard Law Review, 93,* 518–533.

Bell, D. (1992). *Faces at the bottom of the well: The permanence of racism*. New York, NY: Basic Books.

Bell, D. (2004). *Silent covenants*. New York, NY: Oxford University Press.

Brah, A., & Phoenix, A. (2004). Ain't I a woman? Revisiting Intersectionality. *Journal of International Women's Studies*, *5*(3), 75–86.

Brown, A. L., & Brown, K. D. (2010). Strange fruit indeed: Interrogating contemporary textbook representations of racial violence toward African Americans. *Teachers College Record*, *112*(1), 31–67.

Crenshaw, K. W. (1995). Mapping the margins: Intersectionality, identity politics, and violence against women of color. In K. Crenshaw, N. Gotanda, G. Peller, & K. Thomas (Eds.), *Critical race theory: The key writings that formed the movement* (pp. 357–383). New York, NY: New Press.

Crenshaw, K. W. (2002). The first decade: critical reflections, or "a foot in the closing door." *UCLA Law Review, 49,* 1343–1372.

Crenshaw, K., Gotanda, N., Peller, G., & Thomas, K. (Eds.). (1995). *Critical race theory: The key writings that formed the movement*. New York, NY: New Press.

Delgado, R. (1989). Storytelling for oppositionists and others: A plea for narrative. *Michigan Law Review, 87,* 2411–2441.

Delgado, R., & Stefancic, J. (2000). *Introduction: Critical race theory: The cutting edge* (2nd ed.), Philadelphia, PA: Temple University Press.

Delgado, R., & Stefancic, J. (2001). *Critical race theory: An introduction*. New York, NY: New York University Press.

Dixson, A. D., & Rousseau, C. K. (Eds.). (2006). *Critical race theory in education: All God's children got a song*. New York, NY: Routledge.

Epstein, K. K. (2006). A different view of urban schools: Civil rights, critical race theory, and unexplored realities. *Counterpoints: Studies in the Postmodern Theory of Education* (Vol. 291). Oxford England: Peter Lang.

Gillborn, D. (2005). Education policy as an act of white supremacy: Whiteness, critical race theory and education reform. *Journal of Education Policy, 20*(4), 485–505.

Gillborn, D. (2008). *Racism and education: Coincidence or conspiracy?* London: Routledge.

Gillborn, D. (2009). Who's afraid of critical race theory in education? A reply to Mike Cole's "The Color-Line and the Class Struggle." *Power and Education, 1*(1), 125–131.

Gillborn, D., & Youdell, D. (2000). *Rationing education: Policy, practice, reform and equity.* Buckingham, England: Open University Press.

Hylton, K. (2008). *"Race" and sport: Critical race theory.* London: Routledge.

Irvine, J. J., & Irvine, R. W. (2007). The impact of the desegregation process on the education of Black Students: A retrospective analysis. *Journal of Negro Education, 76*(3), 297–305.

Knight, G. W. (2003). *The layman's Bible handbook.* Uhrichsville, OH: Barbour.

Ladson-Billings, G. (2011). Race still matters: Critical race theory in education In M. W. Apple, W. Au, & L. A. Gandin (Eds.), *The Routledge international handbook of critical education.* New York, NY: Routledge.

Ladson-Billings, G. (2006). They're trying to wash us away: The adolescence of critical race theory in education. In A. D. Dixson & C. K. Rousseau (Eds.), *Critical race theory in education: ALL God's children got a song* (pp. v-xiii). New York, NY: Routledge.

Ladson-Billings, G. (Ed.). (2003). *Critical race perspectives on social studies education: The profession, policies, and curriculum.* Charlotte, NC: Information Age Publishing.

Ladson-Billings, G., & Tate, W. F., IV. (1995). Toward a critical race theory of education. *Teachers College Record, 97,* 47–68.

Ladson-Billings, G., & Tate, W. F., IV. (Eds). (2006). *Education Research in the Public Interest: Social justice, action, and policy.* New York, NY: Teachers College Press

Lee, I. (1995). Nomination of Derrick A. Bell, Jr., to be an Associate Justice of the Supreme Court of the United States: The chronicles of Civil Rights activist. *Ohio Northern University Law Review, 22,* 363–448.

Lopez, G. R., & Parker, L. (Eds.). (2003) *Interrogating racism in qualitative research methodology.* New York, NY: Peter Lang.

Loutzenheiser, L. W., & MacIntosh, L. B. (2004). Citizenships, sexualities, and education. *Theory Into Practice, 43,* 151–158. Columbus, OH: Ohio State University.

Macpherson, W. (1999). *The Stephen Lawrence inquiry: CM 4262-I.* London: The Stationery Office.

Marx, S. (2004). Regarding Whiteness: Exploring and intervening in the effects of White racism in teacher education. *Equity and Excellence in Education, 37*(1), 31–43.

Mills, C.W. (2003). *From class to race.* New York, NY: Rowman & Littlefield.

Milner, H. R., & Howard, T. C. (2004). Black teachers, Black students, Black communities, and Brown: Perspectives and insights from experts. *Journal of Negro Education, 73*(3), 285–297.

Parker, L., Deyhle, D., & Villenas, S. (1999). *Race is ... race isn't: Critical race theory and qualitative studies in education.* Boulder, CO: Westview.

Pennington, J. L. (2007). Silence in the classroom/whispers in the halls: Autoethnography as pedagogy in White pre-service teacher education. *Race Ethnicity and Education, 10*(1), 93–113.

Pilkington, A., Housee, S., & Hylton, S. (Eds.). (2009). *Race(ing) forward: Transitions in theorising "race" in education.* Birmingham, England: Higher Education Academy, Sociology, Anthropology, Politics.

Prendergast, C. (2003). *Literacy and racial justice: The Politics of learning after Brown v. Board of Education.* Carbondale, IL: Southern Illinois University Press.

Preston, J. (2007). *Whiteness and class in education.* Dordrecht, The Netherlands: Springer.

Prime minister's questions. (1999, Feb). *Hansard,* column 379–387. Retrieved from http://www.publications.parliament.uk/pa/cm199899/cmhansrd/vo990224/debtext/90224-20.htm#90224-20_spmin0

Rogers, R., & Mosley, M. (2006). Racial literacy in a second-grade classroom: Critical race theory, Whiteness studies, and literacy research. *Reading Research Quarterly, 41*(4), 462–495.

Stovall, D. (2006). Forging community in race and class. *Race Ethnicity & Education, 9*(3), 243–259.

Stovall, D., Lynn, M., Danley, L., & Martin, D. (2009). Critical Race Praxis In Education: Introduction. *Race Ethnicity and Education, 12*(2), 131–132.

Tate, W.F. (1997). Critical race theory and education: History, theory, and implications. In M. W. Apple (Ed.), *Review of Research in Education* (Vol. 22, pp. 195–247). Washington DC: AERA.

Taylor, E. (1998). A primer on critical race theory: Who are the critical race theorists and what are they saying? *Journal of Blacks in Higher Education, 19,* 122–124.

Taylor, E., Gillborn, D., & Ladson-Billings, G. (Eds.). (2009). *Foundations of critical race theory in education.* New York, NY: Routledge.

Tomlinson, S. (2008). *Race and education.* Maidenhead, England: Open University Press.

West, C. (1995). Foreword. In K. Crenshaw, N. Gotanda, G. Peller, & K. Thomas (Eds.), *Critical race theory: The key writings that formed the movement* (pp. xi-xii). New York, NY: New Press

Wing, A. K. (Ed.). (1997). *Critical race feminism: A reader.* New York, NY: New York University Press.

Yosso, T. J. (2006). *Critical race counterstories along the Chicana/Chicano educational pipeline.* New York, NY: Routledge.

Zamudio, M. M., Russell, C., Rios, F. A., & Bridgeman, J. L. (2011). *Critical race theory matters: Education and ideology.* New York, NY: Routledge.

UNIT 2. GENDER AND LGBTQIA+ ISSUES

A Brief Overview of Gender and LGBT in History

In the 19th and early 20th centuries, women organized primarily in churches and neighborhood areas and addressed issues such as the price of food, sexuality, and morality. Some women became activists in the domains of antislavery and labor—challenging their own oppression in contrast to the wishes of their male allies. The status of the family became a central question in the early women's rights movement. Some women organized to protect the traditional roles of families; others protested the traditional model of the family and advocated that wives should be able to own property and control the finances, being on equal terms as men; while some women worked to abolish the family and set up communes. These women have been labeled first wave feminists, with the first wave of feminism beginning in 1848 with the Seneca Falls Convention and ending in 1920 with the right to vote. Because different women worked toward different goals during the early women's movement, historians question the proposition whether all of the women in these social movements were indeed feminists. "In Western Europe and the Americas, historians typically use the word 'feminist' to describe women's collective activities to advance the women's condition, but the meaning of feminism is neither stable nor fixed" (Goldberg Moses, 2012, p. 760). Historically, "feminism" is assigned to "women's collective actions before the word even existed" (Goldberg Moses, 2012, p. 760).

Second Wave Feminism

After the election of John F. Kennedy in 1960, women with connections to both his administration and Congress focused on education and employment to advance the women's movement in what is now regarded as the second wave of the feminist movement. These women were successful in initiating progressive polices: "a 1963 law insisted that women be paid the same as men when they worked the same jobs; a 1964 law stated that all employment must be open to women and men alike; and a 1972 law made unequal treatment of women and men in education illegal" (Goldberg Moses, 2012, p. 766). During the 1960s, the women's liberation movement formed based on the slogan "the personal is political," with an emphasis on the previously overlooked and depoliticized private domain that was central to relationships between women and men. Informal small groups would gather and participate in so-called consciousness raising (CR). Among other things, the CR groups encouraged women to, in effect, name the forms of oppression they experienced in the private, domestic sphere, and this was seen as the first step toward individual and social empowerment. By the 1970s, new scholarship in women's studies was connecting women back to the historical tradition such as voting rights (Goldberg Moses, 2012). This was the era when feminist was the most agreed upon term between the women in the movement. These second wave feminists emerged during the 1960s, 1970s, and 1980s. During this era, a myriad of different types of feminists who held different interpretations of patriarchy emerged:

> Liberal feminists aim to achieve full equality with men in all spheres of life without radically transforming social and political systems. In contrast radical feminism aims for a new social order in which women are not subordinated to men, and femaleness and femininity are not debased. The way in which radical feminism assert autonomy from men and recover their true and natural femininity is by separation from men and patriarchal society. For socialist feminists patriarchy is inseparable from class and race oppression and can only be abolished through the transformation of the social system. Socialist feminism sees gender as socially produced and historically shifting. (Parry, 2002, p. 91).

Second wave White feminists were concerned about race, too, but they could be awkward in working with people of color. "As the women's movement developed, it was rooted in anti-capitalist and anti-racist civil rights movement, but black women found themselves alienated from the central platforms of the mainstream women's movement" (Grady, 2018, para. 34). Black women fought to work outside the home, but most Black women had to work outside the home anyway. While White women and Black women were equally concerned about reproductive rights, Black women advocated for the cessation of forced sterilization of Black women with disabilities, which was not an objective of the mainstream women's movement. In response to the alienation to the central platforms of the women's movement, some Black women departed from feminism to create womanism (Grady, 2018): "Womanist is to feminist as purple is to lavender" (Walker, 1983, as cited in Grady, 2018, para. 36).

Black Feminism

Black feminism emerged at the intersection of antiracist and antisexist struggles during first wave and second wave feminism. During the first wave, "Julia Cooper, Ida B. Wells, and Pauline Hopkins deconstructed the relationship between race and gender" (White, 2001, p. 32). During the second wave, Black feminism was recognized in the writings of Ntozake Shange, Alice Walker, and Toni Cade Bambara. As noted by White (2001), "As long as black feminist voices remained invisible, white feminists could be dismissed as lacking the approval of the authentic black woman. Indeed, angry at the racism they had experienced from white women, many black women charged that feminism is foreign to black culture and participated in the silencing of black feminism" (p. 38). In response, "Black feminists began to realize that they were either misrepresented or not represented at all, and they worked to remedy the situation" (White, 2001, p. 45). Black feminists became authors and rewrote history, literary criticism, and theory. Along the way, they realized that both the mainstream feminist movement and the Black power movement acknowledged them inadequately. During second wave feminism, the most important contribution to Black women's identity came with the 1981 publication of "A Black Feminist Statement," by Combahee River Collective, a group founded in Boston in 1974 (White, 2001). This group helped create a space for Black feminists to speak about their relationship with White feminists and Black liberation organizations. Black nationalism's celebration of Black manhood alienated some Black women. "Considering the number of early black feminists who were lesbian, among them, Audre Lorde, Cheryl Clarke, and Barbara Smith, sexual orientation must have played a role in their alienation from a strongly heterosexist movement" (White, 2001, pp. 41–42).

Third Wave Feminism

Third wave feminism began roughly in the 1990s and featured hotly contested debates between scholars over whether how to conceptualize how these successive waves were both separable in distinct ways yet also historically continuous. Third wave feminism gained momentum with the controversial Supreme Court candidacy of Clarence Thomas, an African American nominee who had to defend himself against claims made by Anita Hill, an African American lawyer, who testified that Thomas has sexually harassed Hill a decade earlier when they worked together. The Anita Hill case led to a litany of sexual harassment complaints filed by other women and a conversation about the overrepresentation of men in national leadership roles (Grady, 2018). The momentum also increased as a consequence of "riot grrrl" groups in the music scene during the early 1990s (Grady, 2018).

History of LBGT

LBGT people have existed since the beginning of time, across all cultures, even if no formal classification was devised to acknowledge this fact. The scope of this overview cannot hope to cover the entirety of LBGT history in the United States. What follows, then, is an abbreviated attempt to highlight some of the defining features of LBGT history and social movements.

In indigenous cultures, a herdache, a young woman or man who took on the dress and tribal duties of the other sex, was sometimes placed in an elevated position in the tribe (Bronski, 2011). These practices were in direct conflict with the values of puritanism and religious and social thought of the time, which "held that people who did not adhere to Christian concepts of sexual behavior, gender affect or modesty were less than human; they were like animals" (Bronski, 2011, p. 5).

The treatment of homosexuals was tied to the treatment of African Americans. The social purity movement merged together race and sex "as the battlefield on which American sexuality was defined" (Bronski, 2011, p. 90). As noted by Bronski (2011), "The sanitary utopia of the social purists was the nightmarish opposite of the utopian visions of the more radical strands of the labor movement and the

African American civil rights movement" (p. 91). The 1886 Haymarket riot and the Supreme Court case *Plessy v. Ferguson* (1896) marked future use of civil disobedience to resist state-sanctioned authority.

The labor movement had influence over the LGBT population. Harry Hay started the Industrial Workers of the World, also known as the Wobblies, which had over a million members in 1923 (Bronski, 2011). Hay then founded the Mattachine Society, an early homosexual rights group, in 1950.

World War II ushered in opportunities for homosexuals who enlisted in military service—both male and female. The benefits of serving their country outweighed the reality that sodomy was prohibited by Article 125 of the Uniform Code of Military Justice (Bronski, 2011). The new ways of thinking about homosexuality during this era shifted the literature and writing generated during this time.

Gay culture started having an effect on mainstream culture. Homosexuality was beginning to be discussed on Broadway in John Van Druten's 1950 *Bell, Book, and Candle*, Christopher Isherwood's 1952 *Berlin Stories*, and Robert Anderson's 1953 *Tea and Sympathy* (Bronski, 2011). During this time, openly gay artists were presenting their work without the interference of producers or directors.

In 1969, Carl Wittman, the son of Communist Party members and a drafter of the Port Huron Statement, composed "A Gay Manifesto" while living in San Francisco (Bronski, 2011). It became a significant piece for a new movement. Wittman's directive in the manifesto was to come out. "For gay liberation, coming out was not simply a matter of self-identification. It was a radical, public act that would impact every aspect of a person's life" (Bronski, 2011, p. 209).

On Saturday, June 28, 1969, police entered the Stonewall Inn at 53 Christopher Street in Greenwich Village. They cleared out the patrons and arrested some of the staff. Protesters gathered outside and confronted the police. After a few days of silence, protests resumed and some violent clashes with the police occurred. The slogans that emerged after Stonewall reflect the larger culture of political militance that emerged such as Gay Power and They Want Us to Fight for Our Country [But] They Invade Our Rights (Bronski, 2011).

Between 1969 and 1979, more than 30,000 gay people migrated to San Francisco. This was "vital in remaking a minority culture and formed one of the most important gay political and cultural centers in the United States" (Bronski, 2011, p. 216). Huey Newton, chairman of the Black Panther Party, said in a speech that the party should "try to form a working coalition with the gay liberation and women's liberation groups" and that "homosexuals are not given freedom and liberty by anyone in society. They might be the most oppressed people in society" (Bronski, 2011, p. 216). This was the first time that a political group asked for coalition with gay liberation groups.

In the 1980s, the AIDS epidemic led to further stigmatization of the gay population. Because of this stigma, medical research, prevention education, and basic care for people suffering from the virus started far too late. This delay caused the epidemic to spread quickly. "The mortality rate from HIV/AIDS during the 1980s and 1990s was staggering: the total number of reported deaths was 1,476 in 1983, 11,932 by 1987, and 31,129 by 1990" (Bronski, 2011, p. 229). In response to the AIDS epidemic, a major innovation which occurred was the phrase "safe sex" as a new response to sexual regulation.

Playwright and activist Larry Kramer planned for a new, grassroots AIDS organization that would "demand the basic health care, civil rights, legal protections, and respect that Americans were guaranteed under the Constitution" (Bronski, 2011, p. 231). Three hundred people came to a meeting to form this group, which they named the AIDS Coalition to Unleash Power (ACT UP). Kramer was adamant in his speech that the other activist groups for AIDS were doing necessary legal work, but instances of discrimination were so widespread and enforcement often so limited, that they still needed to do more work (Bronski, 2011). ACT UP members protested profiteering by drug companies and demanded easier access to experimental HIV drugs almost immediately. The Food and Drug Administration responded that it would shorten the drug approval process by 2 years (Bronski, 2011). "It has been less than forty years since Harry Hay met with his friends to start the Mattachine Society, but sexuality identity, political activism, and the world has changed tremendously. ACT UP, in an age of new technologies, was able to reach a wider audience and get its message across with more sophistication and media flair" (Bronski, 2011, p. 232).

Conclusion

In summary, the common denominator linking the women's rights movement and the LGBT movement resides in their struggle for equal rights, political activism, social justice, and human dignity. While our brief overview of these movements cannot possibly treat the immense scope of their respective origins and development, the intention has been to provide a general sense of each of the movement's pivotal moments in their ongoing historical development.

References

Bronski, M. (2011). *A queer history of the United States*. Beacon Press.

Goldberg Moses, C. (2012). "What's in a name?" On writing the history of feminism. *Feminist Studies, 38*(3), 757–779.

Grady, C. (2018). "The waves of feminism and why people keep fighting over them, explained." *Vox*. Retrieved on May 20, 2020, from https://www.vox.com/2018/3/20/16955588/feminism-waves-explained-first-second-third-fourth

Parry, O. (2002). Gendered methodologies and feminist awakenings. In P. Mohammed (Ed.), *Gendered realities: Essays in Caribbean feminist thought* (pp. 83–106). University of West Indies Press.

White, F. E. (2001). Black feminist interventions. In E. F. White (Ed.), *Dark continent of our bodies: Black feminism and politics of respectability (pp. 25–80)*. Temple University Press.

Feminism, Philosophy, and Education

Nel Noddings

Nel Noddings, "Feminism, Philosophy and Education," *Philosophy of Education*, pp. 217–238, 254–256. Copyright © 2016 by Taylor & Francis Group. Reprinted with permission.

This reading will serve three purposes: It will revisit some of the problems considered in earlier chapters and thus serve as a review; it will elaborate some feminist themes merely hinted at previously; and it will extend a particular feminist view, the ethic of care, and use it to examine some basic ideas in education.

Feminist Critiques of Philosophy

One of the great contributions of contemporary feminist thought is its powerful criticism of traditional philosophy. I have previously written about Jane Roland Martin's criticism of Plato's recommendations for education.[1] Her strongest objection centers on Plato's neglect of the tasks and values traditionally associated with women. Plato, in an argument that was remarkable for his time, took the position that women were not, by their sex alone, unqualified to be guardians of the republic. However, in the selection of guardians, only those traits and competencies long associated with male public leadership were sought. Plato held that some highly talented women could develop these traits and competencies, but he scorned the traits and competencies usually identified with women. To become a guardian, a woman had to become like a man. Clearly, even today, some feminists take a similar position—highly valuing work done in the public sphere and devaluing work in the home and neighborhood community.

Martin objects that such an approach entirely neglects the central importance of "reproductive" work—bearing and raising children, caring for the ill and elderly, maintaining a home, and responding to the physical and psychological needs of families. All of these tasks are

1. Jane Roland Martin, *Reclaiming a Conversation* (New Haven, Conn.: Yale University Press, 1985).

59

brushed aside by Plato. Indeed, his female guardians were to be relieved of these jobs, and their children were to be raised by other, presumably lesser, women.

In contrast to Plato, Martin would educate both female and male children for both "productive" and "reproductive" life. Like other feminists, she wants girls to have opportunities in mathematics and science, but she also wants boys to learn care, compassion, and connection. She wants to put a higher value on women's traditional tasks, not simply liberate the "most able" women from them. Her argument raises a crucial social issue. If all able women become like traditional men, who will raise the children, care for the ill and elderly, and maintain supportive home environments? Martin is not, of course, arguing that women should stay home and accede to their continued exploitation. Rather, she wants us to realize how vital these traditional tasks are and to prepare all of our children to do them well. I have argued along similar lines in suggesting that much of the school curriculum should be organized around themes of care: caring for self; caring for intimate others; caring for strangers and global others; caring for plants, animals, and the natural environment; caring for the human-made environment; and caring for ideas.[2]

One can argue as Martin and I do without being an essentialist. An *essentialist* is one who holds that men and women have essential natures, natures that are essentially different. Contemporary followers of Carl Jung are essentialists. They posit essential masculine and feminine traits, strengths, and weaknesses. However, they also urge a balance—men must accept guidance from their "anima" or feminine aspect, and women must listen to their "animus" or masculine spirit.[3]

Many current feminists abhor the essentialist position because they believe it has long been used to exclude women from the public and professional world. Further, some believe that it is simply wrong, that biological evidence does not support it,[4] but the scientific argument rages on. There is no question about the political use of essentialism; the doctrine has not worked for the betterment of women.

Recognizing the harm done in the name of essentialism, most feminists reject the position. However, one can argue that centuries of experience have left their mark on women's ways of thinking and on the values they espouse, and not all of these ways and values are to be rejected as part of the legacy of oppression. This observation underscores Martin's point that we must think about our values and include them in our designs for education. Many contemporary feminists have become almost phobic over the word *essence*. However, even John Dewey allowed its use insofar as it refers to an enduring quality or attribute and not one fixed for all time in an unchangeable nature. Most feminists find the word too inflammatory, but if I were to use it, I would use it in the Deweyan sense. Indeed, I think it would be remarkable if thousands of years of very different experience did not produce some enduring differences between males and females. But that is not to say that these will endure forever, that they are not subject to alteration through education, or that there is no overlap between males and females in their manifestation. Nor is it to say that one set of traits is superior to the other.

2. Nel Noddings, *The Challenge to Care in Schools* (New York: Teachers College Press, 1992).

3. See, for example, M. Esther Harding, *Woman's Mysteries* (New York: Harper Colophon Books, 1976).

4. Foremost here is Ruth Hubbard. See Ruth Hubbard, Mary Sue Henifin, and Barbara Fried, eds., *Biological Woman: The Convenient Myth* (Cambridge, Mass.: Schenkman, 1982); and Hubbard, *The Politics of Women's Biology* (New Brunswick, N.J.: Rutgers University Press, 1990).

Having mentioned essentialism and the fiery debates it triggers, I should now say more about the educational philosophy of Rousseau. Rousseau recommended an education for boys that would, so far as possible, preserve their natural freedom and goodness and, at the same time, make them into solid, independent citizens. For girls, Rousseau recommended an education for chastity, docility, and subservience. You can see how this fits an essentialist theory. If women are, by nature, intellectually inferior and dependent on men, then their education should be designed to help them make the most of their nonintellectual gifts, particularly the special charm that grows out of their weakness. Because they must please men in order to live comfortably and with some respect, they must be taught how to do this. Above all, they must be chaste, and yet they must be sexually alluring to their husband. They must be able to converse sensibly, but they must not express what seem to be original ideas. They must spend considerable time on their appearance so that they will have a "natural" look. Whereas boys were to be educated for freedom,

> girls should be restricted from a young age.... They will be subjected all their lives to the most severe and perpetual restraint, that of propriety; one must impose restraint on them from the start, so that it will never be a hardship for them, so as to master all their fantasies and make them submit to the wills of other people.... This habitual restraint results in a docility in women which they need all their lives, since they will always be in subjection to a man or to men's judgments, and will never be allowed to set themselves above these judgments.[5]

Susan Okin, after reviewing these comments and those suggesting that Sophie and her peers be nevertheless schooled in coquetry so that their husbands will not be tempted to wander, remarks, "Sophie is indeed to be both concubine and nun."[6]

Perhaps you can see from this brief discussion why so many feminists shun essentialism. One of the earliest feminists, Mary Wollstonecraft, protested that women are not naturally (or essentially) docile, empty-headed, vain, frivolous, and less fair-minded than men.[7] She insisted that women had been made that way by their education, both formal and informal. Give women a chance, Wollstonecraft argued, and society might find women every bit as intellectually and morally capable as men. Further, she said, women need the same education as men if they are to run complex households efficiently and raise sons as well as daughters. Notice that one could accept the basic ideas of essentialism and argue that women's gifts far outweigh their weaknesses. Many Jungians argue this way, and some feminists even argue that women are, by virtue of essential traits, superior to men especially in the moral domain.[8] However, I think it is clear that claims of superiority do not carry far when they are made from a position of subordination, and such claims merely

5. Rousseau quoted in Susan Moller Okin, *Women in Western Political Thought* (Princeton, N.J.: Princeton University Press, 1979), pp. 163–164.
6. Ibid., p. 164.
7. Mary Wollstonecraft, *A Vindication of the Rights of Woman*, ed. Carol H. Poston (New York: W. W. Norton, 1975).
8. Sara Blaffer Hrdy, for example, extols the craftiness evolution has conferred on women. Similarly, many nineteenth-century feminists called on women, thought to be morally superior to men, to save both men and themselves. See Hrdy, *The Woman That Never Evolved* (Cambridge, Mass.: Harvard University Press, 1981).

sidestep the hard work of identifying and valorizing those qualities we want to promote. Let's now continue the discussion of feminism's influence on philosophy and education.

Epistemology

As we have seen, traditional epistemology—an epistemology that has searched for or claimed a foundation for all knowledge—has been attacked from several perspectives, and foundationalism seems to be on the defensive. Pragmatists, postmodernists, and feminists all reject the notion that knowledge can be firmly anchored in an antecedent set of premises or conditions. Most of us no longer believe that truth can be derived from initial self-evident propositions or from basic observation statements, although neither position has been entirely vacated. Mathematics is still generated from initial premises; we have just given up the claim that these are necessarily or self-evidently true. Science still depends on observation statements, but we accept as a fact that observation is theory-laden. Philosophers can and do take these positions without being feminists, and some women philosophers believe that a naturalized epistemology as described by Dewey or Quine is entirely adequate for feminist purposes.[9] From this perspective, no special feminist philosophy is required.

Other feminist philosophers argue that the vestiges of Cartesianism are still too strong even in current naturalistic epistemology. For example, some contend that the epistemological emphasis on rational autonomy and on the one acceptable method that accompanies such rationality excludes many who have legitimate claims to knowledge. We noted Naomi Scheman's claim that there is something schizophrenic about the Cartesian model.[10] On the one hand, it purports to elevate the individual knower; it frees knowers from authority and dogma. On the other hand, the individual knower with all her or his desires, allegiances, projects, and concrete history is reduced to a *method*. From the Cartesian perspective, it is not a full-bodied subject who creates knowledge; it is, rather, an epistemological subject—a mental mechanism.

Many feminists deny that knowledge claims are somehow vitiated when they are colored by the personal aims and interests of the knower. Often called "standpoint" epistemologists, these thinkers insist that a certain privilege is acquired by those who experience oppression. Thus, women have access to privileged knowledge with respect to issues of gender, the poor with respect to poverty, blacks and other ethnic minorities with respect to race, and perhaps students with respect to schooling. Notice that whereas many philosophers agree that scientific knowledge can be and probably is contaminated with such influences, standpoint theorists do not believe that we get closer to "truth" by confessing our biases and rooting them out. On the contrary, they claim that such standpoint-laden claims and reports are epistemically richer and more accurate than those generated through traditionally objective methods.

Feminist epistemology also intersects with and may modify postmodernism. In agreement with postmodernists, some feminists reject most claims to universality, the traditional notion of objectivity, the search for universal truth and certainty, and the creation and use of "grand narratives." However, the

9. On Quine, see, for example, Louise Antony, "Quine as Feminist: The Radical Import of Naturalized Epistemology," in Louise Antony and Charlotte Witt, eds., *A Mind of One's Own* (Boulder, Colo.: Westview Press, 1993), pp. 185–226.

10. Naomi Scheman, "Though This Be Method, Yet There Is Madness in It," in ibid., pp. 145–170.

postmodern rejection of the subject worries many feminists. Although they may agree that the constituting subject growing out of the Cartesian tradition is a myth, many are not ready to speak of a constituted subject or to abandon the concept of a subject entirely.[11] To these feminists, it is ironic that just as women are beginning to claim their subjecthood, some philosophers declare the death of the subject! Of course, this objection is political, not strictly epistemological. But then, these feminists have already argued that there is no epistemology entirely free of the political broadly construed. Thus it seems more prudent to many of us to speak of a partially constituted subject—one who is shaped in large part by her situation in time and place but also at least in part by her own decisions and actions.

Another interesting contribution to epistemology has been made by black feminists. Instead of judging claims—especially claims in the social sciences—by referring them to the traditional criteria of justified true belief, some black feminists prefer to ask who is speaking. This is a variety of standpoint epistemology that puts great emphasis on the experiential credentials of the speaker/knower and correspondingly less on the speaker's argument. Thus, in answer to the question "How do you know?" these feminists expect a narrative-like response emphasizing personal experience. Even when an argument is necessary, its force is judged in part by the passion of expression and the commitment of the speaker, not solely by its internal logic.[12]

A note of caution should be sounded here. The view just mentioned could lead to one in which only the oppressed are allowed to speak on their condition. This is sometimes interpreted to mean that only blacks can speak about the lives of black people, only women on women's oppression, and so on. Standpoint theory does not lead inevitably to this position, and it is easy to show that the position fails the test of internal logic. If, for example, only women can speak credibly on women's condition, then men would either have to remain silent on such issues or merely parrot what women say. But if we insist that objectivity in the best sense is achieved by including all voices that have a stake in a given matter, we would have to include men's voices as well as women's. Men and women, blacks and whites, oppressors and oppressed, speak from different perspectives—different standpoints—but each may contribute something valuable to a discussion of the issues that arise in interaction.

Feminist thinking in epistemology has obvious connections to educational thought and practice. If we consider standpoint epistemology seriously, we will certainly seek out and give more credence to the stories of students and teachers about the phenomena of teaching. For example, students have been telling us for years that social studies is the most boring subject in the high school curriculum. Educators have responded by tinkering with methods and exploring more entertaining modes of presentation. But we have rarely worked with students to help them develop their own themes, and we have done little to raise their consciousness about their own situations. Instead we try to motivate them to study material already designed by others for the purposes of others.[13]

---

11. See the discussion in Susan J. Hekman, *Gender and Knowledge* (Boston: Northeastern University Press, 1990).

12. See Patricia Hill Collins, *Black Feminist Thought* (Boston: Unwin Hyman, 1990).

13. For a discussion of the generation of themes in education, see Paulo Freire, *Pedagogy of the Oppressed*, trans. Myra Bergman Ramos (New York: Herder and Herder, 1970). For an alternative view of what might be taught in schools, see Nel Noddings, *Critical Lessons: What Our Schools Should Teach* (Cambridge: Cambridge University Press, 2006).

Similarly, we are just awakening to the power of teachers' stories in educational research.[14] Teachers, like students, do not know everything about the phenomena of teaching, but they know some things, and they, too, can be encouraged to develop their own themes and to probe deeply into their own situations. They do not have to be researchers. Instead they should be credited with the special knowledge of teachers, and interaction with researchers should raise the consciousness of both groups.

Philosophy of Social Science

As in epistemology, there is a current trend away from the notion of science as normatively controlled and objective. Many philosophers now construe science as a social practice, one influenced by group biases as well as individual ones. In social science, the biases of both the scientist and the scientific community are further aggravated by the fact that its objects of research are themselves subjects replete with their own biases and idiosyncratic responses. Recognizing the multiplicity of interactions in social science research, Lee Cronbach some time ago advised limiting research claims to what feminist and postmodern thinkers now call "local truth," that is, educational researchers and other social scientists should seek results that are accurate for particular groups under particular conditions for particular purposes.[15] These "local" truths are, nevertheless, truths. Their recognition echoes Rorty's claim that changes are more often brought about by changes in the candidates for truth-value than changes in truth-value.

Feminist philosophers of science have shown that the group biases of scientists have included a masculinist ideology that objectifies its human subjects and genderizes nature. Its treatment of nature as "she" has expressed the dual desires to control both nature and women—to force nature to disclose her ways and to dominate women.[16] The exposure of masculinist ideology in science, accomplished largely through the analysis of language, has led to a critique of both the methods and results of science. With respect to method, feminists have questioned the sharp separation between subject and object (is total detachment either necessary or desirable?), control as a primary purpose, objectivity as an ideal achievable by an individual investigator, replicability as the main criterion of acceptable method, and the habit of ignoring anomalies and discarding outliers. With respect to results, feminists have challenged, among other conclusions, the notion that "only men have evolved" and that males are inherently more variable than females in intelligence.[17]

14. See D. Jean Clandinin, Annie Davies, Pat Hogan, and Barbara Kennard, eds., *Learning to Teach, Teaching to Learn* (New York: Teachers College Press, 1993).

15. See Lee J. Cronbach, "The Logic of Experiments on Discovery," in Lee S. Shulman and Evan R. Keislar, eds., *Learning by Discovery* (Chicago: Rand McNally, 1966), pp. 77–92.

16. See, for example, Ruth Bleier, ed., *Feminist Approaches to Science* (New York: Pergamon Press, 1988); Ruth Hubbard, M. S. Henefin, and B. Fried, eds., *Women Look at Biology Looking at Women* (Cambridge, Mass.: Schenkman, 1979); Evelyn Fox Keller, *A Feeling for the Organism: The Life and Work of Barbara McClintock* (New York: Freeman, 1983); also Keller, *Reflections on Gender and Science* (New Haven, Conn.: Yale University Press, 1985).

17. On evolution, see Ruth Hubbard, "Have Only Men Evolved?" in Hubbard, Henefin, and Fried, *Women Look at Biology*, pp. 17–46; on variability, see Nel Noddings, "Variability: A Pernicious Hypothesis," *Review of Educational Research* 62, no. 1 (1992): 85–88.

Feminists have suggested alternative methods, and, as in epistemology, they have allies who agree that these methods are often preferable. Sociologist John O'Neill recommended some time ago that the subjects of sociological research be treated as authentic subjects and that research be conducted within a relation of trust and cooperation.[18] Similarly, feminist sociologist Dorothy Smith calls for research *for* women, not *on* women.[19]

Evelyn Fox Keller, in her biography of Nobelist Barbara McClintock, shows how attachment to the object of study (a "feeling for the organism") can enhance research.[20] So, too, careful attention to anomalies or outliers can lead to the discovery of significant properties and principles. One does not have to seek general principles in central tendencies, nor does one have to engage in reductionism to investigate complex phenomena. The acceptance of pluralism in the physical sciences has its counterpart in the social sciences, ethics, and theology. In theology, for example, feminist "thealogians" are bringing a new respectability to polytheism.

Feminist philosophers of science, ethics, epistemology, and theology all face a thorny problem. If the masculinist traditions in all of these domains are legitimately criticized for claiming right methods and true conclusions, by what criteria do we pronounce them wrong? If we offer alternatives, by what criteria do we defend the alternatives? Feminist theologians, for example, have accused male theologians of illegitimately positing one god described in the image of men of their own culture. The criticism seems justifiable. However, some feminist theologians go on to describe a god created in the image of women in their own culture. What justifies this move?[21] It may well be that the initial criticism can be justified only by allowing a pluralistic conception of deity. Similarly, an attack on the central methods of traditional science can only be sustained contextually, not by the substitution of an alternative, singular method.[22] Again, these ideas are not unique to current feminism; an argument for a pluralistic universe was made years ago by William James,[23] and it is sometimes made by contemporary mathematicians as well.[24]

What can feminist philosophy of social science contribute to educational research? Perhaps the most important contribution is the warning not to substitute "one right way" for another. Qualitative research is not more right than quantitative; narrative no more right than paradigmatic. Rather, the rightness of a research method must be judged by both the purposes of the participants (researchers *and* subjects) and its effects. Instead of asking merely how a study holds up against preestablished criteria of adequacy, we ask now whether purposes are shared and whether the results are both useful and acceptable.

18. John O'Neill, *Making Sense Together: An Introduction to Wild Sociology* (London: Heinemann, 1975).

19. Dorothy E. Smith, *The Everyday World as Problematic: A Feminist Sociology* (Boston: Northeastern University Press, 1987).

20. See Keller, *Feeling for the Organism*.

21. See Sheila Greeve Davaney, "Problems with Feminist Theory: Historicity and the Search for Sure Foundations," in Paula M. Cooey, Sharon A. Farmer, and Mary Ellen Ross, eds., *Embodied Love: Sexuality and Relationship as Feminist Values* (San Francisco: Harper and Row, 1987), pp. 79–96.

22. On this, see Helen Longino, "Essential Tensions—Phase Two: Feminist, Philosophical, and Social Studies of Science," in Antony and Witt, *A Mind of One's Own*, pp. 257–272.

23. William James, *The Varieties of Religious Experience* (New York: Mentor, 1958, 1902).

24. See Rudy Rucker, *Infinity and the Mind* (Boston: Birkhauser, 1982).

Ethics

Feminist ethics, like feminist epistemology and philosophy of science, is varied; there is no unitary position called "feminist ethics." Some feminists concentrate on the liberal agenda and what it should mean for women's rights and justice. Some work from a socialist position and focus on oppression and relief from oppression; these theorists are concerned with racism and classism as well as matters of gender. Some are separatists and seek to develop a female culture quite apart from the social order developed by men.[25] Still others of us are working to articulate an ethic of care, and that is the approach I will say more about here.

Carol Gilligan's *In a Different Voice* has generated an enormous volume of debate—much of it interesting and important but a lot of it irrelevant to the actual development of an ethic of care.[26] Whether the different voice should be exclusively associated with women (whether it can be empirically so linked) is an interesting question but one I find distracting. The main point to consider is whether an ethic of care can lead us to a less violent, more caring way of life. What is this ethic, and why should we think it has such potential?

First, the ethic of care dismisses the old distinction between *is* and *ought* as a pseudoproblem. We do not have to construct elaborate logical rationales to explain why human beings ought to treat one another as positively as our situation permits. Ethical life is not separate from and alien to the physical world. Because we human beings are *in* the world, not mere spectators watching from outside it, our social instincts and the reflective elaboration of them are also in the world. Pragmatists and care theorists agree on this. The ought—better, the "I ought"—arises directly in lived experience. "Oughtness," one might say, is part of our "isness." Anyone who lives beyond infancy has at least an inkling of having been cared for; that inkling may not be enough to really understand what it means to be cared for, and certainly it is often inadequate to produce a fully caring adult. But it is the root of our responsibility to one another. At least in part because of this rootedness in care, in many common human situations, we respond spontaneously to another's plight. I have called this spontaneous response "natural" caring. Perhaps there is a better, less loaded word for it, but what I mean to convey is that the motive to care in many situations arises on its own; it does not have to be summoned.[27]

In contrast, "ethical" caring does have to be summoned. The "I ought" arises but encounters conflict: An inner voice grumbles, "I ought but I don't want to," or "Why should I respond?" or "This guy deserves to suffer, so why should I help?" On these occasions we need not turn to a principle; more effectively, we turn to our memories of caring and being cared for and a picture or ideal of ourselves as carers. I think Kant was right to distinguish between the acts we do spontaneously out of love and those we do from duty or, I would prefer to say, from faithfulness to an ideal picture of ourselves. I think he was wrong—tragically wrong—to elevate ethical caring over natural caring. Ethical caring's great contribution is to guide action long enough for natural caring to be restored and for people once again to interact with mutual and spontaneous regard.

25. For a description of these views, see Alison M. Jaggar, *Feminist Politics and Human Nature* (Totowa, NJ.: Rowman and Allanheld, 1983).

26. See Carol J. Gilligan, *In a Different Voice* (Cambridge, Mass.: Harvard University Press, 1982); also Mary Jeanne Larrabee, ed., *An Ethic of Care* (New York and London: Routledge, 1993).

27. See Nel Noddings, *Caring: A Feminine Approach to Ethics and Moral Education* (Berkeley: University of California Press, 1984).

An interesting debate has arisen over the role of principles in ethics. No one would deny the everyday usefulness of principles as rules of thumb or shortcuts to reliable conclusions. We all learn from experience to respond in certain ways to certain situations, and for the most part these rules or principles save us a great deal of mental labor. But Kantians and rule utilitarians have made principles the very heart of ethics. Kant's categorical imperative has been used (by Kant himself as well as followers) to derive other principles and rules—just as we derive theorems from axioms and postulates in mathematics. Ethical decisions, then, are made on the basis of logico-mathematical reasoning.

In contrast, the ethic of care gives only a minor place to principles and insists instead that ethical discussions must be made in caring interactions with those affected by the discussion. Indeed, it is exactly in the most difficult situations that principles fail us. Thus, instead of turning to a principle for guidance, a carer turns to the cared-for. What does he or she need? Will filling this need harm others in the network of care? Am I competent to fill this need? Will I sacrifice too much of myself? Is the expressed need really in the best interest of the cared-for? If the cared-for is a stranger, I might ask how I would respond to her or him if she or he were a member of my inner circle.

Jean Grimshaw has raised an important question about this kind of thinking.[28] Does it not also proceed from a principle but one of a different sort? Grimshaw imagines her own mother using a principle like this: "Consider whether your behaviour will stand in the way of maintaining care and relationships."[29] The suggestion is that the ethic of care is itself an ethic of principle; its fundamental principle might be: Always act so as to establish, maintain, or enhance caring relations.

On one level, there should be no objection to this. As a descriptive principle, one that describes how carers look to observers outside the caring relation, we hope it will be generally accurate. But it need not be the guiding force behind the carer's response, nor can we derive other principles and rules from it. Kant's moral agent can decide moral questions in solitude. Carers must rub elbows with the recipients of their care. Guiding questions arise, but even these change with the situation, and there are no recipes for caring. Cultural and personal differences will result in different manifestations of care. Thus, at the prescriptive level, there is no universalization—unless it is something so general that it merely reflects the natural tendency mentioned earlier, such as, Do the best you can to keep people from being hurt. But clearly even this cannot be an absolute. The only universals recognized by care theorists are those describing the human condition: the commonalities of birth, death, physical and emotional needs, and the longing to be cared for. This last—whether it is manifested as a need for love, physical care, respect, or mere recognition—is the fundamental starting point for the ethic of care.

Perhaps the greatest contribution of an ethic of care is its emphasis on the relation and the role of the cared-for. Not surprisingly, this is a feature rejected by many traditional ethicists. It insists that caring does not reside entirely in the attitude and intentions of the carer. We must ask about the effects on the cared-for. If A claims to care for B, but B denies that A cares, then the relation between A and B is not one of caring. This does not mean that A is at fault (although A may be), nor does it mean that B is at fault (although B may be). There may be something wrong in the situation.

28. Jean Grimshaw, *Philosophy and Feminist Thinking* (Minneapolis: University of Minnesota Press, 1986).
29. Ibid., p. 209.

This insistence on including the cared-for as an active contributor to the caring relation makes it impossible to codify caring. I cannot retreat to my office and figure out logically what I should do—what principle I should invoke to justify my acts. Nor can I rely on calculation of utilities. Nor can I call upon my virtues and heroically display the behaviors most admired by my community. I may, of course, be influenced by any or all of these considerations. However, at bottom, I have to respond to the cared-for who addresses me in a special way and asks me for something concrete and, perhaps, even unique. Thus what I as a carer do for one person may not satisfy another. I take my cues not from a stable principle but from the living other whom I encounter.

Some feminists have raised a concern that an ethic of care might contribute to the continued exploitation of women. Both Barbara Houston and Sarah Hoagland argue that stress on the maintenance of caring relationships can lead carers to neglect their own welfare and, worse, to blame themselves for the shortcomings of those for whom they try to care.[30] This is a very important objection, and it must be answered carefully. The fear expressed by Houston and Hoagland is certainly borne out historically. Women have in fact been expected to maintain relationships even when the relationships are abusive, and until recently, women were often blamed when their husband and children went wrong. Surely no advocate of an ethic of care wants to endorse such a situation. Does the ethic of care lead logically to this unwanted result? I think the answer is clear that it does not.

First, "carer" and "cared-for" are not permanent labels attached in stable and distinct ways to two different sets of people. They are labels for the parties in an encounter or in a series of encounters in a continuing relationship. Except in structurally unequal relationships (e.g., parent-child, teacher-student, physician-patient), both parties are expected to act as carers when they are so addressed by another. Of course, it can happen that a selfish person will continually make demands on one who tries to respond consistently as carer, but the ethic of care not only allows carers in such a situation to withdraw, it insists that carers must do so to preserve their capacity to care. Houston objects that this way of allowing carers to escape exploitation does not accord them unconditional respect; it values them only as carers. The cared-for, in contrast, enjoys unconditional care. But the concern is, theoretically, unwarranted because each carer is also a potential cared-for and, in addition, the cared-for does not enjoy unconditional respect, either. Both parties, not just one of them, are constrained by the ethic to care.

Second, the ethic is not meant just for women, and there is surely a danger in labeling it a feminine ethic or women's ethic.[31] When I used the word *feminine* (and I probably will not do so again), I intended to point to centuries of female experience and the tasks and values long associated with that experience. I do believe that the care approach is more likely to arise from experience that includes direct, hands-on responsibility for others than from experience more separated from others. The ethic of care is thus "feminine" in the sense that it represents an articulation of one important facet of female experience, but that experience and the moral thought that grows out of it are no more limited to women than scholarly experience and Kantian thought are limited to men. The pertinent question is, which sort of experience and which moral thought will improve the condition of humankind?

30. See the symposium on caring in *Hypatia* 5, no. 1 (Spring 1990): 101–126.
31. See Joan Tronto, "Beyond Gender Difference to a Theory of Care," *Signs* 12, no. 4 (1987): 644–663.

Third, and finally, the ethic of care guards against exploitation by emphasizing moral education. If all children, both girls and boys, are raised to be competent carers and sensitive cared-fors, exploitation should be rare. The ethic of care binds carers and cared-fors in relationships of mutual responsibility. In contrast to the individualism of Kantian ethics wherein every moral agent is wholly responsible for his or her own moral perfection, the ethic of care requires each of us to recognize our own frailty and to bring out the best in one another. It recognizes that we are dependent on one another (and to some degree on good fortune) for our moral goodness. How good I can be depends at least in part on how you treat me. Thus a major aim of the ethic of care is to prevent the very separation that induces the dualisms exploiter/exploited, oppressor/oppressed, moral agent/object, and so on.

An interesting theoretical question about care ethics has arisen. Is the ethic of care a form of virtue ethics? I said very little about virtue ethics in the chapter on ethics and moral education, confining my remarks to its use as a foundation for character education. Contemporary virtue ethicists and care ethicists both rely more on the character, attitudes, and moral resources of moral agents than on the application of principles in making moral decisions. Further, both see a close relationship between human goods and moral virtues.[32] Both, for example, discuss the link between the human desire to be cared for and the moral response of caring. But, as we will see in the discussion of care theory and moral education, there is also a difference; care ethics concentrates more on the relation, virtue ethics on the moral agent.[33]

Care ethics has grown rapidly in the past few decades. Virginia Held notes that "it has given rise to an extensive body of literature and has affected many moral inquiries in many areas."[34] Michael Slote's work attempts "to show that a care-ethical approach makes sense across the whole range of normative moral and political issues that philosophers have sought to deal with."[35] And my own recent work tries to trace care ethics to its earliest evolutionary roots in maternal instinct.[36] Given the scope of current work on care ethics, it probably is no longer appropriate to label it a "feminist" ethic.

Although care theorists are still working on problems centered on human relations within friendships, families, small communities, and schools, interest is growing in its applications to global affairs and justice. There is, for example, lively debate over the primacy of rights or needs in constructing a theory of justice, and care theorists are working to produce a care-driven theory of justice. In the next few years, it is predictable that new work will appear connecting care ethics to peace studies. Indeed, Held closes her book on care ethics with this statement: "A globalization of caring relations would help people of different states and cultures to live in peace, to respect each other's rights, to care together for their environments, and to improve the lives of their children."[37]

32. See Michael Slote, *Morals from Motives* (Oxford: Oxford University Press, 2001).

33. See Michael Slote, "Caring Versus the Philosophers," in Randall Curren, ed., *Philosophy of Education: 1999* (Champaign, Ill.: Philosophy of Education Society, 2000), pp. 25–35. See also my response: Nel Noddings, "Two Concepts of Caring," pp. 36–39.

34. Virginia Held, *The Ethics of Care: Personal, Political, and Global* (Oxford: Oxford University Press, 2006), p. 3.

35. Michael Slote, *The Ethics of Care and Empathy* (London and New York: Rout-ledge, 2007), p. 1.

36. Nel Noddings, *The Maternal Factor: Two Paths to Morality* (Berkeley: University of California Press, 2010).

37. Held, *Ethics of Care*, p. 168.

Care and Education

Because I have mentioned the centrality of moral education in the ethic of care, it makes sense to start our discussion of care and education with the ethic's approach to moral education. Moral education from the care perspective has four major components: modeling, dialogue, practice, and confirmation.

Modeling is important in most schemes of moral education, but in caring, as in character education, it is especially important. In contrast to cognitive developmentalists, we are not primarily concerned with moral reasoning, although, of course, we do not ignore reasoning. We are mainly concerned with the growth of our students as carers and cared-fors. We have to show in our own behavior what it means to care. Thus we do not merely tell them to care and give them texts to read on the subject; we demonstrate our caring in our relations with them. However, we do not care merely for the purpose of modeling. Our caring must be genuine; the inevitable modeling is a by-product.

In addition to showing what it means to care, we engage our students in *dialogue* about caring. On one level, dialogue is such an essential part of caring that we could not model caring without engaging in it. However, it is also important to talk about our caring, because caring can be manifested in very different ways. Students often need help in interpreting the behavior of adults. Is a tough teacher necessarily caring? Might such a teacher be? Is a permissive teacher caring? What does our assessment depend on?

Students can be encouraged to analyze patterns of behavior and reactions to these patterns. If, in the name of fairness, a teacher treats all students exactly alike, do all students feel cared for? Is there a sense of fairness that is compatible with caring? Many students today equate coercion with caring. They believe that a teacher who cares for them will demand that they do certain things. Critical theorists as well as care theorists worry that such thinking may induce a permanent dependency on a strong boss or leader. Thus, one function of dialogue is to help us and our students to reflect upon and critique our own practice. It gives us an opportunity to ask why we are doing certain things and with what effect.

A major difference between virtue ethics and care ethics is revealed in this discussion. As I have described caring, emphasis is on the relation. A person earns the label "caring" by regularly establishing caring relations, and a caring relation requires that the cared-for recognize the caring. But there is a form of caring compatible with virtue ethics but questionable in care ethics. In this form of caring, the main determinant of caring is the motives and conduct of the one said to care. Teachers who act in what they suppose to be the best interests of their students (whether or not they recognize their teachers' conduct as caring) may be said to care. This is a very important difference, and you might want to read more on it.[38] If you, as a teacher, force students to do things they hate because you believe these things are good for them, should you be credited with caring? Can you claim to have established caring relations? Notice that these are two very different questions and may require different answers. To establish caring relations, dialogue is necessary.

Dialogue is implied by the phenomenology of caring. When we care, we receive the other in an open and genuine way. I've called this receptivity "engrossment," but that term is not meant to suggest infatuation, obsession, or single-mindedness. It suggests, rather, a nonselective form of attention that allows the other

---

38. See Nel Noddings, "Caring as Relation and Virtue in Teaching," in P. J. Ivanhoe and Rebecca Walker, eds., *Working Virtue: Virtue Ethics and Contemporary Moral Problems* (Oxford: Oxford University Press, 2006).

to establish a frame of reference and invite us to enter it. As dialogue unfolds, we participate in a mutual construction of the frame of reference, but this is always a sensitive task that involves total receptivity, reflection, invitation, assessment, revision, and further exploration.

Dialogue is essential in moral education from the care perspective. It is a means by which we evaluate the effects of our attempts to care. Through dialogue we learn more about the other, and we need this knowledge to act effectively as carers. As we try to care, we are helped in our efforts by the feedback we get from the recipients of our care.

Finally, dialogue contributes to the growth of cared-fors. All sorts of questions, information, points of view, and attitudes are conveyed in dialogue. Teachers engaged in dialogue with their students can invite their students to participate in the "immortal conversation."[39] Here care theorists agree with Socrates (and Adler) that an education worthy of the name must help students to examine their own lives and explore the great questions human beings have always asked. There is a caveat on this, however. Care theorists would not *force* students to grapple with the so-called eternal questions. Rather, we would *invite* such conversation and allow students to codirect the line of investigation. We would not declare that the unexamined life is not worth living, but we would raise questions: Is the unexamined life worth living? Should we decide this for others? How do we feel about our own?

Practice is also vital in moral education. The experiences in which we immerse ourselves tend to produce a "mentality." Much talk of mentalities is a product of stereotyping, but some of it is real and useful. Those who educate business executives, military leaders, and lawyers, for example, often believe that they are teaching far more than a batch of content; they are training minds with a certain outlook. If we want to produce people who will care for one another, then it makes sense to give students practice in caring and reflecting on that practice.

Sometimes practice in care is translated into a specific requirement for community service. Such experience can contribute to a growing competence in caring, but a perfunctorily satisfied requirement does not ensure the desired growth. Children need to participate in caring with adult models who show them how to care, talk with them about the difficulties and rewards of such work, and demonstrate in their own work that caring is important.

Current curriculum recommendations put a great emphasis on cooperative learning, and cooperative learning can be used to promote competence in caring. However, as we saw in our earlier discussion, cooperative learning can be used for a wide variety of purposes, and it can be defined in many different ways. Teachers should be explicit in telling students that a primary purpose of cooperative work is helping one another—to understand, to share, and to support. The aim is not always or primarily academic learning.

The fourth component, *confirmation*, sets caring apart from other approaches to moral education. Martin Buber described confirmation as an act of affirming and encouraging the best in others.[40] When we confirm someone, we identify a better self and encourage its development. To do this, we must know the other reasonably well. Otherwise, we cannot see what the other is really striving for, what ideal he or she may long to make real. Formulas and slogans have no place in confirmation. We do not posit a single ideal for everyone and then announce "high expectations for all." Rather we recognize something admirable, or at least

39. See Nel Noddings, "Conversation as Moral Education," *Journal of Moral Education* 23, no. 2 (1994): 107–118.
40. Martin Buber, "Education," in Buber, *Between Man and Man* (New York: Macmillan, 1965).

acceptable, struggling to emerge in each person we encounter. The goal or attribute must be seen as worthy both by the person trying to achieve it and by us. We do not confirm people in ways we judge to be wrong.

> Confirmation requires attribution of the best possible motive consonant with reality. When someone commits an act we find reprehensible, we ask ourselves what might have motivated such an act. Often, it is not hard to identify an array of possible motives ranging from the gross and grubby to some that are acceptable or even admirable. This array is not constructed in abstraction. We build it from a knowledge of this particular other and by listening carefully to what she or he tells us. The motive we attribute has to be a real, a genuine, possibility. Then we can open our dialogue with something like, "I know you were trying to help your friend," or "I know what you're trying to accomplish...." It will be clear that we disapprove of this particular act, but it will also be clear to the other that we see a self that is better than this act. Often the other will respond with enormous relief. *Here is this significant and percipient other who sees through the smallness or meanness of my present behavior a self that is better and a real possibility.* Confirmation lifts us toward a vision of a better self.[41]

Trust and continuity are required for confirmation. Continuity is needed because we require knowledge of the other. Trust is required for the carer to be credible and also to sustain the search for an acceptable motive. Because trust and continuity are required, I have suggested that teachers and students should stay together, by mutual consent, for several years. Moral life guided by an ethic of care must attend to the establishment, maintenance, and enhancement of caring relations.

The discussion of moral education can be usefully extended to thinking on multiculturalism. Instead of encouraging an atmosphere in which subgroups compete for time in the curriculum and space for sharply separate political action, we invite dialogue and genuine meetings. Ann Diller has discussed pluralism in education from the perspective of an ethic of care.[42] She calls for reciprocity of understanding, coexploring, and coenjoyment. These aims go well beyond the usual aims of mere coexistence and cooperation. Clearly, these aims reflect our emphasis on authentic dialogue in which both parties are fully receptive; if either turns a deaf ear or listens only to extract words out of context, there can be no reciprocity of understanding. Similarly, to "coexplore" requires both dialogue and practice. Students from different cultures need opportunities to work together not only on intergroup problems and disputes but also on activities with a common aim. Coexploration can reveal common values and interests, and the activities themselves can yield enjoyment.

Often people who are not enthusiastic about multicultural education identify it with ethnic studies. Even some minority scholars express deep reservations about ethnic studies because they believe that there are "higher" human values than those tightly tied to a particular ethnic group. Such scholars speak of "transcendent" values, "higher" values, and "universal" values. Their arguments suggest that people must reach beyond their own ethnic identities toward a higher vision of what it means to be fully human. Most of

---

41. Noddings, *Challenge to Care in Schools*, p. 25.

42. See Ann Diller, "Pluralisms for Education: An Ethics of Care Perspective," in H. A. Alexander, ed. *Philosophy of Education* (Champaign, Ill.: Philosophy of Education Society, 1993), pp. 22–29.

what they seek is admirable; they want an ethnicity and race-blind civility, respect for persons regardless of origins. They seem to want a new humanism.

Care theorists, along with some postmodernists, wonder whether such transcendence is either necessary or desirable. Do not most cultures recommend civility, kindness to strangers, honesty in interactions, and the like? Is it necessary to get beyond one's ethnic identity to locate and exercise such virtues? The danger in supposing that some kind of transcendence is required is that one group's virtues will be described as universal, and the others will be asked, in the name of some abstract humanism, to assimilate. Their own unique patterns of care, courage, and compassion will be lost in a grand narrative. The coexploration envisioned by Diller can lead instead to a recognition that the virtues we admire can be found in other ways of life, and that the evils we deplore can be found in ours as well as those of others. Coexploration can lead to mutual transformation.

I think the ethic of care has something in common with the ethics of alterity (otherness) described by Jacques Derrida and Emmanuel Levinas.[43] Both call for respect of the other *as* other. Richard Bernstein says this of Derrida:

> Few writers have written with such nuanced understanding about the suffering, mourning "other." In one of his most beautiful and loving essays, his homage to Levinas (from whom he appropriates so much), Derrida writes of "... the *respect* for the other *as what it is: other.* Without this acknowledgement, which is not a knowledge, or let us say without this 'letting be' of an existent (Other) as something existing outside me in the essence of what is (first in its alterity), no ethics would be possible."[44]

The ethic of care approaches the other in a similar fashion. A newborn child is not just "flesh of my flesh" but a genuine other whose appearance may or may not mirror mine, whose interests may be different, and whose fate is tied up with yet somehow separate from mine. I look at her face not as a reflection but as a genuine, unique subject who gazes back at me. The very heart of this ethic is the receptivity that allows the other to enter my consciousness in all his or her own fullness—not as a set of facts I have gathered. The result of our encounters will not necessarily be love, and we do not start with an impossible commandment to love—one that in essence presupposes that we are all "children of one God." Rather, we are prepared for the whole range of human emotions when we meet the other, but recognizing our mutual otherness, we reject violence. We "stay with" the other and pass beyond the potential violence of a particular moment.[45]

Derrida's "letting the other be" and the confirmation advocated by the ethic of care are often misunderstood. "Letting be" does not imply mere coexistence. It does not mean neglecting the other or abstaining from any intervention or attempt to persuade. Similarly, confirmation does not imply making excuses for the other or pretending that an ill-motivated act was done with good intentions. On the contrary, both attitudes suggest an understanding of the other that respects that other's ideal. As we intervene, as we

43. For a lucid account of Derrida's ethical position, see Richard J. Bernstein, *The New Constellation* (Cambridge, Mass.: MIT Press, 1992); for an introduction to Levinas, see *The Levinas Reader*, ed. Sean Hand (Oxford: Blackwell, 1989).

44. Bernstein, *New Constellation,* pp. 184–185; the embedded Derrida quotation is from "Violence and Metaphysics," p. 138.

45. For a discussion of staying with and holding, see Sara Ruddick, *Maternal Thinking: Towards a Politics of Peace* (Boston: Beacon Press, 1989).

attempt to persuade, we help the other to do better *as other*, not as a mere shadow of ourselves. Similarly, when we see evil in the other, we withhold judgment long enough to be sure that the evil is in the other and not a projection of evil in ourselves. Thus the receptivity of caring is directed not only outward but inward as well.

Receptivity directed inward suggests a new dimension to critical thinking. Recall that Richard Paul, too, calls for self-understanding as part of critical thinking, but as Barbara Thayer-Bacon points out, Paul's emphasis is on helping critical thinkers to separate themselves from their own biases.[46] Thayer-Bacon wants a more appreciative acceptance of subjectivity and the richness it contributes to critical thinking.

Two goals might be pursued in this extension of critical thinking. First, as both Thayer-Bacon and Jane Roland Martin (see the discussion in Chapter 5) urge, critical thinking might be turned from its largely negative role to a more generous and positive one. Second, a positive form of critical thinking should lead to greater study and use of interpersonal reasoning. As we understand ourselves better, we may increase our motivation to understand others; similarly, as we engage in caring forms of interpersonal reasoning, we should gain a deeper understanding of ourselves. Thus, the two pursuits should be synergistic.

A positive form of critical thinking would be directed at our own emotional lives and patterns of response, not at just our beliefs and arguments. For example, German youth during the Nazi era might have been helped to understand the effects of martial music and smart uniforms. Youth today might consider what they feel as they watch sporting events, listen to rap music, or view violent films. As we inquire into human behavior and our own in particular, we may find that the reasons for our behavior are rarely beliefs. More often it is something we feel that impels us to action; and what we feel is often triggered, as Rorty said, by language. Traditional views of critical thinking try to overcome this tendency to act on feeling. The result, as Martin pointed out so forcefully, is often a highly rationalized coldness and meanness toward others. Critical thinking guided by an ethic of care encourages us to stay in touch with our own feelings and accept our embodied condition. Such acceptance does not imply approval of every emotional reaction. On the contrary, our hope is that the identification and acceptance of our own emotional states should help us to set them aside (not overcome them) and replace them, first, with a tragic sense that we too are vulnerable to error and evil and, second, with more positive feelings for those we encounter.

As we understand the emotional roots of our own behavior, we may learn when to abandon conventional critical thinking and engage in interpersonal reasoning. There are many occasions in human affairs when argumentation fails to advance negotiation; there are even times when it induces hatred, and, as Richard Bernstein noted, we can rarely agree on the "force of the better argument."

Interpersonal reasoning is concerned primarily with the relationship between participants in conversation or dialogue.[47] It is characterized by an attitude of solicitude or care, and it does not aim to defeat the other or even to keep the other "on the point." As part of a caring encounter, it requires the engrossment

46. Barbara J. Thayer-Bacon, *Transforming Critical Thinking* (New York: Teachers College Press, 2000).

47. See Nel Noddings, "Stories in Dialogue: Caring and Interpersonal Reasoning," in Carol Witherell and Nel Noddings, eds.,
   Stories Lives Tell (New York: Teachers College Press, 1991), pp. 157–170.

or attention described in the phenomenology of care. It asks the other, explicitly or implicitly, What are you going through?[48]

Because the primary aim of interpersonal reasoning is to maintain or to move the relationship in a positive direction, it is flexible. It may exhibit remarks that would be judged non sequiturs in argumentation, but these remarks have a purpose: They defuse anger or irritation, support the partner with reminders of more affectionate or happy times, relieve tension with humor, provide breathing time, and the like. Sometimes such "off the point" remarks are used to gather information about a partner's feelings or mood, and, depending on what is learned, a topic may be explored in the conventional mode of argumentation or postponed indefinitely. Interpersonal reasoning often involves a search for an appropriate response. In the usual pattern of critical thinking, appropriate responses are built into an argument. One uses logic to decide the response. Even in "strong" critical thinking, the response is determined by the logic of the argument or by a challenge to one's own premises. In interpersonal reasoning, one seeks an appropriate response to a living other, not to an argument.

You can see that many of the topics we have explored together could be considerably enlarged if we revisited them from the care perspective. For example, although I have already argued against the establishment of national goals and a national curriculum, we could add to the argument by looking at that program through the lens of care. Genuine education must engage the purposes and energies of those being educated. To secure such engagement, teachers must build relationships of care and trust, and within such relationships, students and teachers construct educational objectives cooperatively.

Of course, there should be standards in any enterprise, and students should be encouraged to achieve mastery in their chosen fields of study. But the key here is choice of enterprise. In both the ethic of alterity and the ethic of care, we seek to enhance the other's growth, but we do not threaten the other's Otherness, and we do not define for another exactly what he or she must do or be. If we are to avoid the dull uniformity described by Rousseau, we must encourage multiple ideals of what it means to be educated. Just as it recognizes the contribution of the cared-for to every caring relation, the ethic of care recognizes the contribution of the student to the teaching relation. The odd notion that establishing national goals will make teachers work harder and more effectively, thereby making students work harder and more effectively, is part of a long, long tradition that assumes an autonomous agent can logically plot a course of action and, through personal competence, somehow carry it out, even if others are intimately involved. Such agents, like Scheman's Cartesian knower, are somewhat schizophrenic, for in claiming their own autonomy, they forget that the human objects of their project must also be autonomous.

The ethic of care rejects the notion of a truly autonomous moral agent and accepts the reality of moral interdependence. Our goodness and our growth are inextricably bound to that of others we encounter. As teachers, we are as dependent on our students as they are on us.

48. See Simone Weil, "Reflections on the Right Use of School Studies with a View to the Love of God," in *Simone Weil Reader,* ed. George A. Panichas (Mt. Kisco, N.Y.: Moyer Bell Limited, 1977), pp. 44–52.

Summary Questions

1. Is objectivity possible? How should objectivity be defined?
2. What are some arguments in favor of essentialism? What are the arguments against it?
3. Can Rousseau's recommendation for Sophie's education be defended?
4. Is Cartesian epistemology a model of rationality, or is it, as Naomi Scheman suggests, schizophrenic?
5. Does one have to be a woman to speak credibly on women's condition? Does one have to be black to talk about the condition of blacks?
6. Why do some philosophers object to "grand narratives"?
7. What do we mean by "local truth"?
8. Is it reasonable or irrelevant to challenge an argument by asking who is speaking?
9. What might be meant by research *for* women rather than research *on* women?
10. Is detachment a virtue in research?
11. How might feminists argue against a male vision of God and for a female one?
12. Are qualitative research and quantitative research commensurable?
13. Why (and how) might we argue against the concept of moral autonomy?
14. Do we need principles in ethics? For what purpose?
15. What is the contribution of the cared-for in a caring relation?
16. How can women avoid continued exploitation if they embrace an ethic of care?
17. How does moral education in the care perspective differ from other forms of moral education?
18. How does interpersonal reasoning differ from analytical reasoning?
19. How might teachers "confirm" their students?
20. What might it mean to "let the other be"?

Introduction to the Literature

On feminist epistemology, see Sandra Harding, *The Science Question in Feminism*; also Louise Antony and Charlotte Witt, eds., *A Mind of One's Own*; on feminist philosophy of science, see Ruth Bleier, ed., *Feminist Approaches to Science*; and Evelyn Fox Keller, *Reflections on Gender and Science*; on feminist ethics, see Nel Noddings, *Caring: A Feminine Approach to Ethics and Moral Education*; Nel Noddings, *Starting at Home: Caring and Social Policy*; also Jean Grimshaw, *Philosophy and Feminist Thinking*; on caring in education, see Nel Noddings, *The Challenge to Care in Schools*.

Learning to Remember the Things We've Learned to Forget

Endarkened Feminisms and the Sacred Nature of Research

Cynthia B. Dillard

(Nana Mansa II of Mpeasem, Ghana)

The Question of Memory

I can remember the day as if it were yesterday.... Ma Vic, with whom I stayed during my time in the village, was not only my dear friend, but my guide in the maze of the market. She had her favorite sellers: the woman from whom she bought baskets of plump red tomatoes; another woman her plantain, another yam; still another, her spices and food staples. And as a regular customer, her loyalty was rewarded with the expected "dash" of a few extra onions or an additional handful of rice. As Vic very confidently maneuvered her way through the market, I warily negotiated the open sewers, the sharp corners of the metal roofs, and the young market women who, without a stall, carried their store—big trays of fish or mango or other goods—on their heads. So my eyes faced downward most of the time, tenuously watching every step. My observations of the market were primarily at the places where we stopped to make a purchase, the places where my eyes could focus on what was around me and not on my feet.

We stopped at the plantain woman's stall. "My sister!" the woman exclaimed, greeting Vic with the enthusiasm of someone who knows she's going to make a big sale. "You are welcome," she said to me, the customary greeting in Ghana when you haven't seen someone for a while. Her smile was warm, seeming to remember my presence on previous visits to her stall. Exchanging more small talk in Twi, Vic and the woman began their search for the biggest and the best plantains in the pile. And that's when our eyes met. About 70 years old, this woman (possibly the aunt or mother of the seller) was sitting in the shadows of the stall. She stared at me, a clear combination of curiosity and suspicion in her eyes, yellowed with age. She looked me up and down. I smiled at her, very uncomfortable with her unwavering gaze. As Vic and the seller were finishing their transaction, the old woman reached over and touched Vic's arm, her face now absolutely perplexed, nodding in my direction: "What *is* she (me)? Is she a white woman?" I nearly fell over, a rush of emotions running through me, from absolute horror to disgust to disbelief to sadness. Vic giggled and explained to the woman (who had still not quit staring at me) that I was not a white woman but a black American.

That evening in my researcher's journal (and through confused, angry, and sad tears that could've filled a river), I wondered aloud as I wrote: "How could she see *me* as a white woman?" "Couldn't she see the African woman I could see in myself?" "Didn't she know what had happened to millions of Africans who'd been forcibly taken from the shores of Ghana and other West African countries?" "Where did she think we had gone?" "Had she never imagined that some of us would return?" "How can this sister/mother see me this way?" On reflection, what frightened me most about her question was that, at that very moment, I couldn't answer it myself:

> What had been the rather solid taken-for-granted nature of my African American identity—an identity that I'd used to make sense of myself—melted down like butter on a hot summer's day in that moment in Ghana. Something very rich that I loved dearly had become useless fat on the sidewalk, no help whatsoever in explaining and understanding what she saw, or who I was. But I know there is wisdom in her question or it wouldn't have come to teach me a lesson. If I'm to "be" a researcher in this space, I will have to struggle with the butter on the sidewalk, the shifting ground of African identity through Ghanaian eyes. Neither here nor there (Ghana or the US), neither African nor American, neither recognizably Black nor white. Maybe it's not either/or: Maybe it's both/and? Somehow, it feels like it's beyond these dualities. They seem too simple. Regardless, it hurts to do this work. (Journal, 1/22/98)

And this pain stayed with me until the following week, when market day came again:

> Today is market day again. Honestly, I'm dreading it. But I don't think there's an acceptable excuse not to go and help. ... As we approached the plantain seller's stall, my stomach churned and my nerves were shattered, afraid of what "insult" (however innocent) would come from the old lady. Vic, oblivious to my inner turmoil, again greeted the plantain woman and went about her business. But before I could properly greet the seller, I glanced to my right and caught the eye—and the smile—of the old lady. "Morning Black American lady! How are you?" she says happily, clearly concentrating hard to speak to me in her heavily accented English. I replied in my equally faltering Twi: "Me ho ye," ("I'm fine.") And she reached over and grabbed my wrist. "Black American. Yea." (Journal, 1/29/98)

This story is from my book *On Spiritual Strivings* (Dillard, 2006a). In the book, I sought to examine the ways that centering spirituality in an academic life transforms its very foundations, creating the site for spiritual healing and service to the world. And I chose to begin this talk with that story because it is still on my mind and in my heart, gnawing in the pit of my gut. "*What is she?* Is she a white woman? A black

American—yea!" Both the question and the way the old lady asked it threw my entire sense of who I was into confusion. Yet, in retrospect, it is in the answer to that question that I have come to better understand my self, my life's purpose and a new direction for my work.

What I would like to do in this chapter is to try to reflexively read and remember this story and so many others created and lived by black women everywhere, to make visible the spiritual, cultural, and ritual memories that are necessary to appreciate the complex and contested spaces and places of black women's lives in our fullness. What I am also suggesting here is that you too must travel with me/with us in this journey, in the same engaged process of re-membering and seeing what Busia (1989) calls our "icons of significance" as well. This is our re-search *together*, in community, the goal being to develop a better sense of reading the Diaspora, of truly being able to see Africa's children at home and in the New World. And although this may seem like a very private and singular her/story of travel, journey, awakening, and cultural memory, it might also be read/considered as a metaphor of the history/herstory of African people as we traverse and settle, move, and create homeplace in the New World and Africa as well.

These memories are about the concrete aspects of our lives, where meaning—within our memories—"becomes what we can read and what we can no longer or could never read about ourselves and our lives" (Busia, p. 198). Busia goes on to say: "This act of reading becomes an exercise in identifications—to recognize life experiences and historic transformations that point the way toward a celebration, a coming together attainable only through an understanding and acceptance of the demands of the past, which are transformed into a gift of the future" (p. 198).

And as researchers, we will read and hear differently, and at varying depths, depending on our ability to read productively, to read the signs along the way.

Central to my thinking about the meanings of culture and race in research and other decolonizing projects is an often unnamed element of identity, one that is inherent in the acts of research and teaching. And both are *deeply embedded in the act of memory and of re-membering*. Often in research by scholars of color and others, we see that racial/cultural memory is at least part of what is raised up in our on-going quest to be "seen" and "heard" and "unlimited" in the myriad ways we approach our questions, our scholarship (see Alexander, 2005; Coloma, 2008; Daza, 2008; Strong-Wilson, 2008; Subedi, 2008; and Subreendeth, 2008 for examples). In common, memory can be thought of as a thing, person, or event that brings to mind and heart a past experience—and with it, the ability to "re"-member, to recall and think of *again*. The *American Heritage Dictionary* (2000) goes so far as to say that to remember is "to bear in mind, as deserving a gift or reward" (p. 597). And the very intimate nature of research narratives like the story from Ghana suggests that memory is also about an *awakening*, an opening to the spirit of something that has, until that moment, been asleep within us.

For many researchers of color, embracing an ethic that opens to spirit is fundamental to the nature of learning, teaching, and by extension, research. We seem to inherently recognize that such spaces and acts—and our memories and ways of being with/in them—are always and in all ways also political, cultural, situated, embodied, spiritual: They are alive and present within us. However, all too often, we have been seduced into forgetting (or have chosen to do so), given the weight and power of our memories and the often radical act of re-membering in our present lives and work, that is remembering as a decolonizing project. And if we assume, as I do, that the knowledge, wisdom, and ways of our ancestors are a central and present part of everything that has existed, is existing, and will exist in the future, then teaching and research must also undertake an often unnamed, unrecognized, unarticulated, and forgotten task that is important for individuals who yearn to understand ways of being and knowing that have been marginalized in the world and in formal education. Simply put, *we must learn to re-member the things that we've learned to forget.* Whether through wandering into unfamiliar/always familiar contexts, making conscious choices to use/not use languages and cultural wisdom, or strategically choosing to cover or uncover, in returning to and re-membering, an awakening in research and teaching is possible and powerful. And there are several lessons we must learn to remember, to answer the question asked by the old lady: *What is she?* The first lesson we must recognize and remember is embedded in this very story, a lesson that many African-ascendent people already know:

> Being scattered in diaspora is an act of dispossession from our past, from our original homeland, from our languages and from each other. We must re-member, "to see again the fragments that make up the whole, not as isolated individual and even redundant fragments, but as part of a creative and sustaining whole." (Busia, 1989, p. 197)

So part of the old lady's questions is about remembering as an act of piece-gathering. But the bigger part of this lesson is about seeing ourselves in the gaze of another and not looking away, but looking deeper. It is fundamentally to answer the question: Who are we in relation to others—and staying long enough to find out.

A Memory in Time: Praisesong for the Queen Mother[1]

You woke me this morning

And I became part of Your divine plan

Chosen on this day

To be among the living.

You dressed me in a purple kaba[2]

And I became the color of royalty,

Traveling to the village in a dirty old van

That felt like my royal carriage,

The curtains drawn for the privacy

Of the new Queen Mother.

---

1. Becoming a Queen Mother is part of a collection of meditations from an unpublished manuscript entitled Living Africa: A Book of Meditations. This is also in honor of Paule Marshall's *Praisesong for the Widow* (1984), a book that has had a profound influence on my thoughts on the endarkened nature of memory.
2. Kaba is a style of dress worn by Ghanaian women made from batik/wax print cloth. It consists of a fitted top, often embellished with very elaborate necklines, sleeves, and waist and a form-fitting skirt with a slit and a head wrap.

You introduced "Professor Cynthia Dillard"

To the Chiefs of the kingdom,

And I became my own desire

To know as I am known,

You honored my family name

On the front of the community center and preschool,

And I became my parents, their parents, parents, parents,

Those who, by virtue of the Blackness of Africa

Were considered by some

Not to be fully human,

But whose depth of humanity shone like the sun in this moment.

You brought my sister-mothers to bathe me in the soothing waters of life,

And I once again became the child of all my mothers

Marion Lucille Cook Dillard

Wanda Amaker Williams

Florence Mary Miller

Nana Mansa, the first,

And those unknown to me.

You wrapped me in the swath of traditional kente,

And I became the weavers of that cloth,

The men who learned from their fathers and their fathers' fathers,

An art so special that had taken months and months

Of skill, patience, and love in its creation.

You sat me on my Queen's stool

And I became Nana Mansa II, Nkosua Ohemaa[3]

The spirit of Nana Mansa, the first, now residing

not in my head,

But in the stool,

She speaks centuries of cultural memories

directly to my heart, as an African American,

"I had many children, but you are the only one who has returned."

You lovingly dress me in beads old and new,

Adorning my fingers with gold rings, my Queen's chain around my neck,

And I became the precious riches and treasures of the

Universe

Now and then.

You fanned me with cloth and palms and bare hands,

And I became the wind

Carrying Your voice:

"Don't be afraid, Nana.

Trust me.

You have all that you need.

I will show you what you already know."

You poured libation

And called me into the sacred ritual of remembering,

And I became my own full circle as a researcher,

A searcher again, honoring the knowledge of

Who and what is here and there

Of what's been and is to be,

Inseparable realities, united by Your gift of breath,

3. Queen Mother of Development

A committed teacher and student of my own becoming.

You drummed and we danced

And with each beat,

I became the rhythms of my passed on ancestors,

Who gathered with us on that day

Brothers and sisters of the village, the community, the diaspora,

A holy encounter indeed!

You gave food to feed the whole village,

And I became my own full belly,

And the too often empty bellies of the village children and families,

For that moment, we were all satisfied.

Full.

Happy.

Joyful in Your bounty.

You've blessed me with life,

A chance to manifest extraordinary works

Through You.

By becoming all of myself

I can live not into the smallness of the world's expectations

But into the greatness of the true names

You've given to me.

Praisesongs are traditional types of poems, sung in various places all over the continent of Africa. They are ceremonial and social poems, recited or sung in public at celebrations such as outdoorings (in Ghana, a christening or naming ceremony) or anniversaries or funerals. Embracing the history, legends, and traditions of a community of people, praisesongs can be used to celebrate triumph over adversity, bravery and courage, both in life and death. They can also mark social transition, upward movement culturally, socially, or spiritually. While the meditation above is a praisesong to my ascent as a queen mother in Ghana, here's the question: How might our memories, our encounters and representations of those, act as praisesongs in the world? As we teach, conduct research, and examine and create texts—whether the research narrative, the lesson plan, the interview transcript, the representational text in publication—our sense of who we are, our identity, our very selves and spirits are seen/understood/recognized/grounded in our past: They make sense to us based on something that has happened (in memory) versus simply as a present moment or a future not yet come. I am arguing here that it is from our memories that we can recognize and answer the question: "Who am I?" and collectively "Who are we?" This isn't just about being able to recognize times past on a calendar or datebook. This is fundamentally to see that our known and unknown and yet-to-be-known lives as human being are deeply imbued with meaning that is based in our memory. Booth (2006) suggests that to answer the question of who we are, we have to go deep into the well of memory:

> to draw a boundary between group members and others; to provide a basis for collective action; and to call attention to life-in-common, a shared history and future. ... All of these involve claims about identity across time and change, and about identity and responsibility as well. ... Statement[s] of identity turn out to involve a strong *temporal* dimension. (p. 3; emphasis added)

This is also fundamental to an African cosmology, one that is based on understanding one's place, space, and purpose in time through recognition of a common destiny: I am because we are. And for those of us who think and feel ourselves into our scholarship through frameworks and paradigms that are African in nature and that just "*feels* right" to us[4] (Lorde, 1984, p. 37; emphasis added), we also recognize that we cannot feel or engage our scholarship without seeing that, as singer Dianne Reeves (1999) suggests in her song "Testify": "God and time are synonymous/and in time God reveals all things/Be still/Stand in love/and pay attention." Within African spaces, time is not thought of in the abstract, but in relation to Spirit. Time is what has happened here, what continues to happen here, and the honoring of "the relationships that linger [here]" (Bargna, 2000, p. 25). This is one of the major ways that African cosmology challenges Western conceptions of time, space, and location: It is circular, based in past, present, and future as intricate connective, and collective webs of meaning making:

> You honored my family name
>
> On the front of the community center and preschool,
>
> And I became my parents, their parents, parents, parents,
>
> Those who, by virtue of the Blackness of Africa
>
> Were considered by some
>
> Not to be fully human...

That brings us to the second lesson: Our memories are based in a sense of connective and collective time, from which we both re-cognize our identities and from which we can trans-form those identities.

---

4. See Dillard (2006b) for a full discussion of paradigms and endarkened feminist thought.

For example, any research of the African American might need to explicitly acknowledge the importance of the transatlantic slave trade and the Middle Passage as relevant experiences in the collective memory of African-ascendent personhood. The Middle Passage was the forced enslavement and forced journey of millions of Africans from Africa to the New World. Spaces associated with this trade in human beings—the slave dungeons that dot the western coast of Africa, the routes and rivers that were used for the inland walk to the coastal forts and dungeons, sites in the United States that commemorate the places where enslaved African people resisted and created new homes, new communities—are ripe with memory and with meaning for African-ascendent peoples who *chose* to remember, who *choose* to make pilgrimage to these spaces to feel, see, and better understand the place of such memories in the formations of our identities, our personhood.[5]

And although the events of the Middle Passage and slavery in the New World are now centuries old (and often unrecognized in the memories of many both on the continent of Africa and in the Diaspora), for those who choose to remember, these engagements have the profound ability to transform us, to bring us back to places (both literally and spiritually) that we hear in the praisesong*: "I had many children, but you were the one who returned."* How do we see these recognitions in our scholarship? *"Everything* about the placing of the questions of research is important here, as our lives and those of the participants we study are full of 'icons of significance'" (Busia, 1989, p. 201; emphasis in the original). With every question we ask, don't ask, answer, don't answer, it is crucial for us to recognize and remember that our participants are being forced to ask central questions of their lives as well. As we are "studying" literacy practices, or teacher education or the ways that African American culture shapes mathematics instruction, what does it really mean to say: "Tell me about yourself." Where is the place of racial/cultural memory of the Middle Passage there, both for the researched and the researcher? This is key, as so many "study" with/in/about African-ascendent communities. How do we—or might we—re-cognize the child you are observing as an *African* American, as connected to and collectively a part of the circle of African time? How is our entire enterprise shaped by the lack of memory of an event so very traumatic that it forever changed the very time, space, and spirit of humanity, that there would be no African American without it?

Irwin-Zarecka (1994) states that "personal relevance of the traumatic memory and not personal witness to the trauma [is what] defines community" (p. 49). But the power and relevance of the memory endures. It matters. An African cosmology requires that we see and better understand this persistence across time (it's enduringness, as described by Booth, 2006), as its presence describes one of the ways that the African community is bounded and has borders and cultural understandings that bind and define its members. Such boundedness within community when conscious and connected transforms one's identity such that the question "Who am I?" is no longer a total and bewildering mystery for African Americans and others in Diaspora. It may become, as we see in my praisesong imbued with meaning and with response-ability, both at the core of claims to membership from an endarkened feminist epistemology (see Dillard, 2000; Dillard & Bell, 2011; Dillard & Okpalaoka, 2011). It is the time where we find ourselves a part of something bigger than what we already are.

5. For further explorations of these memories, see Dillard & Bell (2011). See also Dillard. (2008).

One of the many ways that African feminist scholars working from/through endarkened frameworks are re-membering, or putting back together notions of time that honor and lift up "the relationships that linger there," is to attempt to ask a different set of questions, starting first with ourselves. These are the echoes that you heard in the praisesong, an interrogation of the ways that memory is always already there. It is the way that the sacred also shapes memory and is inseparable in memory. Within the temporal and physical movement that Africans in Diaspora have undergone, it is also what gives the memory shape within Western epistemological frameworks, including frameworks of feminism.[6] It is embedded in the ways that a researcher like myself can remember, put it back together again:

> By becoming all of myself
>
> I can live not into the smallness of the world's expectations
>
> But into the greatness of the true names
>
> You've given to me.

What is needed are models of inquiry that truly honor the complexities of memories. Of indigenous and the "modern" time, experienced not just in our minds, but in our bodies and spirits as well. Frameworks that approach research as sacred practice, worthy of reverence. A way of thinking and feeling and doing research that honors the fluidity of time and space, of the material world and the spiritual one. Mostly, as we point out in recent work located in the slave dungeons in Ghana (Dillard & Bell, 2011), we need a way to inquire that acknowledges both the joy and pain of location/dislocation and the transformation of both in our stories: African women are not stories of a singular self, but are stories of *we*, collective stories deeply embedded in African women's wisdom and indigenous knowledges. In his discussion of the Middle Passage, Tom Feelings (1995) further and eloquently states:

> I began to see how important the telling of this particular story could be for Africans all over the world, many who consciously or unconsciously share this race memory, this painful experience of the Middle Passage. ... But if this part of history could be told in such a way that those chains of the past ... could, in the telling, become spiritual links that willingly bind us together now and into the future, then that painful Middle Passage could become, ironically, a positive connecting line to all of us, whether living inside or outside the continent of Africa. (p. ii)

Formed as a question, what do such memories mean for the teacher/scholar of color (and conscience), and how might we more explicitly and systematically engage them, re-member what we have forgotten as a way toward healing not just ourselves but those with whom we teach and research? Turning back to Feelings (1995) above, he suggests first that such memories, from a spiritual framework, have the potential to connect those on the continent of Africa to those in the Diaspora, the result of the traumatic acts of the trans-Atlantic slave trade. This is a central characteristic of racial/cultural memories for all who live with/in Diaspora. So,

---

6. See Dillard & Okpalaoka (2011) for an in-depth look at the sacred and the spiritual in endarkened transnational feminist praxis and research.

first, *these are memories [that] acknowledge an ever present thread between the Diaspora and the continent, a heritage "homeplace."*

It is not accidental that many scholars of color take up the exploration and research into/about connections to or with/in some version of an ancestral, heritage, or cultural homeplace and that our representations—in art, in inquiry, in personhood and identity—represent those cultural spaces and places. Second, *racial/cultural memories are intimate*: They are memories that, good or bad, make you ache with desire "to find the marriage of meaning and matter in our lives, in the world" (Mountain Dreamer, 2005, p. 42). I believe this may be true for Whites and others who have not carried or been politically or culturally marked or "racialized"—and it is worthy of being explored by all researchers, regardless of race. Such intimacy is inextricably linked to racial and cultural identities; that is, memories are part and parcel of the meanings of identity, of the meaning of who we are and how we are in the world. Husband (2007), in his work on African American male teacher identity, suggests that cultural memories are those memories of experiences and/or events related to collective and or individual racial/cultural identity "that are either too significant to easily forget or so salient that one strives to forget" (p. 10). He goes on to describe the fundamental nature and character of racial/cultural memories:

> In the case of the former, cultural memories can be thought of as memories of events as racial/cultural beings that are/were so remarkable that we consider them to be defining moments in our life histories. ... Pertaining to the latter, race/cultural memories are those related to our racial/cultural identities that are so potent [often painful] that we tend to suppress [them] in order to function as human beings. (p. 10)

What we see here is that the intimate nature of racial/cultural memories and their work in identity creation is inseparable from what it means to be vulnerable in our work, from reaching down inside of one's self and across toward others to places that may "break your heart" (Behar, 1996)—but, like many courageous researchers, choosing to go there anyhow.

That brings us to the final part of a definition of racial/cultural memories: ... *They are memories that change our ways of being (ontology) and knowing (epistemology) in what we call the present.* They are inspirational, breathing new life into the work of teaching, research, and living. They are the roots we must first grow in order to have our leaves. They are memories that *transform* us, a place within and without that feeds our ability to engage new metaphors and practices in our work (Dillard, 2000).

The Claim of Memory

Here's lesson #3:

While remembering is about claiming, it is also about being claimed in a space of recognition that has "[held] your people to this earth" (McElroy, 1997, p. 2; emphasis added).

It's been lights off (no electricity) since about 7 pm. Around 7:30 pm, the seamstress arrives with my dresses. They are both really beautiful. But so was what happened with the purple kaba. The seamstress asked me to go and try it on so she could make any adjustments that might be needed. Given my experience with the old lady in the market, I was a little leery about what she might say once I put the dress on. I carefully tied my head wrap and tentatively came out of the side room. "Mmmmmm," she exclaimed, looking at me in my kaba, clearly in admiration. "Who tied it for you?' she said, pointing to my head wrap. "I did it," I said, realizing that I had done so in a manner that surprised her. "Turn around," she said sternly. And as her hand brushed down the back side of my body, I knew that, like the brothers earlier in the day, she too recognized [another] one of the many carry-overs of African womanhood that could not be oppressed or suppressed, even through the violence of the slave trade: The African woman's ass [as she wears the slit skirt]. She turned to Vic: "She is an African woman." So, however weak were our identifications of these links between us, as African women, they were clear and apparent to her and to me in that moment. And her look of recognition is one I will never, ever forget. (Journal, 1/22/98)

Irwin-Zarecka (1994) speaks brilliantly of how people make sense of the past, particularly relevant to this discussion of memories and personhood of African people. That is that, in a wholly racialized society, our collective memories are less about an intellectual "truth" about what we are referencing, what we are working to construct, what we desire to put back together again. That is spiritual and sacred work, the "rules" of which will be different for different groups of people. Mostly, these memories bear weight on the experiences being remembered for these different groups shape our claims to "mine," "theirs," "ours." I'm arguing here that this memory-work is critical for marginalized peoples, to be able to see ourselves more clearly in order to see how we are mutually recognized, mutually remembered, mutually mediated. Such memories are reference to the place that holds us to this Earth, the ways we are because we have been. And as researchers, while our claims to knowing are always subjective,

> it is the definition shared by people we study that matters. In many cases there is a rather radical difference between the observer's and the participants realities. ... But whether the past as we understand it and the part as understood by our subjects are closer or further apart, we ought to consider both in our analysis. Our baseline is a needed standard for critical judgment and their baseline is what informs remembrance [and hence, the answers]. (Irwin-Zarecka, 1994, p. 19)

In many ways, this positions the qualitative researcher as a narrator and creator of memory, both her and his own and the collective memory of, the hearts and soul of humanity, in all its variations. However, for the black or endarkened feminist researcher, whose work is often deliberately situated in indigenous spaces and places, and focused on knowledge and cultural production, this is not simply the narration of a story: It is the *deliberate* work of engaging and *preserving* these stories, both of the "thing" itself and our engagements and experiences with it. But mostly, it is also our *duty*—our responsibility—to *remember*: We are those who can bear witness to our African "past," diasporic "present," and future as a full circle: That is, after all, what it means to be in community, to be in the spirit collectively. Let it be so.

References

Alexander, M. J. (2005). *Pedagogies of crossing: Meditations of feminism, sexual politics, memory, and the sacred.* Durham, NC: Duke University Press.
American Heritage Dictionary of the English Language. (2000). Boston: Delta Books.

Bargna, I. (2000). *African art*. Milan, Italy: Jaca Books.

Behar, R. (1996). *The vulnerable observer: Anthropology that breaks your heart*. Boston: Beacon.

Booth, W. J. (2006). *Communities of memory: On witness, identity, and justice*. Ithaca, NY: Cornell University Press.

Busia, A. (1989). What is your nation? Reconnecting Africa and her diaspora through Paule Marshall's *Praisesong for the widow*. In C. Wall (Ed.), *Changing our own words: Essays on criticism, theory, and writing by black women* (pp. 116–129). New Bruswick, NJ: Rutgers University Press.

Coloma, R. (2008). Border crossing subjectivities and research: Through the prism of feminists of color. *Race, Ethnicity and Education, 11*, 1, 11–28.

Daza, S. (2008). Decolonizing researcher authenticity. *Race, Ethnicity and Education, 11*, 1, 71–86.

Dillard, C.B. (2000). The substance of things hoped for, the evidence of things not seen: Examining an endarkened feminist epistemology in educational research and leadership. *International Journal of Qualitative Studies in Education, 13*, 6, 661–681.

Dillard, C. B. (2000). The substance of things hoped for, the evidence of things not seen: Examining an endarkened feminist epistemology in educational research and leadership. *International Journal of Qualitative Studies in Education, 13*, 6, 661–681.

Dillard, C. B. (2006a). *On spiritual strivings: Transforming an African American woman's academic life*. Albany: State University of New York Press.

Dillard, C. B. (2006b). When the music changes, so should the dance: Cultural and spiritual considerations in paradigm "proliferation." *International Journal of Qualitative Studies in Education, 19*, 1, 59–76.

Dillard, C. B. (2008). When the ground is black, the ground is fertile: Exploring endarkened feminist epistemology and healing methodologies of the spirit. In N. K. Denzin, Y. S. Lincoln, & L. Tuhiwai-Smith (Eds.), *Handbook of critical and indigenous methodologies* (pp. 277–292). Thousand Oaks, CA: Sage.

Dillard, C. B., & Bell, C. (2011). Endarkened feminism and sacred praxis: Troubling (auto)ethnography through critical engagements with African indigenous knowledges. In G. Dei (Ed.), *Indigenous philosophies and critical education* (pp. 337–349). New York: Peter Lang.

Dillard, C. B., & Okpalaoka, C. L. (2011). The sacred and spiritual nature of endarkened transnational feminist praxis in qualitative research. In N. K. Denzin & Y. S. Lincoln (Eds.), *Handbook of qualitative research* (4th ed.). Thousand Oaks, CA: Sage.

Feelings, T. (1995). *The middle passage*. New York: Dial Books.

Husband, T. (2007). Always black, always male: Race/cultural recollections and the qualitative researcher. Unpublished paper presented at The Congress of Qualitative Inquiry, May 3–6, University of Illinois, Champaign-Urbana.

Irwin-Zarecka, I. (1994). *Frames of remembrance: The dynamics of collective memory*. New Brunswick, NJ: Transaction Publishers.

Lorde, A. (1984). *Sister outsider: Essays and speeches by Audre Lorde*. Freedom, CA: The Crossing Press.

Marshall, P. (1984). *Praisesong for the widow*. New York: Dutton.

McElroy, C. J. (1997). *A long way from St. Louie: Travel memoirs*. Minneapolis: Coffee House Press.

Mountain Dreamer, O. (2005). *What we ache for: Creativity and the unfolding of the soul*. San Francisco: Harper Collins.

Reeves, D. (singer). (1999). Testify (audio recording). On album "Bridges." New York: Blue Note Records.

Strong-Wilson, T. (2008). *Bringing memory forward: Storied remembrance in social justice education with teachers*. New York: Peter Lang.

Subedi, B. (2008). Contesting racialization: Asian immigrant teachers' critiques and claims of teacher authenticity. *Race, Ethnicity and Education, 11*, 1, 57–70.

LGBT Oppression

Sandy Watson & Ted Miller

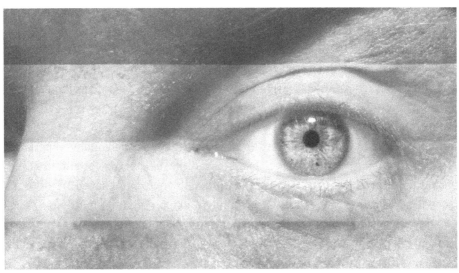

IMAGE 2.3.1

My Back Pages

Yes, my guard stood hard
when abstract threats
Too noble to neglect
Deceived me into thinking
I had something to protect
Good and bad, I define these terms
Quite clear, no doubt, somehow.

Ah, but I was so much older then,
I'm younger than that now.
(Bob Dylan, 1964)

> *I kept myself to myself so I got the grief of being bullied. I twice nearly killed myself because of the bullying...I still get the usual, "Hey puffer...what u doing still alive?" And crap like that.* (Gary, n.d.)
>
> *When I started to realize in 5th grade that being gay wasn't accepted, and that most people believed it wasn't real, I started my hiding.* (Cody, n.d.)
>
> *I want to come out of the closet but I'm too scared. My whole school is filled with people that just take the piss out of gays and I wouldn't be able to stand it.* (Dani, n.d.)

There is no question that Lesbian, Gay, Bisexual, and Transgender (LGBT) students are routinely verbally, emotionally, and physically bullied by their classmates in school contexts as the aforementioned statements from a gay student internet message board demonstrate (Meyer, 2008; Nansel et al., 2001; Pellegrini, Bartini, & Brooks, 2001; Stockdale, Hangaduambo, Duys, Larson, & Sarvela, 2002; U.S. Department of Education and U.S. Department of Justice, 2006).

Just how often LGBT students suffer abuse at the hands of their peers in schools varies across studies cited in the literature since the issue was first explored in the early 1990s. Human Rights Watch (2001) concluded that as many as two million U.S. students have been harassed by peers at school due to their sexual orientation, while the Gay Lesbian Straight Educational Network (GLSEN) National School Climate Survey (NSCS, 2005) results indicated that approximately 75% of students reported hearing anti-gay slurs used by their peers (such as "dyke" and "faggot") regularly in the school setting. In fact, the results indicated that approximately 90% of students frequently heard their peers utter the expressions "that's so gay" or "you're so gay" during the course of every school day.

Further, over one-third of students reported that they had personally experienced verbal or gestural harassment at the hands of their school peers based on their sexual orientation and over 25% indicated experiencing physical abuse (as examples, getting spit on, being chased by other students in their cars in the school parking lot, being touched or grabbed inappropriately) by their classmates. More alarming, approximately 38% of students reported experiencing incidents of physical assault at school simply because of their sexual orientation (GLSEN NSCS, 2005). Physical assaults reported run the gamut from getting shoved into lockers, pushed down stairs, beat up, and even shot.

One of the prevailing reasons why LGBT students perceive their schools to be unsafe is that many of their teachers do not intervene when they (the teachers) witness peer-on-peer LGBT bullying and harassment, effectively allowing the berating and or violent behaviors to continue. One alarming report indicated, "... teachers fail to intervene in 97% of incidents involving anti-gay slurs at school" (Carter, 1997).

Recently, Kosciw and Diaz (2006) stated that 83% of LGBT students report that their teachers rarely, if ever, intervened when students made homophobic remarks. Teachers who turn a deaf ear to anti-LGBT harassment directed toward one student by another, who don't take corrective action when LGBT students report peers' acts of violence inflicted upon them, and who don't intervene when they witness acts of violence against LGBT students are complicit in their silence.

These actions from authority sanction the harassers dehumanizing treatment of LGBT peers and convey that the behaviors are not only acceptable, but welcome (Buston & Hart, 2001; Jordan, Vaughan, & Woodworth, 1997; Kosciw & Cullen, 2001). Shor and Freire (1987) stated:

> The ideology of the "neutral" teacher fits in, then, with support for the status quo, because society itself is not benign. Consciousness is not a blank page; school and society are not neutral fields of social equals. Not acknowledging or not challenging inequality in society is to cooperate in hiding reality, hiding conditions that would weaken dominate ideology. The teacher who pretends that reality is not problematic thus reduces the students' own power to perceive and to act on social issues. An opaque reality disempowers people, by holding a screen in front of what they need to see to begin transformation. "Neutral" teaching is another name for an opaque curriculum, and an opaque curriculum is another name for a domesticating education. (p. 174)

IMAGE 2.3.2

According to Meyer (2008) many studies (Buston & Hart, 2001; California Safe Schools Coaltion, 2004; Chambers, van Loon, & Tincknell, 2004; GLSEN and Harris Interactive 2005; Kosciw & Cullen, 2001; Peters, 2003; Renold, 2000; Wilson, Griffin & Wren, 2005), have shown that homophobic harassment has become "... accepted parts of school culture where faculty and staff rarely or never intervene" (p. 555). This has happened despite the fact that in 2003 a federal appeals court ruled that schools can be held liable when they do not intervene in the harassment of LGBT students (*Flores v Morgan Hill Unified School District*, 2003).

When peer-on-peer verbal and gestural anti-LGBT harassment is allowed to continue because teachers and administrators choose not to intervene, the chances of such abuse escalating into physical harassment and assault increases dramatically (Human Rights Watch, 2001). Paulo Freire stated, "Washing one's hands of the conflict between the powerful and the powerless means to side with the powerful, not to be neutral."

Understanding the (Mis)Behavior

To understand why LGBT harassment and abuse is so prevalent one must explore the way one thinks about sexuality and how the societal norms regarding sexuality came about. Gender scholars such as queer theorists posit "... it is the hegemony of heteronormative patriarchy that constructs dominant notions of sex, gender, and sexual orientation in very oppressive ways" (Meyer, 2008, p. 556). What light to cast an examination of the phenomenon in? Foucault (1978) stated that when one way of being is cast as "normal," it becomes privileged and legitimized, and all other ways of being default to "deviance" and "deviance" is often perceived as taboo, other, abnormal, unacceptable, and/or pathological.

Queer theory proclaims that heterosexuality is socially constructed as the prevalent, natural sexual orientation and thus does not call attention to itself, allowing it to become invisible and unquestionable (Robinson & Ferjola, 2008). Heteronormativity is an institution that maintains the status quo and "... keeps people in their places" (Blackburn & Smith, 2010). Atkinson and DePalma (2008) describe it as a "... tautology that explains things must be this way because that's the way they are" (p. 27). Rich (1980) casts the heteronomative institution as oppressive, and likens it to classism and racism.

When one way of existence is accepted as natural and normal (in this case heteronormativity), then, unless evidence exists or statements are made to indicate otherwise, all people are generally thought to exist within those constructs of heteronormativity. Thus, in keeping with queer theory, and Foucault's thoughts on deviance in the school setting, students who are perceived as existing within the "normalcy" of heterosexuality are invisible; they are not harassed, abused, or assaulted by teachers or peers for being heterosexual. Openly LGBT students however, (and those perceived to be so, correctly or not) because they are not sheltered within the invisible safety net of heteronormativity, are subject to identification as deviants, resulting in an increased potential for harassment, abuse, and or assault by their peers and teachers (Rich, 1980).

It is really no surprise, therefore, why so many teachers fail to intervene when LGBT students suffer harassment and abuse at the hands of their peers and why many teachers even participate in such harassment because the very institutions who employ teachers serve to "... enforce the institution of heteronormativity" (Blackburn & Smith, 2010). From as early as the pre-kindergarten years, students are subject to a variety of routines, procedures, curricula, and pedagogy that enforce heteronormativity to include gender segregation, gender role enforcement, exposure to literature in which heterosexuality is centrally positioned, and the heteronormative performances of school faculty, administration and staff displayed as models to be emulated (Blackburn & Smith, 2010).

Further evidence of the heteronormativity of schools was revealed by Bower and Klecka (2009), who conducted a study (from a queer theory perspective) in which they explored the social norms possessed by teachers in the context of sexuality. Two of their key findings were that teachers generally "... operate within heteronormative frameworks" and the most dominant teacher norm was "... that educators do not contradict personal, moral, or religious beliefs of families" (p. 367). These results are not surprising since most schools operate in a heteronormative system within a heteronormative society (Browne, Browne, & Lim, 2007).

Thus, educators have quite a task set before them: the dismantling of heteronormative frames via the utilization of anti-oppressive practices and pedagogies (Goldstein, Russell, & Daley, 2007; Grace & Wells, 2007; Kumashiro, 2002) so that oppression due to sexual orientation can no longer take place.

A Freirean Approach Toward Reformational Dialogue

Clearly, our schools are in the midst of a crisis of dehumanization when anti-LGBT harassment and abuse occurs with such frequency and at such degree that the victims become "… so oppressed by dehumanizing social structures and conditions that they succumb to a sense of fatalism" (McInerney, 2009, p. 26). Paulo Freire's passion for social justice and his philosophies regarding oppression are sources of hope for many who witness or experience dehumanization. And although Freire was addressing oppression in a mostly socioeconomic context in his book, *Pedagogy of the Oppressed* (1970), we can apply his liberatory strategies in the context of the tragedy that is anti-LGBT harassment, abuse, and assault in our nation's schools.

Freire (1970) posited that dehumanization "… is the result of an unjust order that engenders violence in the oppressors, which in turn dehumanizes the oppressed" (p. 26). He further stated:

> Being less human leads the oppressed to struggle against those who made them so. In order for this struggle to have meaning, the oppressed must not, in seeking to regain their humanity (which is a way to create it), become in turn oppressors of the oppressors, but rather restorers of the humanity of both.
>
> This, then, is the great humanistic and historical task of the oppressed: to liberate themselves and their oppressors as well. The oppressors, who oppress, exploit, and rape, by virtue of their power, cannot find in this power the strength to liberate either the oppressed or themselves. Only power that springs from the weakness of the oppressed will be sufficiently strong to free both. (p. 26)

It is important to note that not all LGBT youth feel oppressed; in fact, Morris (2005) posits that much LGBT (now collectively known as queer) thinking and activism has made a shift to "parody, acting out, acting up, rude, and ludic performance" (p. 10). But for those LGBT youth who do feel oppressed, liberation could come from a Freirean perspective.

Freire (1970) indicated that the first steps toward liberation must be made by the oppressed and their authentic allies because it is only the oppressed who truly understand what it is like to exist in an oppressive society, and it is only the oppressed who understand the absolute necessity for liberation. Freire cautioned, however, against attempts to weaken the oppressors' power. In such instances what results is false generosity or false charity, which serves to "… constrain the fearful and subdue, the 'rejects of life,' to extend their trembling hands" (p. 27). Oppressors will go to great measures to maintain injustice, even perpetuating it themselves so that they can continue as powerful "generosity" givers.

It is only when the oppressors relinquish their charity work and instead work tirelessly together with the oppressed in a true partnership toward a mission to liberate that authentic transformation takes place. Freire (1970) also warned that this working partnership between oppressed and oppressor is only successful when initiated by the oppressed and their allies, and as the oppressed fight "… for the restoration of their humanity they will be attempting the restoration of true generosity" (p. 27). So not only do the oppressed initiate the conversation, they assume "… total responsibility for the struggle" (p. 50).

Unfortunately, at least in the beginning stages of the struggle, the oppressed, in their quest for liberation, themselves often become oppressors or "sub-oppressors." According to Freire (1970), this movement from oppressed to oppressor occurs because the oppressed have operated under the guidelines of the oppressors for so long that they have often internalized the guidelines, causing the oppressed to become fearful of their own liberation. To fully liberate themselves the oppressed must reject the urge to adopt the guidelines of the oppressor, and instead they must work to "... replace them with autonomy and responsibility" (p. 27). This is accomplished, according to Friere, by utilizing the pedagogy of the oppressed, beginning with its first stage, which requires the oppressed "... unveil the world of oppression and through the praxis commit themselves to its transformation" (p. 36).

A Dialogical Meeting

Therefore, applying the first stage of Freire's (1970) pedagogy to the problem of oppression of LGBT youth must involve a request by the oppressed (LGBT students)—because for success, the oppressed must initiate the need for action—for an assembly of LGBT youth, their peers, and teachers for a dialogue about the issue. There is some preparatory foundational cognition required of the oppressed though before the dialogue can commence.

They must first recognize that, through their oppression, they "... have been destroyed precisely because their situation has reduced them to things;" they cannot effectively "... enter into the struggle" without this acknowledgement (p. 50). Once the oppressed acknowledge their existence as objects rather than subjects and realize that they have been dehumanized, they must then commit to taking complete responsibility for the forthcoming struggle and enter into the struggle as humans for their own humanization (Freire, 1970).

Once a dialogical meeting is called, and stakeholders are present, the setting should ideally be arranged in such a way that oppressed and oppressors face one another at the same physical level (preferably in a circular fashion) so that the oppressed become subjects rather than objects in the environment and to facilitate looking inward together toward a shared concentration.

Identifying and Describing the Problem

Next, the oppressed must open a dialogue by identifying and describing the problem for reflection. Ideally, a few LGBT student leaders (Friere's revolutionaries) would begin the discussion by naming the problem (revealing it) and by personalizing it for the oppressors and sharing their individual experiences of harassment, discrimination, and abuse, and including how those experiences have influenced their self-esteem, educational progress, feelings of safety at school, health and well-being, world-views, consciousness, and ethics.

Freire (1970) stated:

> It is only when the oppressed find the oppressor out and become involved in the organized struggle for their liberation that they begin to believe in themselves. This discovery cannot be purely intellectual but must involve action; nor can it be limited to mere activism, but must include serious reflection; only then will it be a praxis. (p. 47)

Oppressed individuals must include authentic reflection as they describe their experiences (objects), for as Freire states, "... to speak a true word is to transform the world" (p. 87) by naming the reality (reflection) and altering it (action). It is also critical that the language of the oppressed incorporate humility, faith in humanization, equality, hope, love for the world, and critical thinking. This humanization of the dialogue allows for a horizontal (equitable) relationship between oppressed and oppressors—without humanization the dialogue becomes hierarchical (vertical and oppressive). The oppressed should also encourage oppressors to examine and share their own consciousness, "... their behavior, their view of the world, and their ethics" (p. 37), and encourage questions, commentary and critical object engagement (Freire, 1970). This Freirean methodology provides an opportunity for both oppressors and the oppressed to become empowered to experience transformative knowledge.

Using a Mediator

An interesting addition to consider for Freire's methodology toward critical consciousness is the utilization of a mediator (one who acts at the middle level of an intervention), as is often used in victim offender mediation programs. Schehr (2000) posited that such mediators (completely objective non-stakeholders) should not remain neutral parties, but rather should enter into the dialogue by creating spaces for the deconstruction and reconstruction of harm in the context of schools as cultural institutions while empowering the oppressed within the dialogue.

Friere (1985), referred to this as conscientization, a process whereby the oppressed "... achieve a deepening awareness both of the sociocultural reality that shapes their lives and of their capacity to transform that reality" (p. 93). Thus, mediators in this context would be known as transformative mediators, whose goal would be to empower both parties. Bush and Folger (1994) identify two means by which transformative mediators might empower both oppressed and oppressors: (1) listening during the dialogue for opportunities for those involved to make decisions that will empower them in the context of the conflict, and (2) encouraging and supporting stakeholders in the careful deliberation of any options available for resolution.

According to Freire (1970), "In the second stage, in which the reality of the oppression has already been transformed, this pedagogy ceases to belong to the oppressed and becomes a pedagogy of all people in the process of permanent liberation" (p. 36). At this point, the oppressed and oppressors enter into a co-intentional relationship where both are subjects working together to "... re-create knowledge" and in the process "... discover themselves as its permanent re-creators" (p. 51).

How Schools are Responding

Many school systems have finally recognized that the bullying of LGBT students is unacceptable and have begun to implement various programs and strategies to counteract such behavior. Unfortunately, many of these strategies are isolationistic, oppositional to what we know about the hidden curriculum, non-transformational, and counteract Freire's work.

For example, in response to the bullying of LGBT students, some districts have opted to open schools that primarily serve LGBT students who have been identified as high risk for dropping out of the educational system. One such initiative is the Harvey Milk School, supported by the Hetrick-Martin Institute, a gay-rights youth advocacy organization, that opened in 1985 in New York City. The school's mission is to "... establish and promote a community of successful, independent learners by creating a safe educational environment for all young people" (as cited in Bethard, R., 2002, p. 419). In addition, in Milwaukee in 2004, a gay-friendly school called Alliance opened its doors.

The removal of LGBT youth from traditional school settings does help ensure their safety, but the action is itself heteronormative, and classifies these individuals as so radically different from their heterosexual peers, that they must be schooled in a completely different setting. It does not address the behavior of the harassers; it removes the "cultural space for possibility" (Margolis, Soldatenko, Acker, & Gair, 2001, p. 15) in which the possibility for transformational dialogue could occur. Sadly, the outcomes of these efforts are that the harassers' homophobia is reinforced.

Somewhat more hopeful, but still not in line with Freire's approach, is Project 10, a counseling and education program that addresses the needs of LGBT youth, that was tested in 1985 at Fairfax High School in Los Angeles in response to a gay student's decision to quit school due to repeated harassment. Project 10 is an initiative that provides school staff training on LGBT youth issues, funds to purchase library materials related to LGBT concerns, assistance with nondiscrimination compliance, and various other services, none of which appear to encourage dialogue between LGBT youth and their heterosexual peers and teachers that might spur transformational change.

In addition, the literature is rife with many other recommendations to address LGBT mistreatment in the school setting (Jeltova & Fish, 2005; McFarland, 2001; Munoz-Plaza, Quinn, & Ronds, 2002; Winter, 2008). Graybill et. al. (2009) recommend:

> First, educators should include LGBT issues in the curriculum to increase the visibility and accomplishments of the population. Second, advocates should provide staff development related to LGBT issues. Third, advocates should support the organization of a gay-straight alliance (GSA), or an after school student club, to provide a safe space for LGBT students and their heterosexual allies. Fourth, sexual orientation should be included in existing antidiscrimination policies. Fifth, the visibility of LGBT populations should be increase by displaying supportive posters and resource fliers around school, in addition to including LGBT-related media in school libraries. (p. 571)

Numerous other recommendations have been made, including (a) schools establishing LGBT Parent Affinity Groups, (b) planning and delivering events that serve to deconstruct heteronormativity (such as an event that celebrates all family types), (c) informing new hires of the expectation to support LGBT students and their families (Winter, 2008), (d) offering "safe spaces" where LGBT students can go for counseling and encouragement (Mayberry, 2006), (e) naming a particular school administrator to handle all anti-LGBT complaints, (f) establishing a student sexual orientation confidentiality policy of nondisclosure for all school workers, (g) providing specialized training related to issues specific to LGBT students for guidance and counseling staff, (h) developing recommended reading lists that include texts on gay issues, (i) having information available for LGBT students and their families regarding local resources and organizations that support or aid LGBT youth, (j) maintaining gender neutral dress codes, and (h) evaluating curricular materials for discrimination and stereotyping (Human Rights Watch, 2001). While all of these recommendations are steps in the right direction, and many of the recommended strategies will decrease LGBT bullying, none serve to liberate the oppressed.

Summary

LGBT youth represent a population in schools at risk to bullying in and by the schools. Evidence does suggest that the practice is widespread and emanates from both peers and professional staff. We have examined some of the causes of maintenance structures for this current climate and forcefully argued for immediate change in policies and activities to protect students.

But going a step further, we conclude that true liberation and acceptance cannot be attained by these policies alone. Indeed, from a Freirean perspective, many common and apparently well intentioned practices actually support and extend the misbehaviors directed toward LGBT. But this is unnoticed as separation reduces surface conflict.

Perhaps we have seen this phenomenon before in schools and failed to take heed from the outcomes. In many ways the initial civil rights struggles associated with school integration followed similar paths in bullying and the reduction of full humanity. Only when integration in schools began to take hold was an actual dialogue across racial perspectives achieved.

In addition, the struggles of LGBT are not dissimilar from the struggle to educate special needs students with others. The current push for inclusion masks the decades of self contained classes and outright denial of services in public schools. There is no doubt special needs students suffered bullying and only with the advent of litigation and legislation has this been reduced as proximity with normal (general education) peers became the norm.

Progress in both of these instances followed closely the requirements described by Freire (1970). We find this abbreviated history of previous instances of bullying and harassment distressing, and yet, potentially comforting. It is certainly a distressing event because it seems difference promotes a negative response, including bullying and abuse, and seemingly we have difficulty learning from previous events. But both situations, the integration of students by race and full inclusion for special needs services, have been initiated and continue to evolve.

In many places integration, unquestioned acceptance, full acknowledgement of basic rights and privileges are the norm and, as we look forward, will certainly become the norm. Can it be otherwise for LGBT? We think not, and that is, we believe, a comforting precedent.

References

Bethard, R. (2002). New York's Harvey Milk School: A viable alternative. *Journal of Law and Education, 33*(3), 417–423.

Blackburn, M. V., & Smith, J. M. (2010). Moving beyond the inclusion of LGBT-themed literature in English language arts classrooms: Interrogating heteronormativity and exploring intersectionality. *Journal of Adolescent and Adult Literacy, 53*(8), 625–634. doi:10.1598/JAAL.53.8.1

Bower, L., & Klecka, C. (2009). (Re)considering normal: Queering social norms for parents and teachers. *Teaching Education, 20*(4), 357–373. Doi:10.1080/10476210902862605

Browne, G., Browne, K., & Lim, J. (2007). Introduction or Why have a book on geographies of sexualities? In K. Browen, J. Lim, & G. Brown (Eds.), *Geographies of sexualities: Theory, practices and politics* (pp. 1–20). Aldershot, UK: Ashgate.

Bush, R. B., & Folger, J. P. (1994). *The promise of mediation: Responding to conflict through empowerment and recognition.* San Francisco: Jossey-Bass.

Buston, K., & Hart, G. (2001). Heterosexuals' use of "fag" and "queer" to deride one another: A contributor to heterosexism and stigma. *Journal of Homosexuality, 40*(2), 1–11.

California Safe Schools Coalition. (2004). *Consequences of harassment based on actual or perceived sexual orientation and gender non-conformity and steps for making schools safer.* Davis, CA: University of California.

Carter, K. (1997). Gay slurs abound. *The Des Moines Register*, March 7, 1997, p. 1.

Chambers, D., van Loon, J., & Tincknell, E. (2004). Teachers' views of teenage sexual morality. *British Journal of Sociology of Education, 25*(5), 563–76.doi:10.1080/01425 69042000252053

Cody. (n.d). Re: The effects of prejudice in schools [online forum comment]. Retrieved from http://www.avert.org/gay-school.htm

Dani. (n.d.). Re: The effects of prejudice in schools [online forum comment]. Retrieved from http://www.avert.org/gay-school.htm

Dylan, B. (1964). My back pages. On *Another side of Bob Dylan* (record). New York: Columbia Records.

Flores vs. Morgan Hill United School District, 324 F.3d 1130 (9th Cir. 2003)

Freire, P. (1970). *Pedagogy of the oppressed*. New York: Continuum Publishing.

Friere, P. (1985). *The politics of education: Culture, power, and liberation*. South Hadley, MA: Bergin & Garvey.

Foucault, M. (1978). *The history of sexuality* (Vol. 1). (R. Hurley, Trans.). New York: Random House.

Gary. (n.d.). Re: The effects of prejudice in schools [online forum comment]. Retrieved from http://www.avert.org/gay-school.htm

Gay, Lesbian, and Straight Education Network (GLSEN). (1999). *National school climate survey*. New York: Author.

Gay, Lesbian, and Straight Education Network (GLSEN) (2005). *National school climate survey*. New York: Author.

Gay, Lesbian, and Straight Education Network (GLSEN) and Harris Interactive. (2005). *From teasing to torment: School climate in America, a survey of students and teachers*. New York: GLSEN.

Goldstein, T., Russell, V., & Daley, A. (2007). Safe, positive and queering moments in teaching education and schooling: A conceptual framework. *Teaching Education, 18*, 183–199. Doi:10.1080/10476210701533035

Grace, A., & Wells, K. (2007). Using Freirean pedagogy of Just Ire to inform critical social learning in arts-informed community education for sexual minorities. *Adult Education Quarterly, 57*, 95–114. Doi:10.11 77/0741713606294539

Graybill, E. C., Varjas, K., Meyers, J., & Watson, L. (2009). Content-specific strategies to advocate for lesbian, gay, bisexual, and transgender youth: An exploratory study. *School Psychology Review, 38*(4), 570–584.

Human Rights Watch. (2001). *Hatred in the hallways: Violence and discrimination against lesbian, gay, bisexual, and transgender students in U.S. schools*. New York: Author.

Jeltova, I., & Fish, M. C. (2005). Creating school environments responsive to gay, lesbian, bisexual, and transgender families: Traditional and systemic approaches for consultation. *Journal of Educational and Psychological Consultation, 16*, 17–33. Doi:10.1207/s1532768xjepc161&2_2

Jordan, K. M., Vaughan, J. S., & Woodworth, K. J. (1997). I will survive: Lesbian, gay and bisexual youths' experience of high school. *Journal of Gay and Lesbian Social Services, 7*(4), 17–33.

Kosciw, J. G., & Cullen, M. (2001). *The GLSEN 2001 National School Climate Survey: The school-related experiences of our nation's lesbian, gay, bisexual, and transgender youth*. New York: The Office for Public Policy of the Gay, Lesbian, and Straight Education Network.

Kosciw, J. G., & Diaz, E. M. (2006). *The 2005 National School Climate Survey: The experiences of lesbian, gay, bisexual, and transgender youth in our nation's schools*. New York: Gay, Lesbian and Straight Education Network. Retrieved November 18, 2010 from http://www.glsen.org

Kumashiro, K. (2002). *Troubling education: Queer activism and anti-oppressive pedagogy*. New York: Rutledge Falmer.

Margolis, E., Soldatenko, M., Acker, S., & Gair, M. (2001). Hiding and outing the curriculum. In E. Margolis (Ed.), *The hidden curriculum in higher education* (pp. 1–19). New York: Routledge.

Mayberry, M. (2006). School reform efforts for lesbian, gay, bisexual, and transgendered students. *The Clearing House, 79*(6), 262–264. Doi:10.3200/TCHS.79.6.262-264

McFarland, W. P. (2001). The legal duty to protect gay and lesbian students from violence in school. *Professional School Counseling, 4*, 171–178.

McInerney, P. (2009). Toward a critical pedagogy of engagement for alienated youth: Insights from Freire and school-based research. *Critical Studies in Education, 50*(1), 23–35. doi:10.1080/17508480802526637

Meyer, E. J. (2008). Gendered harassment in secondary schools: Understanding teachers' (non) interventions. *Gender and Education, 20*(6), pp. 555–570. doi: 10.1080/09540250802213115

Morris, M. (2005). Queer life and school culture: Troubling genders. *Multicultural Education,12*(3), pp. 8–13.

Munoz-Plaza, C., Quinn, S. C., & Rounds, K. A. (2002). Lesbian, gay, bisexual and transgender students: Perceived social support in the high school environment. *The High School Journal*, (Apr/May). doi:10.1353/hsj.2002.0011

Nansel, T. R., Overpeck, M., Pilla, R. S., Ruan, W. J., Simons-Morton, B., & Scheidt, P. (2001). Bullying behaviors among U.S. youth: Prevalence and association with psychological adjustment. *Journal of American Medical Association, 285*(16), 2094–2100. doi:10.1001/jama.285.16.2094

Pellegrini, A. d., Bartini, M., & Brooks, F. (2001). School bullies, victims, and aggressive victims: Factors relating to group affiliation and victimization in early adolescence. *Journal of Educational Psychology, 91*, 216–224.

Peters, A. J. (2003). Isolation or inclusion: Creating safe spaces for lesbian and gay youth. *Families in Society: The Journal of Contemporary Human Services, 84*, 85–110.

Renold, E. (2000). "Coming out": Gender (hetero)sexuality and the primary school. *Gender and Education, 12*(3), 309–326. doi:10.1080/713668299

Rich, A. (1980). Compulsory heterosexuality and lesbian existence. *Signs: Journal of Women in Culture and Society, 5*(4), 631–660. doi:10.1086/493756

Robinson, K. H., & Ferfolja, T. (2008). Playing it up, playing it safe: Queering teacher education. *Teaching and Teacher Education, 24*, 846–858. Doi:10.1016/j.tate.2007.11.004

Schehr, R.C. (2000). From restoration to transformation: Victim-offender mediation as transformative justice. *Conflict Resolution Quarterly, 18*(20), 151–169. Doi:10.1002/crq.3890180205

Shor, I., & Freire, P. (1987). *A pedagogy for liberation: Dialogues on transforming education*. Westport, CT: Bergin & Garvey.

Stockdale, M. S., Hangaduambo, S., Duys, D., Larson, K., & Sarvela, P.D. (2002). Rural elementary students', parents', and teachers' perceptions of bullying. *American Journal of Health Behavior, 26*, 266–277.

U.S. Department of Education and U.S. Department of Justice. (2006). *Indicators of school crime and safety.* Washington, DC: Authors.

Wilson, I., Griffin, C., & Wren, B. (2005). The interaction between young people with atypical gender identity organization and their peers. *Journal of Health Psychology, 10*(3), 307–15. Doi:10.1177/135910530505 1417

Winter, E. (2008). The new constituency: Welcoming LGBT-headed families into our schools. *Independent Schools, 68*(1), 95–99.

UNIT 3. SPIRITUALITY IN EDUCATION

There are a plethora of educational researchers, authors, and scholars who support and defend the notion of nonreligious spirituality in education (Hill, 1989; hooks, 1994; Lewis, 2000; Mayes, 2005; Palmer, 1983; Tisdell, 2006; White, 1996). One scholar, Brian Hill (1989), elevates the word *spiritual* to an esteemed position in the field of education, which he believes cannot be collapsed into "safer" categories. He defends his threefold thesis, which addresses those who subscribe to a religious tradition and those who do not, stating:

> The word "spiritual" does point to aspects of human nature and learning which are not subsumed by other adjectives; that it can be unpacked in a way which is specific enough for curriculum implementation and potentially acceptable both to those who take a religious view of life and those who do not; and that it is not merely desirable but essential that these aspects receive due attention in the education of all children. (p. 165)

Affirming Hill's argument, Mayes (2005) argues for the inclusion of spirituality in the classroom. "In a word, education must be *spiritual*. But by spirituality, Jung did not mean self-absorption or airy disengagement from the world" (p. 177). Mayes also insists that spirituality can be pedagogically powerful in legally appropriate ways with respect to the establishment clause as he appeals to the archetypal aspects of teaching in the realms of moral, philosophical, ontological, and civic development.

Another supporter of spiritual education, Jeff Lewis (2000), interprets spirituality outside of the religious dimension by arguing that schools can incorporate spiritual practices into the curriculum without having to rely upon definitive answers to the many questions such practices raise. For Lewis, the spiritual dimension of education necessitates that it serve an interrogatory purpose:

> The well-rehearsed lists of features associated with spiritual experience, feelings of awe, wonder, transcendence, of unity and wholeness reports of those who have experienced them. If these aspects of human sensibility can be seen as important and enriching, as part of what it is to be fully human, then it is possible to include aspects of spirituality in our programs of education without awaiting the final answer to their mysterious source and genesis. (p. 266)

Lewis (2000) likens the aspects of human nature—physical, emotional, intellectual, and spiritual—to the ancient Hindu view that compares our being to a house with four rooms. If we do not pay attention to all four metaphorical rooms, the whole house will become rotten, soiled by the filthy room we have chosen to ignore. In the same way, human beings must pay attention to all four aspects of their being, including the spiritual, to function as whole persons. Lewis (2000) develops this crucial point:

> Further, if one room becomes overly neglected, then the foul air, damp and rot will eventually spread to the other rooms, making them in turn less wholesome. This analogy suggests that we need to develop all four of our aspects[;] otherwise harm will come to the whole. (p. 266)

This analogy clearly illuminates the importance of addressing the spiritual aspects of students in schools. Consequently, controversies arise over the use of the word spiritual in education because of the complicated connotations inherent in the definition. Many scholars argue that we should stay away from the word and value of spiritual and just focus on using a safer term, such as whole person.

As a result of these interpretive dilemmas, Lewis (2000) maintained that educators should continue to use the word *spiritual* in relation to their pedagogical aims and practices. He writes:

> I am merely suggesting that at the moment the term *spiritual* can be conveniently used to describe this area of human experience. Stipulating a common term to denote a reasonable well defined area of human experience does not commit any of the users to a particular view of the nature of those experiences. It does not entail the acceptance of actual spirits or essences, or of a non-material world. For some people it may mean all, some or none of these things. For all of us, however, the term can be used to signify, and allow discussion of a particular human phenomenon. (Lewis, 2000; emphasis added)

While Lewis (2000) acknowledges the difficulties surrounding the acceptance of spirituality as a legitimate pedagogical category, he also points out that the acceptance of such a term does not bind users to a particular way of thinking about it (i.e., thinking about spirituality in terms "of actual spirits or essences, or a non-material world"). Another scholar, Mike Newby (1996), who shares the same conviction as Lewis about the term *spiritual* in education, suggests that there is a deeper reason at stake in the debate over which term to use. He writes:

> There is, however, a pressing reason why we would do well to preserve the term "spiritual" for this draws attention to the development of an ultimate, overriding perspective on life that influences all one's values and decisions. It is the reality of the importance of the

areas of human functioning, and their perceived neglect in formal education that is of importance, not an argument about which word we prefer in order to discuss. (Newby, 1996, p. 106)

In this case, the word *spiritual* itself helps preserve the nonmaterial area of human functioning, which cannot be substituted with lesser, more safe terms. Furthermore, I believe the neglect of the spiritual arena in formal education and the substitution of safer terms may diminish opportunities for personal growth and development. In fact, educators can use the word spirituality to describe an area of human experience that other neutral terms like moral cannot capture in relation to the process of learning and knowing.

Critics such as Lambourn (1996) and MacKenzie (1998) have argued that the term spiritual is an empty category whose entire contents can be subsumed by other categories such as moral or personal. Similar critics of nonreligious spirituality in education argue that the ambiguous origins of pedagogical practices rooted in spirituality can create moral conflicts for students regarding their own personal belief systems. Students may feel that their own personal belief systems are threatened if they do have definitive answers as to the source of certain nonreligious spiritual practices. Families steeped in religious tradition may not be able to separate their identity as religious beings from their identity as spiritual beings. Therefore, they may view nonreligious practices as threatening to their current religious belief system and may favor the complete abandonment of a spiritual discourse in education for the substitution of safer curricular terms like moral education and holistic education.

One of the more vocal critics of spirituality in education, Nigel Blake (1996), argues that "spirituality is a close neighbor to vulgarity, and one could frame any spiritual practice as an example of embarrassing foolishness (p. 2)." He also argues that spiritual education should only occur in religious institutions despite any attempts to secularize it. Blake (1996) contends:

> There is something peculiarly inapposite in the secular institutionalization of spirituality. Only within the context of some particular faith, I suggest, can we make sense of an institutionalization of spirituality and justify it. Outside the most specific religious traditions and religious institutional contexts, spiritual education is almost a contradiction in terms. (p. 2)

Despite evidence of spiritual practices which encourage the development of the whole person in the classroom, critics like Blake continue to argue for the displacement of the term spiritual due to its controversial nature.

Eckhart Tolle (1999; 2005), a modern-day metaphysician, illuminates this phenomenon. He discusses the problem of attaching too much significance to a personal belief system. Parents, teachers, or scholars opposed to nonreligious spiritual practices in schools may protest in part out of habit—one steeped in an attachment to dogma and the notion of "being right."

> Many people are already aware of the difference between spirituality and religion. They realize that having a belief system—a set of thoughts that you regard as the absolute truth—does not make you spiritual no matter what the nature of those beliefs is. In fact, the more you make your thoughts (beliefs) into your identity, the more cut off you are from the spiritual dimension within yourself. Many "religious" people are stuck at that level.

They equate truth with thought, and as they are completely identified with thought (their mind), they claim to be in sole possession of the truth in an unconscious attempt to protect their identity. They do not realize the limitations of thought. Unless you believe (think) exactly as they do, you are wrong in their eyes, and in the not-too-distant past, they would have felt justified in killing you for that. And some still do, even now. (Tolle, 2005, p. 17)

When students let go of their complete identification with their beliefs and the beliefs of others, they can embrace the paradoxical nature of humanity. This opens a door to a heightened awareness about personal actions and higher levels of cognition. If students are so completely identified with their own belief system, they may not even recognize when they deviate from it or when they commit acts of violence because of it. In an unconscious attempt to protect "their identity," they may commit acts of social injustice.

If, within their respective pedagogies, teachers were to develop a greater conceptual grasp of how passions and desires for learning actually involve the spiritual dimension of life, they may tap into what scholars have framed as "spiritual intelligence." Danah Zohar and Ian Marshall (2000) contend that the whole picture of human intelligence cannot be understood without a dialogue about our spiritual intelligence.

Spiritual intelligence is the intelligence with which we address and solve problems of meaning and value, the intelligence with which we can place our actions and our lives in a wider, richer, meaning giving context, the intelligence with which we can assess that one course of action or one life-path is more meaningful than another. (Zohar & Marshall, 2000, pp. 3–4)

If Zohar and Marshall (2000) are correct, then we must take into consideration the possibility that our students possess this type of human intelligence and would benefit from lessons that would facilitate it. Zohar and Marshall (2000) also describe the primary function of spiritual intelligence, which "gives us our moral sense, an ability to temper rigid rules with understanding and compassion and an equal ability to see when compassion and understanding have their limits" (p. 5). They emphasize the value and meaning that we derive from recognizing our spiritual intelligence. "We also use spiritual intelligence to wrestle with questions of good and evil and to envision unrealized possibilities—to dream, to aspire, to raise ourselves out of the mud" (p. 5).

Zohar and Marshall (2000) offer insight into the limitations of rational and emotional intelligence. They assert that people seek reasons beyond the emotional or intellectual for living their lives. If we believe in the process of educating the whole person, then we should consider adopting an alternative framework outside the conventional paradigm of education. In this regard, Zohar and Marshall (2000) contend:

It isn't enough for people to find happiness within their existing framework. They want to question the framework itself, to question the value of how they are living their lives, and to find new value, that elusive "more." Just by asking such questions, they are showing a need to use their spiritual intelligence. (p. 21)

However, as Howard Gardner (2000) has written, the typical American educator primarily values linguistic intelligence and logical-mathematical intelligence over other types of intelligences (p. 47). Students who show proficiency in other types of intelligences have little or no opportunities to develop them more fully in the classroom setting.

I believe one cultural problem that contributes to this overemphasis on educating only part of the child (i.e., the linguistic and logical-mathematical) is what Zohar and Marshall (2000) call the "missing middle." Drawing on Freud, Ken Wilber, and Jung, Zohar and Marshall (2000) compare Western culture to cultures of the "'healthy middle,' because their strengths and weaknesses are those of the self's middle layer" (p. 24). The self, represented by the lotus image, contains an ego (rational) periphery, an associative (emotional) middle and a unitive (spiritual) center (p. 24).

Zohar and Marshall (2000) argue that shared community has nearly ceased to exist. "We are deeply undernourished in that whole associative, middle layer of the self. We have few collective traditions that point beyond the prosaic everyday level of life that ground us in the deeper origin and meaning of our communities and of our life within them" (p. 25).

In cultures stripped of the "healthy middle," citizens are left to create or discover more superficial meanings. They may resort to attention-seeking or self-destructive behaviors such as materialism, promiscuous sex, drug abuse, or violence. In order to counter the effect of the "missing middle" at the pedagogical level, teachers can facilitate discussions that help students deal with the existential/spiritual questions of life.

Howard Gardner (2000) writes about "two new candidate intelligences" in his book Intelligence Reframed: a spiritual intelligence and an existential intelligence (p. 47). These two intelligences overlap in their relationship to one another. The first candidate, a spiritual intelligence, involves a great amount of complexity and controversy in the field of education. Gardner (2000) observes, "Many of us do not recognize the spirit as we recognize the mind and the body, and many of us do not grant the same ontological status to the transcendent or the spiritual as we do to, say, the mathematical or the musical" (p. 53).

Gardner (2000) points out that the majority of scholars working in the field of cognitive and biological science dismiss questions that are spiritual in nature—designating these questions to religious followers or quacks. However, the decision to omit such questions is just as dangerous as admitting the same questions on the basis of "fiat or faith" (p. 53).

Gardner (2000) outlines three distinct senses of the spiritual, pointing out the difference between "spiritual concerns that are approached through a traditional or organized means (such as participation in a formal religion) and spiritual concerns that are approached in a more personal, idiosyncratic, or creative manner" (p. 54).

In the book *Jung and Education*, Clifford Mayes (2005) differentiates the spiritual approaches in a similar way as Gardner. Mayes refers to spiritual in the traditional sense as "incarnational spirituality" and in the personal sense as "ontological spirituality." He posits, "'Incarnation spirituality' differs from 'ontological spirituality' in that the former rests *specific doctrinal commitments* involving a personal God whereas the latter is non-theistically interested in cultivating *ontological presence as such* in the classroom" (p. 170; emphasis in original).

Consequently, my inquiry will not touch on spiritual concerns approached from an incarnational way, since my intention is to examine spiritual concerns that might be approached in a secular, nondoctrinaire manner that upholds the Establishment Clause of the First Amendment. As Gardner (2000) explicitly states, the spiritual concerns that are approached in a "more personal, idiosyncratic, or creative manner" should be the ones considered in the curriculum of schools today. The first spiritual concern, "spiritual as concern with cosmic or existential issues," overlaps with one of Gardner's other forms of intelligence—existential intelligence.

Gardner (2000) posits that the realms of mythology and art have inspired our attempts to "grasp the ultimate questions, mysteries and meanings in life: Who are we? Where do we come from? What does the future hold for us? Why do we exist? What is the meaning of life, of love, of tragic losses, of death?" (p. 54).

From these existential questions, human beings grapple with life's meaning and purpose. Teachers who are passionate about teaching the whole person do not want to deny students the opportunity to discuss questions of such pivotal importance. The second spiritual concern expressed by Gardner (2000), "spiritual as achievement of a state of being," suggests the achievement of an ontological status inherent in spiritual intelligence. Gardner (2000) distinguishes between the two classical senses of knowing—*knowing how* and *knowing that*—in his discussion of this concern (p. 55). "The first sense delineates the realms of experience, or domains of existence that people seek to understand" (p. 55). Mystics, yogis, and meditators may have more success attaining this sense of spirituality. The second variety may involve a more traditional or personalized route—religion or hallucinogenic substances, which can also evoke this form of consciousness. This particular variety of spirituality has no relevance to my inquiry.

However, the acknowledgment of its existence should be included to honor a more comprehensive analysis of the term. The third spiritual concern, "spiritual as an effect on others," involves the meaningful interactions that students may have with specific individuals or music. For example, knowing about the life of Mother Theresa and Gandhi or listening to classical music may help "some people feel more whole and more in touch with themselves, and the cosmos" (Gardner, 2000, p. 57).

Marsha Sinetar (2000), who focuses on the relationship between education and spiritual growth, asserts that spirituality in education can facilitate a transcultural rebirth in a child's life.

> Much of the absorbing play of any boy's or girl's life is guided by bursts of self-awareness by piercing enthusiasms and wonderings: "Who am I?" "Who shall I be?" and "Which I is the real me?" Heeding love begins with the spiritual musings that turn children toward their truths. Eventually that truth helps them transcend what appears to be their lot in life. (Sinetar, 2000, p. 66)

Sinetar (2000) also emphasizes the importance of growing whole through the development of spiritual intelligence. She writes:

> To the extent we and our children become whole, we and our children feel capable, worthwhile, genuine, ready to express our truest ideas. We pull out the stops and encounter each delicious moment. That progression is spiritually bright. Inspired. Something within catches on fire, is alive with intelligible purpose. (Sinetar, 2000, p. 21)

From a place of inspiration, children can develop their spiritual intelligence and taste a "victory" that never fades. For example, Ryan White, a young boy rejected by his community and classmates because of his diagnosis of AIDS in the 1980s, discovered a more meaningful, more graceful way of being, which some observers may call "spiritual" in nature (Sinetar, 2000, p. 21). Ryan White used his disease as a vehicle to communicate a message of self-respect and celebration that transcended his suffering. He traveled around the country giving inspirational speeches to his peers from the age of 13 until his tragic death at 16. In a sense, this boy had an evolved sense of spiritual intelligence.

In contrast to the tenets described above used to justify facilitating spiritual intelligence in the classroom, the dominant curriculum in public schools teaches students to attach themselves to education as a means to an end: the future degree, the future career, the future in general. Rarely do students or teachers have the opportunity to reflect on the value of the present moment during regular school hours. They have infrequent opportunities, if any, to enter the present moment or develop an awareness of the mind (Tolle, 1999).

Therefore, as an educator committed to furthering the development of whole persons, I must consider the inclusion of spiritual activities in education—activities that encourage students to live in the present moment and develop mind awareness. Opportunities to "enter the present moment" or "develop an awareness of the mind" can take place in public institutions without any attachment to a religious prayer or tradition. For example, the state of Illinois requires public school teachers in K–12 settings to facilitate a daily moment of silence after the Pledge of Allegiance. This required moment of silence is one tiny departure from the usual future-orientated rhetoric and activities which dominate the contemporary school curriculum.

References

Blake, N. (1996). Against spiritual education. *Oxford Review of Education, 22*(4), 443–456.

Gardner, H. (2000). *Intelligence reframed: Multiple intelligences for the 21st century.* Basic Books.

Hill, B. (1989). "Spiritual development" in the Education Reform Act: A source of acrimony, apathy, or accord? *British Journal of Educational Studies, 37*(2), 169–182.

hooks, b. (1994). *Teaching to transgress.* Routledge.

Lambourn, D. (1996). "Spiritual" minus "personal-social"?: A critical note on an "empty" category. In R. Best (Ed.), *Education, spirituality and the whole child* (pp. 150–158). Cassell.

Lewis, J. (2000). Spiritual education as the cultivation of qualities of the heart and mind. *Oxford Review of Education, 26*(3), 266.

MacKenzie, J. (1998). David Carr on religious knowledge and spiritual education. *Journal of Philosophy of Education, 32*(3), 409–428.

Mayes, C. (2005). *Jung and education.* Rowman & Littlefield Education.

Newby, M. (1996). Towards a secular concept of spiritual maturity. In R. Best (Ed.), *Education, spirituality and the whole child* (pp. 99–107). Cassell.

Palmer, P. (1983). *To know as we are known: Education as a spiritual journey.* Harper.

Sinetar, M. (2000). *Spiritual intelligence: What we can learn from the early awakening child.* Orbis.

Tisdell, E. J. (2006). Spirituality, cultural identity, and epistemology in culturally responsive teaching in higher education. *Multicultural Perspectives, 8*(3), 19–25.

Tolle, E. (1999). *Practicing the power of now.* New World Library.

Tolle, E. (2005). *A new earth: Awakening to your life's purpose.* Dutton/Penguin Group.

White, J. (1996). Education, spirituality and the whole child: A humanist perspective. In R. Best (Ed.), *Education, spirituality and the whole child* (pp. 30–42). Cassell.

Zohar, D., & Marshall, I. N. (2000). *SQ: Connecting with our spiritual intelligence.* Bloomsbury.

Towards an Education That (Re)members

Centering Identity, Race, and Spirituality in Education

Cynthia B. Dillard
(Nana Mansa II of Mpeasem, Ghana)

Cynthia B. Dillard, "Towards an Education That (Re)members: Centering Identity, Race, and Spirituality in Education," *Tikkun*, vol. 31, no. 4, pp. 50–53. Copyright © 2016 by Institute of Labor and Mental Health. Reprinted with permission. Provided by ProQuest LLC. All rights reserved.

Why we (re)member

Jacqueline is a twenty-one-year-old Black female. She is introspective and soft-spoken, reflecting her modest, humble Christian upbringing where one speaks only when spoken to and lowers one's eyes in the presence of elders. Her curly brown hair is often straightened or pulled back in a bun and dark-rimmed glasses frame her skin, the color of butterscotch. Often dressed in university apparel, she came to the university from a community college. When we first met, she was a junior studying early childhood education and minoring in sociology. Through much hard work on both of our parts, she received a scholarship that enabled her to study abroad in Ghana. That was the beginning of her transformative experience.

When Jacqueline shared with me the reasons she wanted to travel to Ghana, she raised her eyes and looked deeply into mine: She knew that the stories she'd heard about Black people—from continent to diaspora—did not accurately describe what she knew experientially in her bones. She had a spiritual longing to understand the deeper meaning of blackness and to understand herself as a Black person. "I have to go to Ghana. It's a spiritual calling," she said. "When you came into my … class discussing the Ghana study abroad trip, something told me that I needed to be on that trip to Ghana. As the only African American girl in that class, I knew that I would have a deep connection to Africa."

When applying to study abroad, she spoke of the importance of being around other Black women as mentors and guides. In her view, this was critical to understanding herself as a Black woman teacher. But there was sadness on her face as we talked further. "I have never had a Black teacher," she whispered. "But this trip would guarantee that I'd finally have an African American teacher (professor), a role model to look up to that looks like me, since there are so few."

As might be imagined, experiences in Ghana were life-changing for Jacqueline, as demonstrated by this excerpt from her final paper:

> Ghana was so essential because I learned and found my identity through culture and history of my race. From exiting 'The Door of No Return' and coming back and entering through 'The Door of Return' I had proven that a descendant, at least one, could just briefly return to Africa, and that despite the cruel betrayals, bitter ocean voyages, and hurtful centuries, we were still recognizable. Despite the horrid, inhumane dungeons, I received the word, the connection of my people, healing my wounds of self-doubt and low esteem and feeling proud, having a sense of empowerment, and loving my blackness as a woman.

IMAGE 3.1.1   Past Tense Present

Maya Freelon Asante | Courtesy of the artist and Morton Fine Art | maya-freelonasante.squarespace.com and www.mortonfineart.com

Why Race, Identity, and Spirit in Education

Jacqueline's narrative raises a number of troubling issues in the education of Black girls and women and the ways our minds, bodies, and spirits continue to be harmed by educational experiences that: 1) fail to acknowledge the visibility and centrality of our culture, race, and gender historically or contemporarily; 2) render invisible or totally disregards spirit and spirituality as animating forces in our lives; 3) do little to honor the creativity and contributions of Black people from the African continent including African Americans and others in the African diaspora. Patricia Williams argues that this disregard murders the spirit of Blacks in school and society. With racism as a foundational fact of the U.S., education too often continues to alienate Blacks from our culture and teaches us in ways that cause injury to our spirits. Many argue that such assaults on Black children's lives are grounded in a deliberate and collective national amnesia about who we are, the events that have happened in the various (and often troubled) histories of this nation and the world, who has benefited from telling particular stories of those histories, and the absent dialogues that our collective society has been unwilling to have. Still others argue racism is a permanent part of the landscape of this nation and is a continued barrier to creating the beloved communities across differences, that Dr. Martin Luther King, Jr. called for decades ago. Still other marginalized peoples, including Native Americans and Latinos, also face similar spirit-murder and destruction of memory in the education system.

What is the education that can help us heal these deep wounds and help us to see each other across our differences more clearly? In my book, *Learning to (Re)member the Things We've Learned to Forget*, I examined the ways that centering spirituality in education transforms the very foundations of education, creating sites for spiritual healing and service to the world. While such a stance is particularly important in the education of Blacks and other people of color, I am suggesting that centering culture, race, identity, and spirituality is work that has the potential to heal and serve us all. Looking back, a central thread in Jacqueline's story is that identities matter: social identities (i.e., racial, gender, sexual, ability, etc.), identities embedded in roles (i.e., teacher, mother, mentor, etc.), and spiritual identities or identities that may be based in religion, but may also be "the evidence of things unseen," matter. I am also suggesting here that the work of constructing identities is deeply embedded in acts of memory and of (re)membering. Memory can be thought of as a thing, person, or event that brings to mind and heart a past experience. But (re)membering is both the ability to recall that experience (or think of again) and the ability to put it back together again (to re-"member"). From my view, as spiritual beings having a human experience, we already know in spirit who we are and our work in the world. Thus our human experience provides us space and time to act like we know that.

For many students of color, embracing an ethic that opens to spirit is fundamental to the nature of learning and education. But educational spaces like schools are always and in all ways also political, cultural, situated, embodied, and spiritual. Too often, Black students like Jacqueline are encouraged or forced to forget who they are (or have chosen to do so), given the weight and power of memories in their present lives. This is where study abroad programs like the one Jacqueline experienced in Ghana can be so important. But they are not enough. Teaching those most marginalized by society must begin with an alternative orientation to traditional education: it must embrace a new sense of the world. Thus, education that addresses inequality begins within local lived experiences of Black students, with local communities serving as bridges to understanding one's place in the world. Such understandings arise through critically examining the knowledge and cultural productions of Black people's historical, economic, and cultural stories and struggles. This expansive examination can cultivate learning and teaching based in new ways of seeing, feeling, hearing, understanding, and links to global understandings of education, contributions, and engagements of Black peoples. Assume that the knowledge, wisdom, and ways of our ancestors are a central and present part of everything that has existed, is existing, and will exist in what we call the future. If so, then education that addresses the harm and injury of exclusions and oppressions must also undertake an often unnamed and oft-forgotten task that is important for individuals like Jacqueline who want to understand ways of being and knowing that have been marginalized in the world and in formal education. Simply put, we must learn to (re)member the things that we've learned to forget.

When Learning to (Re)member is the Process of Education

Ghanaian writer Ayi Kwei Armah, in his book *KMT in the house of life: An epistemic novel,* says that Black people are and have always been thinkers and sharers. But we think, he says, in order to share. This is a crucial first step in creating and sharing counter-stories of the brilliance and beauty of Black life. (Re)membering our identities is like weaving kente, the magnificently beautiful cloth of Ghana. Kente is a useful metaphor for (re)membering and weaving identity together again. The processes of (re)membering identity are like the warp of kente cloth: they literally hold the cloth (and our personhood) together. Like kente, the work of constructing one's identity also creates unique designs and "colors" given a person's upbringing, education, and experiences. Like the weft of woven cloth, this process of (re)membering identities (particularly racial and ethnic identities) also creates unique designs and individual ways of being as we engage the processes of education.

[filename=Image 3.1.2 caption=Nurture filename=FIG_3.1.2.jpg source=Maya Freelon Asante | Courtesy of the artist and Morton Fine Art | maya-freelonasante.squarespace.com and www.mortonfineart.com]

Jacqueline's process of (re)membering Black identity, like so many Black youth and adults in schools and universities today, shows us several powerful transformations of body, mind, and spirit. She shows us that both recalling who we are and putting ourselves back together is our education. Each person enacts processes of (re)membering differently based on who they are. Enacting a sacred and spiritual process of (re)membering who we are in relation to diverse knowledges, cultures, places, and people is work we do from the inside out and from one soul to another. This is not necessarily a linear process, as engagements and enactments are shaped by the life experiences of each person. However, in learning to (re)member, we are acknowledging that there are important spiritual lessons we may have once known as people, but that we have learned or been forced to forget. As we learn to (re)member through uncovering and discovering our diverse identities, we initially engage in the process of (re)searching, seeking, looking, and searching again. In Jacqueline's case, she was searching for Black heritage to teach her something new about herself—and about others. But I am suggesting here that, as we engage with one another across our diverse identities, everyone is engaged in (re)search, in trying to understand and be aware of another. And what we are searching for is what Thich Nhat Hanh calls our true identity, with the goal to see ourselves as spiritual beings engaging in a human experience, on purpose for a purpose.

This process of learning to (re)member also involves (re)visioning, expanding our vision and worldview beyond just what we can see towards what womanist scholar Oyèrónkẹ́ Oyěwùmí calls a world sense. This involves an awakening to what we hear, touch, feel, and intuit and acknowledging the spiritual "evidence of things unseen." We read this as Jacqueline articulated her new visions of Africa and herself. Another part of the processes of learning to (re)member is (re)cognizing, the process of changing our thinking and our minds about who we are in relation to one another. In Jacqueline's case, she quite literally changed her mind about who Black people were, what Black people have accomplished, and the sociocultural brilliance of Black people from Africa to the diaspora and back again. While (re)cognizing is often manifest as a change in mind, it also includes shifts in our heart: it involves thinking about our very selves again in light of our encounters. In this process of learning, we also begin (re)presenting ourselves differently in the world, literally putting our understandings of our own and other's identities and culture in the world in new and fuller ways. There is an African proverb that says, "Until the lion tells his own story, the story will always glorify the hunter."

These acts of (re)presention are where the lion begins to speak his or her own story, a kind of truth-telling that disrupts what has passed as universal narratives of humanity towards more specific stories as they have been lived by very diverse peoples. Finally, there is a (re)claiming, where we (re)member in order to claim and embrace the multiple legacies we are a part of (in Jacqueline's case, of African people and history) and to take our place within these legacies. The Akan people of Ghana describe this process of (re)membering as *sankofa*: where we learn from our gatherings of the past in order to build for the future.

When the Child is Black: A Note for Teachers

In an interview with Bernice Johnson Reagan, of acapella group Sweet Honey in the Rock, J.M. Latta spoke of an important consideration in creating spaces for an education that (re)members: "History is sacred because it is the only chance that you have of knowing who you are outside of what's been rained down upon you from a hostile environment. And when you go to the documents created inside the culture, you get another story. You get another history. The history is sacred and the highest, most hallowed songs in tones are pulled into service to deliver that story."

We heard through Jacqueline's encounters with African knowledge and culture in Ghana that those encounters mattered deeply to her sense of being as a Black woman teacher. We heard in her voice (re)claimations of connection, kinship, and healed identities. Learning to (re)member in Ghana allowed her to resist the oppressive narratives of Black women's lives that have been constructed worldwide and to create new identities that empowered and changed her view of Black life. Through her processes of (re)membering, she created an identity drawing on the past. We witnessed in Jacqueline's voice what it meant to take up the sacred operationally, to wrestle and (re)member as deeply situated and healing processes which implied several engagements that are instructive for teachers of Black children.

The first lesson was that she was drawn into and present in a spiritual heritage homeland, in this case, Ghana, West Africa. It is critical that we provide opportunities for Black students to very explicitly experience their heritage and culture, not simply as an important engagement, but as a human right. Whether through experiential global engagements with African and other Black heritage sites such as monuments and museums or bringing the world into our classrooms in other exciting ways, children should have the opportunity to learn and to be in spaces that affirm their heritage, their culture, and their spirits. In Jacqueline's story, we also learned that these engagements are not just important for our students, they are critical for Black teachers and those who care about Black teachers and students. As teachers, one question we might ask of our practice is this: in what ways do I provide learning spaces for my students (assignments, experiences, resources, materials) that affirm the heritage, culture, and spirit of all of my students?

Second, Jacqueline was engaged with the rituals, people, and places (of Ghana) in intimate and authentic ways. As we examine our teaching practices, we might ask in what ways our students engage curriculum and lessons in authentic and intimate ways, especially in relation to Black heritage, culture, and spiritualities. For many Black children, post-integration schooling has done little to affirm the contributions, knowledges, and spiritual perspectives of African and African diasporic heritage, leaving our children without the recognition of themselves as builders of civilizations and producers of knowledge and culture from a long line of Black brilliance and legacy. A question for teachers is this: how might I engage and learn about the rituals, people, and culture of Africa (and by extension, African Americans and others in the African diaspora) in ways that are authentic, intimate, and life-affirming? This is not a question of "adding on" to the common core or other curricular mandates. As we saw in Jacqueline's (re)membering processes, it is a matter of (re)visioning the entire curricular process to meet the educational, social, and spiritual needs of Black students and other students whose cultures and heritages are not readily found in curriculum and educational practices today.

Finally, Jacqueline's story helps us see that, as a future Black woman teacher, she was open to being transformed by her education in Ghana and recognized those encounters as purposeful and expansive, as acts of healing. For Jacqueline, the catalyst and context to (re)member was Ghana, West Africa. However, within our schools, universities, and broader society, we have the responsibility to (re)member Black identities and the rich heritage of Black peoples from Africa and her diaspora, and to place our students' learning against a transnational Black backdrop, wherever we might be. I am suggesting that we shift our engagements as Jacqueline did, to embrace more sacred (re)membering that is, at its core, about healing and social justice. As Jacqueline's (re)membering showed us: we must not only engage our teaching differently, we must learn to be differently.

Awakening Education

Toward a Rich Tapestry of Mindful and Contemplative
Engagement for Social/Environmental Transformation

Claudia Eppert

Dwelling in Difficulties

American philosopher and educational theorist Maxine Greene (1977) importantly argues for an arts and humanities education of "wide-awakeness" in contemporary times. Referencing the philosopher Søren Kierkegaard and writer Henry David Thoreau among others, she articulates "wide-awakeness" as an educational experience that counters an intense civilizational preoccupation with making existence "easy." A wide-awake education, she asserts, is committed to creating difficulties (p. 119). It asks what it means to live deliberately, and aspires to "move people to a critical awareness, to a sense of moral agency, and to a conscious engagement with the world" (p. 120). In what follows, I re-affirm Greene's understanding of awakening and the value of an arts and humanities education, but I consider these further from within the contexts of the increasing prominence in North America of contemplative studies and, more specifically, a philosophy of mindfulness that informs many of these studies. I seek to illustrate how a foundational higher education humanities and arts study of and engagement with such contemplative practices as meditation and yoga can be enriching in and across all academic fields. This engagement, in turn, has the potential to unsettle certain assumptions and approaches with regard to current instrumental educational trends, contemporary contemplative pedagogies among them. It additionally addresses us to rethink dominant North American social currencies and educational initiatives oriented toward social and ecological justice and transformation. In sum, my primary hope is to draw attention to the elemental radicalism of becoming wide-awake. A mindful, awakening education requires us anew to be responsive to and take responsibility for personal and societal slumbering or, alternately put, the potential domestication of education and the public sphere in an era of late capitalism.

Witnessing the Contemplative Turn in North America

It is remarkable to witness the incredible rise of North American interest in contemplative practices and pedagogies, practices and pedagogies which were once so central to educational life in classical Greek times and were integral to ancient Asian wisdom traditions. While a continued mainstay of indigenous wisdom and insight around the world, they were largely marginalized and dismissed by many modern Western philosophical and cultural shifts. Broadly defined, contemplative practices seek to cultivate deeper awareness into the nature of the mind, facilitate empathy and compassion, support wisdom and the active realization of the inter-connectivity of life.[1] These practices are diverse, and include soma arts such as yoga or tai chi, visual arts, dance, music, rituals and ceremonies, nonviolent activism, meditation, storytelling and other relational modes of dialogue and deep listening.[2] Resonating interdependent worldviews and mindfulness philosophies underlie these practices. Increasingly, contemplative practices are being incorporated into schools, colleges, and universities, in multiple content areas and academic fields.

What might account for this growing abundance of enthusiasm for contemplative practices within the North American educational mainstream? Certainly institutions such as Naropa University in Colorado, founded in 1974, and non-profit organizations such as *The Center for Contemplative Mind in Society* (contemplativemind.org), established in 1991, have been contributors. *The Center for Contemplative Mind* has been particularly focused on promoting contemplative studies in higher education. As its website states, it envisions "higher education as an opportunity to cultivate deep personal and social awareness: an exploration of meaning, purpose, and values in service to our common human future." In addition to being very active organizing retreats, conferences, summer pedagogy institutes, workshops, lectures, webinars, and so on, they have provided numerous scholarships over the years for academics to research contemplative practices and incorporate them into their teaching. This center is affiliated with the Association for Contemplative Mind in Higher Education (ACMHE), and also draws attention to other conferences and organizations with similar or more specific interests.

The growing popularity of these organizations, however, might be regarded as themselves responsive to a current North American social malaise and need. Indeed, ours are turbulent times, inscribed with disease, poverty, violence, and the destruction of our ecosystems on an unprecedented scale (Macy, 2007, pp. 91–92). Modern life, with its incessant corporate demands, consumerist preoccupations, and media technologies, increasingly pull many of us into distraction, distress, disengagement, and despair. Pressures to compete in societies that prize power, fame, and possessions and to thrive in a global market with its inherited logics and grammars of progress, productivity, and profit are showing themselves to be unbalancing, as evidenced

1. *The Center for Contemplative Mind in Society,* http://www.contemplativemind.org/.
2. See Tree of Contemplative Practices on http://www.contemplativemind.org.

in the wealth of daily media accounts of manifestations of twenty-first century psycho-social and moral disease.

Contemplative pedagogies and practices are becoming more and more identified as vehicles well primed to help us cope with contemporary pressures. Indeed, supports for the inclusion of contemplative practices within K-12 schools and higher education across disciplines, for instance, often speak to just this. It is attested that students are calmer and more focused following activities such as meditation and yoga, better equipped to manage stress, to develop their study skills, and so on. These accounts are significantly bolstered by scientific and medical research and initiatives undertaken these last years, which have been hugely instrumental in moving contemplative practices from margin to mainstream. Contemplative practices are becoming an indelible part of hospitals and other sites of healing and care inasmuch as they are becoming part of regular educational life. While I am much enthused by this widening embrace, and hope to witness contemplative practices and pedagogies become a normative part and parcel of educational programs and policies, I am eager to see more attention devoted to engagement with the multiple ancestries of these practices and pedagogies, to the preservation of their qualitative integrity, and to their radical roles with regard to both personal and social transformation and renewal.

In other words, as these practices are increasingly engaged in North America, I worry that they are standing in danger of being "used and abused," diluted and commodified, packaged and made "easy," designed to fit into society rather than rigorously question and re-imagine it. I am not alone in this concern. As these practices and pedagogies are mainstreaming, it is notable to observe the measure in which they are being redressed in modern Western secular and scientific fashion. As educational philosopher Donald L. Nelson (2012) points out, for example, "a scientific re-conceptualization... serves to secularize the practice of meditation by positioning it outside of religious tradition...thereby rendering it acceptable in schools that could not or would not promote a specific religious practice in their curriculum" (p. 5). Even though traditions such as Buddhism, as Nelson also emphasizes, are non-theist and only devotional in a religious sense in certain respects, associations with these traditions in "public schools would be difficult or impossible because they would be seen as 'teaching religion'" (p. 5). The same problem exists in the health care professions, in which Vedic, Buddhist, and Taoist and other influences are variously acknowledged and not. Some health care professionals, while advocating such adaptations, have expressed some concerns and tensions they experience in pressures to engage in empirical research and be widely accessible (Mahabodhi, 2010, p. 220).

In some respects, that changes are happening today in the growth of contemplative studies in North America is natural. As history shows, inasmuch as people importantly aspire to hold onto the specificities and essences of their traditions, traditions are also inevitably in continual flux, travelling through time and space, relocating in different geographies, and acquiring alternate forms and expressions in processes of integrating with prior traditions and dynamic local social, geographical, economic, and cultural exigencies, expression, and knowledge. Certainly Buddhism is a prime illustration of this, having begun in India, subsequently moving northward and eastward, and now emerging and taking hold in the West (Bresnan, 2003). To add to the realization of the inevitability of change, wisdom holds that what is wise and beneficial tends to be intuitively recognized as such and thus inevitably perseveres and/or re-emerges, while that which isn't tends to be discarded over time. It is re-assuring that wisdom will continue on, despite any contrary efforts. Concurrently, it is by now well-known how Western colonial and imperial movements have appropriated, oppressed, exoticized, distorted, and disavowed many wisdom traditions. The contemplative arts of meditation and yoga, among many others, are re-emerging and becoming a staple in North America in recognition that they offer insight and wisdom that speaks to current times. In concord with Nelson (2012), I believe that in order to receive this insight and wisdom, contemporary North American society is challenged not to isolate and commodify these practices but rather to rigorously immerse itself in and learn from the diverse ancient traditions in which they have been embedded. It is also addressed to learn respectfully from contemporary sages, monks and nuns, elders, teachers, and communities who are rooted in this land and/ or who have been immigrating to the West and variously working to protect, bring awareness to, teach and embed their holistic ways of knowing and being here.

In my view, it is a matter thus of both ethics and learning that North American education at all levels gives sustained attention to the rich and generous tapestry of histories of traditions in which contemplative practices are situated. An intercultural arts and humanities education may help along these lines. Today, the arts and humanities in higher education are becoming smaller as we find ourselves in the midst of a competitive age where what matters most seems to be that which is material, measurable, immediately usable, and monetary. Yet, the arts and humanities provide opportunities for balance and contextualization that can counter current decontextualizing dynamics. And, it can invite dwelling in difficulties that can inspire wide-awakeness. Following Greene, therefore, I seek to give voice to an arts and humanities education that aspires to what I have called the "remembrance-learning" of and engagement with diverse historical, philosophical, social, and aesthetic entanglements. I emphasize the value of such remembrance and entanglement within and across diverse academic fields and in the embrace of interdisciplinarity. Indeed, it is interesting for me to learn recently that mindfulness, from the Pali word, *Sati,* and the Sanskrit *smrti,* etymologically references a root "to remember."[3] In the remainder of this reading, I consider briefly what wisdom and learning such entangled study might open up for those engaged in contemplative practices, and how this study might spur us to re-envision and re-orient our day-to-day in the direction of a more whole, just, and compassionate future.

Toward Remembrance-Learning

Engagement with the historical, philosophical, social and aesthetic contents and contexts of contemplative practices reveals the measure in which these practices have been embedded within holistic ways of living, knowing, and inter-being in the world. These holistic ways include the embodied cognizance of: the integration of body, heart, and mind; the intimate connectedness rather than sovereignty of self with respect to relations with others, environment, and cosmos; and the integration of inner and outer peace through the cultivation of equilibrium, wisdom, joy, compassion, and loving-kindness, among other qualities. Moreover, as one learns more about the holistic embeddedness of contemplative practices, one also becomes knowledgeable about their intricate linkages with ideas and practices of ethical conduct and rituals of daily living. It is shown that contemplative practice is best accompanied with an ethical sensibility and commitments to social service (Eppert, 2010). To make progress on the path to awakened insight and wisdom,

3. *http://www.vipassana.com*, retrieved April 1, 2013.

it is recognized as important that one clears the way of distraction, deceit and conceit, practices a generosity of spirit, and becomes mentally and emotionally grounded in something beyond one's ego self.

As I discuss elsewhere (Eppert, 2010), Buddhist meditation and also the discussion of yoga in the ancient text, the *Bhagavad Gita,* composed between the fifth and the fourth centuries B.C.E. succinctly indicate interconnected practices. While numerous different Buddhist traditions exist, they each adhere to the four noble truths and the eightfold path identified by the Buddha. The four noble truths hold that life entails suffering, that suffering is caused by attachment, that the cessation of suffering is attainable, and that there is a path to the end of suffering. This path to cessation is the eightfold path, which consists of eight interdependent "right" principles to hold and follow in order to end suffering: right view, intention, speech, action, livelihood, effort, mindfulness, concentration. While the first two concern wisdom and the final three describe practices of mental development, the middle three refer to ethical conduct.[4] Right speech, right action, and right livelihood honour a realization that an enlightened end of suffering and the experience of infinite and abundant compassion and joy proceed through lovingly kind and ethical means. Moreover, as practitioners meditate and follow this path, they bring attention and increasing sensitivity to how, as human beings, we variously carry within us the three poisons of greed, aggression, and delusion. It is precisely this aspect that has drawn me to contemplative studies in the context of critical pedagogy and social justice education; namely the understanding that human-initiated conflict and destruction in the world are manifestations of these poisons (Eppert, 2008). It is, therefore, not only our well-being that is at issue in contemplative cultivation, but the well-being of everything else as well.

The practice of yoga within the tradition of the *Gita* is similarly holistically intertwined. In North America yoga is commonly known as a physical activity, but the *Gita* discusses alternate yogas. The root word of yoga, is to yoke or to link; in other words, to integrate parts of the self, to integrate self with other and world, and to integrate self with Spirit, also understood as Self, writ large. Yogas thus are wisdom practices and rituals that intend to illuminate and support the way to enlightenment and universal consciousness. *Bhakti* is the yoga of fostering loving devotion to a personal God through one's relations with human others. *Karma yoga* is the yoga of compassionate service. *Raja yoga* is the practice of meditation and mental purification, and *jhana yoga* is the way of philosophical inquiry. The physical activity of *hatha yoga,* not mentioned in the *Gita,* is one of the asanas, or practices of bodily purification that intends to prepare the body for meditation (Easwaren, 1985; Eppert, 2010).

Other philosophies and wisdom traditions offer different paths to spiritual insight, inner peace, and connection with self, other, environment, and cosmos. The diversity of wisdom traditions is beautiful and abundant and, as we know from the natural plant and animal world, diversity yields more medicine than does homogeneity. But these traditions vitally recognize contemplative practices as not isolatable and separable. Insight and healing take place in and through manifold relationships and intimacies. As we learn from these traditions, might we not in the process awaken to questioning and re-imagining the dominant discourses in which we live in North America?

4. www.thebigview.com/buddhism/eightfoldpath.html, retrieved July 6, 2013.

Re-Envisioning "Value"

In the midst of learning from multiple traditions and acquiring wisdom and insight, we can become more discerning about our own social currencies and investments. Greene writes that an arts and humanities education may "involve identification of lacks and insufficiencies in [the] world—and some conscious effort to repair those lacks, to choose what *ought* to be" (p. 123, her italics). We can learn, for instance, to unravel the commitments that have forged the composite known as the "West" that has generated the fragmentation and dis-ease that currently begs for contemplative returns. Here we might awaken by coming to recognize a history of classical, medieval, and modern commitments to substantive and autonomous identities, past and present passions for rationalism at the expense of valuing body and emotion, past and present understandings of life and cosmos as composed of dualisms in conflict rather than in complementary harmony with one another, and the rise of market economies and shifts from production oriented to consumer oriented investments. As well, we can explore philosophical commitments that have served to generate greater well-being and senses of responsibility, democratic and social justice commitments, for example. In this process, we might be energized toward healing of self, others, and environment by actively re-imagining and re-engaging our commitments and communities. What socio-cultural, ethical, and communal transformations might be re-vitalizing? Within difficult educational dwelling, we may come to rethink what we most "value," beyond the confines of a narrow utilitarian imagination. Perhaps we can come to recognize and reengage "value" itself in a more multidimensional and balanced way, something I believe is necessary for wise and effective leadership and vision in a time when we are witnessing widespread moral confusion and corruption, an unsustainable consumption of our resources, and the collapse of our once-thriving eco-systems.

As contrasts are explored, and alternatives debated, attention might also be given to the oft-heard assertion that the wisdom of Asian traditions, for example, is inaccessible to Westerners. Insofar as wisdom addresses us to explore dominant Western commitments and continuities, it also calls upon us to deconstruct grand narratives, and to unearth contradictions and counter continuities in the recognition that societies are profoundly complex. For example, as many recent scholars have shown, historical study reveals deep exchange and enmeshment of Western and Eastern ideas dating back to the earliest civilizations and extending to the present (Armstrong, 1993, 2006; Campbell, 1996/2007; Clarke, 1997; Smith, 2008). These authors detail the westward expression of what has been called perennial wisdom during the Axial Age, for example, among the classical Greeks, in the writings of philosopher, mathematician, scientist, and mystic Pythagoras of Samos (570–495 B.C.E.) who may have been influenced by Indian ideas transmitted by way of his travels to Persia and Egypt (Armstrong, 1993, p. 35). Around 300 C.E., mystical and religious neo-platonic philosophy emerges, its first contributor being Plotinus (205–270 C.E.) who maintained that humans experience estrangement and disquiet within themselves, and yearn to experience wholeness. Aspects of neoplatonism significantly influenced Jewish, Islamic, and Christian thinkers of the Middle Ages, and a good deal of the Renaissance. It inspired the philosophers and theologians St. Augustine, Boethius, and Dionysius, living between the fourth to sixth centuries. In the thirteenth century, it influenced St. Thomas Aquinas and the German Christian philosopher, mystic, and theologian Meister Eckhart (Campbell, 1996/2007). Joseph Campbell (1996/2007) and David Smith (2008) observe continuations of interest in East-West perennial wisdom in many eighteenth and nineteenth century Western philosophers, among them the protestant philosopher Immanuel Kant (1742–1804) and the philosopher Arthur Schopenhauer (1788–1860), both of whom similarly apprehended that knowledge is conditioned by our experience and that the mundane world of time and space, of separateness, is an illusion of the mind. As I suggest in considerably more detail elsewhere (Eppert, 2013), knowledge of such exchanges troubles not only narrow essentialist binaries of East and West but also the notion that any one culture is in sole possession of originary truth and wisdom (Mall, 2000). Ram Adhar Mall (2000) asserts, "Today, we cannot carry on as if the ancient classical-occidental mode of history were still valid. It must be stated that Greek historical thought is closer to the Asian than the Christian-European" (p. 121). At the same time, a recent historical study shows that Asian wisdom lies within the Christian European, and within each of the monotheisms. Awareness of deep interchanges and echoes, I believe, opens higher education up more to consideration of the value in balancing studies of differences not with sameness but with resonances.

Spirited Re-groundings and Re-connections

Furthermore, as we study and engage East-West contemplative practices, it becomes apparent how they are immersed in an acknowledgement of and reverence for "spirit." Spirit is variously expressed, and here may be understood, in the words of Smith (2008), as that which breathes in, "over, under, around, through, behind, above, and beyond" (p. 7). It is an ineffability, the expression of which is infinitely creative yet ever partial, fundamentally unthematizable in language and thought. In my view, spirit may be loosely described as that which connects us, animates us, and grounds us. It makes us alive. According to Campbell (1996/ 2007), the message of spiritual awakening is that radiance (radiant energy) is all around and within us. He asserts that when this energy becomes embodied within a human being, as often represented in images depicting humans on a throne of roses or a lotus flower, and one has awakened to the spirit within, one no longer has to work to realize one's identity; one is "it," simply and purely. The "it" is the finding of one's still point. Meditation, he notes, encompasses the literal sitting in an immovable spot in order that one may find the immovable place within; that is, find the place not moved by desire or fear, a deep site of refuge. This notion is represented in the *Gita*, in the lines "when meditation is mastered, the mind is unwavering like the flame of a lamp in a windless place" (Easwaren, 1985, p. 106) as well as in multiple other wisdom texts. It is held that this much practiced grounding can over time open the practitioner more and more to qualities of flexibility, openness, strength, resilience, creativity, compassion, understanding, and wisdom, among others. These qualities are not abstractly conceptualized as much as they are concretely experienced in all their many subtleties within the body and within lived experience. Greene maintains that being grounded, a person "will be far less likely to confuse abstraction with concreteness, formalized and schematized reality with what is 'real'" (p. 124).

In the face of histories of religious abuses and of movements toward secularity, commitments to nurturing mind, body, and spirit together have become lost. Greene (1977) quotes Kierkegaard who writes in 1846 about "the inability of a civilization directed to material improvement—higher incomes, better diets, miracles of medicine, triumphs of applied physics and chemistry—to satisfy the human spirit" (p. 119). Today, in secular educational contexts, we may find the phrase "entrepreneurial spirit" being deployed, but such a representation, in my view, stands in danger of troublingly materializing spirit. As we move forward, perhaps a renewed reverence for spirit, embraced within educational circles, is among what is most essential. Indeed,

I would argue that it is the nurturance and flourishing of a young person's spirit—his or her élan vital—that is of most educational value. Spirit may refer to unique qualities and gifts flowing within and through an individual and to a wholesome intimate relationship with universal creative and ineffable life energies (e.g., Tao/Dao). On such terms, interdependence and sustainable and compassionate existence constitute the grounding essence of contemplative practices.

Cultivating skill in body-based contemplative practices, in the midst of humanities and arts study in higher education, offers an experiential base from which to come to know spirit and also engage more embodied, creative, and relational senses of value. The body can be remembered as an important site of wisdom. Reginald Ray (2008) argues that our forgetting of body wisdom and our loss of touch with nature have led to a global "crisis of disembodiment" with significant consequences (p. 23). He elaborates,

> As I see it, the root cause of impending global catastrophe is the fact that we have completely lost our connection with our bodies and our physical existence.... If to be fully embodied means to be completely present and at one with who and what we are, then modern people are the most disembodied people who have ever lived, because we are not fully present to, or at one with, anything. We are always separate and separating, always trying to find what we seek somewhere else. (p. 23)

Ray identifies all of us living today with a capitalist mindset as exploiters, wittingly or not, noting that we have become cultured to perceive people, things, situations, events, and the earth as objects that could help or hinder us. Too much we approach what we encounter with the question of how he/she/it can serve us (p. 23). He suggests that lurking in our conscious and subconscious the following thoughts; what is in it for me, or, what does this have to do with me? Ray, as well as others such as Christopher Lasch (1979), maintains that a pervasive narcissism and self-aggrandizement, an over-riding focus on "me" and "mine" typifies our age.

Mindfulness and Social/Environmental Transformation

Mindfulness can potentially provide a means to move us out of our narrow self-enclosures, reconnect and re-enchant us with the web of life. It carries an ancient history. Traces are found in the *Rig Veda* (circa 1500 BCE) and it becomes more central in the *Upanishads* (c. 700–200 B.C.E.). The *Upanishads* carries the insight that the "deepest part of oneself and all of existence are in relationship" (Huxley, 1945, p. 8). Mindfulness is part of the eightfold path and, from the Buddha (circa 400 BCE), we have the *Satipatthana Sutta,* a discourse from the Pali Canon of Theravada Buddhism. It describes mindfulness as a practice of developing awareness of body, sensations/feelings, mind/consciousness, and the contents of the mind. It involves practitioners non judgmentally witnessing their thought processes, their feelings, bodily experiences and expressions of pleasure, pain, or neutrality, their senses of disconnection and connection, and other activities (Eppert, 2008). In contrast to processes of reflection, in mindfulness philosophy and practice one does not analyze or evaluate mind, emotion, body, so much as come to apprehend it directly and immediately (Tremmel, 1993, p. 444). Practitioners come to experience that they are not solely the content and form of their thoughts, but rather are also something much deeper and more profound; namely, emptiness/interdependence. The Vietnamese monk Thich Nhat Hanh nicely draws attention to this deeper relationality as he describes a human being as being not only a wave but also an ocean of water and wisdom. In fact, ocean is one's true nature (Eppert, 2009; Hanh, 2002, p. 23). Mindfulness thus entails a practice of forgetting ego-self's constant desire to separate and the remembrance-learning of connectivity. The embodied insight that we are not simply our thoughts can radically open us up to the present moment and the world. Indeed, it is quite radical an awakening, not only personally but also socially, especially when we realize that much of modern Western history and culture has been built on exactly the opposite notion, exemplified by Descartes' oft-quoted phrase, "I think therefore I am." We all have this capacity for awakening. As Thich Nhat Hanh (1987) writes, "[c]hildren understand very well that in each woman, in each man, there is a capacity of waking up, of understanding, and of loving" (p. 9).

Particularly in psychology scholarship, it is held that mindfulness is deeply empowering and healing. It constitutes a therapeutic means for detaching ourselves from and reducing the negative sways and anxiety-ridden reactions of the ego. By becoming more mindful and, in the process, more unconditionally accepting and generously-spirited, we begin to become more receptive, acquire greater capacities for joy and compassion, and transform organically. As Karen Kissel Wegela (2011) comments in her book on mindfulness and compassionate presence as a resource to help others, in contrast to previous Western psychotherapeutic emphasis on the aggressive rooting out of flaws, mindfulness, and the acceptance it cultivates "is actually a much more skillful means for achieving deep, lasting change. Our unconditional yes to what is, to what we feel, and to how we are with others, allows our issues and crises to yield naturally to change.... It turns out that loving acceptance of who we are has a *direction*. It ferries us toward transformation" (p. x, her emphasis).

What I seek to emphasize is that this transformation is about a de-centering radically humility and generosity of spirit rather than egoistic validation, freedom rather than containment, transformation and activism rather than management (although it needs to be remembered that these are not either/ors as Freedom writ large is composed of and balances both freedom and containment). In other words, contemplative practices have the potential to facilitate a basic turn toward a liberatory non-dualistic embodiment. They invite an interminable mindful-bodily exploration of and working with our multi-dimensional, connected embodied nature as a vital ethical practice with the potential to move us out of a narrow conceptualized self-centeredness and open us up to a larger, more interdependent and socially and environmentally participatory worldview. Rather than the body being regarded instrumentally and narrowly for purposes of maintaining strength and longevity, making self happy and successful while disregarding others, or keeping appearances in a highly performative media saturated world, it is recognized as a precious ferry for deep inner, community, and global awakening and peace-creation. Through gradual attunement to one's own body-wisdom and its multiple energies one can become more aware of the interconnectedness of all things, and can come consequently to have greater appreciation for diversity, for senses of the sacred, and for ethical and peaceful relations and transformational possibilities. Ray (2008) contends, "to fully inhabit our bodies...is to discover our embeddedness in the world...we realize we are existing alongside and in connection with a multitude of other subjects, some of who are human like ourselves, some of whom are animals and trees, some of whom are mountains, rivers or stars. To be "with" in this way is so much more present to and respectful of creation, of what is, than the typical modern way of being "over" or "on" (p. 26). I add that to become and be "with" is both difficult and, as children continually manifest, also effortless, simple, and easy. In drawing attention to this interchange, I seek to avoid a false separation between dwelling in difficulties and dwelling in ease, as, again, each is within the other. But this embodiment of "ease" differs radically from the "ease" Greene and Kierkegaard warn against. Ease in a wisdom sense might be understood as the spontaneous expression of wide-awakeness.

New Educational Openings in the Art of Contemplative Engagements

A concluding point. As Shusterman (2008) defines it, somaesthetics is "a discipline that puts the body's experience and artful refashioning back into the heart of philosophy as an art of living" (p. 15). Following Greene, I have discussed the potential roles of the humanities in higher education's engagement with contemplative practices. By humanities and arts studies, as mentioned earlier, I by no means seek to exclude the sciences (which, indeed, would be just yet another reductive practice of separation) Rather, I seek to draw attention to the enlivening potential of foundational philosophical, social, historical and aesthetic engagement in *all* academic fields and to the benefits of imbuing education and culture with multi-dimensional senses of value and wisdom. Which brings me to the subject of the arts a bit more. Wisdom breathes in many places—within nature and land, within the body, within such ordinary daily activities as sweeping the floor, and within the spaces between us. Opening ourselves up to and learning wisdom seems an "art" of engagement in many ways. To me, it seems to include an irreducible immersion in deepening connection and relationships, creating and inviting equilibrium and harmony, and animating and nurturing the soul and spirit. It is in some measure an elusive learning, and can even engage us in more mystical practices. An immediate example that comes to mind references ancient Ayurvedic medicine. In this healing medicine, it is recommended that as one cooks or bakes, one imbues the process and product with good and loving intention. The one who eats the food will then be nourished by this soul warmth. This is a practice the results of which cannot be empirically validated. Yet, it seems a practice of value. Might we benefit from considering how we might restore such soul-full and multi-dimensionally nourishing understanding into all areas of educational policy, theory, and practice?

Along these lines, the twentieth century philosopher Hans Georg Gadamer (1996) distinguishes between what he calls "medicine as science" in contemporary times and "medicine as art" in ancient Greece. Medicine as modern science tends to be oriented toward the isolation, control and management of physical and psychical process and toward to creation of particular artificial effects (p. 35). As such, it tends to sever healing from life-situations and from the natural order of things. In marked contrast, ancient Ionian cosmology emphasized an enigmatic "art of healing." This art encompasses *restoration*; the doctor does not make the health of the sick person but rather restores him or her to health in ways humbly in tune with the harmonic rhythms of nature (p. 19). Ancient Greek medical practice recovers the body to a state of equilibrium, and healing lies within the jurisdiction not of the physician but rather of nature. Gadamer recalls Plato's insight that the body cannot be treated without address to the soul and also to the whole of being. He observes how in Greek, "the whole of being is hole ousia" and how this phrase is connected with "hale" and "healthy being" (p. 73). He asks his readers, "what can intervention, our own actions … contribute towards bringing the achievements of modern society, with all its automated, bureaucratized and technologized apparatus, back into the service of that fundamental rhythm which sustains the proper order of bodily life" (p. 79)? Greene similarly advocates for attention to restorative art as an educational foundation because of the "way in which aesthetic experiences provide a ground for the questioning that launches sense-making and the understanding of what it is to exist in a world" (p. 124). For her, if the arts and humanities "are at the core of curriculum, all kinds of reaching out are likely. The situated person, conscious of his or her freedom, can move outwards to empirical study, analytic study, quantitative study of all kinds" (p. 124). Perhaps an arts and humanities foundational engagement with contemplative practices, pedagogies, and wisdom, in all their fullness, and in all educational areas, can open up meaningful pathways to significant personal, social, and ecological renewal.

Acknowledgments

I am grateful to the editors of this book for their vision and hard work. A version of this paper was presented at the University of Alberta, Faculty of Education Research Forum in March 2013. My many thanks to attendees at this talk for their insightful questions and comments.

References

Armstrong, K. (1993). *A history of God: The 4000-year quest of Judaism, Christianity, and Islam.* New York: Gramercy.

Armstrong, K. (2006). *The great transformation: The beginning of our religious traditions.* New York: Anchor/Random House

Bresnan, P. (2003). *Awakening: An introduction to the history of eastern thought.* Upper Saddle River, New Jersey: Pearson.

Campbell, J. (1996/2007). *Mythos II.* DVD. Joseph Campbell Foundation.

Clarke, J. J. (1997). *Oriental enlightenment: The encounter between Asian and Western thought.* New York: Routledge.

Easwaren, E. (1985). *The Bhagavad Gita.* Berkeley, CA: Nilgiri Press.

Eppert, C. (2008). Fear, (educational) fictions of character, and Buddhist insights for a witnessing curriculum. In C. Eppert & H. Wang (Eds.), *Cross-cultural studies in curriculum: Eastern thought, educational insights.* (1st ed., pp. 55–108). Mahwah, NJ: Lawrence Erlbaum, Taylor and Francis.

Eppert, C. (2009). Remembering our (re)source: Eastern meditations on witnessing the integrity of water. In M. McKenzie, H. Bai, P. Hart, & B. Jickling (Eds), *Fields of green: Re-storying education.* (pp. 191–210). Hampton Press.

Eppert, C. (2010). The war within: Ethical and spiritual responsibilities to children in a time of war and terrorism. *International Journal of Children's Spirituality, 15*(3) (August): 219–232.

Eppert, C. (2013, Unpublished manuscript). *Perennial wisdom, intercultural dialogue, and elemental education: Histories of east-west contemplative journeys to personal and social transformation.*

Gadamer, H. G. (1996). *The enigma of health: The art of healing in a scientific age.* Stanford: Stanford University Press.

Greene, M. (1977). Toward wide-awakeness: An argument for the arts and humanities in education. *Teachers College Record, 79*(1), pp. 119–125.

Huxley, A. (1945). *The perennial philosophy.* London: Chatto and Windus.

Lasch, C. (1979). *The culture of narcissism: American life in an age of diminishing expectations.* New York: Norton.

Macy, J. (2007). *World as lover, world as self: Courage for global justice and ecological renewal.* Parallex Press.

Mahabodhi (2010, manuscript in progress). *What is mindfulness?: Buddhist doctrine and method in the SatipatthanaSutta.* Retrieved April 29, 2010, from http://www.mahabodhi.org.uk/.

Mall, R. A. (2000). *Intercultural philosophy.* Lanham, Maryland: Rowman & Littlefield.

NhatHanh, T. (2002). *No death, No fear: Comforting wisdom for life.* New York: River-head Books

NhatHanh, T. (1987). *Being Peace.* Berkeley, CA: Parallex Press.

Nelson, D. (2012). Implementing mindfulness: Practice as the home of understanding. *Paideusis: Journal of the Canadian Philosophy of Education Society. (Special Themed Issue: Contemplative Practice, Education, and Socio-Political Transformation, Part One), 20*(2), 4–14.

Ray, R. A. (2008) *Touching enlightenment: Finding realization in the body.* Boulder, CO: Sounds True.

Shusterman, R. (2008). *Body consciousness: A philosophy of mindfulness and somaesthetics.* New York: Cambridge University Press.

Smith, D. G. (2008) The farthest west is but the farthest east: The long way of oriental/occidental engagement. In C. Eppert & H. Wang (Eds.), *Cross-cultural studies in curriculum: Eastern thought, educational insights.* Mahwah, NJ.: Lawrence Erlbaum/Routledge, Taylor & Francis.

Tremmel, R. (1993). Zen and the art of reflective practice in teacher education. *Harvard Educational Review, 63*(4, Winter), 434–458.

Wegela, K. K. (2011). *What really helps: Using mindfulness and compassionate presence to help, support, and encourage others.* Boston: Shambhala.

Yoga and Higher Education

Adding Concentration, Clarity, and Compassion to Learning

Ramdas Lamb

E ducation, when used properly, can be one of the most important keys to open the doors to a more peaceful, harmonious, and interdependent global community. This is especially true in the case of higher education, where future community, national, and international leaders are trained. In order to envision how this process can be actualized, we first have to understand what the means and ends of present day higher education are and how they could be modified to achieve that vision.

Contemporary Higher Education

Although issues such as social justice, world peace, etc., are part of the rhetoric of many institutions of higher education, these concepts are largely overshadowed by the promotion of business, science and technology, and other vehicles of material progress and economic profit. Corporations are increasingly financing academic research departments and programs that serve to directly benefit corporate interests. This, in itself is not necessarily negative, but it often results in a tremendous imbalance in what gets taught and what gets overlooked.

As corporate funding increases, so does the potential that the work and findings of some scholars and researchers at the receiving end will be influenced in ways that financially benefit their sponsors, while minimizing or muffling criticism that might be directed against corporate tactics and goals.[1]

Humanities and social science departments—where one is more likely to find discussions about ethics, compassion, and social justice—are among the lowest funded academic programs at most universities. Often, athletic programs receive more financing than do the humanities. This is likely because such departments are not directly connected with profit making endeavors and thus not beneficial to a corporate-centered approach to education. Moreover, they often have instructors who challenge a "profit at all cost" mindset and whose expertise and teachings focus instead on social well-being instead of monetary benefits.

According to the Association of Colleges and Universities, the purpose of a liberal education is to empower individuals and prepare them "to deal with complexity, diversity, and change." and also to help "students develop a sense of social responsibility."[2] Today, however, the stated goal at many institutions is to prepare students to become economically successful and materially productive citizens. In short, universities currently prefer the creation of business professionals, scientists, lawyers, economists, and athletes over students whose primary interests include gaining a sense of social responsibility on the road to the creation of a peace filled and harmonious world. In addition, mass media regularly exposes students to a highly egocentric approach to life, violent imagery and entertainment as the pastime, and an obsession with materialism as the preferred goals of life. More than ever before, there is a need to provide some counterbalances in our education system to these forces and influences.

While most people can appreciate the function of ethical and moral values in the world, it is easy to lose sight of the role that teaching about these can and should play in higher education. Doing so will not only help to create truthful and compassionate social and economic leaders of tomorrow, but the teaching of virtues can have long term benefits in creating a more harmonious society as a whole. From the outset, what must be made clear is that the integration of ethics and values into the curriculum is not the same as sectarian religious indoctrination. The latter has no place in public educational institutions. Unlike religious indoctrination, morality and ethics have been integral to almost every social philosopher's conceptualization of a free and just society since the time of Plato. Unfortunately, the contemporary promotion of material gain at all costs has caused them to be ignored, and many of the world's problems today can be traced back, in part at least, to this ignorance.

In order to inspire our society along ethical lines, we have to begin with our educational system and rethink our current priorities. This does not mean doing away with training of professionals in the fields science, technology, etc. but it does mean approaching education in a manner that integrates ethics and values as fundamental parts of a more comprehensive educational process. One example of how this can occur is the inclusion of teaching about the ancient yoga system of India as a part of the core curriculum.

1. See Slaughter, S. & Rhoades, G. (2004). *Academic capitalism and the new economy: Markets, state, and higher education.* Baltimore; Johns Hopkins University Press.
2. Association of Colleges and Universities website (Retrieved 12/18/12) http://www.aacu.org/leap/What_is_liberal_education.cfm

Yoga and the Western World

The first part of this reading will provide a context for and brief history of the development of the yoga system and its various limbs as elaborated in the *Yoga Sutra* of Patanjali (ca. 3rd–2nd century BCE). It will then look at the introduction of yoga in the west in the early twentieth century, along with a discussion of the three primary methods through which elements of the yoga system have been introduced, taught, and practiced. The last section will address the benefits and shortcomings of the practice of yoga as it exists in higher education settings today. This will include speculation on how the yoga system could be implemented to help facilitate a greater mind-body awareness among students and a more peaceful and harmonious world as well.

As humans, we typically view ourselves as higher on the evolutionary ladder than other forms of life. The first book of the Bible (Genesis: 26–28) states that humans are superior to all other animals and that it is our duty to rule over them. This concept has also been prevalent in most societies throughout history and has extended to almost every facet of life, including intellect, moral standing, right to live, etc.[3] It is why nearly all societies have rules against killing humans but rarely against harming nature or killing other animals. Moreover, in many, the latter has been a form of sport.

We humans also like to believe that our superior intellect has not only led to advancements in physical and behavioral traits that aid in our survival, but it has given us superior moral standing as well. However, if we take a serious look at our species during the last several millennia, it appears that the only area where advancement has occurred is that of technology. We obviously have a greater number and more complex tools and weapons than our ancient ancestors had, but there is no real sign that we have experienced social, intellectual, or moral advancement or growth. We are clearly no closer to creating societies in which oppression of the powerless has ended, where everyone has equal access to knowledge, opportunities, and happiness, or where poverty is non-existent. On the contrary, both individuals and governments now have more powerful tools and means to hurt or kill others en masse, and we do more today to destroy our planet than our ancestors ever thought possible or imaginable.

At the same time, we know from understanding history that there have also long existed the presence of individuals who have attained great wisdom and have desired to promote peace and harmony in the world. Their writings, when available, reveal deep intellectual and practical understanding of human nature, society, ethics, and what we can do to achieve peace. One of the best ways, then, for us to move forward in our attempt to create a harmonious global community is to look back to those who understood the source of our problems and provided teachings to help us solve them.

For more than 4,000 years in India, individuals have sought to understand the human condition and learned and taught methods to transcend the causes and effects of suffering inherent in human existence. Countless Indian ascetics and renunciants have dedicated their lives in search of such wisdom and also of liberation from a life of suffering. Siddhartha Gautama is one of the better known examples. Raised in a royal family in Northern India in the sixth century BCE, he saw and experienced human agony and suffering and

---

3. Thomas Huxley's *Evidence as to Man's Place in Nature*, following on the footsteps of Darwin's seminal work, elucidates the belief in the evolution of humans from primitive to advanced. Many subsequent scholars and others have assumed this view as valid.

sought a path to transcend them. He renounced a life of vast material comfort, became a renunciant, and after years of effort is said to have finally reached his goal of wisdom and enlightenment. In doing so, he came to be known as the Buddha, "the Enlightened One." Thereafter, he set about sharing his wisdom with others. Among his first teachings are the "Four Noble Truths," in which he asserts that suffering is inherent to human existence. He goes on to state that all things are transitory, but as long as we are attached to our bodies and desires related to them that we will continue to experience suffering (Rahula, 1959). History has confirmed that poverty, suffering, hatred, and violence are not simply a product of contemporary existence but have been prevalent since ancient times. Amidst all our tremendous technological and material strides over the millennia, we have yet to transcend suffering, and most of us remain caught in dualistic cycles of pleasure and pain, health and sickness, etc. that perpetuate our suffering and give rise to inner and outer chaos and unhappiness in our lives.

Over several millennia in India, as individuals became involved in the search for inner happiness and peace, many looked to the power and centrality of the mind and the will as major factors in attaining their goals. In the process, they found that the establishment of a moral foundation aids one in gaining control over the functions of body and mind. This, in turn, facilitates an openness to the attainment of self-awareness, wisdom, compassion, and freedom from suffering. This knowledge was understood to be crucial not only for attaining wisdom on the individual level but on a broader level as well, leading to the development and promotion of world of peace and harmony. By the third century BCE, many of the methods and practices that evolved for these purposes came to be grouped together in the system known as *ashtanga* ("eight limbs") *yoga*.

Ashtanga Yoga

The first, and one of the most authoritative of textual sources on *ashtanga yoga* is Patanjali's *Yoga Sutra*. Although diverse understandings and forms of yoga have evolved over the millennia, Patanjali's text and system are still given great deference. As per the name, the system consists of eight limbs. Their combined purpose is to give a systematic direction and guidance to one seeking self-knowledge and self-control. The ultimate goal as presented is realization of the true nature of existence and a state of mental peace and tranquility that manifests as true happiness. The practice of two of these limbs, postures (*asanas*) with some inclusion of breath control (*pranayama*), is what is taught in the west as "yoga." Undertaken alone, these are only designed to help with one's physical health and relaxation and a small degree of mental calm. Without the other limbs, they are essentially seen as incapable of facilitating knowledge of the self and true happiness. Taken together, on the other hand, all the limbs are believed to have the power to bring about the desired goals.

The Eight Limbs

The first two limbs of *ashtanga yoga* each contain five parts and set out the ideal moral and ethical and guidelines for a life of one seeking inner peace, wisdom, and liberation. The importance of these cannot be overemphasized in yoga philosophy, for they are meant to create the foundation, upon which one can construct a life of physical health, mental stability, and emotional calm. Without this foundation, the remaining limbs will have only limited and temporal success, at best. The second two limbs center on the physical body and the control of its functions. Again, they are what define yoga in the minds of most practitioners in the west today. The next pair contain tools to train and focus the mind for gaining self-awareness. The last two limbs can more accurately be seen as states of mind and products of the other limbs than techniques requiring practice and effort. The following is an overview of each limb.

1. *Yama* ("restrictions, cessation")—The five parts are: *truth* (non-lying), *non-violence, non-stealing, non-hoarding*, and *non-waste of one's sexual energy*.[4] These fall in the category of "restrictions" since they all counter negative traits that are common obstacles in most people's lives that inhibit the ability to be truly at peace within and with the world. Lying and avoiding *truth* are among the most frequent deceptive methods used by humans to avoid pain or difficulty, or to fulfill a desire. A recent revelation of large scale cheating at Harvard University is but one example of how both lying and theft are accepted and justified by many in higher education.[5] Studies have shown similar behavior at other colleges and universities as well.

Since violence has been such an integral part of human existence throughout history, the road to a peaceful and harmonious world requires that we make a concerted and conscious effort to practice *non-violence* by diminishing and eventually removing the thoughts, words, and actions in our lives that can and do cause harm to others. Here, yoga philosophy includes the issue of food as well. A diet consisting of food that results from violence is believed to contain subtle residue of that violence, which then has a negative effect on the person who consumes it. Thus, vegetarianism has long been part of the traditional practice of yoga and *non-violence*. Although the diet is typically associated with the philosophical and cultural traditions of India, Greek thinkers like Hesiod (8th c. BCE) and Pythagoras (6th c. BCE) were among the earliest philosophers in the western world to introduce the concept of ethical vegetarianism (Walters & Portmess, 1999).

Theft, the third part, is the expression of a blatant disrespect of others. Thieves ignore the injury and harm they do to their victims, yet many people easily justify and rationalize such actions. *Hoarding* and greed are closely related, with the latter seen as the worst. For this reason, the practice of charity is encouraged to help change one's approach to material attachment and possessiveness. The last of the five is *brahmacharya*, which is normally translated as "celibacy." The term actually refers to the control of one's sexual energy so that it can be used for expanding conscious awareness.

2. *Niyama* ("observances")—Here, too, there are five parts: *cleanliness, contentment, self-study, austerity*, and *surrender to the divine*.[6] The concept and importance of cleanliness have long been integral in the lifestyle of the Indian spiritual aspirant and comprise a fundamental element of the yoga system. *Cleanliness* refers not only to the physical body (inner and outer), but to one's thoughts and actions as well. It is said among traditional practitioners of yoga that truth is one of the best cleansers of the mind. This leads to the cultivation of *contentment*. As one learns to nurture the feeling and practice acceptance of life, one is able to more calmly accept its ups and downs without losing mental and emotional balance. Through the practice, one gains inner strength and peace.

---

4. *Satya, ahimsa, asteya, aparigraha*, and *brahmacharya*.
5. Sarah Green, "Cheating at Harvard, and in the 'Real World.'" *Harvard Business Review*, 9/8/2012. Retrieved December 29, 2012, from http://blogs.hbr.org/hbr/hbreditors/2012/09/cheating_at_harvard_and_in_the html
6. *Shaucha, samtosha, swadhyaya, tapa*, and *ishwara pranidhana*.

Self-study involves pondering questions like "Who or what am I?," "What is the meaning of human existence?," or "Why do I (personally) exist?" Because a lack of self-understanding and self-awareness are among the major sources of unhappiness in our lives, *self-study* is necessary to bring us to a state of self-knowledge and self-actualization. Through efforts to gain such an understanding, we can learn to see ourselves as something far greater and more meaningful than simply material bodies or individual egos. We can also begin to perceive our abiding internal connection with other beings. Many of the more popular programs and workshops today that teach and promote methods to develop self-confidence and positive thinking utilize some of the same approaches found in the traditional yogic practice of *self-study*. An increasing number of universities have begun to experiment with some of these methods.

The value of *austerity* is generally difficult for westerners to conceptualize, for it encourages one to forgo satisfying one's desires as a way to learn self-control. Yoga philosophy teaches that lack of self-control leads to both physical and mental illnesses. Nearly all forms of addiction, including drug abuse, overeating, gambling, overspending, hoarding, etc., stem from an inability to put limits on desires for sensual fulfillment or satisfaction. Those who cannot control their desires become depressed, frustrated, angry, or violent. Also, learning to understand the difference between need and desire is an important step toward gaining mental and emotional balance as well as physical health. Activities like going on a diet, avoiding foods that one enjoys but may be unhealthy, doing daily exercise, putting limits on one's material possessions, etc. can all be seen as positive forms of *austerity* provided they are undertaken as steps toward learning self-control and not solely done for temporal physical or material benefits.

The last of the *niyama* is *surrender to the divine*. Taken at its face value, teaching this can be problematic for a secular institution, as well as for many westerners who reject altogether belief in a divinity. Instead, many contemporary Indian yoga teachers suggest that "*the divine*" should not be interpreted to mean "God" in the western sense. Rather, it should be understood to refer to a transcendental reality and oneness that connects all life together and that is far greater than the personal and temporal ego. One can conceptualize it as a Supreme Being, the Divine nature within, an omnipresent oneness, the inner Self, etc. It should never be confined within narrow a sectarian ideology. When one is able to identify with a larger reality beyond the personal ego, then problems associated with ego identity, such as arrogance, insecurity, jealously, greed, etc. become less of a presence in one's life. As one seeks an internal awareness and relationship with the Self, one leans to identify with that state of being in which all life is connected, where true harmony and peace exist.

3. *Asana* ("posture" or "seat")—Also known as *hatha yoga,* this is primarily what is taught in yoga classes in the west. The various postures are not aerobic in nature, but instead are bodily positions meant to help teach physical and mental control and endurance as well as keep the body limber, balanced, strong, and refreshed. Performing *asana*s aids in a release of stress and tension and thereby promotes health. Another important purpose of doing *asana*s is to help the practitioner to be able to sit comfortably and still for longer periods of time when undertaking the next set of limbs. Moreover, the traditional practice of *asana*s is almost always done in conjunction with *pranayama* and *dharana* for they are meant to work together to bring mind and body into closer connection and harmony.

4. *Pranayama* ("control of the breath")—The root of this Sanskrit term is "*prana*," which means both "breath" and "life force." In the yogic tradition, the relationship between breath and life is inseparable, as is the relationship between breath and mental functioning. The ability to gain control over one's breathing

process is viewed as integral to achieving mental control as well as maintaining or bringing about the health of both body and mind. Most adults breathe unconsciously at a rate of approximately 15 times per minute, and rarely is more than one-fourth of their lung capacity used in the process. As a consequence, much of the potential value and use of breathing are never realized. In *pranayama*, dozens of different methods of breathing are undertaken to strengthen the lungs and increase their capacity, facilitate better oxygen absorption, heat or cool the body, slow down the mind and heart, lessen stress, and aid in healing various illnesses and physical discomforts. More importantly, as one learns to control and use the breath, one also learns control over many of the functions of the body, mind, and emotions typically associated with the autonomic nervous system.

An example of this can be experienced when one has a rapid heartbeat after exercising, when one is excited and the mind is rapid, or when one is emotionally upset and the mind is confused. In such situations, if one concentrates on the breath and begins to take slow, even inhalations and exhalations, gradually increasing their length comfortably, this process will directly aid in bringing about a slower heart rate and/or calmer and more focused mind. Advanced *pranayama* practices can and are used to control pain, diet, bodily temperature, amount of sleep necessary, etc.

5. *Pratyhara* ("withdrawal of the senses")—This is sometimes referred to as the transitional limb from the outer aspects of the yoga system to the inner, mind-centered ones. It is best undertaken in conjunction with *dharana* (the next limb) and is specifically meant to help us gain control over our senses instead of the opposite. For most of us, desires for or aversions to a multiplicity of sense stimuli exert a great deal of control over our lives and actions. We seek fulfillment of some stimuli while attempting to avoid others, and the combination of the two consume much of our time, energy, and attention. In this way, they keep us bound in constant cycles of happiness and sadness, pleasure and pain, etc.

The yoga system provides tools for redirecting and sublimating such urges and aversions. In *pratyhara*, one learns to direct consciousness away from external phenomena and attachment to the sense input they cause and also from the application of dualistic interpretations to these stimuli (pleasant or unpleasant, desirable or undesirable, etc.), for such labeling distracts the mind by causing longing, desire, fear, jealously, anger, etc. By directing attention to the actual process of sensation rather than to what is being sensed, consciousness is gradually turned inward toward one's internal processes and toward awareness of one's inner being. Initially, this can be accomplished by placing attention on the breath, on a particular sensation, on a thought or experience, or on the experience of being, without labeling it as good or bad but simply as being.

Gradually, *pratyhara* helps us to detach from the stimuli and the mental disturbances (positive or negative) they typically cause. Because this focus on one's internal processes is so contrary to the way most people approach life, this is one of the least understood limbs of the yoga system, but it is pivotal for the development of greater and deeper mental and physical awareness. In order to truly develop this ability, the practice of mental focus (*dharana*) is also important, It should be reiterated here that to obtain the results mentioned, these limbs are to be undertaken as part of a holistic approach to the yoga system and not separate from the previous limbs.

6. *Dharana* ("concentration")—The centrality of this limb can be seen by the fact that its main purpose is mentioned in the opening lines of the *Yoga Sutra*, which state, "Yoga is the control of the waves of the mind." In elaborating on *dharana*, Patanjali describes it as the process of "binding of consciousness to a

[single] spot." (Patanjali, III.1) Although this limb is often inaccurately referred to the west as "meditation," it is actually a necessary precursor to it that, when learned, facilitates the mental state in which meditation can occur. Here, mental effort and regular practice for extended periods are typically required. As one learns to concentrate and focus one's mind, one gradually experiences a lessening of mental waves, distraction and wandering, confusion, stress, and tension. In their place, there is an experience of mental calm and a sense of peacefulness and rest.

7. *Dhyana* ("meditation" or "absorption")—While *dharana* is a mental exercise that requires effort to learn and practice, *dhayana* generally refers to a more passive mental state in which awareness is enhanced and one becomes absorbed in and experiences a oneness with the object of meditation. Here, mental waves and fluctuations are replaced with increasing clarity, a deepening sense of self-awareness, and mental and emotional calm. The state of mind is passive yet filled with awareness. When this is combined with a heart that is no longer bound by emotional attachments and aversions, then mind and heart will be naturally more attuned to experiencing selfless compassion and caring for others.

8. *Samadhi*—This is the last limb of the yoga system and the traditional goal of its practitioners. Although there are believed to be several levels or stages of *samadhi,* the term typically refers to a mental/ emotional state that is a deeper and more permanent form of *dhyana*. The mind remains still and perception of all that is occurs in a state of equanimity. The heart experiences genuine compassion and peace. External or internal events or thoughts do not interrupt the inner calm. Experiences previous labeled dualistically (pain or pleasure, etc.) are all accepted as part of the continuous eternal flow of reality. One becomes permanently identified with the inner Self, attains true non-attachment to the temporal things of the world, and thus experiences true and lasting peace. Since one perceives a unified and harmonious world without attachment, all one's actions are done in order to aid others in experiencing this same state of being. With personal needs and desires extinguished, life is then lived for the betterment of others and the world.

Westernization of Yoga

During the last century, elements from the yoga system made their way to and became established in the west, specifically North America, in three primary forms, *hatha yoga*, Transcendental Meditation ("TM," uses aspects of *dharana*, *pratyhara*, and *dhyana*), and *vipassana* (a Buddhist practice utilizing its own form of the three mental limbs found in TM). The first person to introduce *ashtanga yoga* in America in an organized structure was Swami Paramahansa Yogananda, a North Indian Hindu monk.[7] He first visited the U.S. in 1920 to attend an international religion conference. A charismatic individual, many people were attracted by his initial talk and invited him to give a series of subsequent lectures.

Because of the immense and continued interest in him and his teachings, he started a U.S. foundation, Self-Realization Fellowship, to spread an awareness of yoga, establishing a center for that purpose in Los Angeles in 1925. At the same time, he started a publication sent out by mail that eventually went to subscribers all over the country. Originally entitled *East-West,* it was renamed *Self-Realization* in 1948. These

---

7. Lauren Landress, Assistant Director, Public Affairs at Self-Realization Fellowship, has been a major source for information on Swami Yogananda.

booklets contain writings of his on life and spirituality, explanations of most elements of the yoga system, and specific practices related to the first six limbs. In all his teachings, Yogananda stressed the importance of non-attachment, openness, compassion, and love of humanity.

By the time he passed away in 1952, he had inspired countless people from all backgrounds and walks of life to incorporate as much of the yoga system as possible into their lives. In the 1960s, his *Autobiography of a Yogi* was arguably the one book that inspired in westerners an interest in yoga and India more than any other. During the next several decades, many yoga teachers (some quite capable, others not so much) arrived in America to follow the path that Yogananda had forged. However, the more comprehensive and holistic yoga system he had taught was rarely presented in full. Instead, a shortened version was adopted with the emphasis on body and mind and a de-emphasis on the ethical precepts and spirituality. There seems to have been two main reasons for this. The first was that the interest in India and eastern spirituality that had arisen among many young people in the west brought with it a fear and claim among conservative Christians that Hinduism was a pagan religion seeking to take over the youth of America. The second was that the concept of separation of church and state was leading to an increasing number of people being leery of new groups or movements resembling a "religion." In response to both these realities, yoga teachers at the time sought to avoid yoga being labeled as a "religion" and themselves as "religious proselytizers."[8]

In the 1960s, Maharishi Mahesh Yogi, a Hindu swami and yoga teacher, began to lecture in the west and introduced a practice he called Transcendental Meditation, which utilizes elements of the *yoga* system. By the late 1970s, Maharishi, TM, and his organization had become popular both in the U.S. and western Europe. At first, he regularly used religious and spiritual references and quotes in his teachings. However, in 1977 a U.S. federal court judge ruled TM to be a religious practice and thus stopped it from being taught in several New Jersey high schools. This led to a sharp change in the way Maharishi and his organization presented the practice of TM. Reference to religion, spirituality, and ethics was dropped and emphasis was placed instead on TM's physical, mental and emotional benefits. A variety of subsequent individuals wanting to teach elements of the yoga system took note of Maharishi's experience and likewise avoided all or most reference to anything that might be interpreted as religious in their teachings.

By the time of the court ruling against Maharishi and his teachings, scholarly research on the affects of TM was already being conducted at both UCLA and Harvard, so the change in the way TM was being presented aided in the ability for the research and the teaching of TM to continue. During subsequent decades, there have been hundreds of studies of TM at university medical schools and other academic research facilities all over the country, often with very positive results. It continues to be integrated into the curriculum at various institutions of public education. However, avoidance of discussion about the ethical foundations of yoga often remains as well.

Today, the practice of TM is said to be for the development of consciousness and intelligence and for expanded awareness. It is presented as a systematic technique that allows one to experience the unity of mind and matter. The organization's website specifically states that TM is "not a religion, philosophy, or lifestyle. It's the most widely practiced, most researched, and most effective method of self-development."[9]

8. A "documentary" film entitled "Gods of the New Age" and a book, *The Death of a Guru*, are examples of the anti-Hindu rhetoric that was being produced at the time.

9. The Transcendental Meditation Program. Retrieved October 15, 2012, from http://www.tm.org/.

One of the links on the website provides testimony from various Christian and Jewish leaders, as well as a Muslim woman, on the efficacy of the practice as well as assurances to members of their respective faith communities that TM is not a religion and thus does not conflict with their existing religious beliefs and affiliations. The goals of the practice delineated include stress and tension reduction, wellness, inner peace, expanded consciousness, and enlightenment (awareness of the inner self).

As TM was gaining popularity in the U.S. in the 1970s, a Theravada Buddhist practice called "*vipassana*" was introduced as well. It is a method for developing mental focus and awareness that draws upon elements of the yoga system. In the west, it is also known as "mindfulness" or "insight meditation." Many young Americans became attracted to the teachings of various Buddhist practitioners in India, especially a monk named Anagarika Munindra and a lay *vipassana* teacher, S.N. Goenka. The practices they taught share a similarity with three of the limbs of *ashtanga yoga* (*pranayama, pratyhara,* and *dhyana*). In 1975, three of Munindra's American students started the Insight Meditation Society (IMS) in Massachusetts with the goal of introducing and teaching *vipassana* in the west.

In 1979, the University of Massachusetts Medical Center established its Stress Reduction Program using mindfulness training practices similar to those taught at IMS. Subsequently, a variety of other universities added stress reduction programs using similar techniques. The University of Minnesota Medical School took a somewhat bold step in 1995 by establishing a Center for Spirituality and Health with the goal of "improving patient care through the integration of spirituality, cross-cultural and complementary healing practice."[10] Over the years, the university has added several certificate programs that utilize mindfulness and other spiritual disciplines, especially those found in various forms of Buddhism. In these, the teaching of *vipassana* is central.

Whenever *vipassana* and "mindfulness" are taught, any direct mention of religion is usually avoided, although some of the programs are less hesitant about allowing their connection with Buddhism to be known. This is because Buddhism is both presented and seen by many to be more of an atheistic or non-religious philosophy and NOT a sectarian religion, which makes it "safe" both for those who have a committed religious orientation like Christianity as well as those who are against any and all religious belief systems. While this approach has helped make *vipassana* quite successful in secular settings like academia and the world of business, it also means that direct discussion of ethics, values, and morality are usually minimized or avoided, except possibly during the ten-day retreats that many *vipassana* teachers conduct.

Currently, all three practices mentioned above utilize aspects of yoga and are being taught in institutions of higher education. Studies conducted on all three suggest both students and faculty tend to have positive results. TM and *vipassana* are typically found in medical schools or wellness centers and focus on relaxation, stress reduction, and related benefits. The teaching of *hatha yoga* classes in higher education are mostly geared toward alleviating physical, mental, and emotional maladies. Among those ailments that the practice of yoga helps include arthritis and stiff joints, chronic pain, digestive problems, fatigue, high blood pressure, headaches, and a weakened immune system. Although all three of these practices draw on elements of the yoga system, the complete system is rarely if ever taught to most audiences and students. As mentioned previously, much of this seems to be out of fear of being labeled a "religion," which would

10. University of Minnesota Center for Spirituality and Healing. Retrieved October 24, 2012 from http://www.csh.umn.edu/
   Education_Programs/minor/home.html

then turn many away from the practices and also prevent their being taught in secular environments such as public universities.

Of the major U.S. institutions of higher education, Loyola Marymount University (LMU) in Los Angeles, a private Catholic institution founded in the Jesuit tradition and approach to education, has the most extensive yoga teaching program in the country. There, certificates are available for a variety of specialized topics related to yoga such as "Yoga and Ecology," "Yoga and the Healing Sciences," etc. Moreover, the university has taken a significant step in acknowledging the broader aspects of yoga by housing its Yoga Studies Program at its Center for Religion and Spirituality.

There are also several non-traditional private institutions of higher education that have for decades been teaching a more holistic approach to yoga like that being adopted by LMU. Schools such as California Institute for Integral Studies (San Francisco), Naropa University (Denver), and Hindu University of America (Orlando) all offer a more comprehensive approach to teaching the entire yoga system. As a result, broader ethical, philosophical, and practical aspects are included in their studies. Significantly, all three of these institutions were started by individuals who were either born or lived in India and who were raised in cultures in which yoga plays an integral role. Among the goals of their programs is to carry one's experiences of unity out into the world to bring about social justice and world transformation.

Including Yoga Ethics in Education

Increasingly, the world and nearly all aspects of life have become dependent on technology and scientific advancement, and institutes of higher education are the primary training centers for those who will influence how these are used, and misused. The knowledge and values students learn at home and through education influence how they will construct the future. The inclusion of ethical instruction would help to create a more comprehensive system of education that could help minimize the misuse of knowledge while advancing the positive benefits.

Yoga could play a pivotal role. The system evolved as a means to gain control over one's physical, mental, and emotional being in order to develop an ego-transcending self-awareness, to realize a deeper meaning of life, and to experience true happiness. It had nothing to do with adherence to or rejection of any sectarian belief system, for actions and conduct matter far more than beliefs in yoga philosophy. The precepts found in the *yama* and *niyama* comprise a foundational set of values that can be adapted to most belief systems but are specifically meant to be integrated into one's life style.

What makes yoga unique in this regards is that it seeks to make ethics practical by locating them in a holistic mind-body system. It also seeks to show how the more one is able to live by these principles, the more one is able to obtain the desired outcomes. Scholarly research into the physical, mental, and emotional benefits from the various aspects of the yoga system have already revealed many positive results, but these in themselves do not automatically make students or others more ethical, moral, or compassionate. Something more is necessary, something that inspires enhanced mind-body awareness and an expanded consciousness of the world.

Today, the majority of those who regularly practice TM, *vipassana*, or yoga are individuals who had inclinations toward experiencing a more peaceful and harmonious world beforehand and found these methods as useful means to help them validate and further those inclinations. Most college students, on the other hand, are not necessarily so inclined, especially in a university environment geared toward personal material benefit and profit making. They are typically focused on the accumulation of knowledge needed to gain material benefits, which they see as the primary goal in life. With this mindset, even when taught practices that can enhance physical, mental, and emotional health, they will not automatically become caring, compassionate, and self-aware individuals. Again, there needs to be something more in the educational process if students are to learn these. In his short essay, "Wisdom and Knowledge," Bertrand Russell suggests that the teaching of wisdom is not only possible but should be "one of the aims of education."[11]

Unless fundamental changes occur in the way education currently happens, it will do little if anything to alter the present course of so much of our world toward environmental destruction, increased poverty, fear of one another, social and economic divisions and antagonism, and the violence that is the consequence. A critical reassessment of our society and values and how we treat each other is necessary if this change is to occur, and it must take place at home and in the society at large, not only at school. The way we are brought up and taught to perceive and interpret our experiences all influence the way we respond to each other and to life. That is why, even though each person is unique, most individuals in a community share many aspects of their personalities with others in that community. These can be seen to some extent in how communities of people collectively respond to pain and pleasure, wealth and poverty, success and failure, etc.

Within the last decade, one can see a stark example of the difference by looking at two of the more extreme natural disasters that took place in the world, the 2005 Hurricane Katrina that hit New Orleans and killed nearly 2,000 people and the 2011 tsunami that hit the east coast of Japan killing 25,000 people. In the former, there were countless reports of chaos, looting, and murders. In the latter, there was, for the most part, orderliness and discipline, people helping of each other, politeness and patience as everyone waited their turn to receive assistance, no looting, etc. In both cases, the existence, or lack thereof of, of strong ethical and cultural values was the determinant. In Japan, such virtues that have become increasingly absent in the U.S. are integral to the way children are raised and people live their lives, and this was vividly revealed after the 2011 disaster.

Parents and educators both have a responsibility. We are not only participating designers as we guide students toward the future that they will construct, but we are role models as well, whether or not we admit to it. If we want students to learn positive and constructive values but are not putting them to practice in our own lives, we will be unsuccessful, since they learn from our actions more than our words. Those of us who seek to help create a more compassionate, harmonious, and non-violent world have to walk that talk. Truth telling, non-violence, and all the virtues discussed are not simply of rhetorical value, they have to be discussed, considered, and exhibited by both parents and teachers.

The inspiration and teachings of so many enlightened individuals of the past are there for us to consider, to learn from, and to utilize. We can either continue to evolve technologically, while ignoring the most important aspects of being, or we can realize that a road lacking in ethics and a vision of the world as a global community will lead us to an abyss. Education is the key, but it has to provide more than external knowledge. It has to unlock the doors of consciousness, awareness, and self-knowledge for it to

11. Bertrand Russell, *Knowledge and Wisdom*. Retrieved January 14, 2013, from http://www.personal.kent.edu/~rmuhamma/ Philosophy/RBwritings/knowlegANDwis.htm

provide us the tools we need to create a world of peace and harmony. The *ashtanga* yoga system lays out a straightforward approach to help accomplish this task.

Henry David Thoreau

Spirituality and Experiential Education

Benjamin C. Ingman

Benjamin C. Ingman, "Henry David Thoreau: Spirituality and Experiential Education," *Curriculum and Teaching Dialogue*, vol. 13, no. 1–2, pp. 143–158. Copyright © 2011 by Information Age Publishing. Reprinted with permission.

This reading uses Thoreau's philosophy of spirituality, experience, and education as an exemplar for contemporary experiential educators. With the help of Thoreau, I expose a conceptual oversight in experiential education; ultimately calling for a reconsideration of spirituality in human experience, and a reevaluation of experiential education in light of the Thoreauvian conception of spiritual-experiential learning.

Hailed by many as America's greatest Nature writer (Harding, 1961), and perhaps the most genuine American Transcendentalist (Hochfield, 2004; Koster 1975), Henry David Thoreau is no doubt a literary and spiritual icon. These qualifications warrant little authority in the domain of educational discourse, yet surprisingly applicable insight for educators can be found amidst his romantic literature. Though it was never his intention (Thoreau, 1854/2004), his philosophy of spirituality, experience and education provides a contemporary guide for reexamining the components of human experience and reevaluating the philosophy and methodology of experience-based education.

To use a dead, White man, whose work can be vague, controversial and contradictory (Bickman, 1999) as a point of referral is an imprecise, difficult, and arguably imprudent undertaking (Gruenewald, 2002). Foerster (as cited in Harding, 1961) may have said it best, "Thoreau will remain forever baffling if we insist on resolving into perfect harmony all his ideas and impulses, since there is every reason to believe he did not himself harmonize them" (p. 131). Accordingly, the value of the Thoreauvian philosophy presented does not depend on the extent that it accurately represents Thoreau; the significance lies in the applicability of this philosophy to contemporary experiential education.

The objective of this chapter is to critique experiential education, embracing Henry David Thoreau's philosophy of spirituality, experience and education as an exemplary reference. I argue that by identifying and accounting for the role of spirituality in experience, the Thoreauvian perspective exposes an oversight in experiential education, justifying the call for a reevaluation of the philosophy and operationalized methodology of experience-based education.

I begin this critique by clarifying a few working definitions, and then identifying the problem with experiential education. Next, a brief overview of the methodology utilized in this research is presented, followed by a review of Thoreauvian philosophy. Through exploring Thoreau's American Transcendental roots, and his philosophies of education, experience, spirituality, and Nature, I present the Thoreauvian conception of spiritual-experiential learning as the natural remedy to the ills of experiential education. Finally I ground these abstract connections to practice by illustrating how this fresh perspective of experience relates to contemporary experiential education.

Important Concepts

Spirituality and Spiritual Experience

Spirituality is often defined by its indefinable properties. An inherently ambiguous concept, such language as "true self" (Palmer, 2004, p. 32), "inner light" (p. 44), and "[full] presence" (p. 61) has been utilized to define the spirit or soul. Though these terms provide little clarity in respect to defining spirituality, they refine spirit as "an attribute of individuals" (Miller & Thoresen, 1999, p. 6). Further, spirituality is understood in this chapter as the vehicle by which individuals connect with that which is beyond the self; providing the medium for personal connections with "a much larger reality" (Denton & Ashton, 2004, p. 11). To further clarify the brand of spirituality adopted in this chapter, it will help to add another layer of context through exploring spiritual experience.

Spiritual experiences are often triggered by solitude, community, or immersion in Nature; frequently associated with experiences of transcendence (Fox, 1999), or holistic engagement in an experience with "the conscious recognition of a connection that goes beyond our own minds or limits" (Lantieri, 2001, p. 8). It is often characterized by a "momentary loss of self " (Frederickson & Anderson, 1999, p. 22) due to the extreme levels of engagement in the experience, and is henceforth likened to "flow" or optimal experience (Csikszentmihalyi, 1990; Heintzman, 2008). Spiritual experiences are also associated with the ineffable, the intangible, timelessness, or heightened sensory awareness and often inspire feelings of empowerment, hope, humility, or wonder (Frederickson & Anderson, 1999).

Though it is often affiliated with religiosity (Denton & Ashton, 2004; Fox, 1999), spirituality is recognized here as separate from religion—as an attribute of individuals (Palmer, 2004). Miller and Thoresen (1999) explained the grounds for this distinction: "Religion is characterized in many ways by its boundaries and spirituality by a difficulty in defining its boundaries" (p. 6). Even Thoreau, "an American Spiritual genius" (John Sylvester Smith as cited in Harding, 1961, p. 141), was "critical of the effect that religion had upon his contemporaries" (p. 142). While there is a definite relation between spirituality and religion, it is important to understand that spirituality is not reliant on religion. Quite to the contrary, religion, and even mental and physical health are perceived as dependent on spiritual wellbeing (Miller & Thoresen, 1999).

I have referenced a variety of definitions here to encourage the reader to arrive at her own personal understanding of spirituality; pinpointing this definition is the responsibility of the reader. Each reader may well read this chapter with a different understanding of spirituality, and find the Thoreauvian conception resonating with her in different ways. Rather than try to dispel the context from which the reader experiences this chapter, I hope to invite the reader's own meaning as a piece of the greater argument.

Experiential Learning and Experiential Education

Experiential learning theory pulls heavily from the philosophies of Kurt Lewin, Jean Piaget, and John Dewey (Kolb, 1984). It is a "reactive process in which learning occurs by reflecting on previous experiences" (Wurdinger, 2005, p. 8), "involving theory and practice, action and reflection" (Gregory, 2006, p. 118). Experiential learning theory is "the sense-making process of active engagement between the inner world of the person and the outer world of the environment" (Beard & Wilson, 2006, p. 19). It is learning that plays a role in the formation of experience, and, with the help of application and reflection, is derived as a result of experience (Kolb, 1984).

Experiential *education* is "an intentional, purposeful approach to teaching and learning" (Breunig, 2008, p. 79) "that has students actively engaged in exploring questions they find relevant and meaningful, and has them trusting that [both] feeling [and] thinking, can lead to knowledge" (Chapman, McPhee, & Proudman, 2008, p. 7). This philosophy and methodology relies heavily on experiential learning; it values the experiences of the learner as both the context and process by which learning occurs. Experiential education encourages an organic relationship between learning and experience, actualized through a process of inquiry, planning, testing and reflecting. It is "holistic in the sense that it addresses students in their entirety—as thinking, feeling, physical, emotional, spiritual, and social beings" (Carver, 1996, p. 8). These holistic experiences are organized by experiential educators to both build on previous experience, and apply to future experiences in normal social life (Dewey, 1938/1997).

The Problem With Experiential Education

Considering the overwhelming similarity between Deweyan educational philosophy and experiential education (Breunig, 2008; Chapman, McPhee, & Proudman, 1992), it is helpful to understand Dewey's perception of spirituality. Surprisingly, Dewey (1938/1997) identified the soul of the learner as a component of the educational process, "What avail is it to win prescribed amounts of information about geography and history, to win ability to read and write, if in the process the individual loses his own soul[?]" (p. 49). Dewey also noted the difference between religion and spirituality (as he called it "the religious"): "the [spiritual] aspect of experience will be free to develop freely on its own account" (as cited in Re'em, 2004, p. 214). He believed spirituality was "brought about by devotion to a cause; sometimes by a passage of poetry that opens a new perspective, sometimes ... through philosophical reflection" (as cited in Re'em, 2004, p. 214). By defining spiritual experience in this way, Dewey (1916/1944) validates spirituality not only as an element of human experience, but as a piece of reflective experience—a brand of experience he identified as among the most important for education.

Unfortunately, Dewey failed to explicitly import this conception of spirituality into pedagogy, paying little attention to the spiritual dimension of the learner in his educational theory (Taggart, 2001). Dewey's relative omission of spirituality in pedagogy is mirrored in contemporary experiential education program practice, which fails to intentionally integrate learner spirituality in experience and education. However, spiritual elements of the learner have remained in the undertones of experiential education discourse for some time. Experiential education scholars have identified spiritual elements of the learner, such as "states of being and presence" (Tosey, 2006, p. 131) and recognition of human "otherness" (p. 138) as deserving consideration in the implementation of experiential education. Some even explicitly name spirituality as an element of the person that experiential education engages (Carver, 1996), arguing that experiential education is the avenue to "connect[ing] the head with the body, heart, spirit and soul" (Chapman, McPhee, & Proudman, 1992, p. 20).

Supporting these claims, several recent studies examine the incorporation of "spirituality" in experiential education, but in reality, many of these effectively measure religiosity as a measurable byproduct of experience (Daniel, 2007; Griffin, 2003; Henderson, Thurber, Whitaker, Bialeschki, & Scanlin, 2006). This chapter makes an important distinction from these studies: not aiming to increase religious affiliation, or produce spirituality as a consequence, but arguing for its recognition as a component of human experience.

Other recent research on the topic of spirituality in experiential education includes a plethora of methodological recommendations for outdoor experiential educators to better engage participants in spiritual experience through leisure (Heintzman, 2009), adventure (Fox, 1999) and wilderness settings (Frederickson & Anderson, 1999; Heintzman, 2003). These studies stand as particularly relevant to this project because of their shared notion of spirituality: as tied to experience, rather than as a byproduct of process. Yet they omit an important conceptual connection this study aims to establish regarding the role spirituality plays within experience.

Despite the claims that spirituality is at the heart of experiential education philosophy, comprehensive application of these ideals is yet to be realized. I argue that experiential education has failed to recognize the role of spirituality within experience, leaving ample room for improvement in the holistic realm of the discipline (Hutchinson & Bosacki, 2000). In short, the call for experiential educators "to re-conceptualize spirituality entirely" (Stringer, 2000, p. 126), has yet gone unanswered. It is this conceptual oversight that I identify as the problem with experiential education. This seemingly distal value of experiential education reaches fruition in Thoreauvian pedagogy.

Methodology

To use Thoreau as an exemplar requires a thorough understanding of Thoreauvian philosophy. Both Thoreau's literature and Thoreauvian scholarly reports (Bickman, 1999; Gruenewald, 2002; Harding, 1961; Koster, 1975) were analyzed to achieve this comprehensive understanding of Thoreauvian philosophy. I was able to identify general themes of Thoreau's philosophy surrounding issues of spirituality, experience and education, and ultimately apply these themes to contemporary experiential education.

Admittedly, this research design has several inherent weaknesses. Perhaps most obviously, synthesizing the written works of a deceased author is an activity prone to error, especially when examining an American Transcendentalist who himself did not value congruity (Harding, 1961). Additionally, I am not an expert Thoreauvian scholar, though this has been somewhat compensated for through reference to Thoreauvian scholars as a point of triangulation. In spite of these weaknesses in design, overarching themes of Thoreauvian philosophy were revealed, sufficient for the purposes of this project.

Thoreauvian Philosophy

Henry David Thoreau (1854/2004) never believed his ideals should be applied to the lives of others, and to blindly adopt Thoreau's beliefs without scrutiny would be reckless. However, Thoreauvian philosophy is included in the construction of this argument to provide an example of a new philosophy of spirituality, experience and education. In order to understand Thoreau, it is beneficial to first be acquainted with the ideological and social movement to which he ascribed: American Transcendentalism.

American Transcendentalism: Individuality and Spirituality

American transcendentalism carries a rich philosophical foundation, the product of a variety of beliefs, social issues, and philosophies (Koster, 1975). It was not a religion marked by rules or boundaries, but a way of thinking, acting and being, which, above all else, celebrated the pursuit of the individual (Gura, 2007). While some transcendentalists defined their ideology romantically, "What is popularly called Transcendentalism among us, is Idealism" (Emerson, 1842/1891, p. 388), a concrete definition was supplied by Charles Ellis (1842, as cited in Gura 2007):

> This, then, is the doctrine of Transcendentalism, the substantive, independent existence of the soul of man, the reality of conscience, the religious sense, the inner light, of man's religious affections, his knowledge of right and truth, his sense of duty ... his love for beauty and holiness, his religious aspiration—with this it starts as something not dependent on education, custom, command, or anything beyond man himself. (p. 10)

To paraphrase, spirituality is a priori to each individual; knowledge of right and wrong, concepts of space and time, and appreciation for beauty, are innate elements of the individual, all realized via the human spirit (Gura, 2007; Kant, 1781/2007). This universal value of spirituality was perhaps the cornerstone of American transcendental philosophy; the human has a spirit, and this spirit has the ability to connect with that which is beyond the self (Newman, 2005). This value of individual spirituality effectively matriculated as a central component of Transcendental educational philosophy: "contemplation of spirit is the first principle of human culture, *the foundation of self-education* [emphasis added]" (Elizabeth Peabody as cited in Hochfield, 2004, p. 188).

For American transcendentalists, the source of education was the learner's interaction with the material, rather than the material itself (Harding, 1961; Hochfield, 2004). Bronson Alcott, perhaps the most outspoken American Transcendentalist on the topic of education, recognized the importance of both lived experience and spirituality as central tenets of education. For Alcott (as cited in Hochfield, 2004), education was the "calling forth and cultivation of the *divinity within a [person]*, [emphasis added] not an imposition of external forms upon a passive intellect" (p. xxiii).

As one of the most celebrated followers of American transcendentalism, Thoreau adopted these primary philosophical tenets of transcendentalism. Yet this chapter refers to Thoreau specifically because of his provocative understanding of the inter-relation of these core ideals; "Thoreau's uniqueness among his peers was his rare integration of spiritual life, the intellect, and concrete everyday experience" (Gruenewald, 2002, p. 534). Accordingly, focus will shift from American transcendental doctrine to the Thoreauvian philosophy of education, experience, and spirituality.

Henry David Thoreau: Education, Experience, and Spirituality

The foundation of Henry David Thoreau's pedagogy is loosely based on distinctions between what is learned, what is known, and what is experienced: "It is only when we forget all our learning that we can begin to know" (Thoreau, 1859 as cited in Bickman, 1999, p. 2). Thoreau held that to *know* something was to forget what one had learned about it, and to approach it as a new and foreign object. Thoreau believed that this voluntary forgetting was a prerequisite for allowing ones-self to fully *experience* something (1859 as cited in Bickman, 1999). This blatant prioritization of experience over knowledge was critical to Thoreau's educational philosophy—education was not just a means to attain information, but a process of human experience (Bickman, 1999). He made numerous arguments regarding the role of experience in education, critiquing the established norms of education at the time, and arguing for the experiential processes.

> I think it would be worth the while to introduce a school of children to [this] grove, that they may get an idea of the primitive oaks before they are all gone, instead of hiring botanists to lecture to them when it is too late. (Thoreau, 1860, as cited in Bickman, 1999, p. 10)
>
> [Students] should not *play* life, or *study* it merely, while the community supports them at this expensive game, but earnestly live it from beginning to end. How could youths better learn to live than by at once trying the experiment of living? (Thoreau, 1854/ 2004, p. 49)

Thoreau "teaches the values of experiencing the world firsthand" (Gruenewald, 2002, p. 530) through lived experience. He implemented this tenet of pedagogy as a teacher at a Concord Public Elementary School and, more successfully, at a private school he opened with his brother (Harding, 1961). While Henry Thoreau struggled as a lecturer (Koster, 1975), he reveled in the more "uncommon schooling" (Standish, 2006, p. 150) of lived experience, bringing Nature studies to children some 50 years before it was popularly accepted in mainstream society (Harding, 1961).

Thoreau scolded the educational institution for not recognizing the importance of the experiential process: "What does education often do! –It makes a straight cut ditch of a free meandering brook" (1850, as cited in Bickman, 1999, p. 39). He believed this "ditch-cutting" method of education was the fault of instructors who believed it their duty to control student behavior.

> The grammarian is often one who can neither cry nor laugh, yet thinks that he can express human emotions. So the posture-masters tell you how you shall walk,—turning your toes

out, perhaps, excessively,—but so the beautiful walkers are not made. (Thoreau, 1859, as cited in Bickman, 1999, p. 70)

Thoreau's educational ideals of learner independence, primary experience, intrinsic motivation, and adaptable objectives, as well as his criticism of didactic methods of education, establishes a clear link between Thoreauvian pedagogy and the educational philosophy of John Dewey (Bickman, 1999; Gruenewald, 2002; Saito, 2006).Footnote] Through the use of Cavell's work, Saito (2006) made a thorough argument that Dewey and Thoreau had both "apparent similarities [and] radical differences" (p. 345) in their perspectives of education; Thoreau viewed things from a more practice-oriented level, while Dewey lost touch with the practical through his intense pragmatism[/Footnote] Both Dewey and Thoreau believed that mere provision of primary experience did not classify an endeavor as worthwhile—an experience needed to meet a set of requirements to establish it as educative. It is within these requisite conditions of experience that Dewey and Thoreau, albeit subtly, differ. Though Thoreau's philosophy of experience was not developed nearly as intentionally as Dewey's (1938/1997), he effectively goes one step further than Dewey in *depth* of human experience. *Thoreau believed experiences needed to achieve a certain degree of intensity to be truly educative, a condition satisfied by the incorporation of learner spirituality.[Footnote]*More recent research supports this notion of flow-like optimal experience as educative (Csikszentmihalyi, 1990, 1997).[/Footnote]

For instance, on the topic of reading, Thoreau explicitly credited spiritual engagement as an enhancing mechanism of experience, "To read well, that is, to read true books in a true spirit, is a noble exercise, and one that will task the reader more than any exercise which the customs of the day esteem" (Thoreau, 1854/2004, p. 99). Thoreau saw the incorporation of spirituality into education not only as the responsibility of the learner, but the duty of the educator, evident in his criticism of those who received their education in Europe:

> Instead of acquiring nutritious and palatable qualities to their pulp [while in Europe], it is all absorbed into a prematurely hardened shell. They went away squashes, and they return gourds. They are all expressed, or squeezed out; their essential oil is gone. They are pronounced for you; they are good to stand before or for a noun or as handles; not even hollow gourds always, but the handle without the mug. They pronounce with the sharp precise report of a rifle, but [their] likeness is in the sound only, for they have no bullets to fire. (Thoreau, 1853 as cited in Bickman, 1999, p. 28)

The symbolism in this excerpt is of paramount importance to further understanding the role of spirituality in education. It appears that Thoreau was referencing what Palmer (2004) would later term the "divided life" (p. 39)—to live a life that runs antithetical to the will or calling of the spirit. Those returning from Europe were divided from their souls; "hollow gourds" or "the handle without the mug," to extrapolate, "the person without the spirit." Blame was not on the students for failing to make this connection, but the fault of the "education" they received in Europe for not connecting with them on a spiritual level.

Thoreau repeatedly called for forms of education that connected with the spirituality and experience of learners, yet the reality of spirituality in education remains ambiguous. To help articulate these connections, spirituality must first be clarified as an element of experience, from here the link to education (informed with the Deweyan/Thoreauvian philosophy of education) will be clear by transitive relation. In other words, through understanding spirituality as an element of human experience, the role of spirituality in an experience-based education is irrefutable. Once again, we turn to Thoreau to bring a level of reality to the spiritual experience, as exemplified through Thoreau's own experiences with Nature.

Nature and Aesthetic Spiritual Experience

More than his role as an instructor, Thoreau is remembered for his years as a student of life, personifying (and arguably inventing) the practice of lifelong learning (Bickman, 1999). After all, his major motivation for going to Walden Pond was to "learn [from life] what it had to teach ..." (Thoreau, 1854/2004, p. 88). Thoreau's time at Walden exposes another element of his personal doctrine, "That health and happiness can best be achieved through living in close contact with Nature" (Koster, 1975, p. 50). He believed Nature had become detached from mainstream human experience (Thoreau, 1863/2008), problematic because of the role Nature played in education:

> A river, with its waterfalls and meadows, a lake, a hill, a cliff or individual rocks, a forest and ancient trees standing singly. Such things are beautiful; they have a high use which dollars and cents never represent. If the inhabitants of a town were wise, they would seek to preserve these things, though at a considerable expense; for such things educate far more than any hired teachers or preachers, or any at present recognized system of school education. (Thoreau, 1861, as cited in Bickman, 1999, p. 46)

Though Thoreau did revel in appreciation of Nature, his reflective literature quickly reveals that passive observation was far from the apex of the experience. He thought his encounters with Nature noteworthy because of the shared experience and interaction between Nature and himself, accrediting the depth and value of these experiences to metaphysical connection. In this regard, Thoreau's relationship with Nature was multifaceted; he perceived himself as the student, spokesman, and admirer of Nature, but also recognized Nature as interconnected to his own humanity (Thoreau, 1861/2010).

"Dominated by [his] senses" (Porte, as cited in Koster, 1975, p. 49), Thoreau recommended "[confining] the observations of his mind as closely as possible to the experience or life of his senses" (Thoreau, as cited in Koster, 1975, p. 49). This value of aesthetic experience achieved its climax, unsurprisingly, in communion with Nature.

> I think that the man of science makes this mistake, and the mass of mankind along with him: that you should coolly give your chief attention to the phenomenon which excites you as something independent of you, and not as it is related to you. The important fact is its effect on me.... With regard to [rainbows] I find that it is not ... they themselves (with which the men of science deal) that concern me; the point of interest is somewhere between me and them (i.e., the objects). (Thoreau, 1857 as cited in Bickman, 1999, pp. 61–62)

These connections were realized through a type of experience seemingly unique to Thoreau. His integration of aesthetic consciousness and spiritual engagement, as realized in the context of Nature, resulted in a new brand of *aesthetic spirituality*. Thoreau made his deepest spiritual connections with Nature through cognizance of his own sensuous experience; spirituality was couched *within* the aesthetic experience of Nature. This aesthetic spirituality provides both a palatable example of spiritual experience, and a convenient metaphor for the innate sensibilities of holistic experience. In calling us back to Nature, Thoreau calls us back to the *natural*; back to the wilderness, and back to a more organic understanding of spirituality, experience, and learning.

Spiritual-Experiential Learning

Through this overview of Thoreauvian philosophy surrounding themes of education, spirituality, and experience, it is evident that the three are impossibly interrelated; "Thoreau teaches what schools flatly deny: learning involves the whole person, body, mind, spirit, and the total environment with which a person interacts" (Gruenewald, 2002, p. 534). However, I have yet to elucidate exactly *how* the three are related.

For Thoreau, the presence of learner spirituality acted as a catalyst, turning otherwise ordinary experiences into rich, meaningful *experiences*. By inviting spirituality into the conversation, Thoreau was able to "experience the extraordinary in the ordinary" (Saito, 2006, p. 352) resulting in *spiritual-experiential learning*: experiential learning enhanced through spiritual involvement. What's more, if we apply this conception of experience to Thoreauvian (or Deweyan) educational philosophy, we deduce that spirituality is a critical element of education; acknowledging spirituality as a component of human experience validates spirituality as deserving consideration in experience-based education.

Application to Contemporary Experiential Education

Earlier in this chapter, I argued that contemporary experiential education pays insufficient attention to the spiritual dimension of human experience. Through exploring Thoreauvian philosophy, we have witnessed his "commitment to the wholeness of human experience" (p. 538), as a primal tenet of pedagogy (Gruenewald, 2002). When we incorporate spirituality into experience, we intensify the experience to a holistic level, and amplify the call for meaning and learning (spiritual-experiential learning).

If we embrace the Thoreauvian philosophy and reevaluate experiential education with this new perspective, we find an agreeable similarity in the value of experience in education, but a discerning conceptual oversight regarding the spiritual dimension of experience. In other words, experiential education has effectively adopted half of Thoreauvian pedagogy; acknowledging experience as educative, but misinterpreting the components of human experience. By acknowledging spirituality as a component of human experience, experiential educators can identify and rectify this conceptual oversight through the creative design and implementation of methodologies conducive to spiritual-experiential learning.

Considering the diverse array of programs that utilize experiential education today, provision of precise guidelines for the incorporation of spirituality into experience is impractical and beyond the scope of this chapter. That said, I acknowledge that a more concrete example of how this might operationalize may help bring a degree of reality to these, as yet, abstract concepts. In so doing, it is important to note that I provide this example in light of Dewey's (1916/1944) belief that,

> the only way in which adults consciously control the kind of education which the immature get is by controlling the environment in which they act, and hence think and feel. We never educate directly, but indirectly by means of the environment. (pp. 18–19)

Accordingly, the aim for the Thoreauvian facilitator is to create an environment conducive to spiritual-experiential learning. To reiterate the breadth of potential for conceiving experience in this way, I include an example from a formal educational setting: a reading lesson from Mark Twain's *Huck Finn*. In this reading lesson, I could increase the invitation for holistic engagement (and derivative learning) by doing any of the following:

- Play sounds of a river flowing in the background as students read
- Bring water into the classroom, allowing students to touch the water when Huck dives into the river, perhaps conscious of how the water must have felt for Huck
- Have Huck Finn costumes on hand for students willing to wear them
- Adopt an unhurried pace, calling for occasional silence to listen to the sounds of the water and reflect
- Present the opportunity for students to imagine that they are a character in this book as they read, with opportunities to reflect on their hypothetical position in the storyline
- Incorporate other introspective questions and opportunities for personal or group reflection and connection-making

On the surface, this may seem no different than enhancing the reading lesson through utilizing multiple experiential modalities. But, if our intention is to intensify the experience toward the ends of holistic engagement, we are prone to incorporate those components of experience that invite spiritual involvement. For example: silence, an unhurried pace, a supportive environment, stimulation of a variety of senses, personal questions, and time for reflection and introspection (Fox, 1999; Frederickson & Anderson, 1999; Heintzman, 2008; Palmer, 2004; Stringer & McAvoy, 1992).

I reference these practices tentatively, as my intent is not to deliver absolute methodological recommendations for facilitators, but merely to explain what informed the methods chosen in this hypothetical example. There is no absolute method for actualizing the ends of spiritual-experiential learning, and what works for one student or teacher may well fail for another. The spiritual learning experience is an aim, rather than something we simply execute. Implementing this as a programmatic reality is dependent upon first re-conceptualizing the components of human experience, ultimately acknowledging the capacity for spiritual-experiential learning, and re-evaluating methodology accordingly. By framing learner experiences with the holistic mindset, we can invite students' spirituality to join the conversation, augmenting the experience and enhancing the derivative learning.

As others have argued (Bickman, 1999; Gruenewald, 2002), all educators can pull something from the ideas of Thoreau, and provision of spiritually integrated learning experiences can compliment most any educational program. However, this chapter has focused on the oversight that experiential education has committed through effectively adopting half of Thoreauvian pedagogy; recognizing the value of experience as educative while failing to acknowledge the role of spirituality within experience. Through embracing Thoreau's philosophy of spirituality, experience and education, and altering practices accordingly, experiential educators can facilitate truly holistic spiritual-experiential education.

References

Beard, C., & Wilson, J. P. (2006). *Experiential learning: A best practice handbook for educators and trainers* (2nd ed.). London: Kogan Page.

Bickman, M. (1999). *Uncommon learning: Henry David Thoreau on education.* Boston, MA: Houghton Mifflin.

Breunig, M. (2008). The historical roots of experiential education. In K. Warren, D. Mitten, & T. Loeffler (Eds.), *Theory and practice of experiential education* (pp. 77–92). Boulder, CO: Association for Experiential Education.

Carver, R. (1996). Theory for practice: A framework for thinking about experiential education. *Journal of Experiential Education, 19*(1), 8–13.

Chapman, S., McPhee, P., & Proudman, B. (1992). What is experiential education? *Journal of Experiential Education, 15*(2), 16–23.

Chapman, S., McPhee, P., & Proudman, B. (2008). What is experiential education? In K. Warren, D. Mitten, & T. Loeffler (Eds.), *Theory and practice of Experiential Education* (pp. 3–15). Boulder, CO: Association for Experiential Education.

Csikszentmihalyi, M. (1990). *Flow: The psychology of optimal experience.* New York, NY: Harper & Row.

Csikszentmihalyi, M. (1997). Flow and education. *The NAMTA Journal, 22*(2), 2–35.

Daniel, B. (2007). The life significance of a spiritually oriented, outward bound-type wilderness expedition. *Journal of Experiential Education, 29*(3), 386–389.

Denton, D., & Ashton, W. (Eds.). (2004). *Spirituality, action & pedagogy: Teaching from the heart.* New York, NY: Peter Lang.

Dewey, J. (1944). *Democracy and education: An introduction to the philosophy of education.* New York, NY: Macmillan. (Original work published in 1916)

Dewey, J. (1997). *Experience and education.* New York, NY: Kappa Delta Pi. (Original work published in 1938)

Emerson, R. W. (1891). The Transcendentalist: A lecture read at the Masonic Temple, Boston. *The Prose Works of Ralph Waldo Emerson* (pp. 388–396). Retrieved from the Minerva Library of Famous Books. (Original work published 1842).

Fox, R. (1999). Enhancing spiritual experience in adventure programs. In J. Miles & S. Priest (Eds.), *Adventure programming* (pp. 455–461). State College, PA: Venture.

Frederickson, L. M., & Anderson, D. H. (1999). A qualitative exploration of the wilderness experience as a source of spiritual inspiration. *Journal of Environmental Psychology, 19,* 21–39.

Gregory, J. (2006). Principles of experiential education. In P. Jarvis (Ed.), *The theory and practice of teaching* (pp. 114–129). London: Routledge.

Griffin, J. (2003). The effects of an adventure based program with an explicit spiritual component on the spiritual growth of adolescents. *Journal of Experiential Education, 25*(3), 351.

Gruenewald, D. A. (2002). Teaching and learning with Thoreau: Honoring critique, experimentation, wholeness, and the places where we live. *Harvard Educational Review, 72*(4), 515–541.

Gura, P. F. (2007). *American Transcendentalism.* New York, NY: Hill and Wang.

Harding, W. (1961). *A Thoreau handbook.* New York, NY: New York University Press.

Heintzman, P. (2003). The wilderness experience and spirituality. *The Journal of Physical Education, Recreation & Dance, 74*(6), 27–31.

Heintzman, P. (2008). Spirituality in experiential education. In K. Warren, D. Mitten, & T. Loeffler (Eds.), *Theory and practice of experiential education* (pp. 311–331). Boulder, CO: Association for Experiential Education.

Heintzman, P. (2009). The spiritual benefits of leisure. *Leisure/Loisir, 33*(1), 419–445.

Henderson, K. A., Thurber, C. A., Whitaker, L. S., Bialeschki, M. D., & Scanlin, M. M. (2006). Development and application of a camper growth index for youth. *Journal of Experiential Education, 29*(1), 1–17.

Hochfield, G. (2004). *Selected writings of the American Transcendentalists* (2nd ed.). New Haven, CT: Yale University Press.

Hutchinson, D., & Bosacki, S. (2000). Over the edge: Can holistic education contribute to experiential education? *Journal of Experiential Education, 23*(3), 177–182.

Kant, I. (2007). *Critique of pure reason* (M. Weigelt & M. Muller, Trans.). Harmondsworth, England: Penguin. (Original work published in 1781)

Kolb, D. A. (1984). *Experiential learning: Experience as the source of learning and development.* London: Prentice-Hall.

Koster, D. N. (1975). *Transcendentalism in America.* Boston, MA: Twayne.

Lantieri, L. (Ed.) (2001). *Schools with spirit: Nurturing the inner lives of children and teachers.* Boston, MA: Beacon Press.

Miller, W. R., & Thoresen, C. E. (1999). Spirituality and health. In W. Miller (Ed.) *Integrating spirituality into treatment: Resources for practitioners* (pp. 3–15). Washington, DC: American Psychological Association.

Newman, L. (2005). *Our common dwelling: Henry Thoreau, Transcendentalism, and the class politics of nature.* New York, NY: Palgrave Macmillan.

Palmer, P. J. (2004). *A hidden wholeness: The journey toward an undivided life.* San Francisco, CA: Jossey-Bass.

Re'em, M. (2004). Religion, spirituality and authoritative discourse. In H. Alexander (Ed.), *Spirituality and ethics in education: Philosophical theological and radical perspectives* (pp. 212–222). Brighton, Great Britain: Sussex Academic Press.

Saito, N. (2006). Philosophy as education and education as philosophy: Democracy and education from Dewey to Cavell. *Journal of Philosophy of Education, 40*(3), 345–356.

Standish, P. (2006). Uncommon schools: Stanley Cavell and the teaching of Walden. *Studies in Philosophy and Education, 25*(1–2), 145–157.

Stringer, A. (2000). A sense sublime: Mapping the journey, engaging the mess. *Journal of Experiential Education, 23*(3), 124–127.

Stringer, L. A., & McAvoy, L. H. (1992). The need for something different: Spirituality and wilderness adventure. *Journal of Experiential Education, 15*(1), 13–21.

Taggart, G. (2001). Nurturing spirituality: A rationale for holistic education. *International Journal of Children's Spirituality, 6*(3), 325–339.

Thoreau, H. D. (2004). In J. Cramer (Ed.), *Walden.* London: Yale University Press. (Original work published in 1854).

Thoreau, H. D. (2008). *Life without principle.* Charleston, SC: Forgotten Books. (Original work published 1863).

Thoreau, H. D. (2010). *Walking.* Lexington, KY: Cricket House Books. (Original work published in 1861)

Tosey, P. (2006). Experiential methods of teaching and learning. In P. Jarvis (Ed.) *The theory and practice of teaching* (pp. 130–146). London: Routledge.

Wurdinger, S. D. (2005). *Using experiential learning in the classroom: Practical ideas for all educators.* Lanham, MD: Scarecrow Education.

UNIT 4. PHILOSOPHY AND DEMOCRACY IN EDUCATION

Democracy and Education

In order to understand the relationship between democracy and education, we must study the work of John Dewey, a philosopher and educational reformer whose scholarship is considered foundational to understanding this crucial yet widely overlooked relationship. Dewey wrote extensively about democracy and education for over a half-century, making him the nation's greatest philosopher of democracy. In *Creative Democracy—The Task Before Us*, for example, Dewey (1998) criticizes the commonsense view that democracy is nothing more than an external institution virtually synonymous with government, positing instead "that democracy is a way of life":

> In any case we can escape from this external way of thinking only as we realize in thought and act that democracy is a personal way of individual life; that it signifies the possession and continual use of certain attitudes, forming personal character, and determining desire and purpose in all relations of life. (Dewey, 1998, p. 341)

For Dewey, democracy as a way of life is deeply associated with certain character or personality traits, such as a belief in human equality and equality of opportunity. He insists that "The democratic faith in human equality is belief that every human being, independent of the quantity or range of his personal endowment, has the right to equal opportunity with every other person for development of whatever gifts he has" (Dewey, 1998, p. 341).

Democratic theorists like Dewey have developed a set of dispositions or values that define the overall characteristics of democracy. This set of dispositions or values range from cultivating desires to know, to the ability to revise, to engage in dialogue, to listen, and to have faith in people to be self-governing (Counts, 1933). These personal dispositions, especially when they are considered cumulatively, contrasts rather starkly to more traditional views that tend to reduce democracy to nothing more than a form of government.

For Dewey and others, then, if we do not properly grasp the linkages that connect democracy to education, both institutions will devolve—as they need each other for their mutual development.

In this spirit, Richard J. Bernstein (2008) warns us of the dangers posed to both democracy and education when our schools lose sight of their underlying democratic purposes:

> The danger that I see today for democratic education is that we can be so overwhelmed by nefarious external pressures—regardless of whether they come from "enlightened" administrators who demand to develop metrics to show quantitatively that students are improving their skills, or from political, religious, or ethnic groups that want to dictate what should or should not be taught in our schools—that we will lose our bearings about the democratic goals and aims we are trying to achieve—not in some distant future, but here and now. (p. 29).

To address these ominous trends, Bernstein brings the conversation about democracy and education back to Dewey's call to restore the fundamentally civic purposes of education. "It is Dewey who thought that no matter what crisis we face or how intractable problems may seem, we must honestly and intelligently ask what is to be done and how to do it" (p. 29).

Dewey and other like-minded scholar's contributions to the task of re-democratizing education continue to inspire millions of people as they participate more energetically in the democratic process. This can lead to a deep yearning for hope that together the people can change society and the schools for the good of all who participate.

Philosophy of Education

Philosophy of education is the philosophical study of education within the field of Social Foundations of Education. Philosophers of education are concerned with the established branches of philosophy in ethics, epistemology, ontology, axiology, and politics. "*Sophia* is a Greek word that refers to the kind of knowledge that we associate with wisdom; hence the word philosophy (*philo* + *sophia*) means 'the love of wisdom,'" (Quantz, 2014, p. 57–58). Philosophy of education classes are usually taught in schools of education. "The discipline that we now call Philosophy is built upon the reasoned exploration of concepts and meanings. Its tools include logic, analysis, and critique. As a discourse, Philosophy has existed for more than 2,500 years," (Quantz, 2014, p. 58). The concepts and meanings explored in philosophy can be traced back to the great philosophers of the Western tradition, notably Socrates, who believed that education was inseparable from philosophy and politics.

One contested question in philosophy of education focuses on who should be educated and how. This question interested Plato "as he began his discussion with an analysis of society's needs and the varieties of human talent. In contrast, John Dewey made his recommendations by asking what the consequences might be if we made certain choices" (Noddings, 2016, p. 2).

Conclusion

Today, scholars continue the debate over whether to hold a "narrower or stricter view of philosophical analysis and those who would expand the field to include analysis of literature and episodes taken from daily life" (Noddings, 2016, p. 59). In the latter category, some philosophers proclaim that teachers' "voices and theorizing contribute to much of the data for philosophical analysis" (Noddings, 2016, p. 59). From a different perspective, we can expect to see an interesting blend of "empirical, literary, and philosophical analysis directed at the understanding of educational phenomena" (Noddings, 2016, p. 59).

References

American Education Fellowship. Committee on Social and Economic Problems., Counts, G. S. (1933). *A call to the teachers of the nation*. John Day Co.

Bernstein, R. (2008). Democracy and education. *Philosophy of Education Yearbook*, pp. 21–31.

Dewey, J. (1998). Creative democracy—The task before us. In L. Hickman & T. Alexander (Eds.), *The Essential Dewey: Volume 1: Pragmatism, Education, Democracy* (pp. 340–343). Indiana University Press.

Noddings, N. (2016). *Philosophy of education*. Westview Press.

Quantz, R. A. (2014). *Sociocultural studies in education: Critical thinking for democracy*. Paradigm Publishers.

Overcoming Misconceptions in Actualizing John Dewey's Philosophy of Education

Heidi Ann Lopez Schubert and William H. Schubert

John Dewey's name has been praised, castigated, and almost everything in between, and much of the negative press has resulted from misconceptions of his position. It is our hope to clarify Dewey's sense of possibility for education, and to allay criticisms that do not fit his work. We will offer some criticism, too, not wanting to be classed as *true believers*, as critiqued by longshoreman, Eric Hoffer (1951).

Our tack here is dialogic. William (Bill) has studied John Dewey for 40 years, and Heidi, his 23-year-old daughter, recently has been reading Dewey's work. In the early 1990s, Bill was president of the John Dewey Society for Education and Culture. Heidi's background includes much study of the arts, literature, and culture. She is now interested in educational possibilities for the future of the world via schools and other educative venues. Bill wants to learn about Heidi's perspective on Dewey, to learn from it, since some of her writings have taught him to see aspects of education in new ways. For instance, when Heidi read Paulo Freire's (1970) *Pedagogy of the Oppressed*, which Bill respects and often teaches and cites, she offered a criticism that Bill had not considered. While Heidi, too, respects Freire's call for a *problem-posing* education and an overcoming of *banking education* (Freire, 1970, pp. 57–74), and sees problem-posing consonant with Dewey's progressive organization of subject matter, she pointed out that Freire's text ironically presents problem-posing education in a banking manner. This brought a pause for much reflection by Bill about how to present democratic advocacy without doing so autocratically. He mentioned this to colleague, Gerald Graff, a staunch critic of Freire (see Graff,

2000), who concurred with Heidi's observation. Here is an instance of a young scholar (Heidi) being new to the field, being able to see something that Bill's long involvement in the field may have clouded. To wit, Thomas Kuhn (1970) argued that those who become paradigm setters or contribute to the revision of paradigms (mind-sets that govern inquiry in an area of study) are often newcomers or those who enter a field from another field where different perspectives reign.

Freire and Dewey both advocate a dialectical manner of discourse. Therefore, our tack here is to illustrate dialogue in conversation about Deweyan conceptions and misconceptions of his position. In order to stimulate dialogue, Bill will begin by posing some questions derived from more obscure writings of Dewey in an effort to overcome some misconceptions, and Heidi will draw upon in-depth reading of two classics of Dewey's work, *Democracy and Education* (Dewey, 1916) and *Experience and Education* (1938). It has been some time since Bill has re-read these two germinal sources—often regarded as Dewey's two most important works on education. Thus, he is interested in what Heidi finds that confirms, contradicts, or augments what he finds most intriguing or enlightening in Dewey's work.

With this introduction concluded, we will now move away from talking about ourselves as other, Heidi and Bill, and proceed with the dialogue—not knowing where it might lead. However, we do hope that educators, students of education, or anyone else who reads the dialogue will benefit from the exchange of ideas—applying them in their own dialogic worlds.

Bill: This should be fun. I do want to learn from you. I know you have been reading *Democracy and Education* and *Experience and Education*, so I would expect many of your responses to come from these sources. However, I know that you bought *How We Think* (Dewey, 1910/1933), which has had a big influence on educators. So, please feel free to draw on this source, too, if you wish. Of course, you should feel free to draw upon any of Dewey's works. By the way, I purchased the CD-ROM of Dewey's complete writings,[1] produced by the Southern Illinois University Press in collaboration with the Center for Dewey Studies at Southern Illinois University. We might want to look together for certain key ideas. This is a great resource; however, I await the expertise of your computer skills to help this old *luddite* negotiate the technology and glean the ideas. What do you think of this plan?

Heidi: Sounds like a good plan, Dad. I will also use my own personal experiences in schools to help clarify the points in Dewey's philosophy we discuss.

Bill: One of the greatest misconceptions of Dewey was that he was *laissez faire*, an advocate of anything goes. My take is that he was far from this. The error is probably found in Dewey's emphasis on learner interest. Some educators have taken that superficially to mean that any momentary interest (eating candy, throwing paper wads, running around the classroom) should be condoned because it expresses interest. These are more like whims. A Deweyan education, as I see it, asks students to express their interests and then asks that they probe to deeper meanings of those interests. Some classroom teachers assume that *doing* Dewey is impossible because in a class of 30 students, there would have to be thirty curricula—an impossibility to manage. I am convinced, however that Dewey intended that reflection on one's experience unearths common human interests, such as those Robert Ulich called "great events and mysteries of life: birth, death, love, tradition, society and the crowd, success and failure, salvation, and anxiety" (Ulich, 1955,

---

1. The Center for Dewey Studies and the InteLex has made available *The Collected Works of John Dewey: 1882–1953: The Electronic Edition* on a single CDROM; InteLex, P.O. Box 859, Charlottesville, VA 22902; sales@nlx.com.

p. 255), or those in the deep integration of knowledge and human interest depicted by critical philosopher, Jurgen Habermas (1971) I contend that Dewey thought that momentary interests, explored in depth, would coalesce around such interests—these being examples, not a definitive list. So, students would find that seemingly different interests on the surface level would have common concerns at a deeper level, one shared by other human beings more generally. I am interested in how you respond to this interpretation of Dewey's notion of interests, both from reading Dewey and from your own experience as a learner (in or out of school).

Heidi: I don't believe that Dewey's philosophies of education had no structure (as in "anything goes"). I think that building a curriculum based on the students' interests is a key component of his work. My take on this concept *would*, however, include studying eating of candy or running around the room. If that's what the children were most interested at that time, they should do it. Even simple things, "whims," as you called them, can be gateways to understanding key concepts of life. For example, teacher could help the student ponder why they wanted to eat candy, how is candy made, what are the effects of candy on the human body, how candy is advertised, the history of that candy in this culture, why some candies are more appealing to that particular child than others, and so forth. It could even be the subject of math problems through looking at the cost of candy or counting pieces of candy. The candy could be used as a subject for the student to write an essay on, or write a poem about. The various aspects of the candy and the way it's made could be studied as a science laboratory project. Teachers should come to realize that even the simplest of things, the things which many adults take for granted, and many children are taught should be overlooked or thought of as unimportant facets of life through schooling or through parental influence, those things—if they interest a child—should be indulged. The examples that are arbitrarily chosen for study in traditional school subjects should not be thought of as the only ways to get at the topics of core subjects such as math, history, science, and English.

Bill: I agree, and think your example about candy is well taken. However, by *whim*, I refer to simply letting them eat the candy or run about the room, without making anything of it, that is, without all of the teaching-learning experiences you illustrate. Your imaginative example makes *a lot* of it, indeed, and reminds me of Paul Goodman's small section of a large book, *The Empire City* (1959, pp. 126–128), which he calls "A Thousand and One Lesson Plans." He describes how students walk with teachers through New York City and make lessons from almost everything they see. What they see could remain mere whims, if not built upon by teachers and learners who were curious about how things relate. The prospects of teaching in this way causes many teachers to worry about reaching as many students as they usually have in classes. They also worry about not being prepared and needing to be spontaneous. Their uneasiness is important to consider, isn't it?

Heidi: Yes, a teacher who has a full class of, say, 30 students would have a difficult time focusing on the interests and needs of each student as an individual rather than a mass. This is likely why many teachers continue to use the same ways of teaching a subject for all students, regardless of the students' interests or the match between the teacher's way of teaching and ways a particular student learns. Even if the teacher focused on Ulich's "great events and mysteries of life," there's no way of knowing if those subjects would be taught in a way that means something to each student. So I do not believe that focusing on those topics alone is a panacea to provide a student with a good education, one that will help them self-educate through their entire lives.

Bill: Well, maybe you are right. I have been accused of having too much faith in the Deweyan approach, especially when it comes to schooling, as presently constituted. When I taught in elementary school, I must admit that I reached some students more fully than others. You make a good point. Even if the *great mysteries and events* are the organizing center for curricula, the pathways to them must vary for each student. In working with MEd and PhD students I can do this a little more, perhaps because students come to the program with some semblance of common goals, but still it is difficult to move to the great mysteries at the root of surface interests, even with a seminar of only a dozen students or so. However, in some seminars I feel we can come pretty close to the Deweyan goal. It is a goal that requires a faith in and background for improvisational teaching, much as Bateson (1989) has characterized the improvisational nature of composing a life. That should be the end that education strives toward. Of course, we always need to be in the process of composing our lives. It is a never-ending process, and it is, for me, a challenge that makes life so interesting and worthwhile.

Heidi: I believe that in a school setting students will always—no matter how good and considerate a teacher is—be forced to learn things that are of no consequence to them and will shortly be forgotten once the course has been completed. I don't think that schools can be reformed to change that fact because it is impossible for a teacher to create 30 or so different curricula. The only way to make a truly child-centered curriculum is to educate the child in a non-traditional educational setting. That is, either through home schooling, private tutelage, or in classes where the teacher has ample time, an open mind, and maybe three students at the most.

Bill: Wow, three students! That would take some tax increase! Nevertheless, it reminds me that most of Johann Freidrich Herbart's theories (that had such a great impact on teaching and curriculum in the late nineteenth and early twentieth century Europe and America) were derived from his experiences in teaching, say, two princes. Some of his theory provided precedent for progressive interpretations of Dewey. I guess the enormous question is whether those who govern education are willing to provide for very small numbers in wholly un-school like circumstances. I wonder if that is why the deeper essences of Dewey's theories rarely, if ever, have been practiced on a large scale.

Heidi: Regular schools can try as much as they want to reform their curricula, make their class sizes smaller, or whatever other changes they think might be beneficial, but they will never be able to fully accommodate the interests of each child. So in that way, I agree with the critics of Dewey. Unless schools are drastically changed (which would be an improvement), or a teacher winds up with a classroom full of students who think very much alike, it is impossible to design and put into action, a curriculum that caters to the needs and interests of the individual student. But I think that this ideal proposed by Dewey is very much needed in order for a child to have an entirely meaningful educational experience that has lasting positive effects in that child's life. I don't know if Dewey was familiar with home education, but I believe that that sort of setting, where the parents are their child's teacher and there is no set curriculum, provides the ideal learning environment to put this aspect of Dewey's philosophy into action.

Bill: You are referring to John Holt's (1981) *unschooling*, aren't you? He advocates that parents and their children work together to make the best curriculum they can to facilitate their mutual interests. This might not mean staying at home, but rather using resources of their city or community to create spaces, what Maxine Greene (2001b) calls *public spaces* to enrich their lives, akin to what Dewey refers to as *educative growth*. As you know, many parents choose home schooling for other reasons—to indoctrinate their children in particular religious views, especially fundamentalist; to provide an education that will enable them to score high on college entrance tests; to keep them away from what they might consider unsavory influences. Some criticize home education on grounds that it isolates students from learning to live well socially in the world, and Holt's response seems the most Deweyan of the reasons for education without schooling. It involves creating of public spaces of considerably diverse experiences, which contrasts markedly with being thrust in a school that provides a particular community (one that might not be educative, or that even could be downright harmful) from which the students cannot easily escape. Holt's interpretation also contrasts with several of the other more coercive forms of home schooling I just noted.

Heidi: Yes, this is the kind of progressive education that Mom wrote about in her dissertation (Lopez, 1993),[2] drawing examples from her experience as an educator in an urban public school, a dance school, and our home—giving examples of education that builds upon the plethora of resources available in the Chicago area that give life meaning and growth.

Bill: Some say human beings need to be pushed to learn; however, Dewey (1913) argued for the correlative or reciprocal relationship of interest and effort. He said that any interest pursued in depth carries effort with it—each stimulate and enrich the other. Some argue that learners would not encounter new things, if they only studied their interests. They have a point, although they do not usually consider the immense linkage Dewey asserts between democracy and education. If education is democratic, interests are shared. As they are shared, commonality is not the only dimension—novelty is prominent as well. So, interests can expand naturally; they need not be forced. So, I think Dewey intends that democracy and education are also reciprocal. Do you?

Heidi: I think the notion that any human being needs to be pushed in order to learn is ridiculous. Anyone who is alive and sentient is learning every day through the events of their own life. I agree with Dewey that if one pursues an interest they will do it with effort. Those who think otherwise are either fooling themselves, or have never actually been deeply interested in anything in their lives. When a person has a topic that they find greatly intriguing they will naturally want to know more about it. They will ask others what they know about a subject; they will go to bookstores or libraries and search for more books about that topic; they will do experiments through action and/or thought on the topic—working out new ideas and thinking over old ones; they might watch films or television programs that relate to that topic; and in today's world they can use the internet to find billions of websites that provide countless perspectives on whatever topic is of interest. Any exploration of a topic requires the explorer, the student or learner, to put in effort in order to find satisfying information and to keep on expanding their knowledge. So yes, given such sharing and expanding of interest and effort, I do agree that Dewey saw and democracy and education as reciprocal.

---

2. This dissertation is an autobiographical account of attempts to engage and extrapolate Deweyan forms of education in different settings. Ann, as Bill's wife, Heidi's mother (colleague, confidant, and best friend of Heidi, Henry [Heidi's brother, and son of Ann and Bill], and Bill) is acknowledged for her insightful reading of Dewey's ideas, sharing them in conversations with us over the years, and exemplifying them in her many educational endeavors. In 1981, she received the First Place Prize of the John Dewey Essay Project, sponsored by The John Dewey Foundation for her essay, *John Dewey and Jean Piaget: Artists of Inquiry*. Thus, we express our deep appreciation to Ann Lopez Schubert for her contributions to our ideas about Dewey, education, and life.

Bill: In pursuing interests with concomitant effort, I think you are implying that novelty naturally unfurls. Am I correct in this assumption? Do you think it is consonant with Dewey's ideas? Do you likewise think that exploring bookstores, libraries, and especially the Internet (which I observe is so prominent in your own learning) might be considered participatory democracy—that reading and sharing with others via the web can build a kind of community of expanding interests that fosters growth? I have been thinking that this may be a dimension of participatory democracy that is now available and likely would not have been anticipated by Dewey, since he lived from 1859–1952.

Heidi: Absolutely. When exploring interests, there are bound to be new things that you come across, new ways of looking at things you already knew, or new connections to be drawn between the interest and other things. An example based on my own interests is that following my interest in American comic books, I discovered Japanese animation and Japanese comic books (*anime* and *manga*, respectively) via our regular comic store. My interest in anime and manga made me want to learn more about Japan, and by applying effort in researching those topics I became acquainted (through researching in books, the internet, and talking with others who share my interests) with Japanese music (both popular and traditional), Japanese food, and a variety of aspects of Japanese culture: societal roles, manners, the connotations of different habits I saw characters exhibit, their school structures, mythology, Buddhism and Shinto religions, and so forth. By the time I entered college my interests in anime and manga had grown even stronger, and I wanted to expand my knowledge of all things Japanese, so I decided to study Japanese language, and later I took Early Asian History, which then expanded my interests even further by introducing me to information about China and India, thus making me curious about those countries and their cultures as well. As my interests in anime and manga continue, so does my finding of novelty in those interests as well as the introduction to somewhat related interests. Dewey (1916) reflects this perspective, saying:

> The individual who has a question which being really a question to him instigates his curiosity, which feeds his eagerness for information on that will help him cope with it, and who has at command an equipment which will permit these interests to take effect, is intellectually free. Whatever, initiative and imaginative vision he possesses will be called into play and control his impulses and habits. His own purposes will direct his actions. Otherwise, his seeming attention to his docility, his memorizings and reproductions, will partake of intellectual servility.

Bill: This is a stunning example of the kind of networking of learning, what educators sometimes call learning webs. Further, it implicitly bespeaks the ideal of participatory democracy. This is not just democratic voting, or merely governance by majority rule and protection of minority rights. It is more. It is working out ideas, courses of action, and ways of living together. Is this not where democracy might be seen fundamentally as education?

Heidi: Yes, it is as Dewey (1916, p. 87) says when discussing the *democratic ideal*: "A democracy is more than a form of government; it is primarily a mode of associated living, of conjoint experience." Certainly, exploring interests with effort on the Internet, and sharing those findings with others through the use of the Internet's various communication tools (email, instant messaging, online message boards or forums, mailing lists, websites, etc.) builds a truer sense of community, which furthers growth. Through finding and sharing information in this way, I have personally felt more of a democratic connection with others than I have in classrooms. Perhaps this is because in such online communities, unlike in many school classrooms, everyone is there because they want to be. They're there because that particular topic interests them; they want to learn more about it from others, and to share what they already know.

Oftentimes, in school classrooms teachers have to prod students to get them to share their opinions on the topics being discussed, or the teachers might instead desire to have total control over their subject and dismiss opposing or alternative interpretations from students. But as you said, Dad, in online communities there is often more of a participatory democracy where most members of the community are more than willing to discuss, debate, dismiss, and support whatever is brought up. Sometimes these debates are fueled solely by individual opinions, but other times the debaters cite sources from literature, music, or film, and give links to websites. Though the Internet was well before his time, I have to think that John Dewey would have found it fascinating and appreciated its ability to abet learners in applying effort to find novelty within their interests, as well as to create truer participatory democratic learning environments. Dad, since you have role played as Dewey before, what do you think he would have thought about the Internet and its educational possibilities?

Bill: I have suspected that he would see it as an enriched environment, a *library* beyond his imagination, and an opportunity to enable dialogue among persons of common interest and productive debate among those who see things differently. Your characterization of your own experience confirms what I suspected. Thank you.

Thinking back to the reciprocal relationship between interest and effort and also democracy and education, reminds me of what I take to be a valuable key to understanding Dewey through simple reflection on titles he uses in books, articles, or chapters. He often has two terms joined with the conjunction, *and*; and legend has it that if one substitutes the word *is* for *and*, insight can be gained. Let's consider a few: democracy is education, education is democracy, experience is education, education is experience, human nature is conduct, conduct is human nature, the public is its problems, the problems are the public, liberalism is social action, social action is liberalism, philosophy is civilization, civilization is philosophy, the child is the curriculum, the curriculum is the child. Wow, think of the multiple meanings there! Continuing: the school is the society, and the society is the school.

In his preface to *Experience and Education,* did you notice his example of this crusade on dualistic or either-or thinking? Many of Dewey's disciples misconceived his ideas and they drove a wedge in between progressive and traditional education. However, Dewey said that we should look for the best in both and combine them in new and better ways. I quote: "It is the business of an intelligent theory of education to ascertain the causes for the conflicts that exists and then, instead of taking one side or the other, to indicate a plan of operations proceeding from a level deeper and more inclusive than is represented by the practices and ideas of the contending parties" (Dewey, 1938, p. 5). Am I going overboard?

Heidi: That's intriguing. I am keeping an eye on this key to interpretation as I read. I am noticing that it applies to chapter titles in *Democracy and Education*, not only to the overall title of the book. For example: chapter 10, "Interest and Discipline"; chapter 11, "Experience and Thinking"; Chapter 19, "Labor and Leisure" (can the best labor not be what one would do in one's best leisure?); chapter 20, "Intellectual and Practical Studies" (are they fundamentally the same?); chapter 21, "Physical and Social Studies: Naturalism and Humanism" (two in one title! When one probes deeply in one, it seems to tunnel over to the other); and chapter 22, "The Individual and the World" (microcosm and macrocosm of each other, perhaps. While I am not convinced that the substitution of *is* for *and* always works, I do find it to be a challenging heuristic device. It leads to provocative questions and issues. Similarly, in *Experience and Education*, Dewey (1938) begins by debunking the dualism of progressive and traditional education, and as you quoted from the preface, he seeks to unveil the best of both at a deeper level, a Hegelian synthesis of thesis and antithesis. He concludes by seeing that deeper unity of often separated means and ends in the notion of *experience*, the title of chapter 8 being *Experience: The Means and Goal of Education*.

Bill: Yes, Dewey's life exemplifies this integration. He crusaded against dualistic thought and action all through his long (about 70 years) career (doctorate in 1879 and continued scholarly work until his death in 1952). I really like the way he states it when responding to critics after the progressive movement had about twenty years of experience, following the first publication of *Democracy and Education* in 1916. He is often praised for helping philosophy to break away from Cartesian dualistic (referring to Rene Descartes) tendencies to separate mind and body, thought and feeling, theory and practice, and many more. However, some saw his crusade to be exaggerated. Coming from a background in literature, the arts, and existential philosophy, Maxine Greene (2000) says that while she respects Dewey greatly, he sees every problem as soluble—his faith in the democratic process and scientific inquiry was too great. She goes on to say that the world is a complex and complicated place in which we must learn to live with ambiguities and uncertainties. Maybe we need a Deweyan faith, his secular religion as expressed in *A Common Faith* (1934), and a willingness to deal with the indeterminism of life's exigencies. What do you think?

Heidi: While I do think that Greene is correct, that this world is full of ambiguities and complexities that perhaps need to be viewed as dualistic, I also think that Dewey has an important point trying to bring a focus on viewing things such as body and mind as a whole. The separation of body and mind in schools is one of the emphases (in *Democracy and Education*) that interested me the most. It seems that too often teachers expect children to sit still and be quiet during class, which Dewey says is unnatural, an attempt at teaching only the mind rather than the whole child.

Bill: I just have to mention a study I did once, as part of my dissertation research (Schubert, 1975) I went into a series of elementary classrooms and pretended I was a visitor from another planet in a far off galaxy. My aim was to discover the main purposes of education on Earth so I could write an article on *Earth Education* for the (fictional) *Intergalactic Encyclopedia of Education*. So, I researched ethnographically, and did not merely enter the school scene by asking what their purposes were. Rather, I deduced from what I could see and the time spent on classroom tasks, that Earthlings must believe that a great prerequisite to all learning is to learn that one must be seated and quite, for by far the most time was spent on conveying this to students. If that was accomplished, then a little time could be spent in learning reading and mathematics!

Heidi: Traditional school curriculum also arranges the structure of an elementary students' day so that there are only certain times when it's appropriate to use their bodies such as gym class, sport practices, and recess, and then the rest of the day is meant to have the body inactive and the mind active. This doesn't make a whole lot of sense to me. Why, in academic classes, should a student not be allowed to move around? Why should a child be criticized if they fidget a good deal, or want to stand up and walk around a bit while they listen to the lectures? The only reason, I can think of is that it might be distracting to other students. A child, or any person cannot turn off their body or their mind with the flip of a switch, so mind and body should be treated as a whole.

Bill: I like the "flip of a switch" image! Another reason, besides distracting others (though that would be the most defensible reason), goes back to the numbers of students in typical classes and the need to keep them under control, or to appear as having control to administrators or other visitor who might come by. To top off the lack of emphasis on movement, many schools now have cut recess, physical education, and other active dimensions of schooling, because they are not considered germane to gaining higher test scores. Some pragmatists, writing in the spirit of Dewey, call for oneness of mind and body. Mark Johnson (1987) wrote about the body in the mind, for example, and some feminist writers write about embodied knowing (e.g., Grumet, 1988; Martin, 1987). You might recall meeting Ariel, daughter of Emily Martin, a friend of Sharon Stephens.

Heidi: Yes, I do remember playing with Ariel Martin when I was little. However, I unfortunately have not read her mother's works yet, though I am familiar with the concept of embodied knowledge via my background in cultural studies. I didn't realize that many schools have cut recess and physical education from their school structures. It seems ironic in a way with the push for decreasing childhood obesity that schools would remove time for physical fitness activities. They have a point that it physical activity doesn't play a part in standardized testing. But then again I don't believe that being taught to sit still and be quiet above learning actual subject matter has a positive impact on test scores either. What's the point of a teacher having the appearance of a so-called "controlled" group of students, if none of them have actually learned anything in the class besides how to play dead? Perhaps this is why so many students find it necessary (or their parents do) to enroll in SAT or ACT prep classes run by places like Kaplan or the Princeton Review in addition to their regular schooling—despite how schools claim to focus their efforts on improving standardized test scores?

Bill: Dewey is said to have told a joke that depicted his disapproval of intelligence testing when educators began to view it as the educational equivalent of the medical blood test. He said that he compared intelligence testing with the way farmers weigh hogs. They tie a hog on one end of a board that is on a fulcrum, like a teeter-totter, and then run around the countryside until they find a rock that equally balances with the hog. Then they guess the weight of the rock! The point is that the tests are built on arbitrary concepts or intellectual ideas. In evaluation literature this is called a problem of construct validity. The point applies equally well to achievement tests. Do they test meaningful knowledge and skills, or are they just a mechanism to sort society into those who can have certain opportunities and those who cannot? I think a lot of leaders in politics and business who make school policy want a simple answer to what good education is, something akin to the quarterly report of corporations that simply has a bottom line score on profit margins. Test scores are like that and they are like guessing the weight of an irrelevant rock. They also do not test for feeling, dedication, imagination, commitment, curiosity, and other affective dimensions of cognitive pursuits. The affective and cognitive, like thought and feeling in Dewey's discussion are mindlessly separated.

Heidi: This separation of thought from feeling is a dangerous reality in many classrooms. Frequently teachers do not want to hear what the students feel about subjects or issues discussed in their books or in classroom lectures; rather, they are more interested in knowing the unemotional "thoughts" or hearing simply the facts spouted back at them. Even outside of the traditional school setting in psychology books and personality quizzes found in magazines aimed at teenagers, people are supposed to identify themselves as a "thinker or a feeler," as one who is lead by their "head or their heart." Individuals should be encouraged to listen to their head and heart, to view their thoughts and feelings as coming from the same place, as being of one.

Bill: In this regard, I really like Dewey's *The Sources of a Science of Education* (where *science* could mean theory, as well), in which he concludes: "The sources of an educational science are any portions of ascertained knowledge that enter into the heart, head, and hands of educators, and which, by entering, in, render the performance of the educational function more educational than it was before. But there is no way to discover what *is* 'more truly educational' except by the continuation of the educational act itself. The discovery is never made; it is always making" (Dewey, 1929, pp. 76–77). That really grounds the resolution of these dualisms in experience. How do you think schools do (or could) respond to the need for such grounding?

Heidi: If students are taught to view their mind and body as disconnected, and their thoughts and feelings as separate, it might get to the point where classroom note-taking becomes mechanical and students' minds wander off into more interesting thoughts, such as daydreaming or pondering subjects that interest them. This isn't necessarily a bad thing, especially if they're involved in a class that they couldn't care less about but need to take as part of a required curriculum. But what's the point in that, really? If a subject doesn't mean enough to a student to invest their body and mind, thoughts and feelings, in it, then why bother with the course in the first place? Why should students be forced to learn subjects that cause them to find ways to detach their minds from their bodies? Having such a course could be detrimental to their further learning experiences. They may come to view all subjects as things they can get by on simply going through the motions, but not really putting their minds or hearts into it. This whole concept of duality in education of mind and body, thought and feeling, brings to mind a lyric from a song by the rock band called The White Stripes (2003) about a bad experience in a math class that causes the singer, Jack White, to ask the teacher, "Is it the fingers or the brain that you're teaching a lesson?"

Bill: Some folks defend boredom or drudgery in schooling on the grounds that it prepares students for the drudgery of life. I take it that you find such justification nonsensical.

Heidi: Yes, I do find it nonsensical. Dewey said in *Democracy and Education* that if one does not find interest in their vocation, then they shouldn't be doing it at all. He went on to say that studying or working in a field where you have no interest is harmful to yourself, likening it to slavery—"Slavery only illustrates on an obvious scale what happens in some degree whenever an individual does not find himself in his work. And he cannot completely find himself when vocations are looked upon with contempt, and a conventional ideal of a culture which is essentially the same for all is maintained" (Dewey, 1916, p. 361). I've always believed that there are so many people in the world that for every job that needs doing in this world, there are individuals who would find interest in doing each. Therefore, I don't see the point in anyone having to be prepared to do work that they hate. Yes, everyone, no matter how interesting something is, will likely be bored with it for a transitive period. But that temporary boredom is something different than a lifetime of doing work that never means anything to you. I realize that some people don't appear to have a choice other than to work a job of drudgery, but I think that there have to be more options available. Maybe if schools didn't make students feel accustomed to that sort of lifestyle, people would have more confidence in themselves and know what things they are good at and enjoy doing. Thereby, the feeling of having to do a meaningless job would be eliminated entirely.

Bill: I want to bring up a little known book by Dewey (1931a), aptly entitled *The Way Out of Educational Confusion*. I think it hits squarely on a point about how schools can bring about the lack of meaning and lack of connectedness that students too often experience. Dewey declares that one of the biggest sources of educational confusion is the artificial and arbitrary separation made between school and life. This is manifested in separation among subject of study. Students are forever lamenting the irrelevance of school to their lives, and even that any given subject seems to have little connection to other subjects. However, Dewey is far from being against helping students become acquainted with the disciplines of knowledge. He contends, however, that they should be taught in ways that have meaning. If, for instance, the organizing center of the curriculum is a learner interest or concern, then many different subject matters will be seen necessary to learn in order to pursue that interest or concern. When pursued, that interest leads to other interests and concerns—continuing to grow throughout life, as in the example you gave earlier. The notion of *integrated curriculum* is often hawked by consultants in the educational marketplace today as a mere pasting together or re-mapping of subject matter topics that teachers conjure up out of their interests and impose on learners. Or they may be integrated by themes that educators falsely believe all students share. Instead of such imposition, why not trust learners to take charge of their own growth? Educators often claim that self-education is their ideal end; nevertheless, they teach in an autocratic manner that does not enable learners to make decisions about their own growth. How can autocratic experience prepare for democratic living? Here Dewey's distinction between education and school is of considerable import. He says that education is a continuous reconstruction of experiences and concomitant meanings that guide one's life (Dewey, 1916, p. 76). If school helps to do this, it is education; if not, it is mis-education (Dewey, 1938). So, throughout my career, I have increasingly wondered whether I should be more concerned with schooling or with education, writ large. There are, of course, so many dimensions of our life that build our personal philosophies, identities, or guiding perspectives—school being only one. I have become increasingly concerned with the *outside* (of school) *curricula* in life's many venues (Schubert, 2007). If one is truly interested in enabling education in the best and broadest sense that Dewey depicts, should we not look at all dimensions of the ways in which our guiding ideas, ideals, social commitments and actions are shaped? Is that not what education should be about? For example, good novels and other works of art are all about this shaping of who we are and what we do, aren't they?

Heidi: Yes, certainly novels, even not so good novels, and other works of art help to build the multidimensional philosophies that guide our lives. I believe that any and all experience we come into contact with, good or bad, influences who we are and what we think about the world. One of the things I've found most annoying in classes is when professors would talk to us about *the real world* and about when we would enter this so-called real world, wherein this and that would be different, or such-and-such topic we were studying would come in handy. This even happened in classes that I otherwise enjoyed, learned much from, and held respect for the professor. But I never understood when exactly this *real world* was to begin, for is not school part of the world? Is not childhood? It makes no sense that somehow before you graduate college you are part of someplace that is not the world. Is it some *fake world* that is only set up to prepare you for reality. I highly doubt that educators of kindergarten through undergraduate college would tell other adults that they work in the pretend world, the *fake world*, so why should the students be made to believe these artificial boundaries? Dewey (1916, p. 334) speaks clearly to this concern:

> Outside of school pupils meet with natural facts and principles in connection with various modes of human action…In all the social activities in which they have shared they have had to understand the material and processes involved. To start them in school with a rupture of this intimate association breaks the continuity of mental development, makes

the student feel an indescribable unreality in his studies, and deprives him of the normal motive for interest in them.

Bill: I had not thought much about this, until you presented it so directly. I agree that all of life, in or out of school or any other institution, is part of the world. What else could it be? Besides, the distinction is condescending, isn't it, to those who are treated as if they are not in reality. Thanks for this perspective.

Heidi: You are welcome, Dad. The only understanding I can fathom of why topics are arbitrarily divided into class subjects is that perhaps, breaking things into segments makes it easier for students to handle, or easier for teachers to handle. But I think that it's important for teachers to draw connections between the subjects that their students are enrolled in; similarly, it is important for the teachers to point out how knowing one topic will help them when they learn another. Dewey wrote about the (1916) of subject matter, which I understand as a way of saying that when teaching one arbitrary subject they should be spreading seeds of knowledge for other subjects, which I think is an important point for teachers to understand and put into practice. It is a big mistake to teach a subject with the mindset that it is an entirely isolated field. I think that intelligent individuals—teachers or students—are able to draw these connections on their own. I have learned much from classes about subjects that were not directly intended to be part of the course such as learning about history through literature, advertising, and music. According to Dewey, "We have before us the need of overcoming this separation in education if society is to be truly democratic" (1916, p. 338).

Bill: Is it more a matter of intelligence or simply encouragement and being told that it is valuable to be mindful of connections? I think that some schooling sadly teaches the opposite—that this subject is here and that one is there, and we are not here to relate them. I have known teachers who are afraid to open up the lines of connection, because they think it will take them to places where they have no expertise. Teachers need to see learning as adventure, and in an adventure we never can be sure what connections will occur or be needed until we are immersed in the situation. Our late friend, John Nicholls (Nicholls & Hazzard, 1993) was influenced by Dewey's theories and saw education as an adventure when writing his insightful study of a second grade classroom. He was excited to learn from children, as was evident in a story of a second grader who asked why they did workbooks for science. The child said that scientists don't do worksheets; they examine things in the world! So, what do you think about learners, no matter how young, taking a formative role in their own education?

Heidi: I believe that students should be left in charge of their own education, and that self-education is truly the most meaningful way to learn and grow. Dewey stated the importance of "the rights and responsibilities of the individual in gaining knowledge and personally testing beliefs" (Dewey, 1616, p. 344). This is not to say that I don't think teachers are important, for there are some things that I would never have come across had it not been for the teachers in my life—both formal teachers in classrooms, and also people who have come into my life and influenced me in some way. But I think that the individual should be able to decide what they want to study and how they want to go about doing it. Adults in general seem to have such little faith in children, but I think that children, even very young children are able to make decisions. They are able to tell the adults in their lives what interests them and what does not; they are able to select toys, games, books, and videos, which relate to subjects they want to learn, and therefore are able to direct their own education. If adults would only put more trust in the abilities of children—and of teenagers and young adults too—I think that there would be a lot more willingness and eagerness to learn, and more productive outcomes of the learning experiences. As the legend of Dewey's titles goes, experience *is* education and education *is* experience, the child *is* the curriculum and the curriculum *is* the child.

Bill: This is intriguing, indeed. Can you expand on it—perhaps by telling me how to convince adults to have more trust in the capacity of children and youths to direct their own education, i.e., become their own curriculum directors as your mother has insightfully put it.

Heidi: I think I could expand more on this topic, should I?

Bill: Of course.

Heidi: I don't pretend to have *the* answer to how adults can be taught to trust children, teenagers, and young adults to be their own curriculum directors. I do, however, think that the problem lies within the judgmental discrimination that has irritated me my entire life, which I call *ageism*. Basically *ageism* is the discrimination against those younger than you, or on the other side, discriminating against the elderly. And it isn't a problem of adults only, I think that many teenagers suffer from ageism as well, thinking that they are superior to those younger than them, and thinking that adults are stupid and will never understand them. For the teenage variation of ageism, I think that it stems from wanting to be seen as adults, and therefore, they create a metaphorical gap between themselves and children (even those one or two years younger than themselves). From my observation of this phenomenon, most of their ageist feelings dissipate as they grow up.

This does not answer your question though. With regard to adults moving beyond ageism directed at children, I think that the first step is for adults to acknowledge that there is so much that *children can teach them*. Once adults realize that children/students can be teachers too, then the adults in turn can become teachers and students simultaneously. Accepting that simply being an adult who has had X number of years of formal education does not mean one has finished learning, is a big step forward towards trusting children with being their own curriculum directors. In learning to trust children, I also feel it is important for adults to reflect on their own childhood and what things and people helped them to grow into who they are. That's a point that Fred Rogers always brought up on his television series *Mister Roger's Neighborhood* (1968). Whenever he had an adult stop by his television house, or when he would go on trips around the neighborhood to different businesses (the bakery, the music shop, doctor's office, factories, ...) and performances (dancers, musicians, opera singers, puppeteers, gymnasts ...) Fred Rogers would always ask the adult if they used to play at whatever it is they do for a career now. He would ask them things such as how they became interested in that career, if certain people in their lives influenced or supported them in what they love doing, and note if they got started at, say, playing piano when they were little. Sharing that kind of information with children helps to build a stronger connection between the adults and children, and I think it also helps the adults to reconnect to what it's like being little. Dewey wrote that the transition between play and work should be gradual and not forced: "Moreover, the passage from play to work should be gradual, not involving a radical change of attitude but carrying into work the elements of play, plus continuous reorganization on behalf of greater control" (1916, p. 368).

If adults would only give children a chance to show their capacity for choosing what they want to study, if adults would watch how children play and learn from playing, if only adults could pay attention with an open mind, without set objectives such as a "child must know how to do such-and-such task by such-and-such age," then I think that the adults would come to understand that children are bright. Children want to learn about their environments, the people in them, how things work, and how to get along in the world, and children will actively seek out what they want to and need to learn. They are truly able to design their own curricula, without being forced via schools. Of course, children need some support and guidance, they can't exactly go out to a library, bookstore, museum, or really anywhere, on their own at a young age. Adults can offer encouragement and praise for the child's efforts, which usually makes the child want to explore further. As you know, Dad, I learned to read basically on my own from listening to you and Mom read books, comics, and magazines to me from a very young age. When there came a time that I had materials, which I preferred to read privately, that's exactly what I did, and if I ever had a question about what a particular word was, I would ask you. I never needed to use workbooks or reading primers to get started, I just jumped right in with reading material that interested me.

Adults should be active listeners to a child's questions, concerns, assessments of things, and their ideas. An adult can help the child through make suggestions and ask the child what interests them, what they would like to know more about, learning from the child and teaching the child at the same time, as one might with a colleague or friend. I think the most important thing for adults to realize is that just because someone is a considerable amount younger than another (for example, the *teacher*) doesn't mean that they don't have worthwhile ideas. Age certainly has nothing to do with that.

Bill: We, educational theorists, often talk and write about educational discrimination based on race, class, gender, illness, disability, place, and more, but too seldom focus on age as a key variable. We should do so more. You make a compelling case for this. Existentialist philosopher, Martin Heidegger, said the most important insight for educators is "to let learn … to let them learn" (1968, p. 15). He elaborated, "Teaching is more difficult than learning because what teaching calls for is this: to let learn … to learn to let them learn … the teacher must be capable of being more teachable than the apprentices." Adding to this, our friend Bill Ayers argues that teachers must "be students of their students" (Ayers, 2003). This is, I think commensurate with Dewey, and much that occurs in school attempts to control the learning of others. Nevertheless, I sometimes wonder, however, if this faith of Dewey, Heidegger, or Ayers (and my own) is warranted. Should human beings be trusted to learn and grow on their own, seeking others who will facilitate their growth appropriately? Or is the answer that some can and some cannot be trusted? If so, who should decide who can and cannot be trusted?

Heidi: Individuals should be left to learn, to choose what they want to learn, when they want to learn it, and from whom or what they want to learn. There should still be teachers though, and places and ways to go about locating these teachers who have a large base of knowledge on particular subjects. Like when I was growing up and wanted to study ballet, we were able to locate dance studios and choose what classes I would take, and so forth. While I don't believe in trusting everyone, I do think that each person is able to design their own curriculum, the one that perhaps is best suited for what they want to do in their life. Why would a stranger know what's best for someone else to learn? People shouldn't go around deciding what things are important or unimportant for others to study, because no one learns the same, and not everyone really needs to study the same subjects. Unless of course the aim of education is to create a world full of mind-clones, that is, people who have all read exactly the same books, taken the exact same classes, learned that only one particular set of ideas is important to know and that another set is unimportant. What would be the point of doing that?

Bill: The point might be to control and somehow to profit from that control. Your emphasis on mind-clones is powerful. So is your query about why we should want to have strangers devise our curricula. This made me recall the title of another book by Maxine Greene (remember being at her house when you were about six?); her book title relates to your idea, *Teacher as Stranger* (1973). I wonder why we have moved so far from trusting others, or even if widespread trust ever existed among humans. Such trust or faith in one's fellow human beings would seem a necessary basis for democracy and education, as well as for meaningful experience. What is the culprit that prevents faith in others, and often in oneself? In a little known article in the *New York Times* in 1933, Dewey suggests what the culprit is. He pretended that he had visited a utopian educational future and came back to tell about it.

The first point he makes is that there are no schools at all, although there are homelike centers, enriched environments, where individuals of many ages pursue their interests, interacting with one another to grow and expand their horizons and abilities. He says there are no generic teaching methods, no tests, no grades, no hierarchies in the Utopia he visited. This was justified by the fact that some of the most formidable learning is done in early childhood with no particular tutelage—walking, talking, socializing, learning the processes of inquiry, pursuing curiosity. So why do states, churches, and private collectives all demand rigorous standards, sequences of curriculum, and endless evaluation to control learners? All of this strikes me as does the story of the farmer (you know I grew up on a farm) who weighed a cow. Now satisfied with the weight, he subjected it over and over to the process of weighing, somehow thinking that the weight would improve, when investment in the real need, nourishment, was neglected. The analogy to today's testing and accreditation fetishes seems obvious.

Heidi: The Utopian educational future that Dewey wrote about truly does sound ideal. A world in which there are no schools, no tests, no set curriculum or teaching practices, but rather places where individuals who want to learn the same thing, or the same type of thing can gather on their own accord is exactly what I believe would be the best way for people to learn. Reflecting on Dewey's alleged visit to Utopia causes me to reflect on my own experiences with education, those types of settings where I have had my most enjoyable and meaningful learning experiences: learning at home, learning by going to places around the city and country along side of people who I care about, going to what would generally be considered "after school activities" such as lessons in dance, music, acting, cultures, and sciences (such as those I took at the Field Museum of Natural History, The Museum of Science and Industry (which you remember I used to call "The Museum of Science and Interesting"), the Adler Planetarium, and animals (like at the Lincoln Park Zoo and Shedd Aquarium. True, I have had some wonderful classes in college, but in most of those—the real exception being my Japanese classes—it didn't always seem that my classmates wanted to be there, rather it seemed that they felt they had to take the course in order to complete their degree. That was sad to me, and it distracted somewhat from my own learning experience in those classes. I just don't understand why people can't go and study what they want to. Just as you said, people should have more faith in the abilities of themselves and of others to be able to learn on their own, to not have to be forced into learning.

Bill: One big function of education (as schooling) is to credential, so some can go onward with opportunity and others must stay behind, what Joel Spring calls *the sorting machine*. Some see this as a must for a society with limited resources and limited possibilities. Why must we see it so?

Heidi: Why do people feel that education would not occur, if others did not set up a specific plan of what courses need to be studied and at what ages, or years of study? Why does the educational landscape need to be controlled and policed so relentlessly? It is quite true what Dewey said in his article about the Utopian educational future, that some of the hardest things to learn are learned when we are only infants—walking, talking, eating, even breathing. I believe that Alfred North Whitehead (1929) said the same in *The Aims of Education*, that it doesn't really make sense to order subject matter by placing the more difficult tasks in the later years of formal education, because we learned some of the most daunting tasks as babies. When does this distrust in the abilities of human beings to teach themselves, or at least make their own choices on their educational pursuits begin?

Bill: At the conclusion of his *New York Times* piece on Utopia, Dewey tells what the proponents of Utopia told him was the greatest inhibitor to genuine education—the kind of education he advocates in the books you have been reading. He says that the Utopians told him that progress could not be made toward more genuine learning experiences unless the *acquisitive* society is ended. Everything, including education and relationships, is forced into a definition of a thing to be acquired: certifications, credentials, money, possessions, jobs, and so much more—all deemed things to be acquired and somehow banked. It could even be said that this preoccupation with acquisitiveness actually prevents inquisitiveness. Given this position, then, how much can be hoped for within the framework of values in a capitalistic and autocratic (should I say oligarchic) system? This is a great source of my wonder. It is wonder about how to keep the great curriculum questions alive, the one too seldom asked by policy makers: What is worthwhile? What is worth knowing, experiencing, needing, becoming, being, overcoming, sharing, and contributing? What life is worth leading? Who does it benefit and who needs to benefit more? How could they be enabled to benefit more? How can I become my own curriculum director?

References

Ayers, W. (2001). *To teach: The journey of a teacher*. New York, NY: Teachers College Press.
Batesson, M. C. (1989). *Composing a life*. New York, NY: Plume.
Dewey, J. (1933). *How we think* (Rev. ed.). New York, NY: D.C. Heath. (Original work published 1910)
Dewey, J. (1913). *Interest and effort in education*. Boston: Houghton Mifflin.
Dewey, J. (1916). *Democracy and education*. New York, NY: Macmillan.
Dewey, J. (1929). *The sources of a science of education*. New York, NY: Liveright.
Dewey, J. (1931a). *Philosophy and civilization*. New York, NY: Minton, Balch & Co.
Dewey, J. (1931b). *The way out of educational confusion*. Cambridge, MA: Harvard.
Dewey, J. (1933). Dewey outlines utopian schools. *New York Times*, April 23.
Dewey, J. (1934). *A common faith*. New Haven, CT: Yale.
Dewey, J. (1938). *Experience and education*. New York, NY: Macmillan.
Freire, P. (1970). Pedagogy of the oppressed. New York, NY: Macmillan
Goodman, P. (1959). *The empire city*. New York, NY: Macmillan.
Graff, G. (2000). Teaching politically without political correctness. *Radical Teacher, 58,* 26–30.
Greene, M. (1973). *Teacher as stranger*. New York, NY: Wadsworth.
Greene, M. (2001a). *Exclusions and awakenings: The life of Maxine Greene* (documentary filmmaker, M. Hancock) Hancock Productions, 505 West End Avenue, New York, NY 10024.
Greene, M. (2001b). *Blue guitars*. New York, NY: Teachers College Press.
Grumet, M. R. (1988). *Bitter milk*. Amherst, MA: University of Massachusetts Press.
Haberman, J. (1971). *Knowledge and human interests*. Boston, MA: Beacon.
Heidegger, M. (1968). *What is called thinking?* (J. G. Gray, Trans.). New York, NY: Harper & Row.
Hoffer, E. (1951). *The true believer*. New York, NY: Harper & Row.
Holt, J. (1981). *Teach your own: A hopeful path for education*. New York, NY: Delta Seymour/Lawrence.
Johnson, M. (1987). *The body in the mind*. Chicago, IL: University of Chicago Press.
Kuhn, T. (1970). *The structure of scientific revolutions*. Chicago, IL: University of Chicago Press.
Lopez, A. L. (1993). *Exploring possibilities for progressive teaching and learning in three urban contexts*. Unpublished doctoral dissertation, University of Illinois at Chicago.
Martin, E. (1987). *The woman in the body*. Boston, MA: Beacon Press.
Nicholls, J. G., & Hazzard, S. P. (1993). *Education as adventure: Lessons from the second grade*. New York, NY: Teachers College Press.
Rogers, F. (1968). *Mister Rogers Neighborhood*. Children's Television Workshop, PBS.

Schubert, W. H. (1975). *Imaginative projection: A method of curriculum invention*. Unpublished doctoral dissertation, University of Illinois at Urbana-Champaign.

Schubert, W. H. (2007). Curriculum inquiry. In F. M. Connelly (Ed.), *Handbook of curriculum and instruction* (pp. 399–419). Thousand Oaks, CA: Sage Publications.

Ulich, R. (1995). Response to Ralph Harper's essay. In N. B. Henry (Ed.), Modern philosophies of education, Fifty-fourth yearbook (Part 1) of the National Society of Education (pp. 254–257). Chicago, IL: University of Chicago Press.

Whitehead, A. N. (1929). *The aims of education, and other essays*. New York, NY: Macmillan.

The White Stripes. (2003). *Black math*. By Jack White. Elephant. V2 Recordings.

Introduction to Philosophy for Educators

Richard A. Quantz

> "The unexamined life is not worth living."
>
> —Socrates (as reported by Plato, Apology, 38A)[1]

Whereas most of Chapter 3 addressed text analysis, the last several pages stated that a good critique had to not only analyze a text, it had to interpret it as well. As a reminder, *text interpretation* is the specific and conscious act of bringing outside contexts to the text in order to deepen and broaden our understanding of it. One of the most useful outside contexts to use to interpret many educational texts is that of philosophy, especially the philosophy of education. The next four chapters help clarify and develop philosophy and educational philosophy as interpretive contexts for texts in education. This chapter introduces general philosophy to those interested in education.

Which is more valuable for a person to have: knowledge or wisdom? If we look at the way in which students, teachers, and schools are being assessed these days, we might come to the conclusion that knowledge is valued more than wisdom. After all, we have yet to develop a standardized test that measures wisdom. In fact, wisdom is not really measurable in any standard way. However, I believe that even in this "information age," the truly educated person is the wise, rather than merely knowledgeable, person. So an important question for those who wish to educate and be educated is how does a person gain wisdom?

1. Plato, *Apology*, trans. Benjamin Jowett (Auckland: The Floating Press, 2011).

Many people recognize that a certain amount of wisdom is gained through living one's life. The school of hard knocks, if survived, can lead to the older and wiser person. On the other hand, there sure seem to be a lot of people who are merely older and not one bit wiser than when they were young. What leads to wisdom is not surviving and succeeding in the world but rather reflecting on one's experiences in the world. As one experiences more and reflects carefully on those experiences, wisdom can be produced. Schooling can contribute to this production, but only if its focus is to help people learn how, and to develop the dispositions to, reflect on experience. While all subject areas can help teach us how to reflect on experiences, perhaps more than any other academic discipline, philosophy has claimed living reflectively as its central purpose.

The ancient Greek and Latin languages contained words that acknowledged several different kinds of knowing. *Sophia* is a Greek word that refers to the kind of knowledge that we associate with wisdom; hence the word "philosophy" (*philo* + *sophia*) means "the love of wisdom." While there is much information to be gained in the disciplinary study of philosophy, such as who Socrates was and what Plato's Allegory of the Cave refers to, the real purpose of the study of philosophy is to learn the skills and dispositions to live reflectively.

The discipline that we now call *philosophy* is built upon the reasoned exploration of concepts and meanings. Its tools include logic, analysis, and critique. As a discourse, philosophy has existed for more than 2,500 years. As you might suspect, any conversation that has gone on for that long has developed a large set of terms, ideas, problems, answers, canonical texts, heroes, and villains. We could mistake the knowing of these things as "knowing philosophy," but if one is to gain the love of wisdom, it is more important to develop the tools of "reasoned argument" and the dispositions to use reason than to merely "know" the names and most common beliefs of the most popular philosophers.

In this readubg, *reason* refers to the practice of supporting claims with justifiable premises, and *disposition to use reason* refers to the inclination to actually use reason. When one uses reason, one is being rational. To be rational requires that we be coherent and consistent in our questions and answers. *Consistency* refers to the agreement of each of the parts with each of the other parts. *Coherency* refers to the parts' fitting seamlessly into a unity or a whole. Because of the privileging of coherency and consistency, the kinds of questions philosophers ask and the order in which those questions are asked become quite important because after one asks and answers a question, all other questions and their answers should be coherent and consistent with the first. Sometimes, of course, we find out that our earlier questions or their answers were misplaced or weak, which requires that we go back and ask a different question or develop a new answer in order to remain coherent and consistent with later questions and their answers. Through the process of using reason to develop consistency and coherency, we become more confident in our arguments.

The history of asking and answering philosophical questions is so old that the field has been organized by the types of questions asked. Traditionally there have been four basic philosophical questions: ontology (or, before the modern age, metaphysics), epistemology, ethics, and aesthetics (also sometimes spelled "esthetics" and referring to the questions of art such as what we should consider to be art). This book will address ontology, epistemology, and ethics. I personally have a strong commitment to the importance of aesthetics, but I have had to make many choices of what to include and what to exclude in this book. Unfortunately, from my point of view, aesthetics is too frequently ignored in educational philosophy. The result is a field heavily dominated by ontology, epistemology, and ethics and that is where the next four chapters will focus. If you have an interest in aesthetics and education, an excellent place to begin a study of it is the website of The Maxine Greene Center for Aesthetic Education and Imagination at www.maxinegreene.org/.

Ontology

Ontology is that part of philosophy that addresses the question of what it means "to be." One way we can ask the ontological question is to ask what it means to be fully human (or, perhaps, what the essence of being a human being might be). Below are just a few of the many ways in which philosophers have attempted to address this question. In the spirit of the last section, these ontologies are not presented as a set of answers to be mastered but merely as examples of the kinds of answers to the ontological question that philosophers have considered. By studying a list such as this, the reader may gain a better understanding of the kinds of consideration needed to reflect upon their own developing ontological reasoning. Read through the list in the following section and identify which you think might make for a reasoned starting place for your philosophy.

Homo aestheticus

Some philosophers argue that humans are the only animal that constructs a world marked by value, sentiment, or taste; therefore, to be fully human requires that we become fully "civilized" in the arts of living so as to fully appreciate these aesthetic values. To be fully human requires us to use completely our creative abilities to participate aesthetically in life. Consider the following quotation from Beau Smith, an artist and blogger:

> I have a philosophy. I call it the Science of Originality. A fundamental truth in this philosophy is that art is life. I would go further to equate life with consciousness, perception, and creativity. All that is one for me: consciousness, perception, creativity, art, and life.
>
> What a figurative smack on my head I gave myself when I figured out that my chief goal as an artist was to participate in life! I kind of already knew that. But some things you don't really know until you think about them and give yourself that figurative smack on the forehead.[2]

Smith may not be a professional philosopher, but here we see some of the markings of philosophical thinking that this chapter has already mentioned. Smith not only is experiencing life, but he is reflecting on his experiences and eventually coming to the conclusion that to be fully human, at least for Smith, means to be an artist and to be an artist means to "participate in life." This is a good example of *Homo aestheticus*.

---

2. For an example, see Beau Smith, "Art Is Life," *Ezine @rticles*, February 28, 2008, http://ezinearticles.com/?Art-Is-Life&id=1013832.

Homo bellus

The human is a martial animal. Although we might not wish this, we must acknowledge that committing war on others of our species is central to who we are and to the advancement of civilization. While recent animal studies have found that other species appear to engage in something that resembles war,[3] we cannot escape the centrality of war in human societies throughout history and must understand this characteristic as that which is central to our being and, therefore, the development of the arts of war is central to our becoming fully human. Though the ancient Spartans are best known for developing a public education system for males designed to develop warriors (the *agoge*), the centrality of training in the arts and skills of war has hardly been limited to Sparta. In present-day United States, we find many military academies whose reason for being can only be to develop the warrior skills in their students, even if not every graduate is assumed to become a soldier. Furthermore, consider the role of sports in American society both in and outside of schools. In many ways, sport is ritual war and the characteristics that make for outstanding athletes are often considered equivalent to those that make outstanding soldiers.

Homo economicus

Humans are rational and self-interested animals who engage in social exchanges in a manner that works in their own self-interest. Because of the popularity of *Atlas Shrugged* on Advanced Placement reading lists, Ayn Rand may be the person most students know who advances this ontology, but it is also a central assumption of classical liberalism, an economic-political ideology that will be addressed in a later chapter, as well as libertarianism. Consider these two quotations from Ayn Rand:

> America's abundance was not created by public sacrifices to "the common good," but by the productive genius of free men who pursued their own personal interests and the making of their own private fortunes.

and

> To the glory of mankind, there was, for the first and only time in history, a country of money—and I have no higher, more reverent tribute to pay to America, for this means: a country of reason, justice, freedom, production, achievement. For the first time, man's mind and money were set free, and there were no fortunes-by-conquest, but only fortunes-by-work, and instead of swordsmen and slaves, there appeared the real maker of wealth, the greatest worker, the highest type of human being—the self-made man—the American industrialist.
>
> If you ask me to name the proudest distinction of Americans, I would choose—because it contains all the others—the fact that they were the people who created the phrase "to make money." No other language or nation had ever used these words before; men had always thought of wealth as a static quantity—to be seized, begged,

---

3. Nicholas Wade, "Chimps, Too, Wage War and Annex Rival Territory," *New York Times*, June 21, 2010, www.nytimes.com/2010/06/22/science/22chimp.html?_r=0.

inherited, shared, looted or obtained as a favor. Americans were the first to understand that wealth has to be created.[4]

Many students I have taught are surprised to discover that among the many self-identified conservative politicians, *Homo economicus* may be the most frequently asserted ontology of all.

Homo ethicus

Humans are moral beings. To be fully human requires us to act in a manner that is ethically justified. While there may be many different understandings of what it means to engage in proper conduct, the goal of all persons must be to live a "good life" or to become a "virtuous person" or to "act rightly." Listen to former US secretary of education William J. Bennett speak about the centrality of virtue education for schools:

> It's about the virtues, it's about self-discipline and courage, compassion, faith, friendship, the other virtues. It's about the hard realities that constitute the virtues. We used to teach the virtues in the schools. They are very important things for young people to learn.[5]

Homo faber

Often *Homo faber* refers to humans as tool-users and has been attributed to many people, including Benjamin Franklin and Thomas Carlyle, who wrote "Man is a tool-using animal.... Without tools he is nothing, with tools he is all."[6] But neither Franklin nor Carlyle actually used the term *Homo faber*. And neither did Karl Marx, yet Marx is probably the best known advocate of *Homo faber* as the essential nature of being human. Marx argued that humans realize their full selves when they conceptualize things in their minds and then produce them in the world.[7] Hannah Arendt uses the term explicitly and does so in a manner similar to Marx. Arendt distinguishes between *Homo faber* and what she calls *Animal laborans*. *Homo faber* refers to the creation of humans through their freely conceived work in the world. *Animal laborans* refers to the dehumanization of people as mere labor—used for their body to execute the orders of others. In the following passage Arendt stated that "labor" (as opposed to "work," which is creative and spirit building) leaves people isolated and lonely and is worthy only of totalitarian regimes:

> Isolated man who lost his place in the political realm of action is deserted by the world of things as well, if he is no longer recognized as *homo faber* but treated as *animal laborans* whose necessary "metabolism with nature" is of concern to no one. Isolation then becomes loneliness. Tyranny based on isolation generally leaves the productive capacities

4. Ayn Rand, "What Is Capitalism?" in *Capitalism: The Unknown Ideal*, ed. Nathaniel Branden, Alan Greenspan, and Robert Hessen (New York: Signet, 1967), 29; Ayn Rand, "The Meaning of Money," in *For the New Intellectual: The Philosophy of Ayn Rand* (New York: Signet, 1963), 93.
5. William J. Bennett, "The Book of Virtues," *Booknotes*, C-SPAN, 1994, video interview.
6. Thomas Carlyle, *Sartor Resartus: The Life and Opinions of Herr Teufelsdröckh* (Project Gutenberg, 1890), paragraph 9, chapter 5, book 1, www.gutenberg.org/files/1051/1051-h/1051-h.htm.
7. Karl Marx and Friedrich Engels, *The German Ideology* (New York: International Publishers, 1970).

of man intact; a tyranny over "laborers," however, as for instance the rule over slaves in antiquity, would automatically be a rule over lonely, not only isolated, men and tend to be totalitarian.[8]

Do not confuse *Homo faber* with a simple "vocational man." Though human vocations certainly require the use of tools, in today's world they tend more to "labor" than to "work." In other words, vocational training would be consistent with *Animal laborans*, whereas *Homo faber* requires a more critical and political education than vocational training typically provides.

Homo sapiens

In Aristotle's biological classifications, humans were named the animal that reasons. This ontology emphasizes that the human ability to reason is its most central quality. Given Aristotle's influence during the eighteenth century as the modern biological classification was constructed, the human species was given the Latin name *Homo sapiens* by Aristotelian-influenced scientists.

Homo societus

Humans are social animals. Humans are certainly not the only social animals, but we develop a complicated social and cultural world within which all adult members of our species must participate or find themselves isolated in the world. To be fully human requires individuals to become integrated into the larger community and many educational philosophers, including John Dewey, had at least some allegiance to this conception of human ontology. In Chapter 1, I quoted Dewey as having stated, "I believe that all education proceeds by the participation of the individual in the social consciousness of the [human] race."[9]

Homo spiritus

Humans are spiritual beings. To be fully human requires that we connect to our spiritual self. For many, the spiritual self refers to a religious self and, in the United States, that religious spirit is generally associated with an Abrahamic God, but, of course, there are many highly spiritual Americans who define that spiritual self in a manner different than Christianity, Islam, or Judaism such as Buddhists, Hindi, Wiccas, New Agers, and the traditional religions of the indigenous people of America. Spirituality connects us with our self and with others and with the universe. Surely this is one of the primary reasons for the private religious schools in the United States, but one does not have to attend a religious school to locate the spirit at the center of human life.

It would be a grave mistake to assume that education for spirituality required a commitment to religion at all. Michael Dantley argued,

---

8. Hannah Arendt, *The Origins of Totalitarianism* (New York: Harcourt, 1966), 612.
9. John Dewey, "My Pedagogic Creed," *School Journal* 54 (1897): 77–80, http://dewey.pragmatism.org/creed.htm.

A person's spirituality is that ethereal part that establishes meaning in one's life. It dares to ask the hard ontological and teleological inquiries that help people to determine who they are and what their contributions to life will be. Spirituality is the instrument in our lives through which we build connectivity and community with others. Spirituality differs from religion in that religion is an institutionalized space where spirituality may be nurtured and celebrated. Religion is often used to codify moral behavior that works in collaboration with civil authorities to domesticate a society's citizenry. Religion is the formally recognized space where spirituality is legitimately to reside. However, spirituality far transcends the boundaries of institutional religion. Spirituality may certainly be nurtured through the auspices of the religious experience and may be articulated by some through the use of religious language but the ethereal nature of our lives may also be fostered through life's experiences, a relationship with nature, an appreciation for music and the arts, or even the dynamics of family and friendships. It is from one's spirituality that compassion, a sense of equity, understanding and passion toward others as well as the life's work to which one has been "called" emanate.[10]

Spirituality, according to Dantley, is also a necessary aspect of all education, but most particularly to those, such as African Americans, who often express a spirituality that juxtaposes "the truth of social, cultural, and political realities with a hope of dismantling and constructing a different reality grounded in equity and social justice."[11]

Pragmatism

Above I point out how John Dewey seems to have some allegiance to the *Homo societus* ontology, but much more central to Dewey's conception of human existence was his understanding of humans as problem-solvers who must continue to grow and adjust to new situations if the species is to survive. Failure to learn leads to failure to adjust, and ultimately leads to extinction. Furthermore, because humans cannot be conceived of as essentially isolated individuals (as in *Homo economicus*), Dewey understood humans as always one with the society, so that it is not only individuals who must solve problems and grow and adjust, but societies that must as well. Integrating these ideas, we might suggest that pragmatism's ontology suggests that to live fully as a human, one must not only learn how to learn and solve problems but how to contribute to a democratic society that is geared to solving problems and growing and adjusting to new conditions. Of all the ontologies described here, Dewey's pragmatism requires democracy at its center for humans to realize their full human selves.

10. Michael E. Dantley, "Successful Leadership in Urban Schools: Principals and Critical Spirituality, a New Approach to Reform," *Journal of Negro Education* 79 (2010): 214–215.
11. Ibid., 216.

Existentialism

Existentialism rejects the idea that there is any essential characteristic of human beings but argues, instead, that humans are *radically free*. The idea of being radically free does not refer to political freedom (we know only too well that many people have little political freedom at all), but that we are free from some predetermined essence prescribed by God or Nature or anything else other than what we are free to determine for ourselves both as individuals and as societies. We create what it means to be human as we move through our lives and make choices. Our choices and actions create not only our own individual selves, but contribute to the creation of what it means to be human for all humanity. In other words, when I choose to lie to gain advantage, I not only show through my actions that I am a liar, but that human beings are animals that lie to gain advantage. On the other hand, when I choose to tell the truth, even when it is not to my own advantage, I show through my actions that not only am I an honorable person, but that humans are animals that can maintain honor even when not to their advantage. For this reason, we live in both "possibility" and "dread"—possibility because in any situation, we can always do otherwise—we do not have to conform to that which our society and culture expect of us and dread because in our choices we carry the burden of acting not only for ourselves but for all humanity. Once we realize that "we can do otherwise" (i.e., that we are radically free), we must live in "good faith" by stopping the practice of "lying to ourselves" (i.e., living in "bad faith") and instead choose to "live in truth." When we live as unreflective members of our culture, we live in bad faith. For example, when we become blindly patriotic or complacently accepting of the status quo, we live in bad faith. We must either accept responsibility for the immorality of our society or act against such immorality as war, poverty, child hunger, ignorance, and lack of humane health care.[12]

Postmodernism

To be human means to find that you exist in a symbolically constructed world (i.e., a world of language and media) embedded in power relations that we turn to in order to "name" or "identify" our Self. There is no essence nor is there any existential freedom and we are, therefore, decentered and multivoiced. Of all of the ontological ideas discussed in this chapter, the postmodernists would object the most to the suggestion that they even have an ontology. Because postmodernists point out that all theorizing is trapped in language the suggestion that we can ever claim to get at the essence of what it means to be human ignores the reality that whatever we claim, we do so through language and are, therefore, ultimately trapped by it and in it.

How Ontology Relates to Educational Philosophy

The eleven answers to this ontological question are only some of the possible answers that philosophers and other theorists have advanced as the best and most reasoned claim to the fullness of human existence. Which is correct? That is the wrong question. Trying to decide which of the eleven answers is the correct one suggests that the answer is singular and exists outside of us waiting for us to discover it. Some people are

---

12. For a good discussion of Sartre's work on bad faith/good faith, see Ronald E. Santoni, *Bad Faith, Good Faith, and Authenticity in Sartre's Early Philosophy* (Philadelphia: Temple University Press, 1995).

discouraged by questions that have no single correct answer. Many wonder why we are bothering to ask a question that has no correct answer. Many suggest that it is just a waste of time.

But, to fail to explore this question and commit to one or some combination of answers is to live unreflectively. One way or another, we each commit to an ontology. Our only question is whether or not we are going to do so reflectively or unreflectively. Are we going to reason our way to the best answer we can or are we just going to commit based on nonreason? And make no mistake about it, which answer you pick or that we as a society pick makes profound differences in people's lives. This is particularly true for those who are invested in formal education because some of these ontologies are congruent with the reality of our present schools while others are not. To achieve most of these ontological goals will require a radical change in the nature of schools, because most schools are congruent with only a few of those mentioned in this chapter.

A democratic society requires that its citizens make decisions about the nature of its public education, but when its citizens have not reflected on the very purpose of living a life, how can it possibly decide what its schools should look like? Keep in mind that philosophy commits to a reasoned exploration of problems and that it values consistency and coherency, so, if we start with one or another or some combination of these ontologies or argue for a twelfth or thirteenth, our educational philosophy must be consistent and coherent with our ontology. When we accept one ontology and then work in a school system set up to realize a contradictory ontology, we must either work to change our schools, give in and accept a different ontology, or live in the soul-sucking condition that Jean-Paul Sartre called "bad faith."

For this reason, how you answer the question of what it means to be fully human should help guide your own pursuit of becoming educated and should also guide how we develop our public schools. If you commit to *Homo economicus*, for example, as being the essence of living a fully human life (as so many of our present policy-makers do), then you will pursue one type of education: one that teaches you how to succeed as an economic being. If you commit to pragmatism as the basis of living a fully human life (as many college professors do), you will pursue a different type of education: one that teaches you the skills and dispositions necessary to solve problems through continuous growth as part of a community. The commitment to a particular ontology or the failure to commit to any has real and profound impact on the everyday lives of our public school students even though few Americans, even few teachers, seem to realize it.

Epistemology

Given the importance of coherency and consistency, which philosophical question one asks and answers first becomes quite pivotal in all that follows. While many people will be comfortable asking and answering the ontological question first, others prefer to ask and answer the epistemological question first. *Epistemology* asks what counts as knowledge or, perhaps, how we justify what we claim as knowledge. It also asks how we obtain knowledge. Many people argue that we cannot answer the ontological question until we have developed a justifiable epistemology, because we cannot justify our claim to know what a fully human life is until we have decided what it means "to know." But whether one starts by asking what it means to be fully human or starts with what it means to know, the answer to both questions must be consistent with each other and coherent with the overall philosophy developed.

Below are a few of the ways in which philosophers have attempted to address the question of epistemology. The different epistemologies presented below were selected based on their popularity in educational texts but also to help clarify through comparison one to the others.

Correspondence (Classical)

One of the oldest approaches to epistemology is referred to as "classical" or "correspondence" and is most closely associated with the classical philosophies of the ancient Greeks and Romans. However, it is still found prominently today in a wide range of philosophies and, perhaps more importantly, in the commonsense of ordinary people. There are at least three different versions of classical epistemologies depending on what kind of classical philosophy is utilized: empiricist, idealist, realist. These classical epistemologies differ in some very important ways, but they also share some common conclusions about knowledge.

What is knowledge?

All three classical epistemologies share the claim that *knowledge* is that which we hold in our minds that corresponds to the world as it is. This is why it is called *correspondence epistemology*. The claim here is that there is a world that exists out there that humans can know as it is, and we can claim to know it when our ideas match that world as it actually is.

How do we obtain knowledge?

The three classical epistemologies differ on their understanding of how we obtain knowledge-in-mind that corresponds to the world.

Empiricists. The world is fundamentally material (i.e., the world exists in matter) and so we obtain real knowledge through empirical methods that guide and structure our observations of the material world so that our ideas correspond to the facts of the material world. Empiricists typically privilege science as the best way of knowing.

Idealists. Because the material world is always changing (living things age, nonliving things break down), the eternal world of ideas and concepts (e.g., theoretical knowledge or the world as God knows it) is the most fundamental world, and so we obtain real knowledge through conceptual methods, which guide and structure our reason so that our ideas correspond to the postulates and logic of the conceptual world. Idealists tend to favor philosophy or religion or art as a way of knowing.

Realists. Realism is a form of idealism that agrees that true knowledge is found in the world of ideas but argues that humans can discover those eternal concepts through observation of the empirical world. In other words, realists believe that the ideal world is revealed in the material world. Aristotle is the iconic example of a realist. While we tend to think of him as a philosopher, his work in the physical sciences was a central influence to the birth of modern science starting in the fifteenth century. Realists tend to favor theoretical science.

Pragmatic (Transactional or Interactional)

Pragmatism developed near the end of the nineteenth century and grew out of the American experience. It has been very influential in educational discourses and is often associated with the philosopher John Dewey.

What is knowledge?

Knowledge is constructed as we transact with our world. We act upon our world, and our world acts upon us (transaction). Knowledge helps us negotiate our lives in the world (i.e., solve the problems we identify as we engage our world). We gain knowledge through our reflective experiences with the world. Knowledge only counts when others, who have studied the questions and problems seriously, agree to accept it as knowledge until another idea or data gained from experience requires that we revise our knowledge. In this way, in pragmatism, truth is always tentative, never absolute. Humans can never really know the world as God knows it. It certainly would be arrogant for people to liken ourselves to God; we must settle for the very human, very useful, and very worthy goal of tentative, human, and pragmatic truths.

How do we obtain knowledge?

Because pragmatism claims that knowledge is the result of our transactions with the world, to gain knowledge we must engage our world (transact with it—both the material and the symbolic worlds) in an active and systematic manner. We must act on our world and observe the way the world acts back on us. We must, therefore, be comfortable and confident in the processes of knowledge production. The processes of science can be helpful in organizing this process, but so can the processes of the humanities and the fine arts. What distinguishes the expert from the novice is not that one gains knowledge through transactions with the world and the other does not, but that the expert transacts with the world through a studied and reflective method, whereas the novice does so through less reflective processes.

Phenomenological

Both pragmatism and phenomenology maintain a skepticism toward claims of absolute knowledge, and both understand that knowledge is located in a process of construction. Where they differ is in their understanding of what this constructive process is and how it works. If pragmatism is rooted in the American experience, phenomenology is rooted in the European experience.

What is knowledge?

Knowledge is that which is left after we strip away all our interpretations and get to the basic experience of something in particular. We can never know the world as it is, but only as we experience it. Knowledge is how we experience the world before our language and our culture enter into our interpretations of that experience, but we often fail to recognize the ways in which our culture colors or distorts what we are experiencing directly. The moment we name what is happening or interpret it, we insert culture into it and we distance ourselves from knowledge.

How do we obtain knowledge?

We must put our Self in an experience of something in particular and attempt through reflection or through intuition to "get back to the thing itself" as it presented itself to us before we started to make meaning out of it. We must search for that which the kernel of this experience has in common with the kernel of other experiences. Phenomenology requires much self-reflection of our experiences and the ability to step outside our cultural recipes for making meaning. For example, freedom is known through our experience of freedom. As we experience freedom, we must learn to strip away all of our cultural biases to get to the fundamental experience of freedom itself before we recognize it and called it "freedom."

Hermeneutical

Hermeneutics is a method developed by biblical scholars in the Middle Ages to cull out what were to be considered true books of the Bible from imposters. During the Renaissance, the techniques of hermeneutics began to be applied to all texts, not just the Bible.

What is knowledge?

Knowledge is that which is built up as we experience things in their context and return to them again and again each time with a new set of experiences within which to reconsider those things. Knowledge is a back and forth, circular process of comparing part to whole and whole to part.

How do we obtain knowledge?

We have an experience with "A," which gives us some sense of "A." We then have an experience with "B," which combined with our sense of "A" gives us some sense of "B." But now our knowledge of "B" requires that we reconsider our experience with "A," therefore changing our understanding of "A." We then have an experience with "C," which combined with our sense of both "A" and "B" influences how we understand "C." But now our new experience with "C" requires that we reconsider our understandings of both "A" and "B," resulting in a new understanding of those phenomena. This process is never-ending. All parts must be understood in light of all other parts or of the whole. It is sometimes referred to as the "hermeneutic circle."

Critical Theory

Critical theory is a social philosophy that developed following World War I and centered in Frankfurt, Germany. During World War II, many of the original critical theorists fled Nazi Germany and migrated to England and the United States. It has had much influence in educational philosophy since the 1980s.

What is knowledge?

Knowledge always represents interests and, therefore, is always integral with morality and politics. No knowledge is morally or politically neutral and objective. Much knowledge, especially that knowledge that passes as neutral and objective, actually serves the interests of the powerful to help them maintain the status quo. Critical knowledge results from the demystification of our myths about the world and works to transform our world. Only "critical knowledge" serves the general interest of emancipation and democracy.

How do we obtain knowledge?

Critical knowledge results from the elimination of the way societies make meaning of the world that distorts the way the world actually works. For example, Americans tend to accept an American narrative that the United States is the most socially mobile country in the world, that Americans, regardless of social class, have a better chance to succeed than citizens of any other nation. The facts suggest otherwise.[13] According to critical theory, as long as Americans accept this distortion of the facts, such knowledge will serve only to maintain the nation that has more inequality than any other major industrialized nation. Only when Americans demystify such myths and tell stories that match the actual material facts, will we have critical knowledge that will make it possible to create the democratic nation that we claim to want.

Postmodernism

According to postmodernism, all the epistemologies discussed above are "modern" except the classical epistemologies of correspondence, which are "ancient." Today's world requires a postmodern philosophy. According to postmodern philosophers, so-called modern epistemologies are locked into a mistaken belief that people can actually "know" a world outside of our language. Postmodernism argues that knowledge outside of language is not possible.

What is knowledge?

Knowledge is only that which we are able to convince others to accept as knowledge. There is no "real" knowledge but only that which the powerful have been able to assert as true and get others to accept.

How do we obtain knowledge?

This is the wrong question. What we really need to ask is, how is it that some knowledge has become accepted as true? The answer to this revised question is that some people are able to convince others to accept knowledge claims because they have the power to do so either through control of the institutions that legitimize knowledge or because they have the ability to manipulate the language well enough to "win the game." That which counts as "knowledge" in school, according to some postmodern epistemologies, is that which those scholars, policy-makers, and teachers have determined counts as "knowledge" regardless of whether it is true or not. Whoever writes the textbooks and tests determines what is true. Or, as it is sometimes said, history is written by the victors. Postmodernists might be seen as having ambitions to foster the lions' version of the hunt.

13. Jason DeParle, "Harder for Americans to Rise from Lower Rungs, *New York Times*, January 4, 2012, www.nytimes.com/2012/01/05/us/harder-for-americans-to-rise-from-lower-rungs.html?_r=2&pagewanted=1&hp.

Constructivism

In the field of education, many speak of "constructivist epistemology." Philosophically, *constructivism* is an imprecise term that might include pragmatic, phenomenological, and/or hermeneutic epistemologies. It implies that knowledge must be constructed by the knower or the community of knowers in some way. For this reason, constructivism in educational texts is consistent with pragmatism, phenomenology, hermeneutics, and several others as well.

Summary

The epistemologies discussed above are just some of the possible answers to the questions of what knowledge is and how we obtain it. There are many others, but whichever epistemologies philosophically minded educators might accept, their epistemological reasoning must be consistent with their ontological reasoning and coherent with their philosophy as a whole. One would think that teachers, whose job it is to help students gain knowledge and understanding, would have thought deeply about what knowledge is and how it is produced and learned. Unfortunately, too many teachers simply take a naïve, unphilosophical approach to knowledge. Essentially they accept that knowledge is whatever is tested. But to approach teaching without having reflected upon one's epistemology is, to use Sartre's concept explained above, to live in bad faith. Teachers must think carefully about epistemology and accept their own complicity in the construction of the nation's commonsense understanding as to what counts as knowledge and what does not.

Ethics

Ethics is that area of philosophy that asks about proper human conduct. Most philosophers use the terms *ethics* and *morality* interchangeably as synonyms (though there are some important exceptions among philosophers to this common usage). In contrast, some other fields, such as educational psychology, make clear distinctions between these two terms. This book will typically use these two terms interchangeably. The only exception is when discussing Nel Noddings's ethic of care because Noddings is one of the few who makes a careful distinction between ethics and morality in order to clarify what she believes are important conceptual distinctions.

Ethics versus Efficacy

American professional cultures tend to value efficacy over ethics. When trying to decide what to do, professionals typically ask about what works rather than what is moral. *Efficacy* simply means effectiveness or the power to get something done. In education, for example, many people ask how we can get test scores up. They ask, "What works?" That is a question of efficacy. Much less frequently do they ask an ethical question such as, "Is focusing on test scores good for students?"

To answer a question of efficacy, we make an empirical argument. In other words, if I wanted to argue that to get test scores up, we should have an exercise program in schools, I would be required to provide empirical evidence that showed that exercise programs raise test scores.[14] On the other hand, if I wanted to argue that focusing on test scores was unethical, I would need a normative argument. There is evidence that suggests that the focus on test scores results in a curriculum that emphasizes basic information rather than higher order thinking, and that leads some educators to argue that the focus on test scores is unethical because it diminishes the education of students' higher order thinking.[15]

Public Ethics

Many Americans assume that ethics (or morality) belong in the private sphere: that morality is not a subject for public engagement. Perhaps this excluding of ethics from public discussion follows from confusion over the place of religion in ethics.

If we assume that the only basis for ethical decision-making lies in religion, then we might think that, since religion is supposed to remain in the private sphere, we must also relegate ethics to the private sphere. Certainly there are some ethical problems that lie specifically in religion. For example, whether a man should cover his head or shave his face or a woman should cover her head or face or dress modestly might all indicate adherence to or rejection of specific religious understandings of morality. But one does not have to appeal to a specific religious belief to argue for the moral need to dress modestly in public or to refrain from stealing or murder or to educate our society's children. Contemporary Americans seem to have lost the language necessary for public discussions of ethics.

This book develops a couple of ways in which we can begin to recover such a public language of ethics: one that neither requires a person to bring religion to the conversation nor forbids someone to bring their religion to the debate. While we agree there are some primary questions that apply only to the private sphere and are not issues for public discussion, there are ethical issues in the public sphere that can be addressed from whatever an individual's private religious or personal moral system might be. Chapters 7 and 8 explore two ways to approach ethics that could be used to build a conversation on ethics in public spaces. These ethics neither require nor forbid individuals to bring their own personal religious or nonreligious moral foundation to the discussion, yet provide a basis for an honest debate on the ethics of different schooling practices.

Conclusion

Philosophy is a discipline aimed at developing the skills and dispositions necessary to lead a reflective life. It is the process of asking and seeking answers to age-old questions, such as what does it mean to be fully human? (an ontological question), how can we justify the knowledge we claim? (an epistemological question), and what is proper conduct? (an ethical question). Philosophy privileges reason and demands consistency and coherency. Educators and others interested in education should be interested in basic

---

14. For evidence that exercise does raise test scores, see "Active Living Research: Using Evidence to Prevent Childhood Obesity and Create Active Communities," www.activelivingresearch.org/files/Active_Ed.pdf.

15. Angela Engel, "Exposing the Myths of High Stakes Testing," *FairTest: The National Center for Fair and Open Testing*, 2007, www.fairtest.org/exposing-myths-high-stakes-testing.

philosophical questions because philosophy's requirement of being reasoned requires that any philosophical questions we might ask and answer related to education must be consistent and coherent with the questions we ask and answer in general philosophy. In fact, philosophers have been interested specifically in questions of education at least since Plato, whose *Meno*, written in the fourth century BCE, is one of the first and one of the most important explorations of educational philosophy.[16] Frequently, people confuse the end result of such philosophic reflection for philosophy itself. As Chapters 9–11 will clarify more fully, answers that are separated from the actual process of philosophic reasoning are better labeled "ideology" than "philosophy."

As people seeking education, students have generally not been asked to reflect on what they think they need to become "fully human." Instead, students are typically asked to just go along with the teachers and the rules and the bureaucracy and hope that at the end they will have gotten an education. I am skeptical that such unreflective processes lead to a person's becoming educated. My own educational philosophy requires students to think about where they would like to be *as a human being* when they complete their schooling. Surely they will not yet be fully educated when they graduate from college, but hopefully they will be on their way and, if they have actually reflected on where that path should lead (and *only* if they have reflected on where that path should lead), when their formal schooling is completed, their education will not end but rather continue through a lifetime of reflective living.

---

16. Plato, *Plato's Meno*, trans. Benjamin Jowett (Rockville, MD: Serenity, 2009), http://books.google.com/books?id=5VZYxRiErOOC&printsec=frontcover&dq=meno&hl=en&sa=X&ei=CJs_UdwKgdjSAbyQgcgE&ved=0CDMQuwUwAA.

Waste in Education

John Dewey

The first chapter dealt with the school in its social aspects, and the necessary readjustments that have to be made to render it effective in present social conditions. The second dealt with the school in relation to the growth of individual children. Now the third deals with the school as itself an institution, in relation both to society and to its own members—the children. It deals with the question of organization, because all waste is the result of the lack of it, the motive lying behind organization being promotion of economy and efficiency. This question is not one of the waste of money or the waste of things. These matters count; but the primary waste is that of human life, the life of the children while they are at school, and afterward because of inadequate and perverted preparation.

So, when we speak of organization, we are not to think simply of the externals; of that which goes by the name "school system"—the school board, the superintendent, and the building, the engaging and promotion of teachers, etc. These things enter in, but the fundamental organization is that of the school itself as a community of individuals, in its relations to other forms of social life. All waste is due to isolation. Organization is nothing but getting things into connection with one another, so that they work easily, flexibly, and fully. Therefore in speaking of this question of waste in education I desire to call your attention to the isolation of the various parts of the school system, to the lack of unity in the aims of education, to the lack of coherence in its studies and methods.

I have made a chart (I) which, while I speak of the isolations of the school system itself, may perhaps appeal to the eye and save a little time in verbal explanations. A paradoxical friend of mine says there is nothing so obscure as an illustration, and it is quite possible that my attempt to illustrate my point will simply prove the truth of his statement.

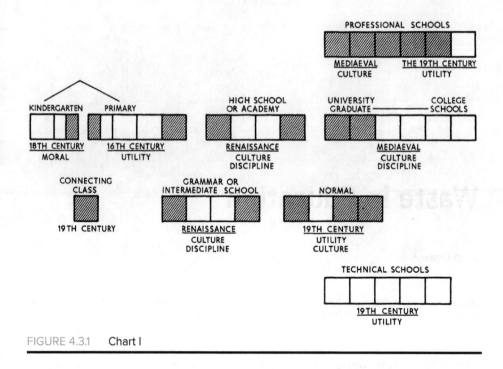

FIGURE 4.3.1   Chart I

The blocks represent the various elements in the school system and are intended to indicate roughly the length of time given to each division, and also the overlapping, both in time and in subjects studied, of the individual parts of the system. With each block is given the historical conditions in which it arose and its ruling ideal.

The school system, upon the whole, has grown from the top down. During the Middle Ages it was essentially a cluster of professional schools—especially law and theology. Our present university comes down to us from the Middle Ages. I will not say that at present it is a mediaeval institution, but it had its roots in the Middle Ages, and it has not outlived all mediaeval traditions regarding learning.

The kindergarten, rising with the present century, was a union of the nursery and of the philosophy of Schelling; a wedding of the plays and games which the mother carried on with her children to Schelling's highly romantic and symbolic philosophy. The elements that came from the actual study of child life—the continuation of the nursery—have remained a life-bringing force in all education; the Schellingesque factors made an obstruction between it and the rest of the school system—brought about isolations.

The line drawn over the top indicates that there is a certain interaction between the kindergarten and the primary school; for, so far as the primary school remained in spirit foreign to the natural interests of child life, it was isolated from the kindergarten, so that it is a problem, at present, to introduce kindergarten methods into the primary school; the problem of the so-called connecting class. The difficulty is that the two are not one from the start. To get a connection the teacher has had to climb over the wall instead of entering in at the gate.

On the side of aims, the ideal of the kindergarten was the moral development of the children, rather than instruction on discipline; an ideal sometimes emphasized to the point of sentimentality. The primary school grew practically out of the popular movement of the sixteenth century, when, along with the invention of printing and the growth of commerce, it became a business necessity to know how to read, write, and figure. The aim was distinctly a practical one; it was utility; getting command of these tools, the symbols of learning, not for the sake of learning, but because they gave access to careers in life otherwise closed.

The division next to the primary school is the grammar school. The term is not much used in the West, but is common in the eastern states. It goes back to the time of the revival of learning—a little earlier perhaps than the conditions out of which the primary school originated, and, even when contemporaneous, having a different ideal. It had to do with the study of language in the higher sense; because, at the time of the Renaissance, Latin and Greek connected people with the culture of the past, with the Roman and Greek world. The classic languages were the only means of escape from the limitations of the Middle Ages. Thus there sprang up the prototype of the grammar school, more liberal than the university (so largely professional in character), for the purpose of putting into the hands of the people the key to the old learning, that men might see a world with a larger horizon. The object was primarily culture, secondarily discipline. It represented much more than the present grammar school. It was the liberal element in the college, which, extending downward, grew into the academy and the high school. Thus the secondary school is still in part just a lower college (having an even higher curriculum than the college of a few centuries ago) or a preparatory department to a college, and in part a rounding up of the utilities of the elementary school.

There appear then two products of the nineteenth century, the technical and normal schools. The schools of technology, engineering, etc., are, of course, mainly the development of nineteenth-century business conditions, as the primary school was the development of business conditions of the sixteenth century. The normal school arose because of the necessity for training teachers, with the idea partly of professional drill and partly that of culture.

Without going more into detail, we have some eight different parts of the school system as represented on the chart, all of which arose historically at different times, having different ideals in view, and consequently different methods. I do not wish to suggest that all of the isolation, all of the separation, that has existed in the past between the different parts of the school system still persists. One must, however, recognize that they have never yet been welded into one complete whole. The great problem in education on the administrative side is how to unite these different parts.

Consider the training schools for teachers—the normal schools. These occupy at present a somewhat anomalous position, intermediate between the high school and the college, requiring the high-school preparation, and covering a certain amount of college work. They are isolated from the higher subject-matter of scholarship, since, upon the whole, their object has been to train persons how to teach, rather than what to teach; while, if we go to the college, we find the other half of this isolation—learning what to teach, with almost a contempt for methods of teaching. The college is shut off from contact with children and youth. Its members, to a great extent, away from home and forgetting their own childhood, become eventually teachers with a large amount of subject-matter at command, and little knowledge of how this is related to the minds of those to whom it is to be taught. In this division between what to teach and how to teach, each side suffers from the separation.

It is interesting to follow out the interrelation between primary, grammar, and high schools. The elementary school has crowded up and taken many subjects previously studied in the old New England grammar school. The high school has pushed its subjects down. Latin and algebra have been put in the upper grades, so that the seventh and eighth grades are, after all, about all that is left of the old grammar school. They are a sort of amorphous composite, being partly a place where children go on learning what they already have learned (to read, write, and figure), and partly a place of preparation for the high school. The name in some parts of New England for these upper grades was "Intermediate School." The term was a happy one; the work was simply intermediate between something that had been and something that was going to be, having no special meaning on its own account.

Just as the parts are separated, so do the ideals differ—moral development, practical utility, general culture, discipline, and professional training. These aims are each especially represented in some distinct part of the system of education; and, with the growing interaction of the parts, each is supposed to afford a certain amount of culture, discipline, and utility. But the lack of fundamental unity is witnessed in the fact that one study is still considered good for discipline, and another for culture; some parts of arithmetic, for example, for discipline and others for use; literature for culture; grammar for discipline; geography partly for utility, partly for culture; and so on. The unity of education is dissipated, and the studies become centrifugal; so much of this study to secure this end, so much of that to secure another, until the whole becomes a sheer compromise and patchwork between contending aims and disparate studies. The great problem in education on the administrative side is to secure the unity of the whole, in the place of a sequence of more or less unrelated and overlapping parts, and thus to reduce the waste arising from friction, reduplication, and transitions that are not properly bridged.

In this second symbolic diagram (II) I wish to suggest that really the only way to unite the parts of the system is to unite each to life. We can get only an artificial unity so long as we confine our gaze to the school system itself. We must look at it as part of the larger whole of social life. This block (A) in the center represents the school system as a whole. (1) At one side we have the home, and the two arrows represent the free interplay of influences, materials, and ideas between the home life and that of the school. (2) Below we have the relation to the natural environment, the great field of geography in the widest sense. The school building has about it a natural environment. It ought to be in a garden, and the children from the garden would be led on to surrounding fields, and then into the wider country, with all its facts and forces. (3) Above is represented business life, and the necessity for free play between the school and the needs and forces of industry. (4) On the other side is the university proper, with its various phases, its laboratories, its resources in the way of libraries, museums, and professional schools.

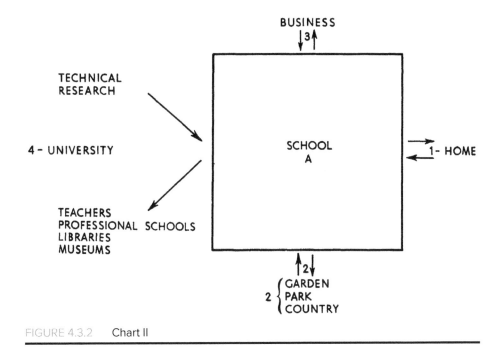

FIGURE 4.3.2   Chart II

From the standpoint of the child, the great waste in the school comes from his inability to utilize the experiences he gets outside the school in any complete and free way within the school itself; while, on the other hand, he is unable to apply in daily life what he is learning at school. That is the isolation of the school—its isolation from life. When the child gets into the schoolroom he has to put out of his mind a large part of the ideas, interests, and activities that predominate in his home and neighborhood. So the school, being unable to utilize this everyday experience, sets painfully to work, on another tack and by a variety of means, to arouse in the child an interest in school studies. While I was visiting in the city of Moline a few years ago, the superintendent told me that they found many children every year who were surprised to learn that the Mississippi river in the textbook had anything to do with the stream of water flowing past their homes. The geography being simply a matter of the schoolroom, it is more or less of an awakening to many children to find that the whole thing is nothing but a more formal and definite statement of the facts which they see, feel, and touch every day. When we think that we all live on the earth, that we live in an atmosphere, that our lives are touched at every point by the influences of the soil, flora, and fauna, by considerations of light and heat, and then think of what the school study of geography has been, we have a typical idea of the gap existing between the everyday experiences of the child and the isolated material supplied in such large measure in the school. This is but an instance, and one upon which most of us may reflect long before we take the present artificiality of the school as other than a matter of course or necessity.

Though there should be organic connection between the school and business life, it is not meant that the school is to prepare the child for any particular business, but that there should be a natural connection of the everyday life of the child with the business environment about him, and that it is the affair of the school to clarify and liberalize this connection, to bring it to consciousness, not by introducing special studies, like commercial geography and arithmetic, but by keeping alive the ordinary bonds of relation. The subject of compound-business-partnership is probably not in many of the arithmetics nowadays, though it was there not a generation ago, for the makers of textbooks said that if they left out anything they could not sell their books. This compound-business-partnership originated as far back as the sixteenth century. The joint-stock company had not been invented, and as large commerce with the Indies and Americas grew up, it was necessary to have an accumulation of capital with which to handle it. One man said, "I will put in this amount of money for six months," and another, "So much for two years," and so on. Thus by joining together they got money enough to float their commercial enterprises. Naturally, then, "compound partnership" was taught in the schools. The joint-stock company was invented; compound partnership disappeared, but the problems relating to it stayed in the arithmetics for two hundred years. They were kept after they had ceased to have practical utility, for the sake of mental discipline—they were "such hard problems, you know." A great deal of what is now in the arithmetics under the head of percentage is of the same nature. Children of twelve and thirteen years of age go through gain and loss calculations, and various forms of bank discount so complicated that the bankers long ago dispensed with them. And when it is pointed out that business is not done this way, we hear again of "mental discipline." And yet there are plenty of real connections between the experience of children and business conditions which need to be utilized and illuminated. The child should study his commercial arithmetic and geography, not as isolated things by themselves, but in their reference to his social environment. The youth needs to become acquainted with the bank as a factor in modern life, with what it does, and how it does it; and then relevant arithmetical processes would have some meaning—quite in contradistinction to the time-absorbing and mind-killing examples in percentage, partial payments, etc., found in all our arithmetics.

The connection with the university, as indicated in this chart, I need not dwell upon. I simply wish to indicate that there ought to be a free interaction between all the parts of the school system. There is much of utter triviality of subject-matter in elementary and secondary education. When we investigate it, we find that it is full of facts taught that are not facts, which have to be unlearned later on. Now, this happens because the "lower" parts of our system are not in vital connection with the "higher." The university or college, in its idea, is a place of research, where investigation is going on: a place of libraries and museums, where the best resources of the past are gathered, maintained, and organized. It is, however, as true in the school as in the university that the spirit of inquiry can be got only through and with the attitude of inquiry. The pupil must learn what has meaning, what enlarges his horizon, instead of mere trivialities. He must become acquainted with truths, instead of things that were regarded as such fifty years ago or that are taken as interesting by the misunderstanding of a partially educated teacher. It is difficult to see how these ends can be reached except as the most advanced part of the educational system is in complete interaction with the most rudimentary.

The next chart (III) is an enlargement of the second. The school building has swelled out, so to speak, the surrounding environment remaining the same, the home, the garden and country, the relation to business life and the university. The object is to show what the school must become to get out of its isolation and secure the organic connection with social life of which we have been speaking. It is not our architect's plan for the school building that we hope to have; but it is a diagrammatic representation of the idea which we want embodied in the school building. On the lower side you see the dining-room and the kitchen, at the top the wood and metal shops and the textile room for sewing and weaving. The center represents the manner in which all come together in the library; that is to say, in a collection of the intellectual resources of all kinds that throw light upon the practical work, that give it meaning and liberal value. If the four corners represent practice, the interior represents the theory of the practical activities. In other words, the object of these forms of practice in the school is not found chiefly in themselves, or in the technical skill of cooks, seamstresses, carpenters, and masons, but in their connection, on the social side, with the life without; while on the individual side they respond to the child's need of action, of expression, of desire to do something, to be constructive and creative, instead of simply passive and conforming. Their great significance is that they keep the balance between the social and individual sides—the chart symbolizing particularly the connection with the social. Here on one side is the home. How naturally the lines of connection play back and forth between the home and the kitchen and the textile room of the school! The child can carry over what he learns in the home and utilize it in the school; and the things learned in the school he applies at home. These are the two great things in breaking down isolation, in getting connection—to have the child come to school with all the experience he has got outside the school, and to leave it with something to be immediately used in his everyday life. The child comes to the traditional school with a healthy body and a more or less unwilling mind, though, in fact, he does not bring both his body and mind with him; he has to leave his mind behind, because there is no way to use it in the school. If he had a purely abstract mind, he could bring it to school with him, but his is a concrete one, interested in concrete things, and unless these things get over into school life he cannot take his mind with him. What we want is to have the child come to school with a whole mind and a whole body, and leave school with a fuller mind and an even healthier body. And speaking of the body suggests that, while there is no gymnasium in these diagrams, the active life carried on in its four corners brings with it constant physical exercise, while our gymnasium proper will deal with the particular weaknesses of children and their correction, and will attempt more consciously to build up the thoroughly sound body as the abode of the sound mind.

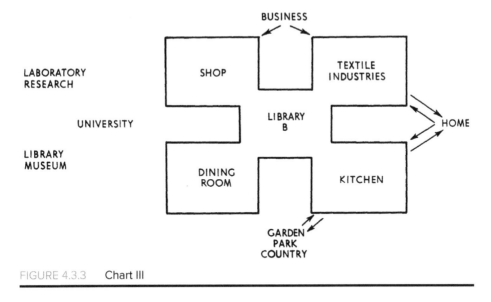

FIGURE 4.3.3   Chart III

That the dining-room and kitchen connect with the country and its processes and products it is hardly necessary to say. Cooking may be so taught that it has no connection with country life and with the sciences that find their unity in geography. Perhaps it generally has been taught without these connections being really made. But all the materials that come into the kitchen have their origin in the country; they come from the soil, are nurtured through the influences of light and water, and represent a great variety of local environments. Through this connection, extending from the garden into the larger world, the child has his most natural introduction to the study of the sciences. Where did these things grow? What was necessary to their growth? What their relation to the soil? What the effect of different climatic conditions? and so on. We all know what the old-fashioned botany was: partly collecting flowers that were pretty, pressing and mounting them; partly pulling these flowers to pieces and giving technical names to the different parts, finding all the different leaves, naming all their different shapes and forms. It was a study of plants without any reference to the soil, to the country, or to growth. In contrast, a real study of plants takes them in their natural environment and in their uses as well, not simply as food, but in all their adaptations to the social life of man. Cooking becomes as well a most natural introduction to the study of chemistry, giving the child here also something which he can at once bring to bear upon his daily experience. I once heard a very intelligent woman say that she could not understand how science could be taught to little children, because she did not see how they could understand atoms and molecules. In other words, since she did not see how highly abstract facts could be presented to the child independently of daily experience, she could not understand how science could be taught at all. Before we smile at this remark, we need to ask ourselves if she is alone in her assumption, or whether it simply formulates the principle of almost all our school practice.

The same relations with the outside world are found in the carpentry and the textile shops. They connect with the country, as the source of their materials, with physics, as the science of applying energy, with commerce and distribution, with art in the development of architecture and decoration. They have also an intimate connection with the university on the side of its technological and engineering schools; with the laboratory and its scientific methods and results.

To go back to the square which is marked the library (Chart III, A): if you imagine rooms half in the four corners and half in the library, you will get the idea of the recitation room. That is the place where the children bring the experiences, the problems, the questions, the particular facts which they have found, and discuss them so that new light may be thrown upon them, particularly new light from the experience of others, the accumulated wisdom of the world—symbolized in the library. Here is the organic relation of theory and practice; the child not simply doing things, but getting also the *idea of* what he does; getting from the start some intellectual conception that enters into his practice and enriches it; while every idea finds, directly or indirectly, some application in experience and has some effect upon life. This, I need hardly say, fixes the position of the "book" or reading in education. Harmful as a substitute for experience, it is all-important in interpreting and expanding experience.

The remaining chart (IV) illustrates precisely the same idea. It gives the symbolic upper story of this ideal school. In the upper corners are the laboratories; in the lower corners are the studios for art work, both the graphic and auditory arts. The questions, the clinical and physical problems, arising in the kitchen and shop, are taken to the laboratories to be worked out. For instance, this past week one of the older groups of children doing practical work in weaving, which involved the use of the spinning wheel, worked out the diagrams of the direction of forces concerned in treadle and wheel, and the ratio of velocities between wheel and spindle. In the same manner, the plants with which the child has to do in cooking afford the basis for a concrete interest in botany and may be taken and studied by themselves. In a certain school in Boston science work for months was centered in the growth of the cotton plant, and yet something new was brought in every day. We hope to do similar work with all the types of plants that furnish materials for sewing and weaving. These examples will suggest, I hope, the relation which the laboratories bear to the rest of the school.

The drawing and music, or the graphic and auditory arts, represent the culmination, the idealization, the highest point of refinement of all the work carried on. I think everybody who has not a purely literary view of the subject recognizes that genuine art grows out of the work of the artisan. The art of the Renaissance was great because it grew out of the manual arts of life. It did not spring up in a separate atmosphere, however ideal, but carried on to their spiritual meaning processes found in homely and everyday forms of life. The school should observe this relationship. The merely artisan side is narrow, but the mere art, taken by itself, and grafted on from without, tends to become forced, empty, sentimental. I do not mean, of course, that all art work must be correlated in detail to the other work of the school, but simply that a spirit of union gives vitality to the art and depth and richness to the other work. All art involves physical organs—the eye and hand, the ear and voice; and yet it is something more than the mere technical skill required by the organs of expression. It involves an idea, a thought, a spiritual rendering of things; and yet it is other than any number of ideas by themselves. It is a living union of thought and the instrument of expression. This union is symbolized by saying that in the ideal school the art work might be considered to be that of the shops, passed through the alembic of library and museum into action again.

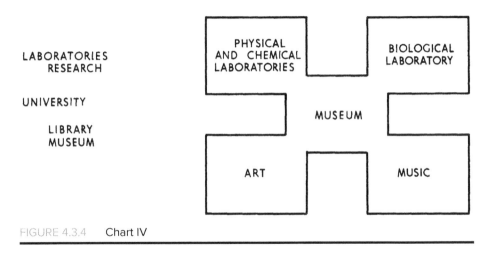

FIGURE 4.3.4   Chart IV

Take the textile room as an illustration of such a synthesis. I am talking about a future school, the one we hope, sometime, to have. The basal fact in that room is that it is a workshop, doing actual things in sewing, spinning, and weaving. The children come into immediate connection with the materials, with various fabrics of silk, cotton, linen, and wool. Information at once appears in connection with these materials; their origin, history, their adaptation to particular uses, and the machines of various kinds by which the raw materials are utilized. Discipline arises in dealing with the problems involved, both theoretical and practical. Whence does the culture arise? Partly from seeing all these things reflected through the medium of their scientific and historic conditions and associations, whereby the child learns to appreciate them as technical achievements, as thoughts precipitated in action; and partly because of the introduction of the art idea into the room itself. In the ideal school there would be something of this sort: first, a complete industrial museum, giving samples of materials in various stages of manufacture, and the implements, from the simplest to the most complex, used in dealing with them; then a collection of photographs and pictures illustrating the landscapes and the scenes from which the materials come, their native homes, and their places of manufacture. Such a collection would be a vivid and continual lesson in the synthesis of art, science, and industry. There would be, also, samples of the more perfect forms of textile work, as Italian, French, Japanese, and Oriental. There would be objects illustrating motives of design and decoration which have entered into production. Literature would contribute its part in its idealized representation of the world-industries, as the Penelope in the Odyssey—a classic in literature because the character is an adequate embodiment of a certain industrial phase of social life. So, from Homer down to the present time, there is a continuous procession of related facts which have been translated into terms of art. Music lends its share, from the Scotch song at the wheel to the spinning song of Marguerite, or of Wagner's Senta. The shop becomes a pictured museum, appealing to the eye. It would have not only materials—beautiful woods and designs—but would give a synopsis of the historical evolution of architecture in its drawings and pictures.

Thus I have attempted to indicate how the school may be connected with life so that the experience gained by the child in a familiar, commonplace way is carried over and made use of there, and what the child learns in the school is carried back and applied in everyday life, making the school an organic whole, instead of a composite of isolated parts. The isolation of studies as well as of parts of the school system disappears. Experience has its geographical aspect, its artistic and its literary, its scientific and its historical sides. All studies arise from aspects of the one earth and the one life lived upon it. We do not have a series of stratified earths, one of which is mathematical, another physical, another historical, and so on. We should not be able to live very long in any one taken by itself. We live in a world where all sides are bound together. All studies grow out of relations in the one great common world. When the child lives in varied but concrete and active relationship to this common world, his studies are naturally unified. It will no longer be a problem to correlate studies. The teacher will not have to resort to all sorts of devices to weave a little arithmetic into the history lesson, and the like. Relate the school to life, and all studies are of necessity correlated.

Moreover, if the school is related as a whole to life as a whole, its various aims and ideals—culture, discipline, information, utility-cease to be variants, for one of which we must select one study and for another another. The growth of the child in the direction of social capacity and service, his larger and more vital union with life, becomes the unifying aim; and discipline, culture, and information fall into place as phases of this growth.

I wish to add one word more about the relationship of our particular school to the University. The problem is to unify, to organize, education, to bring all its various factors together, through putting it as a whole into organic union with everyday life. That which lies back of the pedagogical school of the University is the necessity of working out something to serve as a model for such unification, extending from work beginning with the four-year-old child up through the graduate work of the University. Already we have much help from the University in scientific work planned, sometimes even in detail, by heads of the departments. The graduate student comes to us with his researches and methods, suggesting ideas and problems. The library and museum are at hand. We want to bring all things educational together; to break down the barriers that divide the education of the little child from the instruction of the maturing youth; to identify the lower and the higher education, so that it shall be demonstrated to the eye that there is no lower and higher, but simply education.

Speaking more especially with reference to the pedagogical side of the work: I suppose the oldest university chair of pedagogy in our country is about twenty years old—that of the University of Michigan, founded in the latter seventies. But there are only one or two that have tried to make a connection between theory and practice. They teach for the most part by theory, by lectures, by reference to books, rather than through the actual work of teaching itself. At Columbia, through the Teachers College, there is an extensive and close connection between the University and the training of teachers. Something has been done in one or two other places along the same line. We want an even more intimate union here, so that the University shall put all its resources at the disposition of the elementary school, contributing to the evolution of valuable subject-matter and right method, while the school in turn will be a laboratory in which the student of education sees theories and ideas demonstrated, tested, criticized, enforced, and the evolution of new truths. We want the school in its relation to the University to be a working model of a unified education.

A word as to the relation of the school to educational interests generally. I heard once that the adoption of a certain method in use in our school was objected to by a teacher on this ground: "You know that it is an experimental school. They do not work under the same conditions that we are subject to." Now, the purpose of performing an experiment is that other people need not experiment; at least need not experiment so much, may have something definite and positive to go by. An experiment demands particularly favorable conditions in order that results may be reached both freely and securely. It has to work unhampered, with all the needed resources at command. Laboratories lie back of all the great business enterprises of today, back of every great factory, every railway and steamship system. Yet the laboratory is not a business enterprise; it does not aim to secure for itself the conditions of business life, nor does the commercial undertaking repeat the laboratory. There is a difference between working out and testing a new truth, or a new method, and applying it on a wide scale, making it available for the mass of men, making it commercial. But the first thing is to discover the truth, to afford all necessary facilities, for this is the most practical thing in the world in the long run. We do not expect to have other schools literally imitate what we do. A working model is not something to be copied; it is to afford a demonstration of the feasibility of the principle, and of the methods which make it feasible. So (to come back to our own point) we want here to work out the problem of the unity, the organization of the school system in itself, and to do this by relating it so intimately to life as to demonstrate the possibility and necessity of such organization for all education.

Gramsci and Education

Stanley Aronowitz

Published under the auspices of the Italian Communist Party after the war more than a decade after Antonio Gramsci's death in 1937, the celebrated *Quaderni* (prison notebooks) has not yet been fully translated into English. But the work has had an illustrious career since some pieces of it appeared in the late 1950s. The first of the translations were made by the Italian American trade union and political activist Carl Marzani and appeared under the title *The Open Marxism of Antonio Gramsci* in the wake of the Twentieth Congress of the Soviet Communist Party, at which, it will be recalled, Nikita Khrushchev revealed some of the crimes of Stalin. The significance of the convergence of Gramsci's first publication in English with that explosive speech can be grasped only when we understand the degree to which Gramsci's thought diverged from the orthodoxy Stalin had imposed on the world communist movement. Marzani's introduction of this hitherto obscure Italian Marxist thinker to English-speaking audiences was generally regarded as a "revisionist" document by both the orthodox Leninists and Gramsci's admirers. Gramsci's works seemed to vindicate the anti-Stalinist tenor of Khrushchev's main report to the congress and also, more to the point, suggested a departure from the prevailing Marxist-Leninist orthodoxy that had reigned for forty years.

Perhaps most salient was Gramsci's reconceptualization of civil society. Recall that in *Elements of the Philosophy of Right*, Hegel had made the radical argument that, rather than constituting a sphere of free discussion among equals, in the capitalist epoch every question resolved itself to the cash nexus. Consequently, civil society, which once promised a noncommodified environment for the development of a participatory (middle-class) citizenry, was coterminous with market relations. To the extent that Marx presupposed Hegel's distinction between state and civil society, now transmogrified into the binary categories of infrastructure and superstructure, the Marxist tradition tended to ignore the significance of the public sphere, including such institutions as media, voluntary organizations, and educational institutions. In contrast, Gramsci insisted that since all capitalist societies, even the fascist dictatorships, tend to rule primarily by consent rather than by force, the key to the rule of capital was to be found in its ability to achieve ideological hegemony over "civil society" conceived as the sphere of public life that was neither, strictly speaking, of the economy nor of the state. On the contrary, it was precisely the degree to which contending classes in modern society established their ability to create a "common sense" and thus appeared independent from the coercion of economic and state relations that their rule was made possible.

Marzani's slim volume of some of Gramsci's writings made little impact in the wake of the near collapse of the American and British Communist Parties in the late 1950s. But Gramsci's concepts of revolutionary politics were in sync with many in the New Left who, a few years later, sought an alternative Marxist tradition to that of Stalinism and even Trotskyism, which they viewed as authoritarian. Despite its fragmentary character, the most widely read of Gramsci's works is the second English-language selection, published in 1971 under the title *Selections from the Prison Notebooks*. Much longer and better annotated than the Marzani version, it stood alone until recently as a definitive scholarly rendition. Edited with a long introduction and copious notes by Quintin Hoare, it managed to provide most of Gramsci's central ideas by thematically dividing and synthesizing what were otherwise pithy notes, often provocative but sometimes banal. Despite Hoare's New Left credentials, the volume appeared under the imprint of the UK and U.S. Communist Parties' publishing houses and remains to this day the central source of the "popular" reception of Gramsci's thought. A companion volume extracted the large number of entries on culture. There now exist *Further Selections*, two volumes of the earlier political writings, the prison letters, and two volumes of a projected six-volume edition of the entire *Quaderni*. But the essays that mark Gramsci's most sustained contributions to philosophy; political, social, and cultural theory; and the strategy and tactics of revolutionary struggle are contained in the *Selections*.

Despite the diverse topics that occupied Gramsci's interest during his eleven-year internment (after all, he was himself trained as a "traditional," that is, humanistic intellectual, a designation that refuses the specialization that marks contemporary thought) and the obscurity of many of his references to contemporary Italian writers, most of whom have been long forgotten, activists as much as scholars still find much to fascinate them. Indeed, despite the virtual disappearance of official communism after the collapse of the Soviet Union in 1991, the commentaries continue on almost every aspect of his writings. What can the work of a general secretary of the Italian Communist Party whose major work was done during the fascist era say to us at a time when the political problematic to which Gramsci addressed himself seems to have been surpassed—a condition that perhaps was not evident in the immediate postwar years when the *Notebooks* were published? It is not only that the Soviet Union and its minions have disappeared from the world stage or that the Communist Parties of Eastern as much as Western Europe have degenerated into pale imitations of the social democratic formations they once despised. Or that what is left of official communism—Cuba, China, Vietnam, and North Korea—are social formations that, to say the least, have proven incapable of sustaining autarchic economies even as their political systems are, to one degree or another, Stalinist throwbacks, an asymmetry that is not likely to last. Equally to the point, a strong argument can be made for the historicity of many of Gramsci's formulations, especially his distinction between the war of position and the war of maneuver, where the latter signifies the strategy and tactics of revolutionary struggle. Although socialist revolution may not have been permanently foreclosed in Western countries, the prospects for such events seem dim, at least for the coming decades. What remains are the elaborations of the war of position—the long march through institutions in civil society and in struggles for intermediate power within the capitalist state, where my term "intermediate" signifies an extension of popular power from the institutions of civil society to the state, but still a capitalist state.

There is much in Gramsci's writings to mark him as a significant scholar. Let us stipulate at the outset that just as Marx was among the greatest Hegel commentators, Gramsci must be ranked as a major writer on Machiavelli. And his *Notes on Italian History,* especially his remarks on the so-called Southern Question, are a landmark in our collective understanding of why politics, even of an international variety, must always take national and regional specificities into account. Moreover, his contributions to the development of historical materialism, configured as a critique of Nikolai Bukharin's attempt at a popular manual as well as his other comments on the significance of culture and language in the formation and reproduction of the nation-state (found chiefly in his "Problems of Marxism"), are among the most powerful statements of the nondogmatic Marxism that later transmuted into what Perry Anderson called "western" Marxism (Anderson 1976). These contributions richly deserve the scholarly attention the *Notebooks* continue to receive even after the end of official communism.

There is, of course, a lively debate on Gramsci's ideas about education. I would argue that his remarks on education and the implicit educational issues addressed in many of his writings remain among the most salient for us. In the United States, the conversation has been conducted, in the main, among educational theorists and researchers who, given that they are largely ensconced in universities and work at best within a reformist environment, tend to focus on schools. Indeed, Gramsci's views on the "common school" could easily be inserted into the contemporary curriculum debate. He insisted that the common school should privilege "formative" rather than vocational and technical education on grounds that are familiar today:

> The tendency today [in the public or common schools] is to abolish every type of schooling that is "disinterested" (not serving immediate interests) or "formative"—keeping at most only a small-scale version to serve a tiny elite of ladies and gentlemen who do not have to worry about assuring themselves of a future career. Instead there is a steady growth of specialized vocational schools, in which the pupil's destiny and future activity are determined in advance. A rational solution to the crisis ought to adopt the following lines. First, a common basic education, imparting a general, humanistic, formative culture; this would strike the right balance between development of the capacity for working manually (technically, industrially) and the development of capacities required for intellectual work. (Gramsci 1971, 27)

Gramsci's discussion is directed not only to the existing educational system but to what an educational system must provide under conditions where the key institutions of the economy and civil society are under popular control. Gramsci remarks that contemporary "deliberative bodies" distinguish their work in two "organic" spheres: The first is the essential decisions they must make; the second is the "technical-cultural" activities undertaken by "experts" that precede decision-making. His reference to "deliberative bodies" signifies what popular or workers' councils would have to consider in establishing common schools. Far from denigrating technical education, he calls for a balance so that those at the top levels of political leadership would possess familiarity with problems of production. Although the new society would inevitably require experts and he does not foresee the possibility of abolishing the capitalist division of labor anytime soon, Gramsci insists that "destiny" not be established at the outset of a child's schooling by what we would now term "tracking" and that schools play a role in enabling manual and technical workers to engage in the intellectual work required of members of deliberative bodies that direct the system. In short, his position on the common school embodies his theory of democratic politics and his social philosophy, in which popular participation as well as representatives constitute the twin elements of any future democracy. His educational ideas are directed at improving schools not so much for the sake of reform as for the sake of making possible a new kind of social rule in every institution of the state and civil society.

Gramsci devotes considerable attention to education, among other institutions, because even in the wake of fascism, schools are primary sites for achieving mass consent for social rule. The great Gramscian Louis Althusser argues that among the state's *ideological* apparatuses, as opposed to the *repressive* apparatuses (law, courts, police, army, prisons), educational institutions are the most important. The school is the state institution par excellence that prepares children and youth for their appropriate economic and political niches within the prevailing order (Althusser 1971). It acts as a sorting machine, forming and reproducing the classes of society according to what Pierre Bourdieu terms "degrees of attainment of cultural capital." It transmits the dominant culture and habits of mind and, perhaps most important of all, inculcates in a large portion of the population the knowledges and values that are deemed appropriate for citizenship in a given social formation. But technical and manual workers are formed not only by specialized curricula (Bourdieu and Passeron 1977). A plethora of commentators, notably Paul Willis, have added that school "failure" is a crucial marker of working-class formation at the level of everyday life (Willis 1981). Manual or low-level service workers are formed by their refusal (coded as failure) of the standard curriculum that constitutes the basis for the accumulation of cultural capital.

Gramsci-inspired writers on schools in advanced capitalism have, with some notable exceptions, taken education to mean schooling. Although many writers have engaged in a sharp critique of the role and function of schooling in terms of what Henry Giroux and I have called "reproductive" theory, there is considerable reluctance to reveal the inner tensions of schools, that is, the degree to which movements within schools have attempted to offer both resistance and alternatives to the dominant program of technicization and the systematic devaluation of formative education (Aronowitz and Giroux 1985). Indeed, there is considerable evidence that many contemporary Gramscians recoil, on populist or libertarian grounds, at Gramsci's call for a curriculum that brings forward some of the features of the "old school of grammatical study of Latin and Greek together with the study of their respective literatures and political histories" (37). Gramsci extols the old school, admittedly reserved for a tiny elite, as a guide for a new common educational program:

> Individual facts were not learnt for immediate practical or professional end. The end seemed disinterested, because the real interest was the interior development of personality, the formation of character by means of the absorption and assimilation of the whole cultural past of modern European civilization. Pupils did not learn Latin and Greek in order to speak them, to become waiters, interpreters or commercial letter-writers. They learnt in order to know at first hand the civilization of Greece and of Rome, a civilization that was a necessary precondition of our modern civilization; in other words, they learnt them in order to be themselves and know themselves consciously. (37)

Gramsci defends the old common school for its ability to impart habits of "diligence, precision, poise (even physical poise), ability to concentrate on specific subjects, which cannot be acquired without the mechanical repetition of disciplined and methodical acts. If one wants to produce great scholars, one still has to start at this point and apply pressure throughout the educational system in order to succeed in creating those thousands or hundreds or even dozens of scholars of the highest quality which are necessary to every civilization" (37).

Clearly, if the criteria of contemporary relevance, of practical scientific and technical knowledge, and of specialization guide the educational system, these scholars are not likely to be produced, and the consequences for civilization would be deleterious. To form scholars, he argues, one must master more than one language and civilization in order to engage in the "analysis of distincts" (38), Croce's emendation of the dialectic to signify difference without contradiction. The student becomes an intellectual—no less than a scholar—by "plunging" into knowledge and life, by being subjected to the discipline of learning.

The old school was intended for the education of the ruling class. Its restriction to the upper reaches of society was intended not only to train succeeding generations of elites but to subject the subalterns to technical and vocational niches, a "destiny" that deprives them of the means by which any democracy may emerge. For Gramsci, democracy "by definition" means that the distinction between the ruler and ruled narrows, that "citizenship" beyond consent is broadened to mean active participation, is widely instituted. Yet, apart from providing in his prescription for school reform a common curriculum of early, disinterested education, he hesitates to draw the logical conclusion of his own analysis: the mass intellectual education of the subalterns. Or, in another locution of his terminology, the transformation of the masses from "spontaneous philosophers" to philosophically as well as technically educated social actors.

Gramsci despairs of translating old elite schooling to a mass education system, chiefly because workers and peasants lack the time and the cultural preconditions for study. Until the establishment of a new social order, his recommended strategy is to put education in the service of the formation of an intellectual "elite," where the concept of elite is transformed from its class-specific location in the traditional rulers to social groups in whose interest the formation of a new, egalitarian social order may come into being—the historical bloc of discontented social groups led by the working class. But short of an extensive program of formative schooling conducted by the revolutionary party itself, a task that may be necessary under conditions of the surrender of the public schools to occupational priorities, the struggle for reform of the common school curriculum in the direction of formative education is a necessary precondition for producing this elite.

Gramsci's concept of education is, however, only secondarily directed to schooling. The key is the formation of an "intellectual moral bloc" capable of contesting the prevailing common sense and providing in its stead, more or less systematically, a "scientific" understanding of the social world and of politics that can be widely disseminated in the institutions and other social spaces of civil society. Here the concept "science" signifies not the common usage of industrial societies, in which the object of knowledge is nature or a naturalized social world and the methods of knowing are experimental and mathematical, which strictly excludes intuition and speculation. Gramsci invokes a more traditional idea of science—the preindustrial, according to which science signifies only the effort to achieve systematic knowledge in which philosophy as much as the traditional natural and social sciences is a legitimate mode of knowledge acquisition.

Under the gaze of the censors, the term Gramsci employed to designate social science was "the philosophy of praxis." For nearly all commentators, it stood in for Marxism, and indeed, his texts provide some confirmation of this view. But there is a sense in which the philosophy of praxis may be understood as the unity of theory and practice. Unlike Leninist orthodoxy, in which theory is conceived as being in "the service" of practice, its "handmaid" or "guide," Gramsci understands the unity of the concepts as two sides of the same totality, and there is no structure of dominance. For, as his essays "The Study of Philosophy" and the compendium of comments from the *Notebooks* grouped under the title "Problems of Marxism" make clear, Gramsci's historical materialism and philosophy are directed principally and highly polemically against "mechanical materialism"—the dominant ideology of the Third, Stalinist International—especially ideas of historical inevitability with which Bukharin had, no doubt under pressure from Stalin, identified himself, as did many in the leadership of the Italian Communist Party. The philosophy of praxis is the core paradigm, if you will, from which the intellectual moral bloc needs to be formed to assist the masses to overcome the simple reductionism of bourgeois or Catholic common sense, both of which are content to leave them at a "low level" of understanding. The point of the bloc is "to make politically possible the progress of the mass and not only small intellectual groups":

> The active man-in-the-mass has a practical activity, but has no clear theoretical consciousness of his practical activity, which nonetheless involves understanding the world in so far as it transforms it. His theoretical consciousness can indeed be historically in opposition to his activity. One might almost say that he has two theoretical consciousnesses (or one contradictory consciousness): one which is implicit in his activity and which in reality unites him with his fellow workers in the practical transformation of the real world; and one, superficially implicit or verbal, which he has inherited from the past and uncritically absorbed. It holds together a specific social group, it influences moral conduct and the direction of will ... but often powerfully enough to produce a situation in which the contradictory state of consciousness does not permit of any action, any decision or any choice, and produces a condition of moral and political passivity. Critical understanding of self takes place therefore through struggle of political "hegemonies" and of opposing directions, first in the ethical field and a higher level of one's own conception of reality. Consciousness of being part of a particular hegemonic force (that is to say political consciousness) in the first stage toward a further progressive self-consciousness in which theory and practice will finally be one. (333)

It is evident that the crucial educational issue is how to address the political hegemonies, how to bring the practical and theoretical consciousness of the most "advanced" political actors together. In short, beyond the "masses," how to overcome the power of common sense among those who are charged with political leadership within the great social movements. For Gramsci, the intellectuals are to be conceived not as the technicians of power but as its sinews. No class in modern society, he argues, can organize itself for power—for the war of maneuver, that is, the revolutionary activity—without the participation of intellectuals whose ultimate task is to embody the unity of theory and organization. It is they who contest in the institutions of civil society and the trade unions as well as the universities.

Which brings us to the central question of how to achieve scientific understanding in ever wider groups of the underlying population. In "The Modern Prince," Gramsci offers a particularly clear formulation of the task. He speaks of the need for "intellectual and moral reform" and suggests that the key is the development of a "national popular collective" that replaces the "divinity and the categorical imperative" by linking moral with economic reform. This at the cultural level.

But perhaps Gramsci's major innovation was to have recalled Machiavelli's insistence on the science of politics as an autonomous discourse and the idea that politics is the main science. Thus the struggle for a new scientific understanding as a new common sense always entails taking the point of view of "the man of action" rather than that of the scholar or, in current fashion, the nomadic intellectual.

References

Althusser, Louis. 1971. "Ideology and Ideological Apparatuses." In *Lenin and Philosophy*. New York: Monthly Review Press.

Anderson, Perry. 1976. *Considerations on Western Marxism*. London: New Left Books.

Aronowitz, Stanley, and Henry Giroux. 1985. *Education Under Siege*. South Hadley, MA: Bergin and Garvey.

Bourdieu, Pierre, and Jean-Claude Passeron. 1977. *Reproduction in Education, Culture and Society*. London: Sage Publications.

Gramsci, Antonio. 1971. *Selections from the Prison Notebooks*, ed. and trans. with an introduction by Quintin Hoare. New York: International Publishers.

Willis, Paul. 1981. *Learning to Labor: How Working Class Kids Get Working Class Jobs*. New York: Columbia University Press.

UNIT 5. ECOLOGICAL LITERACY

Over the past 40 years, scholars in the Social Foundations field have increasingly turned their attention to environmental matters. These scholars recognize that the needs in the field have radically shifted along with the needs of the planet to warrant the study of ecological literacy. Ecological literacy has been added to the traditional study of philosophy, sociology, educational policy, and comparative education within the canon of Social Foundations of Education. "To a large extent, social foundation scholars interested in eco-justice pedagogy are consistent with their overall commitment to developing critiques of dominant ideological beliefs and to promoting socially responsive educational reforms" (Tozer et al., 2011, p. 289).

Many professors of Social Foundations interested in educational reform have creatively implemented environmental justice issues into the readings, activities, and discussions in their classrooms. This shift in pedagogical focus is justified owing to the growing recognition of our planet's ecological deterioration. David Orr (2004) captures this decline in great detail:

> If today is a typical day on planet earth, we will lose 116 square miles of rain forest, or about an acre a second. We will lose another 72 miles to encroaching deserts, the results of human mismanagement and overpopulation. We will lose 40 to 250 species and no one know whether that number is 40 or 250. Today the human population will increase by 250,000. And today we will add 2,700 tons of chlorofluoro-carbons and 15 million tons of carbon dioxide to the atmosphere. Tonight, the earth will be a little hotter, its waters more acidic, and the fabric of life a little more threadbare. (p. 7)

Thus, the study of ecological literacy or environmental matters within the Social Foundations curriculum is recommended for all students in order to broaden their knowledge base and enhance their eco-consciousness. The question remains: What does it mean to be ecologically literate? Pilgrim, Smith, and Pretty (2007) define persons as ecoliterate if "they are able to identify local plants and animals, name their uses and tell stories about them" (p. 1742). In this way students who spend time outdoors are more likely to develop an ecological literacy.

Pilgrim, Smith, and Pretty (2007) "define ecoliteracy as a cumulative knowledge base that describes local ecosystem components and their interactions most commonly derived from a pool of accumulated observations" (p. 1742). There are four levels of ecological knowledge:

> (1) the names of living (e.g., plants, animals) and physical (e.g., soils, water, weather) components of ecosystems; (2) the functions and uses of each component; (3) the land and resource management systems and the social institutions that govern them; and (4) the worldviews and cosmologies that guide the ethics of the people in the system. (Pilgrim et al., 2007, pp. 1743–1744)

Professors who teach ecological knowledge in their classrooms contribute to increasing their student's eco-consciousness. Martusewicz and Edmundson (2005) describe a cultural-ecological approach to teacher education and outline an ecojustice framework to help guide educators. They reframe what scholars may define as an eco-consciousness as an eco-ethical consciousness. "We define eco-ethical consciousness as the awareness of and ability to respond carefully to the fundamentally independence among all forms of life on the planet" (Martusewicz & Edmundson, 2005, p. 73). Eco-ethical consciousness involves responsibility and intelligence, along with an ability to take action as a consequence of one's new ecological awareness.

Conclusion

The addition of ecological literacy as an emergent area of study has increased the relevance of the Social Foundations because it addresses the development of new human needs. As Pilgrim, Smith, and Pretty (2007) have stated, "ecoliteracy as a knowledge base offers some solutions to local, national, and global environmental challenges by providing information on the use of locally available resources" (p. 1742). Offering solutions to global environmental crises in the classroom will foster the eco-ethical consciousness of students, and thus will also foster their citizenship. This recent trend can only increase students' awareness of the grave threats posed to the planet by global climate change.

References

Martusewicz, R., & Edmundson, J. (2005). Social foundations as pedagogies of responsibility and eco-ethical commitment. In D. Butin (Ed.), *Teaching social foundations of education: Contexts, theories, and issues.* Routledge.

Orr, D. W. (2004). *Earth in mind: On education, environment, and the human prospect.* Island Press.

Pilgrim, S., Smith, D., & Pretty, J. (2007). A cross-regional assessment of the factors affecting ecoliteracy: Implications for policy and practice. *Ecological Applications, 17*(6), 1742–1751. Retrieved July 7, 2020, from https://www.jstor.org/stable/40062071

Tozer, S., Gallegos, B., Henry, A., Greiner, M., & Price, P. (Eds.). (2011). *Handbook of research in social foundations of education.* Routledge.

Towards an Animal Standpoint

Vegan Education and the Epistemology of Ignorance

Richard Kahn

Towards an Animal Standpoint: Vegan Education and the Epistemology of Ignorance

> historia ... II. an account of one's inquiries, a narrative, history....
> —Liddell and Scott. *An Intermediate Greek-English Lexicon* (1889)

> A Klee painting named "Angelus Novus" shows an angel looking as though he is about to move away from something he is fixedly contemplating. His eyes are staring, his mouth is open, his wings are spread. This is how one pictures the angel of history. His face is turned toward the past. Where we perceive a chain of events, he sees one single catastrophe which keeps piling wreckage and hurls it in front of his feet. The angel would like to stay, awaken the dead, and make whole what has been smashed. But a storm is blowing in from Paradise; it has got caught in his wings with such a violence that the angel can no longer close them. The storm irresistibly propels him into the future to which his back is turned, while the pile of debris before him grows skyward. This storm is what we call progress.
> —Walter Benjamin (1970, pp. 259–260)

> Looking at the immediacies of the colonial context, it is clear that what divides this world is first and foremost what species, what race one belongs to.
>
> —Frantz Fanon (2004, p. 5)

I became a member of the vegan movement[1] in 1998, after quitting my job in New York and having adventurously moved cross-country to Los Angeles, the City of Angels, in the search for love and some newfound direction. Up to that point, my whole life had been a sort of haphazard series of fragments in which my ethical commitment to nonhuman animals repeatedly attempted to articulate and realize itself in a manner akin to the way one tunes in a radio or satellite feed of relatively poor signal strength, there were pieces of a message I kept receiving, but always through a veil of immense feedback that muddied my comprehension and ultimately made me change the channel. In the years prior, I had committed to vegetarianism and even served as an unwitting diplomat of sorts for the philosophy, having introduced it to the small rural town of Szabadszállás, Hungary, when I lived there for a year in the mid-90s ("Ah, vegetáriánus," people would say to me dolefully and half-perplexed when I tried to politely refuse the honor, as a visiting American, to strike the first blow in a ritual pig slaughter or to eat the sheep intestines stew that had been painstakingly crafted for me as a sometimes dinner guest). I also became more political about my lifestyle as I grew steadily more responsive to the fact that my deployment of vegetarianism as a personal dietary choice, one often locked in the private confines of my lonely kitchen or occasional restaurant outings, was at best a meager remedy to a social and ethical atrocity of such huge proportions that I feared to seriously contemplate it in any sort of systematic fashion.[2] In part, my increased sensitivity toward the need for a more radical form of vegetarianism was undoubtedly catalyzed by those friends and acquaintances in my everyday life who were invariably curious as to how I had arrived at the decision to stop eating meat and therefore commonly put questions to me such as "Is this for health reasons or your love of animals?" Now I

1. The vegan movement began in 1944 when Donald Watson and Elsie Shrigley founded the U.K. Vegan Society in response to frustrations that vegetarians were increasingly normalizing the practice of consuming dairy products linked to highly exploitative and oppressive animal husbandry practices (Rodger, 2004). The society defines veganism as "a philosophy and way of living which seeks to exclude, as far as is possible and practical, all forms of exploitation of, and cruelty to, animals for food, clothing or any other purpose; and by extension, promotes the development and use of animal-free alternatives for the benefit of humans, animals and the environment. In dietary terms it denotes the practice of dispensing with all products derived wholly or partly from animals" (Vegan Society, 1979). News media tend to characterize vegans as "avoiding" animal products of any kind, but do not emphasize that they do this as a form of political boycott.

2. A summary of the many aspects and broad extent of the evolving catastrophe for animal-kind, both human and nonhuman, can be found in Kahn (2008, 2010a). For a powerful filmic treatment of this horror, see the movie *Earthlings* (2003). Like most people I only became gradually familiar with the realities behind the conditions in industrial factory farms, slaughterhouses, and other institutional practices responsible for the standard American diet such as the overfishing of the oceans and the destruction of the Amazonian rain forests in order to grow endless acres of monocropped soybeans for cheap beef production. Interestingly, people's first response to consciousness of these problems is often to respond by saying something like, "If I had to know where my food came from, I don't think I could eat it." This is a profound articulation of the need for vegan education and the epistemological role that ignorance plays in allowing for grossly unsustainable cultural practices to continue without challenge.

can only chuckle at the supposed dichotomy of the query, but at the time these inquiries into my beliefs seriously troubled me as I lacked a convincingly coherent answer for them. I remained lodged, at least partially, within an epistemology of ignorance (Tuana, 2004; McHugh, 2004; Mills, 2007) that served to occlude the full extent of my membership within a speciesist society and so I was without the critical literacy necessary to voice my dawning conscientization into the need for animal liberation as part of my own emancipatory journey. Yet, my initial succession from the hegemony of the standard American diet had granted me certain epistemological privileges as well such that I began to read my interrogators on another level. Hence, I learned to interpret their questions about my vegetarian lifestyle as implicit attempts to elicit my re-enculturation into mainstream values and the dominant culture. But, even more importantly, I also perceived others' suspicion of my motives as a continual opportunity to better grasp exactly why and how I came to stand in the particular social, cultural and historical position I in fact occupied.

In this way, I was led to follow an educational path that I remain upon today, the development of an "animal standpoint" (Donovan, 2006), a mode of "oppositional consciousness" (Collins, 1989) that I define variously as: (1) the "cognitive praxis" (Eyerman & Jamison, 1991) of the animal and earth liberation movements, which works to rupture and transform academic discourse in order to establish relevant knowledge interests that are held by movement members (Kahn, 2006); (2) the recognition of the sociopolitical and cultural agency of nonhuman animals that coconstructs our shared reality (Haraway, 2003; Latour, 2004); and (3) the attempt to radically shift our gestalt away from a Western cosmological legacy informed by the history of speciesist relations that has functioned ideologically to inscribe reified notions of "humanity" and "animality" throughout society (Kahn, 2007, 2010a; Lewis & Kahn, 2009). The critical theorist Steven Best (2009) writes:

> Whereas nearly all histories, even so-called "radical" narratives, have been written from the human standpoint, a growing number of theorists have broken free of the speciesist straightjacket to examine history and society from the standpoint of animals. This approach ... considers the interaction between human and nonhuman animals—past, present, and future—and the need for profound changes in the way human beings define themselves and relate to other sentient species and to the natural world as a whole. (para. 14)

Accordingly, a primary concern of the animal standpoint is to provide counterhistories to what Ivan Illich called "modern certainties," or the "epoch-specific apriorisms which generate not only our mental conceptions but also our sensual perceptions and feelings in our hearts about what constitutes social reality" (Cayley, 1992, pp. 172–173). These counter-histories can help to illuminate profound silences on the animal standpoint in the sociohistorical record as being often nonaccidental, and institutionally perpetrated and organized, in order to legitimate hegemonic regimes of truth and ways of knowing that are foundational to our present moment's "dialectic of enlightenment" (Horkheimer & Adorno, 2002).

Of course, as we continue to live under the hegemony of speciesism in which animal liberation is not the norm, and in fact is considered an act of "ecoterrorism" (Federal Bureau of Investigation, 2008), it is impossible to produce a definitive and unified chronicle of the animal standpoint at this time. Instead, the animal standpoint is very much anticipatory of a future possibility that is only realizable now to a certain extent. As the epigram by Benjamin alludes, those who would speak from the animal standpoint occupy something of a morally eschatological space in which they are left to piece together clues out of the catastrophic rubble of the past in order to map the prospects of hope. In this way, the animal standpoint actually seeks to understand the world from multiple evolving locations, and so there are at present a multitude of heterogeneous and contradictory animal standpoint situations, not a singular universal standpoint that can be utilized like a cryptographic key for a theory of everything. But as Sandra Harding (2004, pp. 127–138) has argued, while this form of subjugated knowledge may be unable to escape being pluralist and partial in nature, it can thereby serve positively as a powerful resource to increase our objective understanding of society and provide for a more robustly democratic public sphere beyond majoritarian accounts.

Lately, I have become interested in the ways in which the act of counterstorytelling as a methodological element of critical race theory can provide a compelling model for historical research from the animal standpoint. As Tara Yosso (2006) writes, by interpretatively blending social science data and critical theory with personal reflections, autobiography, and the experiences of colleagues and other acquaintances, counterstory telling strengthens marginalized traditions of resistance, draws attention to the victims of systemic oppression, and documents the workings of this oppression from the epistemological standpoint of the victimized (pp. 10–11). This essay therefore attempts to employ a form of counterstorytelling to provide some summative exploration of my formal and nonformal educational experiences as a vegan academic working on animal standpoint theory.

On Becoming a Vegan

I remember the day I told my father I had made the decision to become a vegan. "Congratulations, Rich," he said dryly over the phone, "you've officially found a way to get even weirder. Why do you have to be such a pain the ass?" His reaction continued: "A vay-gun, huh?" he muttered, sarcastically emphasizing his mispronunciation of the term (which is pronounced "vee-gun"). "Well, give my regards to planet Vega." Over the years, my father's stance has softened somewhat and, upon recent visits to him, he has shown real concern about how to provide proper hospitality and has even gone out of his way to cook special vegan desserts for the occasions. Further, to a small degree, he allows some discussion about social matters from a vegan perspective such as my own.

On the other hand, he is also clear about drawing a firm line in the sand where he will not cross over into discussions that require self-critique or transformation around his own viewpoints on nonhuman animals or their status in society. For instance, I can eat a vegan meal in relative peace next to him, he seems to have decided, but in order to do so I must silently tolerate his meat and dairy-based food choices and listen obediently to his stories about how he relates to nonhuman animals and the natural world, regardless of how far they might transgress my own ethical commitments. An analogy for this might be that an abolitionist could be considered welcome at a slave auction as long as she did not openly question the reason for being there in the first place.

When in my father's company I am also consistently needled by his "jokes" that I send my vegan children to spend time under his care so that he can "teach them how to eat hamburgers, hotdogs, and all other sorts of yucky stuff." Invariably, this line of half-comedy ends with his dramatic guffaws and an attempt to form the hand salute used by the *Star Trek* character, Mr. Spock the Vulcan. Only a few times has my father actually done the gesture correctly, spreading his fingers apart into a "V" at the middle and ring finger, while intoning, "live long and prosper." In any event, his point is clearly not to offer salutary blessings, but rather to remind me of my alien and outsider status as an invader of his normal cultural routine. I relate this story not because I intend to paint my father as a uniquely unfeeling ogre who is deserving of public scrutiny, but rather because I have found that my relations with him on this matter are broadly representative of how vegans (who comprise approximately 1.4% of the general population[3]) are generally treated in their day-to-day lives by the great mass of other people. In fact, I think dealings with him are somewhat better even.

Microaggressions

The vegan in a speciesist society is ubiquitously on the receiving end of an unending volley of "microaggressions," the "subtle insults (verbal, nonverbal, and/or visual) directed toward people … often automatically or unconsciously" (Solórzano, Ceja, & Yosso, 2000) in situations when those who are the microaggressions' target are members of a marginalized class. Part of what makes pedagogy against microaggressions so difficult is that these acts are often perpetrated by people who are unaware of the repressive nature of their behavior and who may not even consciously intend to communicate hostile messages through their actions. In other words, such microaggressions are part of the transactional fabric of the conflictual encounter between standpoint epistemologies and the larger epistemology of ignorance that is manufactured to support the conservation of the social status quo.

Many times these microaggressions arise indirectly against vegans through people's everyday use of speciesist language (Dunayer, 2001), in which nonhuman animals are spoken of as unthinking, unfeeling, and lesser objects instead of rational, sentient, and equal beings. As part of common parlance, which socially reproduces desensitization, vegans are required literally to stop conversation and challenge these assumptions if communication is to take place in good faith. However, to do so is often highly impractical as communication does not take place in a political vacuum and so vegans can easily be outnumbered or outranked by their interlocutors. Moreover, if they do in fact raise questions about the assumptions buried in people's language, they run the risk of being tagged as strident, irrational, or otherwise extreme.

In other instances, vegans can be more directly singled out for microaggressions against them. A case in point took place in 2002, in a truck stop outside of San Bernardino, CA, when my wife (then an ovo-lacto vegetarian) and I stopped to investigate whether the Burger King located there was offering the new "BK Veggie" sandwich. The context for our decision was a raucous debate that was taking place within the animal advocacy community at the time about the food item. Liberal vegan ideologues like Erik Marcus and major animal rights groups like PETA openly celebrated its arrival and encouraged everyone to buy as many as possible, believing it to be a strategic opportunity to get vegetarianism solidly established within popular culture. On the other hand, a significant number of vegans (including myself) were highly skeptical that fast-food corporations like Burger King held liberatory potentials for anything beyond perhaps a highly contradictory and strategically useless form of vegetarianism as personal lifestyle addendum. Indeed, as with

---

3. This number is according to a 2006 poll conducted by Harris Interactive for the Vegetarian Resource Group, see:
   http://www.vrg.org/journal/vj2006issue4/vj2006issue4poll.htm

McDonald's fries that were revealed to be quietly slathered in meat juices, so too it was eventually found that Burger King's veggie burger was not even vegetarian unless one asked to have its standard mayonnaise and bun removed, for these contained polysorbate-60, a fatty-acid emulsifier, derived from animals. Further, some vegans pointed out that, unless Burger King also microwaved the patty on a separate plate instead of flame-broiling it, the veggie burger would share grill fats and residue from the other meat products that are cooked there. With these points being actively discussed between us as we drove down the I-10, upon seeing the Burger King sign listed for an upcoming truck stop, my wife and I decided to stop in and see for ourselves whether or not to believe all the hype.

A sprawling and somewhat unsanitary place for drivers to fill up on a wide-range of commodities in a hurry, it was at first difficult to even locate the Burger King within the travel center. Having eventually found it tucked in the back of the building, near the bathrooms and a small array of video game consoles, we stepped up cautiously toward the lone order-taker as we scanned the menu to see if the BK Veggie was an available item there. I had bet it would not be. The place was deafeningly quiet and seemed almost to be staged for our experiment. "Can I help you?" the young woman behind the cash register asked. We did not see the item on the menu. "Do you have the BK Veggie?" we inquired. "Uhm … the what?" she replied. Our order-taker was baffled and so we quickly provided a run-down as to the national announcement of the new sandwich. "I'm not sure if we have that or not," she muttered confusedly, "I'd better check with the manager." With that she was off and disappeared into a back area behind the equipment. A minute later she returned with a smile, "Yes, we do have it!" Since it was available, my wife was determined to taste one and placed an order, careful to spell out that it should not have either the bun or mayonnaise and that it should be microwaved, as she was a vegetarian. "I don't think we can do that" the cashier wondered out loud. In a friendly but direct manner, my wife insisted, "I thought the motto of this company is "Have it your way" The young woman behind the counter disappeared again, this time to return with the manager himself.

"What seems to be the trouble here?" he drawled, "So you want one of those BK Veggies, but how do you want it?" I noticed that he had raised one of his eyebrows, as if doubtfully examining the strange customers before him, wondering if we were troublemakers with our out of the ordinary request. My wife reiterated her desire, calmly providing the philosophical explanation for it along the way. "Oh. Hmmm. So you want just a microwaved veggie patty nothing on it? Alright we can do that," the manager concluded, as he directed to the order-taker that he would take care of it and then headed off to find the frozen patty for microwaving. Two minutes later he returned with a grayish, wet-looking specimen on a small paper plate and handed it to my wife, "One BK Veggie for you." Thinking it looked pretty unappetizing we took it and were about to head back to the car to explore it further when the manager suddenly exclaimed excitedly, "Call me T-Rex!" "What?" we thought, and looked up to see him thumping his chest fiercely with one fist. "Call me T-Rex!" he said again, very pleased with himself and then began to stomp back and forth across the cashier aisle floor like the carnivorous dinosaur. Finally, returning from the Cretaceous period, he turned back toward us, pointed to our order and began to shake his head from side to side. "I don't eat anything unless it's bled. I'd never eat one of those things," the manager resolved.

It was a fascinating reaction on the man's part, one that we had in no obvious way enlisted. Apparently, even the single order of a quasi-vegetarian item that was his to offer for profit had struck at his identity as a happy member of a speciesist society in such a profound manner that he felt compelled to provide a performative rejection of what he took to be our critical countercultural position. Quite literally, through a microaggressive burst, the Burger King manager had to underline for us all that what he knew to be true prior to his customers' order of the veggie burger (with all of its possible background context) had not been put in jeopardy by the encounter. In this way, he sealed any fissures that may have erupted in his epistemology of ignorance and eradicated any possible contextual messaging that might eventually lead him to overturn his cosmological certainties about the order of the universe or his own place in it.

Microinequities

Vegans not only encounter microaggressions across society, but also "microinequities," which Sue et al. (2004, p. 273) define as "the pattern of being overlooked, underrespected, and devalued." Whether it is at the supermarket or the average eatery, shoe store, clothier, or anywhere else that the living animal body is brutally reduced to an unliving article for trade, there is a widespread structural ignorance to vegan issues in most communities in the United States. While tiring and thankless work, an interesting form of vegan education can be to visit these establishments and to inquire of them what they have that is vegan, thereby making shopping a form of "public pedagogy" (Giroux, 2004). As in the Burger King example, this often sends frontline help scrambling for supervisors in a desperate attempt to figure out what a "vegan" is and whether or not one can then be serviced there (the answer typically being, "no"). While the tactic is unlikely to foment thoroughgoing social change from the animal standpoint, it can at least serve to generate critical dialogue with people and possibly raise some metacognitive reflection about multiculturalism, as well as put veganism on their cultural radar thereby.

Businesses are hardly the only purveyor of microinequities, though. Even friends and acquaintances routinely overlook the need to find some way to demonstrate the thought of inclusion to vegan guests at parties or other gatherings. This is frequently revealed when a vegan is offered and rejects the barbeque, cake, or any list of items that is then rapidly produced thereafter, as it becomes more and more apparent to host and guest alike that the vegan attendee had not been considered during the event's preparation. At other times, friends will thoughtlessly engage in talk about the delightful qualities of the nonvegan meal they may recently have had or will display nonvegan merchandise to vegans in the search for their cordial approval, something that of course cannot come without involving the vegan in a fundamental self-contradiction.

Activists for other radical and progressive causes are themselves not above overlooking and devaluing advocates for the animal standpoint. For instance, I have been a part of many meetings where strong critiques of classism, racism, sexism, or other forms of structural oppression are delivered by people who then go on to consume commercial varieties of factory-farmed meat and dairy, entirely blind to the problematical aspects of doing so.[4] Moreover, vegans have had a hard time being heard in some activist communities, as

4. One could easily (and ultimately should) advance critiques of members of the vegan community in this same way. For example, an entire line of vegan-friendly "green" consumer products, including gourmet ice creams, cookies, pizzas, "chicken" nuggets, and the like, have sprung up in the last decade as both vegan manufacturers and other companies have raced to fill the needs of what is demographically considered a niche market with significant buying power. However, exchanging relatively low consumer cost meat for high-priced vegan frozen and boxed food simply assists the capitalist system to effect transformation through a period of potential crisis. It is no surprise, then, that companies selling vegan wares such as Whole Foods, Inc. have been repeatedly tabbed as grossly exploitative of labor. In this

they can be stereotypically characterized therein as White liberals who have adopted a political cause that works to divert them from the need to examine the other forms of prejudice suspected to be rooted within their lives. I myself have been the target of such criticism, and while I would be the first to admit both my own imperfections and that there are some vegans for whom this charge is undeniably apt, it is also overly broad and misleading. Thus, allies in other struggles are sometimes surprised to learn that important vegan figures in the fight for social justice include people like César Chávez, Coretta Scott King, Alice Walker, and Michael Franti. While not a reason to adopt vegan politics in itself, opening dialogue about why vocal leaders like these became vegan or why other activists assumed they were not can serve to sow the seeds for the kind of collective intersectional analyses that are ultimately necessary to understand the "matrix of domination" (Collins, 2000) that is used to divide and conquer counterhegemonic groups by those who would legislate our everyday lives.

Vegan Education in the Public Schools

Vegans can just as easily encounter microaggressions and microinequities in the school as they can in the larger society.[5] While some schools have moved to try to incorporate a consistent vegetarian (and sometimes vegan) offering on the menu, the overall reality is that vegans are still treated like second-class citizens in most school cafeterias. Even when there is food provided for them to eat, the school experience is structured so as to reduce veganism to a personal "special dietary requirement" and not a collective political standpoint from which to mount a transformative critique of society. When exhaustive ingredient lists are not made openly available, or there is not clear transparency as to the manner in which the available food has been cooked, and staff are not properly educated so as to be able to easily answer questions about the food or its preparation, this constitutes a form of microaggression by school administrations against vegans (and by extension, all who eat at the school). It is crucial to remember, however, that behind these dietary microaggressions are macroaggressive institutional logics, not just the careless or uninformed aptitudes of individual administrators.

Consider the recent story of Dave Warwak, a fifth through eighth grade tenured art teacher in the Chicago-area Fox River Grove Middle School, who had previously exhibited at Northern Illinois University but who was suspended and then fired by his public school for teaching art from the animal standpoint.[6] In 2006,

way, veganism that is not also anti-capitalist fails to strike at the larger structural problem and so can itself be a source of continued epistemological ignorance. On Whole Foods, see for example, http://www.wholeworkersunite.org and http://www.ufcw.org/press_room/index.cfm?pressReleaseID=3, as well as http://www.coopamerica.org/programs/responsibleshopper/company.cfm?id=309

5. Due to issues of space, I will not cover the range of issues that might be covered under this idea, which besides issues of school food include in-class dissection, the use of pesticides and rodenticides by schools, in-class pets, as well as the manner in which the history of nonhuman animals (as with women, people of color, the disabled, etc.) has effectively been written out of the majority of the school curriculum.

6. The details of this story are formed out of personal correspondence I had with Warwak in September and October, 2007, as well as the composite evidence and article links archived on Dave Warwak's websites: http://www.inslide.com and http://peepshowforchildrenonly.com. The latter is dedicated to a self-published manuscript in which Warwak chronicles, his pedagogical saga and archives transcripts from resultant legal proceedings that took place when Warwak

Warwak became a vegan and decided to respond to evidence of animal cruelty by students at the school by developing (and gaining approval for) a collective art lesson in which a number of students and teachers created and cared for their own companion animal made out of commercially-available marshmallow "Peeps" chick-shaped candy. As with school exercises in which students care for "baby" eggs, people at the school personalized their Peeps, spoke to them, and treated them as if they were subjects of a life that were deserving of protection. At the end of the lesson, however, Warwak surprised everyone by collecting the marshmallow chicks for a diorama school art exhibit he then created in which the Peeps candies were represented as locked behind zoo cages, hung on the wall as trophy game heads, squashed as road kill, boiled and fried in pots and pans, and enclosed between slices of bread as sandwiches. According to a September 12, 2007 *Chicago Tribune* editorial, this resulted in a rebuke from the school's principal that Warwak was trying to "influence students against the school lunch program" and he was warned to stick to the curriculum. In response, Warwak replied that part of teaching art to students is to get them to think about life and to have them connect their creativity to the social issues that they care very deeply about. He then turned his sights on asking for the removal of the National Dairy Council's "Got Milk?" and other promotional posters which adorned the lunch room walls. When the school's cafeteria manager refused to take them down, Warwak and his students posted their own vegan posters satirizing the issue. He also began a more public campaign to raise consciousness about the quality of school lunches being offered at the school, which resulted in his dismissal.

While one might question Warwak's collegiality, it also seems clear upon studying his case that his firing was not due to his pedagogical style, but rather his unwillingness to relent from using the art curriculum to explore his own school as a location in which to house the animal standpoint. By doing so, he quickly found himself immersed in a hot bed of political issues related to the existence of what could be termed the "school cafeteria-industrial complex" that lay just below the epistemological surface of the school's day-to-day code of normalcy. For instance, we might ask (as he did): Why were the Dairy Council posters in the school? What was the school's food quality? What's wrong with influencing students against the school lunch program if there is a sound educational point to be made in doing so?

Not only at Fox River Grove Middle School but also in thousands of schools across the country, corporate agribusiness has run amok in the attempt to utilize public education as a place to establish the naturalization of commercial meat and dairy as lifelong eating habits, to generate increased sales, to subsidize the food industry against decreased producer prices, as well as to funnel below-health standards food not fit for public sale. Warwak was correct to demand the removal of the Dairy Council's posters as the Federal Trade Commission had in fact already targeted them for removal from approximately 105,000 public schools. In May 2007, the Commission ruled that the advertisements' message on behalf of the dairy industry's "Milk Your Diet" campaign, that claimed that the regular consumption of milk promotes healthy

sued the school district for being improperly fired and for not abiding by mandated state standards for character and humane education.

weight loss, was scientifically misleading and false.[7] A story on the matter in *Alternet* captures the corporate duplicity behind this overt operation to infuse milk propaganda in schools:

> The Milk Your Diet campaign (also called BodyByMilk; Think About Your Drink; Why Milk?; 24oz/24hours; 3-A-Day; and Got Milk? as in, one of these slogans has got to work!) … shipped truck-size posters of 'stache-wearing David Beckham, Carrie Underwood and New York Yankee Alex Rodriguez to 45,000 public middle and high schools and 60,000 public elementary schools last fall and conducted an online auction where students could use milk UPC codes as currency. ("It is an amazing experience," say the web promos, which were still up in May. "Did we mention you have a chance to win an iPod? And a Fender guitar? And cool clothes from Adidas and Baby Phat? All you have to do is drink milk to get it. Any sizes. Any flavors.") The campaign offered $1,000 America's Healthiest Student Bodies Awards to schools with the "most active" students and saluted them with what? Got Milk recognitions. (Rosenberg, 2007)

Schools across the country have utilized dairy industry materials in this fashion because it is tacitly demanded by the USDA's National School Lunch Program, the primary governmental vehicle through which food that is in oversupply is promoted and national prices thereby subsidized. In this case, schools are only reimbursed for their food expenses by the program if they promote items like milk, which it has deemed a nutritional good.

It should be pointed out that this is the same National School Lunch Program that was slammed by a March, 2008 exposé from the *Wall Street Journal*, which uncovered that:

> In reports dating back to 2003, the USDA Office of Inspector General and the Government Accountability Office cited the USDA's lunch-program administrators and inspectors for weak food-safety standards, poor safeguards against bacterial contamination, and choosing lunch-program vendors with known food-safety violations. Auditors singled out problems with controls over E. coli and salmonella contamination. (Williamson, 2008)

Worse still, the above phrase "known food-safety violations" is something of a euphemism. For a prime beef vendor for the National School Lunch Program has been the meat packing company Westland/Hallmark which, via undercover footage shot by the Humane Society of the United States, was revealed to be regularly slaughtering "downer" cows (i.e., mortally sick animals that have also been linked to Mad Cow and other fatal diseases in humans) for popular consumption. Though having repeatedly denied any illegal wrongdoing for years, the ultimate revelation of West-land/Hallmark's practices in turn led to the nation's largest ever recall of beef (Associated Press, 2008). Unfortunately, it was suspected that the large majority of the meat from Westland/Hallmark had already been eaten, much of it by school children. Dave Warwak's art program therefore sought to provide a form of epistemological rupture of the educational status quo in order to call attention to the role being played by this sort of food in his own school. In so doing, however, he threatened

---

7. The Federal Trade Commission ruling, while a victory for democratic science, came on the heels of countless petitions filed against the Dairy Industry campaign by the animal rights organization, Physicians Committee for Responsible Medicine, dating back to 1999. The Commission denied a hearing for all of the previous petitions.

to parade the fact that the dietary norms constructed on behalf of those attending public schools (as well as in the larger society) are generally set in place by an emperor without clothes.

"Ecoterrorists" in the Academy?

In closing, I would like to offer some cursory critical remarks about higher education from the animal standpoint. While many colleges and universities exert greater control over their food purchases than public schools, and have moved to respond to increasing student demand for vegetarian and vegan menu options, there has been far more interest in providing locally-produced foods as part of a potential cost-cutting program legitimated through the language of sustainability (Powers, 2007) than in engaging in campus-wide discussion about the ethical dimensions of dining hall food services. Furthermore, the forms of symptomatic microaggression that take place against vegans in elementary and secondary schools, and in the broader society, routinely occur on college campuses against students and faculty alike as well.

To my mind, the most ominous of these microaggressive themes is the tendency amongst academics to uncritically reproduce the sentiments of corporations and the state about the animal rights movement as being composed of irrational and increasingly criminal elements.[8] This has resulted in a hostile campus climate for vegan scholars working from the animal standpoint, in which their colleagues maintain a psychological disposition that functions institutionally to delegitimate research normatively informed by the unprecedented plight faced by nonhuman animals. Crucially, this also feeds into an atmosphere of repressive tolerance within higher education that stifles meaningful protest and just debate of vivisection practices on campus.[9]

The philosopher Steven Best perhaps represents the bellwether case for what can happen professionally to animal standpoint theorists, as the repercussions for his written inquiries on this matter have involved Best's being branded an "ecoterrorist" in the halls of the United States Senate, his having a permanent ban placed upon his visitation rights by the United Kingdom, and his subsequently having his departmental Chair removed under spurious circumstances that also allegedly involved attempts to revoke his tenure status as a professor (for more on Best's story, see Kahn, 2010b). In my own experience, I have been actively discouraged by mentors, "for my own good," from doing animal standpoint work, and when I have chosen instead to continue with it, have been coached to remove relevant references from my curriculum vitae, and to otherwise deemphasize the research interest publicly wherever possible. I should add that the advice was not without some strategic merit, as my professional references informed me after my being hired last year that prospective employers repeatedly asked for assurances that I was "just studying these things" and was without any correlative background of illegal behavior. In a connected instance, dating back to September 2003, a professor in my PhD program easily wondered out loud with me if I had anything to do with a then recent series of alleged Earth Liberation Front attacks on Humvee vehicles in the San Gabriel

---

8. It should be noted that standpoint theory has been used historically to question the right of capitalist society to define criminality in ways that privilege social leaders and further marginalize the struggle-from-below. See Lukacs (1971).
9. I deal with this issue at length in Kahn (2010b).

Valley. "I figured it must have been you and some of your buddies," he remarked. To this day, I am not sure whether or not he was kidding.

More than ever before, we need students actively engaged in critical animal studies, yet it can be argued that the current academic trend is toward the penalization of animal standpoint research and vegan education. The counterargument might be that we are now witnessing an almost faddish rise of scholarship on nonhuman animals through the development of interdisciplinary posthumanist discourse and the emergence of fields such as "Human-Animal Studies." To be sure, these developments should be pursued as potential opportunities to shatter the long tradition of speciesist scholarship across the disciplines and to end the role that higher education plays in producing an epistemology of ignorance about nonhuman animals at this time. But as Frank Margonis (2007) has written, "One of the key philosophical strategies for maintaining the epistemology of ignorance is ... a tendency to abstract away from social realities" (p. 176). In this sense, I am skeptical that posthumanism or other forms of academese that are detached from the concrete requirements for ani mal liberationist praxis provide much more than a means to undermine the animal standpoint by co-opting its language and tempering its aims on behalf of the quest for professional prestige and more conservative political visions.

My skepticism about the academy's present desire to seriously confront the issues of the animal standpoint should not be considered cynicism about the larger possibility for positive change, however. On the contrary, if the previous century was marked by an assault on the lines of color, class, and gender, the twenty-first century will be defined in large part by the attempt to resolve issues of justice in relation to species. The critical educator Paulo Freire (2000) wrote, "While the problem of humanization has always, from an axiological point of view, been humankind's central problem, it now takes on the character of an inescapable concern" (p. 43). As I have tried to relate, there are significant historical forces at work affecting a culture of silence throughout mainstream society on vegan issues. Yet, in all sectors and levels of education, both formal and nonformal, the struggle for a new paradigm of nonanthropocentric understanding is taking place today at the grassroots. It is true that the end of speciesism cannot be guaranteed but, then again, neither can the conditions that would allow for its unquestioned continuance.

References

Associated Press. (2008). *Beef recall hits school lunch program*. Retrieved August 28, 2008 from http://www.edweek.org/ew/articles/2008/02/19/24beef_ap.h27.html

Benjamin, W. (1970). *Illuminations*. London: Jonathan Cape.

Best, S., (2009). The rise of critical animal studies: Putting theory into action and animal liberation into higher education. *State of Nature* [Electronic version]. Retrieved from http://www.stateofnature.org/theRiseOfCriticalAnimal.html

Cayley, D. (1992). *Ivan Illich in conversation*. Concord, Ontario: House of Anansi Press.

Collins, P. H. (1989). The social construction of black feminist thought. *Signs: Journal of Women in Culture and Society, 14*(4), 745–773.

Collins, P. H. (2000). *Black feminist thought: Knowledge, consciousness, and the politics of empowerment*. New York, NY: Routledge.

Donovan, J. (2006). Feminism and the treatment of animals: From care to dialogue. *Signs: Journal of Women in Culture and Society, 31*(2), 305–330.

Dunayer, J. (2001). *Animal equality: Language and liberation*. Derwood, MD: Ryce.

Eyerman, R., & Jamison, A. (1991). *Social movements: A cognitive approach*. Oxford, England: Polity Press.

Fanon, F. (2004). *The wretched of the earth*. New York, NY: Grove Press.

Federal Bureau of Investigation. (2008). *Putting intel to work: against ELF and ALF terrorists*. Retrieved March 16, 2009, from http://www.fbi.gov/page2/june08/ecoterror_063008.html

Freire, P. (2000). *Pedagogy of the oppressed*. New York, NY: Continuum.

Giroux, H. A. (2004). Cultural studies, public pedagogy, and the responsibility of intellectuals. *Communication and Critical/Cultural Studies, 1*(1), 59–79.

Haraway, D. (2003). *The companion species manifesto: Dogs, people, and significant otherness*. Chicago, IL: Prickly Paradigm Press.

Harding, S. (2004). *The feminist standpoint theory reader: Intellectual & political controversies*. New York, NY: Routledge.

Horkheimer, M., & Adorno, T. (2002). *Dialectic of enlightenment: Philosophical fragments*. Palo Alto, CA: Stanford University Press.

Kahn, R. (2006). The educative potential of ecological militancy in an age of big oil: Towards a Marcusean ecopedagogy. *Policy Futures in Education, 4*(1), 31–44.

Kahn, R. (2007). Toward a critique of paideia and humanitas: (mis)education and the global ecological crisis. In I. Gur Ze'ev & K. Roth (Eds.), *Education in the era of globalization* (pp. 209–230). New York, NY: Springer.

Kahn, R. (2008). Towards ecopedagogy: Weaving a broad-based pedagogy of liberation for animals, nature and the oppressed people of the earth. In A. Darder, M. Baltodano, & R. D. Torres (Eds.), *The critical pedagogy reader* (2nd ed., pp. 522–540). New York, NY: Routledge.

Kahn, R (2010a). *Critical pedagogy, ecoliteracy, and planetary crisis: The ecopedagogy movement*. New York, NY: Peter Lang.

Kahn, R. (2010b). Operation get fired: A chronicle of the academic repression of radical environmentalist and animal rights advocate-scholars. In A. J. Nocella, II, S. Best, & P. McLaren (Eds.), *Academic repression: Reflections from the academic industrial complex* (pp. 200–210). Oakland, CA: AK Press.

Latour, B. (2004). *Politics of nature: How to bring the sciences into democracy*. Cambridge, MA: Harvard University Press.

Lewis, T. & Kahn, R. (2009). Exopedagogies and the utopian imagination: A case study in Faery Subcultures. *Theory & Event, 12*(2). Retrieved January 2, 2010, from http://muse.jhu.edu/journals/theory_and_event/v012/12.2.lewis.html

Liddell, H. C., & Scott, R. (1889). *An intermediate Greek-English lexicon*. Oxford, England. Retrieved from http://www.perseus.tufts.edu/cgi-bin/ptext?doc = Perseus%3Atext%3A1999.04.0058%3Aentry%3D%2316098

Lukacs, G. (1971). *History and class consciousness: Studies in Marxist dialectic*. Cambridge, MA: MIT Press.

Margonis, F. (2007). John Dewey, W. E. B. Du Bois and Alain Locke: A case study in white ignorance and intellectual segregation. In S. Sullivan & N. Tuana (Eds.), *Race and epistemologies of ignorance* (pp. 173–196). New York, NY: SUNY Press.

McHugh, N. (2004). Telling her own truth: June Jordan, standard English and the epistemology of ignorance. In V. Kinloch & M. Grebowicz (Eds.), *Still seeking an attitude: Critical reflections on the work of June Jordan* (pp. 87–100). Lanham, MD: Lexington Books.

Mills, C. (2007). White ignorance. In S. Sullivan & N. Tuana (Eds.), *Race and epistemologies of ignorance* (pp. 11–38). New York, NY: SUNY Press.

Monson, S. (Producer & Director). (2005). *Earthlings:* Making the connections [Film]. Burbank, CA: Nation Earth.

Powers, E. (2007, Nov. 1). Campus food from around the corner. *Inside Higher Ed*. Retrieved August 28, 2008 from http://www.insidehighered.com/news/2007/11/01/local

Rodger, G. D. (2004). *24 carrot award*. Retrieved August 28, 2008, from http://www. vegparadise.com/24carrot610.html

Rosenberg, M. (2007, June 5). Milk is not a diet food. *Alternet*. Retrieved August 28, 2008, from http://www.alternet.org/healthwellness/53102/milk_is_not_a_diet_food/

Solórzano, D., Ceja, M., & Yosso, T. (2000). Critical race theory, racial microaggressions, and campus racial climate: The experiences of African American college students. *Journal of Negro Education, 69*(1/2), 60–73.

Sue, D., Capodilupo, C. M., Torino, G. C., Bucceri, J. M., Holder, A. M. B., Nadal, K. L., et al. (2004). Racial microaggressions in everyday life: implications for clinical practice. *American Psychologist, 62*(4), 271–286.

Tuana, N. (2004, Winter). Coming to understand: Orgasm and the epistemology of ignorance. *Hypatia, 19*(1), 194–232.

Vegan Society. (1979). *Memorandum of Association of the Vegan Society*. Retrieved August 28, 2008, from http://www.vegansociety.com/html/downloads/ArticlesofAssociation.pdf.

Williamson, E. (2008, March 3). School lunch at risk for years. *Wall Street Journal*. Retrieved August 28, 2009, from http://www.greenchange.org/article.php?id=2097

Yosso, T. J. (2006). *Critical race counterstories along the Chicana/Chicano educational pipeline*. New York, NY: Routledge.

What Is Education For?

David W. Orr

If today is a typical day on planet earth, we will lose 116 square miles of rain forest, or about an acre a second. We will lose another 72 square miles to encroaching deserts, the results of human mismanagement and overpopulation. We will lose 40 to 250 species, and no one knows whether the number is 40 or 250. Today the human population will increase by 250,000. And today we will add 2,700 tons of chlorofluorocarbons and 15 million tons of carbon dioxide to the atmosphere. Tonight the earth will be a little hotter, its waters more acidic, and the fabric of life more threadbare. By year's end the numbers are staggering: The total loss of rain forest will equal an area the size of the state of Washington; expanding deserts will equal an area the size of the state of West Virginia; and the global population will have risen by more than 90,000,000. By the year 2000 perhaps as much as 20% of the life forms extant on the planet in the year 1900 will be extinct.

The truth is that many things on which our future health and prosperity depend are in dire jeopardy: climate stability, the resilience and productivity of natural systems, the beauty of the natural world, and biological diversity.

It is worth noting that this is not the work of ignorant people. Rather, it is largely the results of work by people with BAs, BSs, LLBs, MBAs, and PhDs. Elie Wiesel once made the same point, noting that the designers and perpetrators of Auschwitz, Dachau, and Buchenwald—the Holocaust—were the heirs of Kant and Goethe, widely thought to be the best educated people on earth. But their education did not serve as an adequate barrier to barbarity. What was wrong with their education? In Wiesel's (1990) words,

It emphasized theories instead of values, concepts rather than human beings, abstraction rather than consciousness, answers instead of questions, ideology and efficiency rather than conscience.

I believe that the same could be said of our education. Toward the natural world it too emphasizes theories, not values; abstraction rather than consciousness; neat answers instead of questions; and technical efficiency over conscience. It is a matter of no small consequence that the only people who have lived sustainably on the planet for any length of time could not read, or like the Amish do not make a fetish of reading. My point is simply that education is no guarantee of decency, prudence, or wisdom. More of the same kind of education will only compound our problems. This is not an argument for ignorance but rather a statement that the worth of education must now be measured against the standards of decency and human survival—the issues now looming so large before us in the twenty-first century. It is not education, but education of a certain kind, that will save us.

Myth

What went wrong with contemporary culture and education? We can find insight in literature, including Christopher Marlowe's portrayal of Faust who trades his soul for knowledge and power, Mary Shelley's Dr. Frankenstein who refuses to take responsibility for his creation, and Herman Melville's Captain Ahab who says "All my means are sane, my motive and my object mad." In these characters we encounter the essence of the modern drive to dominate nature.

Historically, Francis Bacon's proposed union between knowledge and power foreshadowed the contemporary alliance between government, business, and knowledge that has wrought so much mischief. Galileo's separation of the intellect foreshadowed the dominance of the analytical mind over that part given to creativity, humor, and wholeness. And in Descartes's epistemology, one finds the roots of the radical separation of self and object. Together these three laid the foundations for modern education, foundations that now are enshrined in myths that we have come to accept without question. Let me suggest six.

First, there is the myth that ignorance is a solvable problem. Ignorance is not a solvable problem; it is rather an inescapable part of the human condition. We cannot comprehend the world in its entirety. The advance of knowledge always carried with it the advance of some form of ignorance. For example, in 1929 the knowledge of what a substance like chlorofluorocarbons (CFCs) would do to the stratospheric ozone and climate stability was a piece of trivial ignorance as the compound had not yet been invented. But in 1930 after Thomas Midgely, Jr., discovered CFCs, what had been a piece of trivial ignorance became a critical life-threatening gap in human understanding of the biosphere. Not until the early 1970s did anyone think to ask "What does this substance do to what?" In 1986 we discovered that CFCs had created a hole in the ozone over the South Pole the size of the lower 48 U.S. states; by the early 1990s, CFCs had created a worldwide reduction of ozone. With the discovery of CFCs, knowledge increased, but like the circumference of an expanding circle, ignorance grew as well.

A second myth is that with enough knowledge and technology, we can, in the words of *Scientific American* (1989), "manage planet earth." Higher education has largely been shaped by the drive to extend human domination to its fullest. In this mission, human intelligence may have taken the wrong road. Nonetheless, managing the planet has a nice ring to it. It appeals to our fascination with digital readouts, computers, buttons, and dials. But the complexity of earth and its life systems can never be safely managed. The ecology of the top inch of topsoil is still largely unknown as is its relationship to the larger systems of the biosphere. What might be managed, however, is us: human desires, economies, politics, and communities.

But our attention is caught by those things that avoid the hard choices implied by politics, morality, ethics, and common sense. It makes far better sense to reshape ourselves to fit a finite planet than to attempt to reshape the planet to fit our infinite wants.

A third myth is that knowledge, and by implication human goodness, is increasing. An information explosion, by which I mean a rapid increase of data, words, and paper is taking place. But this explosion should not be mistaken for an increase in knowledge and wisdom, which cannot be measured so easily. What can be said truthfully is that some knowledge is increasing while other kinds of knowledge are being lost. For example, David Ehrenfeld has pointed out that biology departments no longer hire faculty in such areas as systematics, taxonomy, or ornithology (personal communication). In other words, important knowledge is being lost because of the recent overemphasis on molecular biology and genetic engineering, which are more lucrative but not more important areas of inquiry. Despite all of our advances in some areas, we still do not have anything like the science of land health that Aldo Leopold called for a half-century ago.

It is not just knowledge in certain areas that we are losing but also vernacular knowledge, by which I mean the knowledge that people have of their places. According to Barry Lopez (1989),

> it is the chilling nature of modern society to find an ignorance of geography, local or national, as excusable as an ignorance of hand tools; and to find the commitment of people to their home places only momentarily entertaining, and finally naive.

> [I am] forced to the realization that something strange, if not dangerous, is afoot. Year by year the number of people with firsthand experience in the land dwindles. Rural populations continue to shift to the cities.... In the wake of this loss of personal and local knowledge, the knowledge from which a real geography is derived, the knowledge on which a country must ultimately stand, has come something hard to define but I think sinister and unsettling. (p. 55)

The modern university does not consider this kind of knowledge worth knowing except to record it as an oddity "folk culture." Instead, it conceives its mission as that of adding to what is called "the fund of human knowledge" through research. What can be said of research? Historian Page Smith (1990) has offered one answer:

> The vast majority of so-called research turned out in the modern university is essentially worthless. It does not result in any measurable benefit to anything or anybody. It does not push back those omnipresent 'frontiers of knowledge' so confidently evoked; it does not *in the main* result in greater health or happiness among the general populace or any particular segment of it. It is busywork on a vast, almost incomprehensible scale. It is dispiriting; it depresses the whole scholarly enterprise; and most important of all, it deprives the student of what he or she deserves—the thoughtful and considerate attention of a teacher deeply and unequivocally committed to teaching. (p. 7)

In the confusion of data with knowledge is a deeper mistake that learning will make us better people. But learning, as Loren Eiseley (1979) once said, is endless and "in itself... will never make us ethical men" (p. 284). Ultimately, it may be the knowledge of the good that is most threatened by all of our other advances.

All things considered, it is possible that we are becoming more ignorant of the things we must know to live well and sustainably on the earth.

In thinking about the kinds of knowledge and the kinds of research that we will need to build a sustainable society, a distinction needs to be made between intelligence and cleverness. True intelligence is long range and aims toward wholeness. Cleverness is mostly short range and tends to break reality into bits and pieces. Cleverness is personified by the functionally rational technician armed with know-how and methods but without a clue about the higher ends technique should serve. The goal of education should be to connect intelligence with an emphasis on whole systems and the long range with cleverness, which involves being smart about details.

A fourth myth of higher education is that we can adequately restore that which we have dismantled. I am referring to the modern curriculum. We have fragmented the world into bits and pieces called disciplines and subdisciplines, hermetically sealed from other such disciplines. As a result, after 12 or 16 or 20 years of education, most students graduate without any broad, integrated sense of the unity of things. The consequences for their personhood and for the planet are large. For example, we routinely produce economists who lack the most rudimentary understanding of ecology or thermodynamics. This explains why our national accounting systems do not subtract the costs of biotic impoverishment, soil erosion, poisons in our air and water, and resource depletion from gross national product. We add the price of the sale of a bushel of wheat to the gross national product while forgetting to subtract the three bushels of topsoil lost to grow it. As a result of incomplete education, we have fooled ourselves into thinking that we are much richer than we are. The same point could be made about other disciplines and subdisciplines that have become hermetically sealed from life itself.

Fifth, there is a myth that the purpose of education is to give students the means for upward mobility and success. Thomas Merton (1985) once identified this as the "mass production of people literally unfit for anything except to take part in an elaborate and completely artificial charade" (p. 11). When asked to write about his own success, Merton responded by saying that "if it so happened that I had once written a best seller, this was a pure accident, due to inattention and naivete, and I would take very good care never to do the same again" (p. 11). His advice to students was to "be anything you like, be madmen, drunks, and bastards of every shape and form, but at all costs avoid one thing: success" (p. 11). The plain fact is that the planet does not need more successful people. But it does desperately need more peacemakers, healers, restorers, storytellers, and lovers of every kind. It needs people who live well in their places. It needs people of moral courage willing to join the fight to make the world habitable and humane. And these qualities have little to do with success as our culture has defined it.

Finally, there is a myth that our culture represents the pinnacle of human achievement. This, of course, represents cultural arrogance of the worst sort and a gross misreading of history and anthropology. Recently, this view has taken the form that we won the Cold War. Communism failed because it produced too little at too high a cost. But capitalism has also failed because it produces too much, shares too little, also at too high a cost to our children and grandchildren. Communism failed as an ascetic morality. Capitalism has failed because it destroys morality altogether. This is not the happy world that any number of feckless advertisers and politicians describe. We have built a world of sybaritic wealth for a few and Calcuttan poverty for a growing underclass. At its worst, it is a world of crack on the streets, insensate violence, anomie, and the most desperate kind of poverty. The fact is that we live in a disintegrating culture. Ron Miller (1989) stated it this way:

> Our culture does not nourish that which is best or noblest in the human spirit. It does not cultivate vision, imagination, or aesthetic or spiritual sensitivity. It does not encourage gentleness, generosity, caring, or compassion. Increasingly in the late twentieth century, the economic-technocratic-statist worldview has become a monstrous destroyer of what is loving and life-affirming in the human soul. (p. 2)

Rethinking Education

Measured against the agenda of human survival, how might we rethink education? Let me suggest six principles.

First, all education is environmental education. By what is included or excluded, students are taught that they are part of or apart from the natural world. To teach economics, for example, without reference to the laws of thermodynamics or ecology is to teach a fundamentally important ecological lesson: that physics and ecology have nothing to do with the economy. It just happens to be dead wrong. The same is true throughout the curriculum.

A second principle comes from the Greek concept of Paideia. The goal of education is not mastery of subject matter but mastery of one's person. Subject matter is simply the tool. Much as one would use a hammer and a chisel to carve a block of marble, one uses ideas and knowledge to forge one's own personhood. For the most part we labor under a confusion of ends and means, thinking that the goal of education is to stuff all kinds of facts, techniques, methods, and information into the student's mind, regardless of how and with what effect it will be used. The Greeks knew better.

Third, I propose that knowledge carries with it the responsibility to see that it is well used in the world. The results of a great deal of contemporary research bear resemblance to those foreshadowed by Mary Shelley: monsters of technology and its byproducts for which no one takes responsibility or is even expected to take responsibility. Whose responsibility is Love Canal? Chernobyl? Ozone depletion? The *Exxon Valdez* oil spill? Each of these tragedies was possible because of knowledge created for which no one was ultimately responsible. This may finally come to be seen for what I think it is: a problem of scale. Knowledge of how to do vast and risky things has far outrun our ability to use it responsibly. Some of this knowledge cannot be used responsibly, safely, and to consistently good purposes.

Fourth, we cannot say that we know something until we understand the effects of this knowledge on real people and their communities. I grew up near Youngstown, Ohio, which was largely destroyed by corporate decisions to "disinvest" in the economy of the region. In this case MBA graduates, educated in the tools of leveraged buyouts, tax breaks, and capital mobility, have done what no invading army could do: They destroyed an American city with total impunity and did so on behalf of an ideology called the "bottom line." But the bottom line for society includes other costs: those of unemployment, crime, higher divorce rates, alcoholism, child abuse, lost savings, and wrecked lives. In this instance what was taught in the business schools and economics departments did not include the value of good communities or the human costs of a narrow destructive economic rationality that valued efficiency and economic abstractions above people and community (Lynd, 1982).

My fifth principle follows and is drawn from William Blake. It has to do with the importance of "minute particulars" and the power of examples over words. Students hear about global responsibility while being educated in institutions that often spend their budgets and invest their endowments in the most irresponsible things. The lessons being taught are those of hypocrisy and ultimately despair. Students learn, without anyone ever telling them, that they are helpless to overcome the frightening gap between ideals and reality. What is desperately needed are (a) faculty and administrators who provide role models of integrity, care, and thoughtfulness and (b) institutions capable of embodying ideals wholly and completely in all of their operations.

Finally, I propose that the way in which learning occurs is as important as the content of particular courses. Process is important for learning. Courses taught as lecture courses tend to induce passivity. Indoor classes create the illusion that learning only occurs inside four walls, isolated from what students call, without apparent irony, the "real world." Dissecting frogs in biology classes teaches lessons about nature that no one in polite company would verbally profess. Campus architecture is crystallized pedagogy that often reinforces passivity, monologue, domination, and artificiality. My point is simply that students are being taught in various and subtle ways beyond the overt content of courses.

Reconstruction

What can be done? Lots of things, beginning with the goal that no student should graduate from any educational institution without a basic comprehension of things like the following:

- the laws of thermodynamics,
- the basic principles of ecology,
- carrying capacity,
- energetics,
- least-cost, end-use analysis,
- limits of technology,
- appropriate scale,
- sustainable agriculture and forestry,
- steady-state economics, and
- environmental ethics.

I would add to this list of analytical and academic things, practical things necessary to the art of living well in a place: growing food; building shelter; using solar energy; and a knowledge of local soils, flora, fauna, and the local watershed. Collectively, these are the foundation for the capacity to distinguish between health and disease, development and growth, sufficient and efficient, optimum and maximum, and "should do" from "can do."

In Aldo Leopold's words, does the graduate know that "he is only a cog in an ecological mechanism? That if he will work with that mechanism his mental wealth and his material wealth can expand indefinitely?

But that if he refuses to work with it, it will ultimately grind him to dust"? And Leopold asked, "If education does not teach us these things, then what is education for?" (p. 210).

Sources

Eiseley, L. 1979. *The star thrower.* New York: Harcourt Brace Jovanovich.

Leopold, A. 1966. A *Sand County almanac.* New York: Ballantine. (Original work published 1949.)

Lopez, B. 1989, September. American geographies. *Orion.*

Lynd, S. 1982. *The fight against shutdowns.* San Pedro, CA: Singlejack Books.

Merton, T. 1985. *Love and living.* New York: Harcourt Brace Jovanovich.

Miller, R. 1989, Spring. Editorial. *Holistic Education Review.*

Managing Planet Earth. 1989, Sept. *Scientific American, 261,* 3.

Smith, P. 1990. *Killing the spirit.* New York: Viking.

Wiesel, E. 1990. Remarks before the Global Forum. Moscow.

A Wilderness Environmentalism Manifesto: Contesting the Infinite Self-Absorption of Humans

Kevin Michael DeLuca

> The world is nature, and in the long run inevitably wild…. Wilderness is a *place* where the wild potential is fully expressed.
>
> —G. Snyder, *The Practice of the Wild*

For the past two decades, the core of the environmental movement, wilderness preservation, has suffered from a two-pronged assault, one political and the other theoretical. On the front of political practice, the attack has come from the so-called environmental justice movement.[1] This movement is better conceived as the human justice movement. My renaming is not a slight. Human justice is a fine goal, but it is not environmental justice. As even a cursory reading of the environmental justice literature suggests, the main concern of the environmental justice movement is humans. The nonhuman is only of interest insofar as it affects humans. Therefore, although the environmental justice movement is often concerned to clean up the environment, at other times it is content to support practices that harm the environment and the nonhuman in support of some human concern, frequently jobs. Never is the environmental justice movement primarily concerned with wilderness. Fundamentally, the environmental

---

1. Accounts of the environmental justice movement that are good starting points include Bullard (1990), Gottlieb, (1993), and Schwab (1994).

justice movement does not support environmental issues that impinge on human interests or rights. Indeed, the environmental justice movement attacks environmental groups that support wilderness or endangered species as racist and classist.

The environmental movement also has been attacked as being in favor of something that does not exist—namely, wilderness. From a position heavily indebted to postmodernism, wilderness has been savaged as a racist and classist human construct invented by elite whites and corporations. The chief proponent of this position is William Cronon, though roots go to the work of Raymond Williams and many have participated, including myself.[2] This theoretical deconstruction often spawns cruder arguments that (1) wilderness does not exist, (2) the construct of wilderness is discriminatory, and, therefore, (3) it makes no sense to attempt to preserve wilderness.

The response of some in the environmental movement has been, in a word, appeasement. Mainstream environmental organizations, such as the Sierra Club and Greenpeace, have been quick to turn to environmental justice issues. In this chapter, I want to suggest that the environmental movement's surrender of wilderness is premature. There are good reasons to defend wilderness ferociously. In what follows I will review and critique the positions of the environmental justice movement and the postmodern critics of wilderness. I then will defend wilderness as both a crucial rhetorical trope in environmental political battles and an a priori reality that makes possible the human. Finally, I will review two cases that show the benefits and possibilities of wilderness environmentalism.

Environmental Justice: All Humans, All The Time

The environmental justice movement in the United States has achieved extraordinary success. Whether one ties its origin to Lois Gibbs, Love Canal, and the antitoxins movement or to Robert Bullard, Warren County, and the environmental racism movement, the environmental justice movement has raised to a national level public awareness of the disproportionate impact of environmental degradation on minorities and lower classes, changed corporate practices, and transformed government policies. Some of the more obvious successes include the stopping of numerous hazardous waste sites, the establishment of the Superfund law, and the signing of Executive Order 12898. That order mandated that "each Federal agency shall make achieving environmental justice part of its mission by identifying and addressing, as appropriate, disproportionately high and adverse human health or environmental effects of its programs, policies, and activities on minority populations and low-income populations."[3] The federal government established the National Environmental Justice Advisory Council (NEJAC) and the Interagency Working Group on Environmental Justice (IWG) to help implement environmental justice goals, defined as follows:

2. The deconstruction of nature came first and wilderness more recently. For arguments about and accounts of the social construction of nature, see Collingwood (1945), Evernden (1992), Haraway (1989), and Williams (1980). For the argument that wilderness is also a social construction, see, Nash (1973, p. 132), Cronon (1996), Cronon's edited volume (1996), Oelschlaeger (1991), DeLuca (2001), and DeLuca and Demo (2001). Much of the discussion of wilderness is collected in Callicott and Nelson (1998).

3. Available online at www.epa.gov/fedsite/eo12898.htm.

Environmental Justice is the fair treatment and meaningful involvement of all people regardless of race, color, national origin, or income with respect to the development, implementation, and enforcement of environmental laws, regulations, and policies. In sum, environmental justice is the goal to be achieved for all communities and persons across this Nation. Environmental justice is achieved when everyone, regardless of race, culture, or income, enjoys the same degree of protection from environmental and health hazards and equal access to the decision-making process to have a healthy environment in which to live, learn, and work.[4]

This national mandate has trickled down to regional levels. For example, the city of Los Angeles includes environmental justice in its general plan:

Assure the fair treatment of people of all races, cultures, incomes and education levels with respect to the development, implementation and enforcement of environmental laws, regulations, and policies, including affirmative efforts to inform and involve environmental groups, especially environmental justice groups, in early planning stages through notification and two-way communication.[5]

It is clear that the environmental justice movement has benefited thousands of people. It has changed government policies and laws and has helped specific communities protect their homeplaces from the depredations of corporate polluters. For its many successes, for its dedication, and for its effective redress of race and class discrimination, the environmental justice movement is to be celebrated.

As it has gained national stature, the environmental justice movement has also challenged and transformed the environmental movement, especially with respect to its focus on wilderness and nonhuman nature. This challenge has been both implicit and explicit. Environmental justice activists have redefined "environment" to focus on humans. Gibbs articulates this new definition:

Over the past ten years the Movement for Environmental Justice has redefined the word environment. No longer does the media, the general public or our opponents see the environmental movement as one that is focused on open spaces, trees, and endangered species alone. They have finally got it! The Environmental Justice Movement is about people and the places they live, work and play.[6]

Bullard echoes Gibbs: "The environmental justice movement has basically redefined what environmentalism is all about. It basically says that the environment is everything: where we live, work, play, go to school, as well as the physical and natural world."[7]

---

4. Available online at www.epa.gov/region03/environmental_justice/index.htm.
5. Available online at http://www.lacity.org/ead/EADWeb-AboutEAD/environmental_justice.htm.
6. Gibbs (1993, p. 2). The other quotes from Gibbs and the Center for Health and Environmental Justice (CHEJ) are from the CHEJ website online at www.ejrc.cau.edu.
7. Schweizer (1999).

Words have consequences. They direct thoughts and actions. Gibbs and Bullard are right. Environmental justice activists have successfully shifted the meaning of environmentalism from a wilderness focus to a human and human habitat focus. For example, at the landmark first National People of Color Environmental Leadership Summit (Summit I), out of the seventeen Principles of Environmental Justice (Appendix A), only one has a focus on nature not connected to humans. Even the last principle, which focuses on preserving "Mother Earth's resources," connects that preservation to human self-interest: "to insure the health of the natural world for present and future generations." There is no need to explicitly state humans. It is understood.

This shift in environmentalism is manifested in environmental justice actions.[8] Gibbs's Center for Health and Environmental Justice (CHEJ), "the only national environmental organization founded and led by grassroots leaders," is concerned with multiple issues affecting human health but has no room for wilderness issues. Bullard's Environmental Justice Resource Center (EJRC) focuses on "environmental and economic justice, environmental racism, land use and industrial facility permitting, brown-fields redevelopment, community health, transportation equity, suburban sprawl, and smart growth."[9] Wilderness is noticeably invisible. The insignificance of wilderness for environmental justice activists makes sense, in light of their experiences and focus. As Gibbs's CHEJ defines it, environmental justice is "the principle that people have the right to a clean and healthy environment regardless of their race or economic standing."

So, environmental justice activists shift the focus of environmentalism from wilderness and nature to people. On its own, this is neither surprising nor noteworthy. The problem for wilderness advocates is that environmental justice groups, not content to have their own "environmental movement" focused on people, directly challenge and berate the environmental movement for not focusing on people and their problems, in other words, for being environmental groups. In the now famous 1990 letters to the Group of Ten, the Southwest Network for Economic and Environmental Justice indicted wilderness advocacy as racist and colonialist:

> Your organizations continue to support and promote policies which emphasize the clean-up and preservation of the environment on the backs of working people in general and people of color in particular. In the name of eliminating environmental hazards at any cost, across the country industrial and other economic activities which employ us are being shut down, curtailed, or prevented while our survival needs and cultures are ignored.[10]

These charges of racism and classism raise the shibboleth of jobs versus the environment, the ghost that haunts the environmental movement. Far from being a call for environmental justice, this letter demonstrates a most pernicious form of anthropocentrism, wherein only human interests count. From such a position, no wilderness area or national park should be preserved because it would necessarily cost human jobs when the trees cannot be cut, the minerals mined, the grasses grazed. No poisons, such as DDT, could be banned

8. Here I am not considering Native American environmental justice groups. For historical, cultural, and legal reasons, Native American environmental justice groups are markedly different from other environmental justice groups. This difference is perhaps most apparent with respect to attitudes toward nonhuman nature.
9. Environmental Justice Resource Center, www.ejrc.cau.edu
10. Southwest Organizing Project, "The Letter that Shook a Movement," *Sierra*, May/June 1993, 54.

because someone would lose a job when the production line was shut down. Environmental devastation is big business, and stopping it will cost jobs (at least in the short run).

The culture issue is also used to smear the protection of ecosystems and species. For example, if one's culture tends to favor fishing an endangered species, that is their human right, and too bad for the fish: "although these Latino communities support conservation efforts, they are concerned that state restrictions on activities such as fishing 'will deprive them of an opportunity for contact with nature by restricting their ability to use the catch as an occasion for generosity to family, friends, and neighbors.'"[11] The environmental crisis is the result of a multitude of human practices. If we are going to make any progress in stopping environmental destruction, we are going to have to give up many cultural practices, no matter how much we like them. For example, in the South, from where I am writing, cars and the right to drive them whenever and wherever one wants are considered part of one's cultural heritage—note the devotion to NASCAR. When it comes to saving ecosystems and the planet's health, culture is often the problem and should not be a trump card used to stop protecting species and ecosystems.

Indeed, environmental justice responses to protecting endangered species represent another damaging aspect of human self-absorption. Giovanna Di Chiro writes, "So the trademark slogans of mainstream environmentalism, such as 'Save the whales' or 'Extinction is forever,' are seen to reflect concerns of white people who are blind to the problems of people of color."[12] To put it bluntly, from an environmental justice perspective, to be worried about the extinction of nonhuman species is a form of racism. African American journalist Paul Ruffins articulated (with regret) the position of African American environmentalists: "We have attacked white environmentalists for their concern with saving birds and forests and whales while urban children were suffering from lead paint poisoning."[13] The absurdity of this position is obvious. Is the environmental movement not allowed to care for wilderness or other species until every human being is safe and happy? Because humans are so expert at hurting each other, such a position amounts to disbanding all conventional environmental organizations.

Environmental justice groups attempt to claim the moral high ground on this issue by claiming endangered species status for themselves: "We feel that many of these communities are just as much endangered species as any animal species."[14] Although Di Chiro lauds this position—"The question of what (and who) counts as an endangered species is therefore another crucial aspect of the environmental justice movement's reconceptualization of the relationships between nonhuman and human nature and the emergence of new ideas of nature and new forms of environmentalism"[15]—in truth the position represents either a woeful ignorance of science or a stunning example of human self-centeredness. No, humans are not an endangered species and a subset of humans cannot constitute an endangered species. Yes, many species are endangered as a result of human cultural practices.

---

11. Di Chiro (1996, p. 319).
12. Di Chiro (1996, p. 311).
13. Quoted in Di Chiro (1996, p. 312).
14. Environmental justice activist Dana Alston, quoted by Di Chiro (1996, p. 302).
15. Di Chiro (1996, p. 315).

Silencing Wilderness: The Gag of Humanism

Despite the logical inanity of the environmental justice positions and the blatant use of the race and class cards, many environmental movement groups have acquiesced to environmental justice demands.[16] The Sierra Club, America's preeminent environmental organization both historically and politically, is the paramount example.[17] At a Sierra Club centennial celebration, then executive director Michael Fischer called for "a friendly takeover of the Sierra Club by people of color ... [or else it will] remain a middle-class group of backpackers, overwhelmingly white in membership, program, and agenda.... The struggle for environmental justice in this country and around the globe must be the primary goal of the Sierra Club during its second century."[18] This marked turn toward social justice was institutionalized in 1993: "The Board of Directors of the Sierra Club recognizes that to achieve our mission of environmental protection and a sustainable future for the planet, we must attain social justice and human rights at home and around the globe." This utopian humanitarian mission was elaborated upon with a 2001 declaration of their own "Environmental Justice Principles."[19]

So, what is wrong with the Sierra Club and other environmental organizations adopting "environmental justice" as a goal? The problems are both philosophical and practical. The startling innovation that wilderness preservation introduced into modern industrial civilization with Yosemite in 1864 is the idea that other living beings have a right to existence outside of their service to humans. In thinking about Yosemite, David Brower suggested that Frederick Law Olmsted was one of the first to attempt to speak for the trees: "Mountains have a voice, and Olmsted was one of the first to try to speak for them. He proposed the rights for nature implicit in the national park idea."[20] The attempt of the Sierra Club to accommodate environmental justice activists represents a retreat from speaking for the trees to once again speaking for people, just like everyone else. It is, according to Aldo Leopold, to shun the light of Darwin's wisdom:

> that men are only fellow-voyagers with other creatures in the odyssey of evolution. This new knowledge should have given us, by this time, a sense of kinship with fellow-creatures; a wish to live and let live; a sense of wonder over the magnitude and duration of the biotic enterprise. Above all we should, in the century since Darwin, have come to know that man, while now captain of the adventuring ship, is hardly the sole object of its quest,

16. Humanism can be defined as "a philosophy centered on man and human values, exalting human free will and superiority to the rest of nature; man is made the measure of all things" (*The Concord Desk Encyclopedia, Presented by TIME*, 1982, p. 604). Humanism arose in contrast to Christianity.

17. The Sierra Club is the example here because of its prominence and enthusiastic adoption of environmental justice principles. Other important environmental groups have made similar moves, including the World Wildlife Fund, the National Wildlife Federation, Earth First!, and Greenpeace.

18. "A Place at the Table: A *Sierra* Roundtable on Race, Justice, and the Environment," *Sierra* (May/June 1993): 51.

19. Available online at www.sierraclub.org/policy/conservation/justice.asp.

20. David Brower, "David Brower opposes the Yosemite Valley Plan," available online at www.yosemitevalley.org/HTML/Articles/2000_11_20.html.

and that his prior assumptions to this effect arose from the simple necessity of whistling in the dark.[21]

There are many organizations that speak for people and their myriad concerns. I do not insist that they become environmental organizations and speak for the trees. It is important for environmental organizations to retain their unique perspective, speaking primarily for sentient beings that have no human voice. The Sierra Club's board of directors is wrong to claim that, "to achieve our mission of environmental protection and a sustainable future for the planet, we must attain social justice and human rights at home and around the globe."[22]

"I have come to the reluctant conclusion that social justice and environmental sustainability are not always compatible objectives.... The differences between them and not merely tactical but strategic: their objectives differ in fundamental ways." (p. 83)

In fact, Dobson makes the strong claim that there is no evidence of such a relation: "The US environmental justice movement is, therefore, simultaneously a site for extravagant claims regarding the compatibility of the justice and environmental agendas and a black hole as far as empirical studies designed to substantiate those claims are concerned" (p. 86). Indeed, in the case of population control, the nondemocratic Chinese government provides a clear counter-example. It is highly doubtful that a democratic China could have curbed its population as effectively as China has through its strict one-child policy. Democratic India has been an abject failure at controlling its population. Population control is not a popular idea. Democracy is not an a priori condition for environmental integrity.[23] Social justice and human rights around the globe are not a priori conditions for environmental protection. Indeed, the protection of endangered species around the globe often requires the violation of human rights and social justice. Environmental protection often increases human suffering. When people are prevented from hunting rhinos for money to feed their families or poaching turtle eggs for profit and food, human suffering is increased. Some environmental protection requires the shutting down of destructive industries and the loss of jobs. If the environmental movement adopts the human-centered perspective of the environmental justice movement, they will be unable to make the hard decisions that increase human suffering, that require putting other beings and ecosystems, not humans, first. Putting humans always first is a crucial cause of the environmental crisis we now face.

In practical terms, abandoning wilderness and environmental protection as a first principle leads environmental groups to abandon environmental criteria as a means of judging practices and policies. Environmental justice activists quite explicitly put human, cultural, and economic concerns over environmental concerns. Gibbs's and Bullard's definitions of "environment" make that clear. The berating of wilderness activists moved to save whales and trees while there are still children suffering from lead paint poisoning or starvation makes that clear. When environmental groups put human rights, social justice, economic concerns, and respect for cultural diversity ahead of wilderness preservation and ecosystem health,

21. Leopold (1949/1968, pp. 109–110).
22. A reviewer alerted me that Andrew Dobson (2003) makes a similar argument with respect to socialism and environmentalism. Dobson argues:
23. Kate Soper (1996) also makes this argument.

it becomes impossible to condemn human practices on environmental grounds and judge among competing cultural practices. For example, backpacking, off-road four-wheeling, recreational vehicle "camping," and fishing are all cultural practices, but they have different environmental consequences and should be judged in light of those consequences, not their importance to the groups that practice them. When the right of minorities to have jobs is the paramount concern, it becomes difficult to condemn jobs and work practices harmful to the environment.

The controversy in California and Canada over leaf blowers is another example. When local groups tried to convince towns to do something as simple as ban leaf blowers, a recent extraneous and ecodamaging invention, they were charged with being elitist and racist, because many landscape workers in California are Latino. Despite the environmental and human health costs, especially for workers, groups such as the Association of Latin American Gardeners of Los Angeles and the Bay Area Gardeners Association insisted on a right to leaf blowers. As one proponent of the ban noted, "To convince urban gardeners that it is their God given right to work with leaf blowers is akin to the United Farm Workers demanding the retention of the short handled hoe and DDT in their day."[24] Sheldon Ridout, a veteran of what he terms "combat gardening," started a landscaping company called the Silent Gardener. He was motivated by "coming home smelling like fuel every day, always being in a cloud of dust and being surrounded by noise."[25]

The point cannot be emphasized enough. The world is facing a catastrophe of historic and unique proportions, and it is not a crisis of social justice and human rights. Arguably the state of social justice and human rights is better now than at any other time in human history. Regardless, social injustices and human rights violations are not new. As documented annually by the World Watch Institute and others, however, humans are threatening the vital signs of planetary health in a manner and scale unprecedented in human history. Air and water pollution, chemical contamination, topsoil loss, collapse of multiple fisheries, forest loss, desertification, and loss of biological diversity are the threats that must be confronted if we are to achieve the environmental movement's mission of environmental protection and a sustainable future for the planet.[26]

Another important consequence of the ethos of environmental justice groups is the deferment to the local. Following the lead of environmental justice groups, environmental groups like the Sierra Club and Green-peace not only agree to take on environmental justice issues, but also agree to defer absolutely to the experiences and decisions of local environmental justice groups. This is a problem. Although local groups can have insights peculiar to their experiences and place, they are by no means the sole repository of wisdom and can often act for short-sighted self-interests against the interests of the greater community and the larger good. An obvious and painful example comes from recent U.S. history. If left up to the "wisdom" of the local majority in the South in the 1960s, Jim Crow segregation would have remained the law of the region. With respect to environmental issues, the intervention of national or international bodies is often necessary to overcome the resistance of the local. In the controversy over the slaughter of ancient forests in the Pacific Northwest, local communities often vociferously have opposed any protections of trees or animals that

24. Michalowski (1998).

25. Lorraine Johnson, "Sound and Fury," available online at www.canadiangardening.com/sound_fury2.shtml.

26. Available online at www.worldwatch.org. The World Wildlife Fund puts out a Living Planet Report available online at www.panda.org/news_facts/publications/general/livingplanet/index.cfm.

impinge on what they perceive to be their self-interests. Locals have physically assaulted environmentalists and proudly displayed their feelings toward the endangered spotted owl on bumper stickers: "Kill an owl. Save a logger."[27] On the global level, nations repeatedly have asserted their local self-interests over global interests. Paramount examples in this respect would be the U.S. refusal to ratify the Kyoto Protocol on global warming and Brazil's refusal to heed international suggestions for protecting the Amazon rainforest. To idealize the local is a dangerous act for environmental groups. Leopold's famous story about shooting a wolf is instructive. "I thought that because fewer wolves meant more deer, that no wolves would mean hunters' paradise. But after seeing the green fire die, I sensed that neither the wolf nor the mountain agreed with such a view."[28] It is difficult for people facing pressing local needs (hunger and employment) to "think like a mountain."

Even romanticizing "native peoples" is problematic. Americans' romanticization of Native Americans is both racist and historically inaccurate.[29] In Thailand, grassroots activists idealize the hill tribes, arguing that they live in harmony with the forests while ignoring the damage hill tribes are doing to headwaters forests. As Buddhist monk Achan Pongsak Techadhammo, a leader of Green Buddhism, notes, "Man coexisting with the forest: that's a romantic idea, little more than wishful thinking. People still talk about it because that's the way they'd like things to be. The hill tribe population is growing rapidly. They just don't farm to live; they farm to sell and with the support of vested interest groups. They have TVs, motorcycles, and cars."[30]

A final concern with the turn to environmental justice issues at the expense of wilderness is brutally political. Although Fischer argues that the Sierra Club needs to turn away from backpacker issues to environmental justice issues to avoid "losing influence in an increasingly multicultural country,"[31] such a stance is either politically naïve or utopian. The United States is not a democracy with power equally divided among each person and his or her vote. Quite clearly, political power rests in the hands of corporations and the upper and middle classes (largely white) and will continue to do so for many more decades. To these groups, wilderness issues and preservation appeals are more likely to be persuasive then discussions of toxic waste sites. The environmental movement makes this political reality an implicit calculation in their widespread rhetorical appeals through calendars, photography, books, and wilderness vacations. In a recent year, the Sierra Club's five calendar entries were *Wilderness*, *Wildlife*, *Birds*, *Butterflies*, and *Adventure Travel*. I have yet to see the toxic-waste-site calendar.

Wilderness is a Fiction: Your Point?

The environmental justice denigration or neglect of wilderness is echoed and reinforced by the postmodern deconstruction of wilderness. From this perspective, wilderness is a fiction, a social construction of a particular time, place, and people. More to the point, wilderness is the invention of rich, white European and American males in the 1800s, which involved practices that excluded woman, other classes, and nonwhite

27. For an accounting of attacks on environmental activists, see Helvarg (1994, p. 130).
28. Leopold (1949/1968, pp. 129–130).
29. Spence (1999) and Darnovsky (1991).
30. Quoted in Fahn (2004, p. 138).
31. *Sierra* (1993).

races and visited genocidal destruction upon Native Americans. The upshot is that, if wilderness is not natural, what is the point of preserving it, especially if such preservation entails racist, classist, and sexist practices? The source of much of this critique of wilderness is William Cronon's essay, "The Trouble with Wilderness; or, Getting Back to the Wrong Nature." Cronon's polemical title encourages dismissing wilderness, which is a misreading of his essay and a misunderstanding of the postmodern theories undergirding his own writing.

In deconstructing wilderness, Cronon is advancing the deconstruction of nature more broadly, suggested by Clarence Glacken, R. G. Collingwood, Raymond Williams, Donna Haraway, and Neil Evernden, among others, to the idea of wilderness. His essay continues in a more pointed fashion from work such as Roderick Nash's groundbreaking *Wilderness and the American Mind* and Max Oelschlaeger's comprehensive *The Idea of Wilderness*. In a nutshell, Cronon argues, "Far from being the one place on earth that stands apart from humanity, it is quite profoundly a human creation—indeed the creation of very particular human cultures at very particular moments in human history.... [T]here is nothing natural about the concept of wilderness."[32]

In much of my own work I have detailed how a "white wilderness" was created in the United States. Through Carleton Watkins' Yosemite photographs, William Henry Jackson's Yellowstone photographs, Thomas Moran's paintings, and John Muir's writings, among others, the values of elite "white" culture were inscribed in a vision of pristine, sublime wilderness that subsequently became a foundational value of the preservation movement.[33] To move from the deconstruction of wilderness to the dismissal of wilderness in favor of privileging humans and their concerns, however, is to misunderstand postmodernism. If postmodernism can be reduced to a central impulse, arguably, it would be the questioning of modernism's foundational concepts and Truths.[34] Far from privileging the human, postmodernism represents an even more sustained questioning of the human than of wilderness. Foucault puts this questioning most succinctly at the end of *The Order of Things*: "Taking a relatively short chronological sample from within a restricted geographical area—European culture since the sixteenth century—one can be certain that man is a recent invention within it.... As the archaeology of our thought easily shows, man is an invention of recent date. And one perhaps nearing its end." Foucault concludes that, if the cultural discourses that made possible "man" were to change, "then one can certainly wager that man would be erased, like a face drawn in sand at the edge of the sea."[35]

If one accepts the postmodern deconstruction of wilderness, the same logic dictates the deconstruction of the human. Our contact with the world, with the Real, is always already mediated through multiple discourses. This is the meaning of Jacques Derrida's infamous line, "*il n'y a pas de hors-texte* [There is nothing outside of the text]."[36] The response, then, is not to dismiss wilderness as a fiction and turn to the human, but, rather, to ask what are the benefits and costs of the fiction of wilderness. To Cronon's credit, despite

32. Cronon (1996, 69, 79). See note 2, above, for citations on the wilderness debate.
33. DeLuca (1999, pp. 217–246), DeLuca (2001), and DeLuca and Demo (2001).
34. There are many good accounts of postmodernism. Besides Lyotard's (1984) seminal account, *The Postmodern Condition*, useful summaries are provided by Calinescu (1987) and Harvey (1989).
35. Foucault (1973, p. 386–387).
36. Derrida (1976, p. 158).

his polemical title, this is what he does. The very first sentence of his essay, which stands alone as its own paragraph, reads, "The time has come to rethink wilderness."[37]

Cronon calls for this rethinking because of the importance of wilderness: "Although wilderness may today seem to be just one environmental concern among many, it in fact serves as the foundation for a long list of other such concerns that on their face seem quite remote from it. That is why its influence is so pervasive and, potentially, so insidious."[38] Cronon points to several insidious effects. The idea of pristine, sublime wilderness posits an ontological separation between humans and wilderness, because the very presence of humans destroys wilderness. A focus on pristine wilderness condemns civilization to being a narrative of environmental devastation, the despoiling of the Garden of Eden. Valorizing pristine wilderness devalues other habitats. A focus on wilderness leads environmental groups to ignore other issues, such as pollution and social justice.

It is important to recognize, therefore, that Cronon is critiquing the *idea* or *concept* of wilderness: "By now I hope it is clear that my criticism in this essay is not directed at wild nature per se, or even at efforts to set aside large tracts of wild land, but rather at the specific habits of thinking that flow from this complex cultural construction called wilderness. It is not the things we label as wilderness that are the problem—for nonhuman nature and large tracts of the natural world *do* deserve protection." For Cronon, the deconstruction of wilderness provides an opportunity to figure out and nuance our appreciation of the ecological, social, and political value of wilderness, not to analyze away its worth. Perhaps the greatest value of wilderness is that it prods us humans out of our infinite self-absorption. "The striking power of the wild is that wonder in the face of it requires no act of will, but forces itself upon us as proof that ours is not the only presence in the universe. Wilderness gets us into trouble only if we imagine that this experience of wonder and otherness is limited to the remote corners of the planet, or that it somehow depends on pristine landscapes we ourselves do not inhabit."[39]

Cronon and I agree on both the deconstruction and vital nature of wilderness, though we disagree on the ecological and political valuation of wilderness. In a later lecture tellingly titled "Humanist Environmentalism: A Manifesto," Cronon reaffirms the value of wilderness but reduces it to one among many humanist values: "A humanist environmentalism strives to protect nature but also other, equally important values: responsible (wise?) use, social justice, democracy, fairness, tolerance, community, generosity (forgiveness of the other), love, humane living, beauty, good humor, joy. Wilderness is a crucial measure of our success in building a more just and humane environmentalism."[40] Instead of a humanist environmentalism, I want to propose a wilderness environmentalism, wherein wilderness is the measure of all things.[41]

37. Cronon (1996, p. 69).
38. Cronon (1996, p. 73).
39. Cronon (1996, pp. 81, 88).
40. Available online at www.lib.duke.edu/forest/lecture99.html.
41. The dead Greek I am thinking of and defacing here is Protagoras: "Man is the measure of all things."

Salvaging Wilderness

I propose a wilderness environmentalism because I think it is crucial that the environmental movement be grounded in wilderness, not humanism. That said, in proposing a wilderness environmentalism, I acknowledge the deconstruction of wilderness and suggest wilderness not as the pristine and sublime ideal, but as the a priori condition of our being that surrounds and grounds us. The resources for such a move come from a surprising list of both famous environmentalists and social theorists. After briefly noting these thinkers, I will look at wilderness environmentalism on the ground and in the trees, with the examples of Julia Butterfly Hill and WildAid.

In his essay "Walking" Thoreau elaborates on his sentiment, "In Wildness is the preservation of the World": "I wish to speak a word for Nature, for absolute freedom and wildness, as contrasted with a freedom and culture merely civil—to regard man as an inhabitant, or a part and parcel of Nature, rather than a member of society."[42] Karl Marx, even while noting that nature is "not a thing given directly from all eternity, remaining ever the same, but the product of industry and the state of society" also admonishes, "Man *lives* from nature, i.e., nature is his *body*, and he must maintain a continuing dialogue with it if he is not to die."[43] It is important to keep in mind that both Thoreau and Marx note not only humanity's essential connection to nature, but also that humans are not apart from but a part of nature/wilderness. Even Muir, often credited as a chief architect of sublime wilderness as a realm apart from humans, writes, "Mountains are fountains not only of rivers and fertile soils, but of men. Therefore, we are all, in some sense, mountaineers, and going to the mountains is going home.... [W]ildness is a necessity."[44] Here Muir is advocating wilderness as home, not as vacation destination.

Writing in exile from Germany during World War II, Frankfurt School theorists Max Horkheimer and Theodor Adorno proposed that the domination of nature results in such horrors as the Holocaust, so that "the fully enlightened earth radiates disaster triumphant." For Horkheimer and Adorno, "world domination over nature turns against the thinking subject himself.... As soon as man discards his awareness that he himself is nature, all the aims for which he keeps himself alive—social progress, the intensification of all his spiritual and material powers, even consciousness itself—are nullified."[45] It is important to emphasize here that Horkheimer and Adorno, urban Jewish intellectuals who in no way supported the Nazi romanticization of the earth, insist that the very possibility of social progress depends on how humans relate to nature. Their position exactly reverses the claim of environmental justice groups and the Sierra Club that "to achieve our mission of environmental protection and a sustainable future for the planet, we must attain social justice and human rights at home and around the globe."

Aldo Leopold echoes the primacy of wilderness: "Wilderness is the raw material out of which man has hammered the artifact called civilization.... Wilderness gives definition and meaning to the human enterprise." In advocating for the primacy of wilderness, Leopold also prescribes humanity's place in the wild with his famous land ethic, which "changes the role of *Homo sapiens* from conqueror of the land-community

---

42. Thoreau, (1906, p. 205).
43. Marx (1975, p. 328).
44. Muir (1888/1976, p. 202); Muir (1901, p. 3).
45. Horkheimer and Adorno (1972, pp. 3, 26, 54).

to plain member and citizen of it."[46] Lacking Leopold's poetic sensibility, ecoactivist Dave Foreman puts it bluntly, "It [wilderness] is the natural world, the arena for evolution, the caldron from which humans emerged, the home of the others with whom we share this planet.... The preservation of wildness and native diversity is *the* most important issue. Issues directly affecting only humans pale in comparison."[47]

These theorists do not suggest neglecting the human, but, rather, recognizing that wilderness/nature grounds and circumscribes the human. What does such a perspective look like in practice? The practices of Julia Butterfly Hill and WildAid suggest another response to the specter of jobs and the incessant cry of humanity that seem to so easily defeat environmentalism—one that does not abandon wilderness. It is a response that does not ignore human issues, but also does not turn the environment into another subset of the human domain. It is a response that respects the nonhuman and humbles humanity in relation to the rest of creation. It is a response that honors Thoreau's dictum, "In Wildness is the preservation of the World," in its most fundamental senses.

Speaking for Trees and People

Julia Butterfly Hill lived for two years in Luna, a 1,000-year-old redwood targeted for cutting, descending only when Pacific Lumber agreed to spare the tree. Tree-sitting is a tactic made popular by the radical environmental group Earth First! as a way of saving ancient forests. The particular tree-sit that Butterfly joined had started in October 1997 and was significant for its location. It was not in pristine wilderness but on a hillside above the town of Stafford, California. The members of Earth First! chose this location after a mudslide caused by clearcutting destroyed seven homes in Stafford. Significantly, Stafford is a lumber town. The site of this Earth First! tree-sit links wilderness and social concerns. This linkage is echoed in Butterfly's rhetoric, which explicitly articulates the inextricable twining of wilderness and social issues.[48]

In numerous interviews, Butterfly deftly weaves wilderness issues with human concerns and a critique of corporate practices that manages to displace the jobs-versus-environment debate. Instead of letting jobs or social justice be the test of all wilderness issues, Butterfly places wilderness as the grounds for environmental and social concerns. Further, she does this all the while consistently claiming that she and her actions are merely symbols for larger struggles against environmental devastation and corporate avarice.

Speaking to *Time Magazine Online*, Butterfly said, "After being up here a few days, I realized that what was happening here was not only destroying the environment, but people's lives as well. I gave my word to this tree, the forest, and to all the people whose lives are being destroyed by the lumber companies, that my

46. Leopold (1949/1968, pp. 188, 200, 204).
47. Foreman (1991, p. 27).
48. Butterfly's ubiquitous presence in multiple media is one testament to her effectiveness. Besides her international presence in outlets from Europe to Japan, she has appeared repeatedly in every major newspaper in the United States, including the *New York Times*, the *Washington Post*, the *San Francisco Chronicle*, the *Los Angeles Times*, and *USA Today*, as well as news weeklies such as *Time* and *Newsweek*. She has been featured in women's magazines ranging from *Family Circle* to *Ms.* She has been interviewed on many Internet sites and radio stations. She has appeared on major television news programs, including an extended segment on *NBC Dateline*. In environmental circles she has become something of a folk hero and spokesperson, as well as the subject of several independent documentaries.

feet would not touch the ground and until I had done everything in my power to make the world aware of this problem and to stop the destruction." In an interview with Monica Mehta on *MOJO Wire*, Butterfly elaborated on many of these points:

> I feel pretty good. It's been really, really hard, but as hard as it's been on me physically, all I have to do is think about the seven families in the town of Stafford who no longer have a home. And all I have to do is think about the animals whose homes are these forests that are being destroyed. I felt raising public worldwide awareness is very important. And right now this sit has gained a much-needed spotlight that we can shine on the forests and on the issues and love and respect. I look at *Earth First!* more as a movement than as an organization, in that when we put ourselves first we suffer, but when we put the Earth first then everyone is helped.[49]

Butterfly presents an engaging and sophisticated analysis of justice that encompasses environmental and social dimensions through a grounding in wilderness. Instead of people first, it is wilderness first but with a recognition that caring for wilderness *is* caring for people. For Butterfly, adding people is not merely a polite gesture, but a recognition of the essential connection between wilderness and people. Consistently, Butterfly links the tree *and* forest *and* people. She is a tree-hugger and a people-hugger. In this position Butterfly is reaffirming the fundamental insight of the Frankfurt School's analysis of the domination of nature: that in the domination of nature people are inevitably dominated. Clearcutting the redwoods destroys people's homes. Butterfly is also proffering a complicated notion of wilderness. It is not out there, far away. It is in many places and it is intimately connected to human lives. Indeed, wilderness is the ground of our being. We do not so much live in an environment as dwell in wilderness.

The position Butterfly advocates fundamentally transforms Cronon's "humanist environmentalism" by moving the emphasis from "humanist" to "wilderness" so that wilderness is not merely an important value and a crucial measure of our success but the ground that makes possible our existence. Wilderness environmentalism holds out hope for shifting away from the multiple anthropocentric worldviews that have done enough harm. In the end, Butterfly is offering and enacting a wilderness environmentalism that grounds caring for people in caring for wilderness. This is a different vision than the myth of pristine wilderness and offers the possibility of reimagining human-wilderness relations.[50]

Founded in 1999, the radical, direct-action group WildAid uses armed confrontations with poachers, undercover espionage, and high-profile media campaigns in an attempt "to decimate the illegal wildlife trade within our lifetimes." Using such tactics, WildAid cofounders Steve Galster, Suwanna Gauntlett, Steve Trent, and Pete Knights have helped save tens of thousands of wild animals, reduced consumption of shark-fin soup in Thailand by 30 percent, and solicited millions of dollars to put armed patrols in parks and wildernesses. WildAid is a good case study for two reasons. First, it is confronting one of the main threats to global ecosystem health: loss of biodiversity. As E. O. Wilson explains, "The sixth great extinction spasm of

49. I attained the transcripts of these two online interviews at Julia Butterfly Hill's tree-sit website, www.lunaturu.org. Another current site of information about her activities is www.circleoflifefoundation.org.
50. For a fuller treatment of Butterfly's tree-sit, see DeLuca (2003).

geological time is upon us, grace of mankind. Earth has at last acquired a force that can break the crucible of biodiversity."[51]

Second, WildAid is working in regions (largely in Southeast Asia) where endangered animals are at risk from desperate people and embedded cultural traditions. The $5 billion annual illegal trade in "protected" wildlife is largely supplied by poor villagers. In Myanmar (Burma), where annual per capita income is $300, one clouded leopard skin fetches $114, aloe wood can wholesale for $1,000 per kilo, and Malayan sun bear skins and gall bladders sell for $1,000 each.[52] The largest source of consumer demand is from China, where there is a cultural belief in *ye wei*, or wild taste: "the belief that exotic fare endows them with added social status and the traits of the animal consumed, such as bravery, long life or sexual prowess."[53] China's increasing economic wealth has led to a sort of economic democracy that is devastating to wildlife and ecosystems. Wild fare that was once the province of only the wealthy is now accessible to the many. Roughly 20 million seahorses are used each year to "treat" asthma, heart disease, and impotence. In just eight months in 2003, 10,000 pangolins (scaly anteaters) were seized on their way to China from Indonesia. In Southeast Asia, up to 10,000 tons of freshwater turtles are used annually.[54] As Galster describes it, the fauna and flora of the region face "the Chinese vacuum cleaner, sucking up Southeast Asia's wildlife left and right."[55]

In this human war on wildlife and wild places, WildAid is clearly on the side of the wild. Cofounder Gauntlett explains, "There are 30,000 parks in the world, most of which are not protected at all. That's why we dedicate ourselves to direct protection of wildlife preserves in developing countries."[56] A *New York Times* reporter states it a bit more harshly in describing WildAid's work in Cambodia: "In a country where there is little help for the people, a new generation of environmentalists is trying to protect the ebbing populations of wildlife in Southeast Asian bush. And they are doing it the way so much gets done these days: with troops and guns."[57] WildAid's work in Asia puts in stark relief the consequences of giving up on wilderness in favor of an environmental justice approach to people, their work, and their cultural practices. If we put people first, we will stand by and watch as the last rhino horn, the last tiger penis, and the last seahorse are ground up and consumed in desperate attempts to increase the world's human overpopulation. If we put people first, we will stand by and watch as a poor villager eradicates the last clouded leopard in a futile attempt to eradicate poverty.

Putting wilderness first, as WildAid does, involves brutal choices. While raiding a Cambodian wildlife restaurant at gunpoint and rescuing long-tail macaques, turtles, and cobras, WildAid does not concern itself with the young teenage girls working as waitresses and prostitutes. As the accompanying reporter notes, "I can't resist the rude observation that while we have saved some turtles, we have left the girls behind ... punishing a lady for having a turtle while abandoning child prostitutes."[58] This example, however, suggests

51. Quoted in Singer (2004).
52. Singer (2004).
53. Gray (2003).
54. Gray (2003).
55. Singer (2004).
56. Singer (2004).
57. Hitt (2003).
58. Hitt (2003).

the futility of the Sierra Club position that to achieve environmental protection "we must attain social justice and human rights at home and around the globe." If environmental protection depends on eradicating prostitution, we may as well all go buy SUVs and retire to the beach.

Putting humans first dilutes the focus and efforts of environmental groups. Further, because many human issues involve abstractions, such as social justice and human rights, they are Sisyphean tasks with no clear way to even define victory. Putting wilderness first, however, does not mean abandoning humans, as the case of Butterfly suggests. Though not as eloquent as Butterfly, WildAid definitely attends to human issues by attending to wilderness issues. WildAid lists five goals: to decimate the illegal wildlife trade in our lifetimes; to bring wildlife conservation to the top of the international agenda; to protect wilderness areas effectively and affordably; to ensure that endangered species populations rebound; and to enable people and wildlife to survive together. WildAid elaborates: "We want a world where our invaluable natural resources are not ravaged, one in which local communities can improve their lives without destroying their environment, and where humanity can survive together with wildlife for generations to come."[59] More then just words on a website, WildAid has put humans and wilderness in dialogue through several practices under the rubric "Surviving Together." First, many of the park rangers that WildAid hires and trains are former poachers. Second, WildAid hires local people to act as staff and informants. Galster hopes, by 2030, to be "turning its overseas offices into locally run NGOs [nongovernmental organizations] with all-local staffs, as he has already done with the Phoenix Fund in Russia."[60] Third, WildAid helps former poachers turn to more sustainable practices, such as mushroom and flower farming. As former poacher Sampong Prachopchan explains, "When I was a poacher, a middleman sent me into the forest to get aloe wood. We all knew that if we shot an elephant or tiger, he would buy that, too. But after I was arrested, I decided to leave poaching. If we keep on destroying the forest, there will be none left for the next generation."[61]

The Upshot

Understanding is always a dicey proposition. I want to be as clear as I can here. The environmental justice movement is a good thing. The work that environmental justice groups perform is needed and makes a significant difference for human health and well-being. I am in no way suggesting that environmental justice groups should change their focus on human health, toxic wastes, and race and class bias. For people living in the midst of severely degraded environments, such a focus makes perfect sense. That said, accusations of racism against groups that support wilderness issues and encouraging the environmental movement to move away from wilderness are both wrong and a mistake.

The Sierra Club is an amazing organization that has done invaluable work for decades. Their move to adopt the principles of environmental justice at the expense of a focus on wilderness, however, is a grievous error. The Sierra Club is not unique in this error. In a promotional video celebrating thirty years of "Making a World of Difference," the World Wildlife Fund spends roughly half of the program discussing

59. Online at http://wildaid.org.
60. Singer (2004).
61. Singer (2004).

the problems of people and tells contributors, "[Y]ou've enabled local people to improve their lives today and preserve the earth's irreplaceable natural resources for future generations." Even Earth First!, originally a no-compromise radical wilderness group, so turned to human issues like jobs for loggers in the 1990s that cofounder Foreman left to start an organization with a focus on wilderness (The Wildlands Project).

To make alliances with diverse groups is important. The stances of environmental justice advocate Bullard and wilderness advocate Foreman are instructive. In an interview with Earth First!, Bullard says, "I don't think you can get any more radical than fighting racism."[62] Foreman argues, "The idea of wilderness, after all, is the most radical in human thought—more radical than Paine, than Marx, than Mao. Wilderness says: Human beings are not paramount, Earth is not for *Homo sapiens* alone."[63] While retaining their radically different positions, both Bullard and Foreman advocate alliances with others. In speaking with Earth First!, Bullard says, "I'm not saying that you are gonna get a lot of people of color inundating your organization with membership but we can work together without being members and that's where the I think the collaboration, coalitions and signing onto supporting specific campaigns has really made a difference."[64] Although insisting that, "[i]n everything human society does, the primary consideration should be for the long-term health and biological Diversity of Earth," Foreman suggests, "[c]onservationists should try to find common ground with loggers and other workers whenever possible."[65] Such common ground among environmental, human justice, labor, native peoples, civil rights, women's rights, and peace activists is even more crucial now in the face of the onslaught of corporate global trade and the acronyms of that apocalypse (WTO, GATT, NAFTA, IMF/WB).

Still, I think Bullard and Foreman are right. It is important that environmental justice and wilderness environmental groups with different ideas retain their distinct identities and orientations even when forming alliances when it makes strategic sense. For the environmental movement, that identity revolves around wilderness. This is true even if one finds compelling, as I do, the deconstruction of wilderness. The lesson of postmodernism is not that wilderness is a deconstruction and, therefore, we should all be humanists. Rather, the lesson is that the mediated world we think in is necessarily a product of multiple social discourses, so the question is not one of truth but of rhetorical force, not one of ontology but of politics. The human and human rights are just as much social constructions as wilderness. China makes this very point when contesting the United Nations' Universal Declaration of Human Rights as a political ploy by Western nations in the thrall of the ideology of individualism and neglectful of community. The question, with respect to wilderness, then, is what sort of political, ecological, and social work does it enable environmentalists to do?

First, wilderness historically has been a politically effective trope that enables the environmental movement to improve the environment for both wildlife and people. The constant use of wilderness images via photography, calendars, screen savers, books, and ecotourism by the environmental movement testifies to the political and rhetorical force of wilderness. For example, using an image-based strategy proponents of the Arctic National Wildlife Refuge have staved off determined attempts to open the area to drilling. Although the refuge remains under threat, it is important to remember that it has taken the Republicans decades of rancorous struggle, repeated attempts, millions of dollars, appeals to national security in the wake of the

62. Schweizer (1999).
63. Foreman (1991, p. 19).
64. Schweizer (1999).
65. Foreman (1991, pp. 26, 32).

September 11 attacks, and an election that increased the Republican majorities to even approach this goal. In addition, as part of this campaign, pro-drilling advocates realized they would have to portray the area in a way that challenged its worth as wilderness. As Ann Klee, Secretary of the Interior Gale Norton's top advisor, asked department biologists while preparing a slide show, "Don't you have any ugly pictures of ANWR"?[66]

The idea of wilderness also continues to spread around the globe and enables nations and activist groups to save significant areas. Thailand, for example, has preserved roughly 12 percent of its land. The recent awarding of the Nobel Peace Prize to Kenyan environmental activist Wangari Maathai suggests an international recognition of the primacy of nonhuman nature. As Nobel committee chair Ole Danbolt Mjoes explained, "It is clear that with this award, we have expanded the term 'peace' to encompass environmental questions relating to our beloved Earth.... Peace on earth depends on our ability to secure our living environment."[67]

Second, as Dave Foreman and Howie Wolke argue in *The Big Outside*, wilderness, especially when designated over large areas, is crucial to preserving ecosystems and maintaining biodiversity. With mass extinction one of the major threats facing the planet, wilderness is a crucial strategic response: "big wildernesses, particularly if adjacent to or connected via corridors with other wild areas, are best able to support the full array of indigenous species in a given region."[68]

Finally, wilderness provides a context and restraint for humans. With a humanist orientation, humans lose all sense of perspective and place and succumb to the fatal illness of species solipsism, believing "man is the measure of all things." Wilderness as the a priori ground of humanity provides a powerful antidote. Cronon succinctly expresses this important attribute of wilderness:

> I also think it no less crucial for us to recognize and honor nonhuman nature as a world we did not create, a world with its own, independent nonhuman reasons for being as it is. The autonomy of nonhuman nature seems to me an indispensable corrective to human arrogance. Any way of looking at nature that helps us remember—as wilderness also tends to do—that the interests of people are not necessarily identical to those of every other creature or of the earth itself is likely to foster *responsible* behavior.[69]

Abandoning wilderness-centered environmentalism is a disastrous error. The finest moments of environmentalism often involve humans exceeding self-concern and caring for wilderness and other species because of their intrinsic being. To be sure, wilderness was often sold as a balm for harried urban souls and a boon for railroad profits, but one cannot read John Muir, Edward Abbey, Rachel Carson, or Janisse Ray, among others, and not be struck by the love of wilderness for its own sake—the love of something outside of human design. More than love, though, the encounter with wilderness is an encounter with a nonhuman other. When we abandon wilderness we risk losing what Derrida terms "monstrosity," the other that exceeds human

66. Grunwald (2003, p. A3). For a more thorough account of the role of images in the debate over the Arctic National
    Wildlife Refuge, see Check (2005).
67. Tyler (2004).
68. Foreman and Wolke (1989, p. 24).
69. Cronon (1996, p. 87).

sense and economic calculation.[70] We need not decry the loss of the pristine wilderness of the Romantic tradition, with its unfortunate race and class consequences. We do need to salvage wilderness as the excess and otherness that grounds and surrounds us, putting us in our place.

References

Brice, A., *The devil's dictionary* (New York: Dover, 1993).
Bullard, R., *Dumping in Dixie: Race, Class, and Environmental Quality* (Boulder, Colo.: Westview Press, 1990).
Calinescu, M., *Five Faces of Modernity* (Durham, N. C.: Duke University Press, 1987).
Callicott, B., & Nelson, M. P. *The Great New Wilderness Debate* (Athens: University of Georgia Press, 1998).
Check, T., "Visual Enthymemes of Alaskan Wilderness: Television News Coverage of the Arctic National Wildlife Refuge." Presented at the 8th Conference on Communication and the Environment, June 24–27, 2005, Jeckyll Island, GA.
Collingwood, R. G., *The Idea of Nature* (Oxford: Clarendon, 1945).
The Concord Desk Reference, presented by *TIME* (New York: Concord Reference Books, 1982).
Cronon, W. ed., *Uncommon Ground: Rethinking the Human Place in Nature* (New York: W. W. Norton and Company, 1996).
Cronon, W., "The Trouble with Wilderness, or Getting Back to the Wrong Nature," *Environmental History* (January 1996): 69–90.
Darnovsky, M., "Stories Less Told: Histories of U.S. Environmentalism," *Socialist Review* 22 (1991): 11–54.
DeLuca, K., "Meeting in a Redwood: Wilderness on the Public Screen," *Situation Analysis: A Forum for Critical Thought & International Current Affairs* (spring 2003): 32–45.
DeLuca, K., "Trains in the Wilderness: The Corporate Roots of Environmentalism," *Rhetoric and Public Affairs* 4, no. 4 (winter 2001): 633–652.
DeLuca, K., "In the Shadow of Whiteness: The Consequences of Constructions of Nature in Environmental Politics," in T. Nakayamo and J. Martin, eds., *Whiteness* (Thousand Oaks, CA: Sage, 1999), 217–246.
DeLuca, K., and Demo, A., "Imagining Nature and Erasing Class and Race: Carleton Watkins, John Muir, and the Construction of Wilderness." *Environmental History* (2001): 541–560.
Derrida, J., *Of Grammatology* (Baltimore: John Hopkins University Press, 1976).
Di Chiro, G., "Nature as Community: The Convergence of Environment and Social Justice," in W. Cronon, ed., *Uncommon Ground* (New York: W.W. Norton, 1996), 298–320, 527–531.
Dobson, A. "Social Justice and Environmental Sustainability: Ne'er the Twain Shall Meet?" in J. Agyeman, R. Bullard, and B. Evans, eds., *Just sustainabilities* (Oxford: Oxford University Press, 2003), 83–95.
Evernden, N., *The Social Creation of Nature* (Baltimore: John Hopkins University Press, 1992).
Fahn, J. D., *A Land on Fire* (Chiang Mai: Silkworm Books, 2004).
Foreman, D., *Confessions of an Eco-Warrior* (New York: Harmony, 1991).
Foreman, D., and Wolke, H. *The Big Outside* (Tucson: Ned Ludd Books, 1989).
Foucault, M., *The Order of Things* (New York: Vintage, 1973).
Gibbs, L., "Celebrating Ten Years of Triumph," *Everyone's Backyard* 11, no. 2 (1993): 2.
Gottlieb, R., *Forcing the Spring* (Washington, D.C.: Island Press, 1993).
Gray, D., "Consuming Exotic Animals," *Associated Press* (January 1, 2003), available online at http://wildaid.org/index.asp?CID=8&PID=331&SUBID=&TERID=14.
Grunwald, M., "Some Facts Clear in the War of Spin over Arctic Refuge," *Washington Post* (March 6, 2003): A3.
Haraway, D., *Primate Visions: Gender, Race, and Nature in the World of Modern Science* (New York: Routledge, Chapman, & Hall, 1989).
Harvey, D., *The Condition of Postmodernity* (Cambridge, Mass.: Basil Blackwell, 1989).
Helvarg, D., *The War against the Greens* (San Francisco: Sierra Club Books, 1994).
Hitt, J., "The Eco-Mercenaries," *New York Times* (August 4, 2003), available online at http://wildaid.org/index.asp?CID=8&PID=331&SUBID=&TERID=18.
Horkheimer, M., and Adorno, T., *Dialectic of Enlightenment* (New York: Herder, 1972).
Marx, K., "Economic and Philosophical Manuscripts," in Q. Hoare, ed., *Karl Marx: Early Writings* (New York: Vintage, 1975), 279–400.
Leopold, A., *A Sand County Almanac* (New York: Oxford, 1949/1968).
Lyotard, J.-F., *The Postmodern Condition* (Minneapolis: University of Minnesota Press, 1984).
Michalowski, J., "Letter to Adrian Alvarez and the Association of Latin American Gardeners of Los Angeles," (1998), available online at www.nonoise.org/quietnet/cqs/polphil.htm.

70. Derrida (1976, p. 5) is referring to the future as a monstrosity, but I think wilderness must be conceptualized in similar terms: "The future can only be anticipated in the form of an absolute danger. It is that which breaks absolutely with constituted normality and can only be proclaimed, *presented*, as a sort of monstrosity ... which will have put into question the values of sign, word, and writing."

Muir, J., *West of the Rocky Mountains* (Philadelphia: Running, 1888/1976).

Muir, J., *Our National Parks*, (Boston: Houghton Mifflin, 1901).

Nash, R., *Wilderness and the American Mind*, rev. ed. (Binghamton, N.Y.: Vail-Ballou, 1973).

Oelschlaeger, M., *The Idea of Wilderness* (New Haven, Conn.: Yale University Press, 1991).

Schwab, J., *Deeper Shades of Green: The Rise of Blue-Collar and Minority Environmentalism in America* (San Francisco: Sierra Club Books, 1994).

Schweizer, E., "Environmental Justice: An Interview with Robert Bullard," *Earth First! Journal* (July 1999), available online at www.ejnet.org/ej/bullard.html.

Sierra, "A Place at the Table: A *Sierra* Roundtable on Race, Justice, and the Environment," *Sierra* (May/June 1993): 51.

Singer, N., "See the Last Clouded Leopard. See the Last Clouded Leopard Die. See the Last Clouded Leopard Skin on the Black Market. See a Pattern Here?" *Outside Magazine* (May 2004), available online at http://outside.away.com/outside/features/200405/clouded_leopard_wildlife_conservation_l.html

Snyder, G., *The Practice of the Wild* (San Francisco: North Point Press, 1990).

Soper, K., "Nature/'nature'" in G. Robertson, M. Marsh, L. Tickner, J. Bird, B. Curtis, and T. Putnam, eds., *Future/Natural* (New York: Routledge, 1996), 22–34.

Southwest Organizing Project, "The Letter that Shook a Movement," *Sierra*, (May/June 1993), 54.

Spence, M. D., *Dispossessing the Wilderness* (New York: Oxford University Press, 1999).

Thoreau, D. H., "Walking," in *Excursions and Poems* (Boston: Houghton Mifflin, 1906), 205–248.

Tyler, P. E., "Peace Prize Goes to Environmentalist in Kenya," *New York Times* (October 9, 2004): A1.

Williams, R., "Ideas of Nature," in *Problems in Materialism and Culture* (London: Verso, 1980), 67–85.

UNIT 6. A BRIEF HISTORY OF THE EDUCATION OF MARGINALIZED GROUPS

In this unit, we will examine the ways in which historically marginalized racial and ethnic groups have experienced education in the United States. Our analysis cannot possibly include all such marginalized groups, so it will be limited to the following groups: Native Americans, African Americans, Asian Americans, and Latino Americans.

Native Americans

Thomas McKenney, the head of the Office of Indian Affairs, put forth ideas on the schooling of Native Americans through the Civilization Act of 1819. He argued for the creation of a tribal school system controlled by White missionaries to civilize Native Americans in one generation. The "civilizing" included a conversion to Christianity.

In 1821, Sequoyah, a mixed-blood Cherokee brought the Cherokee nation a Cherokee alphabet, using 86 characters (Spring, 2013). He did not speak English, so his approach in developing a written language was different from the literate missionaries. The editor of the first Native American newspaper, Elias Boudinot, printed stories in both English and Cherokee. Unfortunately, the missionaries were resistant to learning the Cherokee language and alphabet, so Sequoyah's discovery was of little use to them (Spring, 2013). In 1841, the Choctaw and Cherokees had successful educational systems. They sent numerous graduates to eastern colleges and used bilingual teachers and Cherokee texts to attain a 100% literacy rate.

Congress started an Indian Peace Commission to handle the warring tribes. The Indian Peace Commission had specific ideas for the education of Native Americans. Thus, the curriculum in schools shifted to teaching in English only, erasing Indian customs, and focusing on allegiance to the U.S. government. The establishment of off-reservation boarding schools became the norm where Indian children left their families to be schooled away from home. The Carlisle Indian School, founded by Richard Pratt in Carlisle Pennsylvania was the first off-reservation boarding school. Between 1879 and 1905, 25 off-reservation boarding schools were opened throughout the country (Spring, 2013). The goal of these boarding schools was to inculcate the Indian children into "fervent patriotism" to the U.S. government and take away any remnants of the children's language and culture. In 1928, the Meriam Report published by the Institute for Government Research at Johns Hopkins University criticized boarding schools and the removal of children from their families and communities. The report supported community day schools that would integrate education with reservation life (Spring, 2013). Native Americans would spend the rest of the century rebuilding what the federal government had destroyed (Spring, 2013).

African Americans

The first African Americans who arrived in Jamestown in 1619 were denied an education during enslavement because plantation owners feared that an educated slave would be incompatible with the system of slavery and ultimately result in increasing the likelihood of slave revolts. Moreover, in the early 19th century, plantation owners also grew to fear that their "property" would be exposed to abolitionist literature. The abolitionist societies would eventually contribute a great deal to the education of the newly-freed in the post–Civil War reconstruction period.

The first public schools to offer desegregated education to Black children were the Boston Public Schools. In 1855, the governor signed a law that basically allowed all children to attend Massachusetts schools, and in September of that year the schools were integrated.

In the 1890s, debates developed between two major leaders, Booker T. Washington and W. E. B. Du Bois, over how to pursue education for Blacks. Washington compromised with White demands and was satisfied with the foundation of segregated industrial education. W. E. B. Du Bois, in contrast, believed that no compromise should be made with Whites and that Black education should focus on building up the future Black leaders of the community through a robust liberal arts curriculum (Spring, 2013).

By 1900, African Americans in the South attended a segregated school system that spent fewer dollars per pupil than the White schools. The NAACP (National Association for the Advancement of Colored People) resisted school segregation since its founding in 1909. In 1954, the NAACP hired Thurgood Marshall to argue the *Brown v. Board of Education* case, which was most concerned with African American children who lived in racially mixed neighborhoods having access to nearby public schools (Militz-Frielink et al., 2019). The White children could walk to their neighborhood schools, but "black children had to walk across dangerous parts of town and ride buses for up to an hour to reach their segregated schools" (Militz-Frielink et al., 2019, p. 364). *Brown* ruled that school segregation was "unconstitutional because it violated the equal protection clause and due process clauses of the Fourteenth Amendment" (Militz-Frielink et al., 2019, p. 366). Although Brown was a civil rights victory, *Brown II* (1955) ruled that schools should desegregate with "all deliberate speed," which southern Whites interpreted as never. Consequently, school desegregation happened at a very slow pace, and Black teachers in segregated schools were laid off as a result.

The resegregation of American schools was recognized as early as 1999 by the Civil Rights Project at Harvard University. (Spring, 2013). The trend for increasing segregation in schools was a catalyst for increasing poverty among African American and Latino students. This trend leads to an overemphasis on test preparation and scripted lessons in schools.

Asian Americans

Asian Americans struggled for an equal educational opportunity before World War II. The California school code of 1872 only provided education for White children between 5 and 21 years old, which subsequently denied education to Asian Americans, Mexican Americans, African Americans, and Native Americans. In 1884, Mamie Tape, a Chinese American born in the United States, challenged the San Francisco school board regarding admittance to the school district, in which she was denied. In response, Superior Court Judge Maguire argued that the Fourteenth Amendment to the Constitution, which guaranteed equal protection, provided for equal access to public schooling for Mamie Tape (Spring, 2013).

The California legislature responded to Judge Maguire's decision by providing education for Chinese children in segregated schools. "The San Francisco school district justified segregation by saying that is was essential 'not only for the purpose of relieving the congestion at present prevailing in our schools, but also for the higher end that our children should not be placed in any position where their youthful impression may be affected by association with pupils of the Mongolian race'" (Spring, 2013, p. 79).

The San Francisco Board of Education created a separate school for Chinese, Japanese, and Korean children in 1906. Japanese parents boycotted the school and tried to win public opinion in Japan as a way of forcing favor with the U.S government (Spring, 2013). Stories appeared in Japanese newspapers stating that segregation was an affront to the nation, and an American ambassador to Japan warned the U.S. government of the unfavorable situation. President Theodore Roosevelt pressured the San Francisco school system to end segregation. However, Japanese students remained segregated and continued to face exclusionary laws and legal actions through World War II (Spring, 2013).

Hispanic/Latino Americans

To justify paying farmworkers low wages, Anglos adopted an attitude of racism against Mexicans and Latin Americans, which then led to the establishment of segregated schooling. Mexicans and Latin Americans faced economic exploitation from the Anglos and racism to justify paying farmworkers lower wages and the establishment of segregated schooling (Spring, 2013). In 1855, the California Bureau of Instruction passed a mandate that school classes be conducted in English. In the last half of the 19th century, many Mexican Americans attended Catholic schools or nonsectarian private schools to avoid the anti-Mexican attitudes of public school authorities (Spring, 2013). In California, some parents wanted a bilingual education for their children so they could have exposure to the cultural traditions of Mexico and Spain—while still learning English. Some local Mexican leaders in Santa Barbara were able to avoid the state requirement on teaching

English only and were able to establish a bilingual school. However, the majority of bilingual schools were maintained by the Catholic Church.

The great immigration of Mexicans into the United States during the early 20th century caused increasing discrimination and segregation. There were two conflicting attitudes toward educating children of immigrants. Farmers did not want Mexican children to attend school because it detracted away from them being able to perform farm work. Public school officials wanted Mexican children to attend school so they could be Americanized. Thus, schools did not enforce attendance laws for Mexican children. The education they received in segregated schools was similar to the education Native American received, in that they lost their customs, culture, and language. Texas passed laws with stricter requirements for the use of English in schools—making it a criminal offense to speak any other language. These laws required that teachers, principals, school board members, and superintendents use only English when working in the school.

In 1929, members from the Mexican American community met in Corpus Christi, Texas, to establish the League of United Latin American Citizens (LULAC). LULAC had a code that showed the desire of middle-class Mexican Americans to integrate the culture of Mexico with that of the United States (Spring, 2013). LULAC was committed to bilingualism and instruction in the cultural traditions of Mexico. It was also committed to fighting school segregation and discrimination. LULAC's first case involving school segregation occurred in 1928 when a child of unknown racial background, adopted by a Mexican family, was denied admission to a local Anglo elementary school. Her father wanted her to attend the Anglo school because of her unknown racial background. School officials justified school segregation of Mexican children because they required special instruction in English (Spring, 2013). This particular child spoke fluent English, so the state superintendent ordered the local school district to enroll the child in the Anglo school (Spring, 2013). LULAC's second case occurred in 1930 when the Del Rio, Texas, independent school district proposed a bond election to construct and improve school buildings (Spring, 2013). Although Mexican schools were included, Mexican American parents complained that the proposal continued the segregation of schools. The court cooperated with the local school district's arguments on segregation. LULAC also turned their attention to the anti-Mexican bias in textbooks, including the racism and the distortions of Mexicans in history. Changes in the textbooks did not occur, however, until the 1960s during the civil rights movement. The civil rights movement also brought the end of segregation of Mexican American students. In Puerto Rico, the following Americanization policies were put in effect in public schools (Spring, 2013):

1. The policy that requires celebration of U.S. patriotic holidays such as Fourth of July.
2. The Pledge of Allegiance to the U.S. flag and study of important historical figures to create allegiance to the United States.
3. The Americanizing of all textbooks used in Puerto Rican schools.
4. The expelling of teachers who engaged in anti-U.S. activities.
5. The use of teachers from the United States as opposed to local teachers.
6. Introduction to organizations such as Boy Scouts of America to promote allegiance to the United States.
7. The replacement of Spanish with English as the language of instruction.

Conclusion

By the 1830s the development of American public schools led to the concept of equality of opportunity, which meant that education should provide everyone with equality of opportunity to gain wealth (Spring, 2013). However, this equality of opportunity excluded African Americans, Native Americans, Asian Americans, and Hispanic/Latino Americans. In 1896, the *Plessy v. Ferguson* decision, while nominally about railroad cars, ratified the legitimacy of all forms of racial segregation throughout the nation, including in those states that practiced racial segregation in the schools, through its odious "separate, but equal" doctrine. This doctrine was overturned in 1954 by the *Brown v. Board of Education* decision. However, the problem of racially segregated schools still persists. Today, American educational policy seems to promote a de facto form of separate but equal even as such racial segregation is de jure illegal. Disappearing from the discourse about equality of opportunity are conversations about language and culture, a gap that our analysis intends to fill. The No Child Left Behind policy has caused a new generation of inequality within the schools, suggesting that the doctrine of separate but equal, while formally illegal, has nevertheless exerted its influence on the schools (Spring, 2013).

References

Militz-Frielink, S., Moore, A. L., & Neal, L. I. (2019). *Brown v. Board of Education* I. In J. Wilson (Ed.), *50 key events that shaped African American history: An encyclopedia of the American mosaic.* ABC-CLIO.

Spring, J. (2013). *Deculturalization and the struggle for equality: A brief history of the education of dominated cultures in the United States* (7th ed.). McGraw Hill.

The White Architects of Mexican American Education

David G. Garcia

> The ignorant are allowed to live and breed under conditions that become a threat and a menace to the welfare of the community. Many cases of filth and disease and contagion are found by us in the school work. We suggest to these Mexican people that they care for themselves, but they do nothing. The personal health of the Mexican children in the grammar school affects every child in the school.
>
> —Richard B. Haydock, January 31, 1917

In January 1917, school superintendent and city trustee Richard B. Haydock[1]

Richard B. Haydock served as inaugural president of the Oxnard City Board of Trustees and Oxnard's first mayor from 1903 to 1906, and simultaneously as superintendent of Oxnard schools from 1903 to 1907. He left these positions to work as school superintendent for Ventura, California, for four years. In 1911, he was reappointed as superintendent by the Oxnard School Board of Trustees, and held this position until his retirement from public service in June 1939. He also resumed service on the city board of trustees from about 1915 to 1919. See *Oxnard School District Board Members' Terms of Office*, Oxnard Elementary School District, Oxnard, CA, 2012–13; *City of Oxnard Elected Officials History, 1903–2014*, Office of the City Clerk, Oxnard, CA. John Steven McGroarty included Haydock in his

---

1. Epigraph: "Policewoman Graduate Nurse for City Health," *Oxnard Daily Courier,* January 31, 1917, front page.

volume of biographical sketches, noting that Haydock had served as an elected member of the Ventura County Board of Education in 1888, and had remained in that position for forty-five years. McGroarty further explained that Haydock was a "Royal Arch Mason and was master of the Oxnard Lodge, F. & A.M. in 1903" and credits Haydock for founding the local chapter of the Red Cross just after World War I. John Steven McGroarty, *California of the South: A History,* vol. 3 (Chicago: S. J. Clarke, 1933), 312–15. made a case for the appointment of a city policewoman deputy nurse, warning that the living conditions of Mexican families posed "a threat and a menace" to the larger school population. In December 1921, when he spoke to the Oxnard Rotary Club, Haydock framed his concerns about "local problems" with remarks about Blacks as a national problem, because, "be it ever so slight, even as in the octoroon, the unfortunate is still a negro.... Few men will say that the American for which we hope and pray can ever be made out of such stock."[2] These 1917 and 1921 newspaper accounts offer a unique vantage point from which to understand the collective project of White supremacy embedded in Oxnard's infrastructure and institutions from the city's founding.

As noted in the Introduction, the White architects of Mexican American education helped craft indelible patterns of racial segregation within and beyond schools.[3] For example, before establishing municipal elections, an elite group of White men appointed each other to serve on the Oxnard City Board of Trustees. Many of these powerbrokers served on the Oxnard School Board of Trustees and had connections with the town's main employer, the American Beet Sugar Company (ABSC).[4] Others conducted business with the schools, providing the land, building materials, and insurance for constructing and maintaining facilities. Some took on each of these roles simultaneously. White men also exerted influence as members of racially exclusive fraternal and civic organizations.[5] White women contributed to and led educational efforts, segregated social clubs, church activities, and volunteer organizations.[6] A small group of White women also wielded power as school leaders.[7]

2. "'Our Schools and the Future American': Principal R. B. Haydock Tells Rotary Club What He Thinks on This Subject," *The Oxnard Daily Courier,* December 30, 1921, front page. *The Oxnard Daily Courier* published his speech in four parts on December 29, 30, 31, 1921, and January 3, 1922.

3. I utilize here the concept originally put forward by William H. Watkins in *The White Architects of Black Education: Ideology and Power in America, 1865–1954* (New York: Teachers College Press, 2001).

4. The American Beet Sugar Company (ABSC) became the American Crystal Sugar Company in 1934 and remained in operation until 1958.

5. See, for example, Oxnard local fraternal organizations such as Elks Lodge, Masonic Temple, Knights of Columbus, and Rotary Club.

6. The *Oxnard Courier* often reported on women participating in social, civic, and charity club meetings. I did not find additional archival records for any individual women's clubs. According to newspaper accounts, a series of women's clubs were named after the day of the week they met (e.g., the Oxnard Monday Club held meetings at the Masonic Temple). Other clubs were directly linked to men's associations (e.g., the Women's Auxiliary of the American Legion). Wives of men who worked for the American Beet Sugar Company also figured centrally in Americanization efforts, aimed at Mexican adults, and in mobilizing playground activities for Mexican children. Women also led the Oxnard Parent-Teachers' Association, Catholic Women's Association, Campfire Council, and organized with social-civic organizations such as Oxnard Community Service.

7. These women were most often widowed or unmarried (see, for example, Ventura County superintendent of schools Blanche T. Reynolds, n132). School board records through the 1930s reference an internal policy in the Oxnard School District of encouraging women teachers and principals to resign once they were married.

Richard Thompson Ford has observed, "public policy and private actors operate together to create and promote racially identified space and the racial segregation that accompanies it."[8] This chapter's close examination of the White architects' public remarks and actions during Oxnard's formative years, from 1903 to 1930 in particular, demonstrates a carefully constructed, ideological architecture aimed to establish Whites at the top of a racial hierarchy. They sought to reproduce this hierarchy through the physical infrastructure of a city demarcated by racial spaces. They manufactured disparate schooling and housing conditions as a central component of these designs. West of Oxnard Boulevard and the railroad tracks meant White, first-class treatment and the promise of prosperity, while east meant Mexican, second-class treatment and little hope for social mobility.[9] The White architects' enactment of mundane racism shaped an interconnected residential and educational system of discrimination that persisted well beyond the 1930s.

In 1903, as the newly elected president of the city board of trustees (i.e., Oxnard's first mayor), Haydock began to oversee all aspects of city planning and school construction.[10] He led efforts to purposefully underdevelop what became the predominately Mexican east-side neighborhoods. He approved plans for substandard housing and neglected to extend basic municipal services such as sewage, electricity, and paved roads to this area. At the same time, he oversaw the development of upscale homes, a sewage and waste system, lighting, and street pavement for the west side of the city, where the White community lived.[11] He also helped plan and place the city's elementary schools west of the tracks, in close proximity to White

8. Richard Thompson Ford, "The Boundaries of Race: Political Geography in Legal Analysis," *Harvard Law Review* 107, no. 8 (1994): 1841–1921, 1845.
9. La Colonia was originally known as Colonia Home Gardens, a neighborhood that was bracketed by Third Street and Cooper Road. As it grew, other neighborhoods such as Ramona Home Gardens became connected to La Colonia. In accordance with how my interviewees referred to the neighborhood, I call the entire area by its popular name, La Colonia. See Map 1, page 38.
10. He was elected June 30, 1903. See City of Oxnard Board of Trustees Meeting Minutes, June 30, 1903, folder 07, file no. 00020476. See also a discussion of his role in building city infrastructure and institutions, in Madeline Miedema, "A Giant Step Forward: A History of the Oxnard Public Library, 1907–1992," *Ventura County Historical Society Quarterly* 37, no. 2 (1992): 3–46, 3.
11. Haydock and the city trustees considered west-side infrastructure actions necessary for the public good, in stark contrast to how they viewed the east side. Routine installation of electricity and paved roads exemplified this unequal treatment; for example, 1903 approval of electric lights to be placed in the alleys on blocks K and U, and installation of lights for the downtown plaza (see City of Oxnard Board of Trustees Meeting Minutes, September 29, 1903, folder OXFCC007, file no. 00020484); 1917 placement of light posts at Fifth and B streets, and at the Southern Pacific Railroad Station (City of Oxnard Board of Trustees Meeting Minutes, August 21, 1917, folder OXFCC006, file no. 00021029); 1921 approvals for lighting along north and south Fifth Street, and on A, B, and C streets—all west-side residential/business streets (City of Oxnard Board of Trustees Meeting Minutes, October 4, 1921, folder OXFCC006, file no. 00021165); and 1922 street improvement along Wooley Road, from the west line of Saviers Road to the east line of C Street, approved because the "public interest and convenience requires" (City of Oxnard Board of Trustees Meeting Minutes, December 19, 1922, folder OXFCC006, file no. 00021222). The city also approved payment for the costs of paving for the "public benefit" the residential area "Beginning on the west line of Saviers Road at the South east corner of Lot 1, Block 1, Wolff, Hill & Laubacher Subdivision" (City of Oxnard Board of Trustees Meeting Minutes, December 19, 1922, folder OXFCC006, file no. 00021223).

neighborhoods. Oxnard Grammar School was constructed in 1908,[12] on Third Street between A and B streets, and enrolled a predominately White student population.[13]

FIGURE 6.1.1   Oxnard Grammar School, circa 1908. Richard B. Haydock (top left corner). Courtesy of the Museum of Ventura County.

Though the school board began recording meetings in 1916, the minutes remain sparse until 1923, when trustees Ben S. Virden, Dr. Harry M. Staire, and Roy B. Witman expressed anxiety about overcrowding.[14] Newspapers and other materials offer insights about the development of the town and schools during this time. Haydock's 1917 remarks, for example, set out a seemingly objective motion for a deputy policewoman

12. Before this time, records indicate the San Pedro School functioned as the city's only school and had been in existence as early as 1870. See Helen Frost, *102 Year History of Oxnard School District* [pamphlet] (Oxnard, CA, 1975). On file with author.

13. The limited integration that did exist in Oxnard schools occurred only at the convenience of Whites and reinforced what Derrick Bell has identified as the "interest convergence" model. Bell conceived of this model in terms of the gains made from civil rights, with the *Brown v. Board* desegregation case as his main example. Applying his analysis to Oxnard, I found examples of "interest convergence" before *Brown* as well. See Derrick A. Bell, "*Brown v. Board of Education* and the Interest-Convergence Dilemma," *Harvard Law Review* 93, no. 3 (1980): 518–33.

14. Ben S. Virden, President, 1916–30; Dr. H. M. Staire, Clerk, 1916–25; Roy B. Witman, Clerk, 1920–34; see *Oxnard School District Board Members' Terms of Office*, Oxnard Elementary School District, Oxnard, CA, 2012–13. The newspaper lists Virden as president of the board in 1939, giving scholarship awards; "Commencement Speaker Urges Graduates to Turn to God to Make Them Stronger in Solving Civilization's Problems," *The Oxnard Daily Courier,* June 10, 1939, front page. Witman also served as chairman of the City Chamber of Commerce; *City of Oxnard Elected Officials History, 1903–2014,* Office of the City Clerk, Oxnard, CA.

nurse, but also offered an argument for segregation. Indeed, he complained, "these Mexican people" purposefully placed "every child in the school" at risk because of supposed contagious diseases. In his proposal to the city trustees, he noted, "We have laws to prevent the abuse of livestock ... but the people are allowed to abuse themselves."[15] In acknowledging that poor parents with sick children would likely not be able to access a doctor, he expressed tolerance for Mexicans. Still, he likened these families to livestock. The city trustees reviewed no actual evidence to corroborate Haydock's presumption of a health "menace" emanating from the Mexican children. Even so, they approved his motion for a deputy policewoman nurse and "insisted that she be able to speak Spanish."[16] Haydock patronizingly noted that if special instruction did not work, he could legally deny Mexican children access to schools altogether: "If possible, these people ought to be taught better. The law provides for the exclusion from school of children infected with a contagion. If we enforce this rule nothing is done for the children."[17] Haydock's claim to be flouting the law by allowing contagious children to attend school belied his role in ensuring the district's funding based on daily attendance, as Mexicans comprised at least 40 percent of elementary school enrollments.

About three weeks later, in February 1917, Haydock selected Policewoman Eloise M. Thornton, a graduate nurse who had "organized school nursing in the city of Los Angeles" and had experience working with police, health, and school departments as a "probation and humane officer."[18] Her appointment, "as a deputy marshal and a deputy health officer,"[19] reified the shared belief among the White architects that educating Mexican children required policing. These unexamined beliefs effectively criminalized Mexican children and their parents.

In 1916, the White architects, led by school superintendent and city trustee Haydock and the president of the school board of trustees and city treasurer Virden,[20] had overseen construction of a new school to accommodate a growing student population. In 1917, the school trustees officially named this facility the "Haydock Grammar School," supported by a petition organized by landowner Charles Donlon. Over thirty people signed the petition "in recognition of the long years of able, faithful, and efficient educational work [Haydock] has done in this community."[21] When the Richard B. Haydock School opened in March 1917, on the corner of Wooley Road and C Street, it enrolled approximately two hundred upper- and lower-grade elementary students who lived in "the south part of town."[22]

15. "Policewoman Graduate Nurse for City Health," *Oxnard Daily Courier*, January 31, 1917, front page.

16. Ibid.

17. Ibid.

18. "Experienced Policewoman Is Chosen," *Oxnard Courier*, February 23, 1917, 3. As a city trustee, Haydock had been authorized to select Thornton, and the chief of police made the official appointment.

19. "Policewoman Graduate Nurse for City Health," *Oxnard Daily Courier*, January 31, 1917, front page. Haydock asserted that the city required a professional nurse because the city health officer "was under no obligation to treat these people. It would take all his time if he attended to them."

20. Virden served as city treasurer, 1910–20; Haydock's city council service overlapped Virden's, from approximately 1915 to 1919 (see n1). See *City of Oxnard Elected Officials History, 1903–2014*, Office of the City Clerk, Oxnard, CA.

21. "Trustees Name New School Haydock Grammar School," *Oxnard Courier*, March 9, 1917, front page.

22. "Grammar Pupils in New Building," *Oxnard Courier*, March 9, 1917, 3. Haydock School enrollments initially included early elementary grades through eighth grade. By the 1950s, Haydock School was designated an intermediate school,

Local claims about Mexican children being a "menace" within schools reverberated with regional and national nativist arguments to halt immigration from Mexico altogether.[23] However, these voices conflicted with those of industrialists and growers, whose successful lobbying between 1917 and 1920 facilitated increases of over seventy-three thousand temporary Mexican immigrants and more than one hundred thousand permanent Mexican immigrants throughout the United States.[24] The very low wages paid to Mexican farmworkers and the seasonal availability of employment meant that families often worked together and followed the crop harvests. Men, women, and children worked in the fields.

Ventura County school officials encouraged such work, knowing that child labor laws exempted agricultural work and that compulsory education laws exempted children working in the fields.[25] For example, in May 1917, the *Oxnard Daily Courier* updated readers about the notices sent out by Ventura County school superintendent James E. Reynolds for assistance in harvesting crops, stating: "More than 300 families in Ventura [C]ounty have responded favorably…. High school children generally are likewise responding in good shape to the request of the officials for aid in harvesting the crops of the county."[26] While the top educational official in the county encouraged children working in the fields, other local officials expressed concern about Mexican children not attending school regularly.

When Policewoman Thornton outlined her initial work in January 1918, she "told of the necessity of keeping the children in school, of poor housing conditions, and advised that only English be spoken to the children."[27] These brief remarks foreshadowed the complex structural inequality shaping Mexican children's experiences, which would not be sufficiently addressed by a policewoman nurse. By August 1918, her report to the city trustees demonstrated she had accepted Haydock's approach to ignore the conditions shaping schooling experiences and focus on Mexican children as the problem. As she discussed her efforts in "Teaching Foreign Children Our Ways," Thornton took on some of Haydock's patronizing tone, remarking, "the Mexican must learn to keep his word if he expects to get help when he needs it…. He is slow to learn some things."[28]

Thornton stepped down from the position after about one year, citing that she could not sustain her own health while engaging in such a difficult job.[29] Haydock complained of the problems occurring in her

enrolling only seventh- and eighth-grade students. See details of enrollments at each school by year from 1916 through 1950 in "Attendance Registers by Years," Oxnard School District Archives, date unknown.

23. For example, Natalia Molina discusses how the case in Los Angeles of officials characterizing Mexicans as diseased, and treating health problems as a criminal matter, paralleled arguments put forward by proponents of restricting Mexican immigration on the floor of the U.S. Congress in 1924. Natalia Molina, *Fit to Be Citizens? Public Health and Race in Los Angeles, 1879–1939* (Berkeley: University of California Press, 2006).

24. Alfredo Mirandé, *Gringo Justice* (South Bend, IN: University of Notre Dame Press, 1987); Julian Samora, "Mexican Immigration," in *Mexican-Americans Tomorrow: Educational and Economic Perspectives,* edited by Gus Taylor (Albuquerque: University of New Mexico Press, 1975), 60–80.

25. Federal Writers' Project, "Child Labor in California Agriculture," *Monographs Prepared for a Documentary History of Migratory Farm Labor in California* [1938], California Digital Library.

26. "County Seat Notes: Harvest Aid," *Oxnard Daily Courier,* May 25, 1917, 3.

27. "To Make Americans of Foreign-Born," *The Oxnard Daily Courier,* January 10, 1918, front page.

28. "Teaching Foreign Children Our Ways," *The Oxnard Daily Courier,* August 8, 1918, front page.

29. "Oxnard Police Woman to Resign," *The Oxnard Daily Courier,* October 25, 1918, front page.

absence, "especially in connection with the grammar schools."[30] He noted several cases of "pinkeye" that caused students to be sent home from school, remarking: "If they had medical care, or any kind of attention … the children would soon be cured, and back to school. As it is they spread the disease and do not get cured easily."[31] Consistent with his previous comments, Haydock could barely muster empathy for the Mexican children, and remained principally focused on the average daily attendance funds these students represented.

Designing Poor Living and Health Conditions

Haydock, along with the other city trustees, actually contributed to the very conditions of "filth" they claimed occurred because of Mexican "ignorance." Two weeks after his motion for a policewoman nurse, in mid-February 1917, he and the city trustees confirmed street paving plans for the town. They purposefully designed the pavement plans to cover only the west side of Oxnard in the commercial and residential sections of the White community.[32] In the meantime, neither city nor school leaders made efforts to secure the safety of the Mexican children who walked daily on dirt- or mud-filled streets and across the railroad tracks to attend west-side schools. These actions and refusals to act exemplified the mundane disregard shown for the tax-paying Mexican community.

30. "Policewoman's Work Missed by Trustees," *The Oxnard Daily Courier,* September 3, 1919, front page.
31. Ibid.
32. "Street Paving Started; Will Cover West Side and Circle about the City," *Oxnard Daily Courier,* February 14, 1917, front page. The *Courier* wrote a special front-page note applauding the decision of the trustees, under the title "The Trustees Did Well." Two years later, the newspaper reported some of the ways priorities were also laid out within the west side: "Beside the pavement, which will cover all of the important residence and business streets, the other streets will be covered with crushed rock and made to harmonize with the rest of the city." "No Protests Filed against City Paving," *The Oxnard Daily Courier,* June 25, 1919, front page.

FIGURE 6.1.2A   West-side residences, Oxnard, circa 1920s. Courtesy of the Museum of Ventura County.

FIGURE 6.1.2B   East-side residences and outhouses off Fifth Street, Oxnard, circa 1940s. Courtesy of the Museum of Ventura County.

Another example came with the flu of 1918, when the newspaper confirmed that Mexicans were not admitted to St. John's Hospital west of the tracks. On November 4, 1918, *The Oxnard Daily Courier* reported front-page health updates about White residents recovering from the flu at St. John's Hospital, and in the next column over announced that Police Chief Murray had opened a "temporary city detention hospital to care for Mexicans stricken with the 'flu.'"[33] Reportedly, in a building on Seventh and Meta streets, east of the boulevard, "homeless and helpless" Mexican flu victims lay on donated cots and bedding, while Murray and an untrained, unnamed male citizen volunteer administered "heroic measures."[34] The article further noted that in the first night the makeshift facility served five patients, though one died because "some were too far gone.... The 'hospital' has been needed badly for several days."[35]

The same night the "hospital" opened, the city trustees directed firemen to wash some of the west-side streets and sidewalks, "as a precautionary health measure."[36] The following week, the superintendent of streets, Charles Green, received the assistance of "some 12 or 14 Mexicans" to clean "the alleys in the Mexican section of the city as a precaution against the spread of influenza, through unnecessary filth."[37] Praising their volunteerism, the newspaper recognized that "a great many Mexicans since the influenza

33. "Temporary Hospital Opened," *The Oxnard Daily Courier,* November 4, 1918, front page.
34. Ibid.
35. Ibid.
36. "Firemen Make Clean City Streets," *The Oxnard Daily Courier,* November 4, 1918, front page.
37. "Mexicans Assist City Officers," *The Oxnard Daily Courier,* November 12, 1918, front page.

epidemic started have been doing splendid work in co-operating with the city authorities."[38] The article did not explain why the city trustees directed firemen to clean the paved streets on the west side of town and left Green alone to sanitize the dirt alleys on the east side. This lack of explanation, and the evidence of Mexicans working to compensate for the lack of city resources or personnel hours, reflects the commonly held understanding that the east side simply would not receive the same treatment as the west side. City and school leaders rarely made public statements justifying this disparate treatment, but when they did, they usually identified Mexicans themselves as the problem. This attribution of blame functioned to absolve the companies recruiting and profiting from the low-wage labor Mexicans provided.[39]

In October 1919, the city's newly hired policewoman nurse, Mrs. May Webb, continued this pattern of casually blaming Mexicans regardless of the facts. She complained almost immediately of the conditions on the east side of town that she believed contributed to a potential health disaster: "If typhoid fever ever broke out in your city I don't see where it would stop on account of these swarms of flies," she declared, detailing, "the conditions here that draw flies and breed flies are 'simply terrible.'"[40] She publicly critiqued "housing conditions in some of the poorer quarters" as "terribly bad," and reminded the trustees that these problems lay "only two blocks from the main part of your city."[41] She also observed "bad" conditions west of the tracks, on C Street, and asserted, "You spend plenty of money … you have a good man on the job. It must be the fault of your people."[42] While detailing her observations, she expressed frustration that while she had expected to be a "nurse inspector," her work in Oxnard took on "more of a social service nature, to teach not only the minds but also the five senses," and "to teach common sense."[43] She condescendingly remarked, "Getting hold of the ever elusive Mexican children, whose parents have no conception whatever of the need of their children going to school," required her to be more of a truant officer than a nurse.[44]

Webb's claim that Mexicans were a problem shifted attention away from the infrastructure issues she had just outlined and back onto familiar ideological territory. In response, the city trustees took some blame for the "torn-up condition of the streets due to paving and gas improvements [on the west side]"[45] and thanked Policewoman Webb for her report. With their silence about the east side, they endorsed Webb's reasoning that lack of "common sense" on the part of Mexicans caused the "terribly bad" conditions.[46]

As Natalia Molina has explained, "Portraying people of Chinese, Mexican, and Japanese ancestry in Los Angeles as threats to public health and civic well-being obscured the real causes of communicable disease

38. Ibid.
39. In his research observations and oral history interviews throughout California and the Southwest, Paul S. Taylor identified patterns of company neglect fostering unsanitary conditions. He also found extensive evidence of Mexicans taking initiative to improve their living conditions through daily cleaning rituals, including sweeping and cleaning dirt floors, creatively insulating tents and wooden shacks, and taking full advantage of any available bathing facilities. Paul S. Taylor, *Mexican Labor in the United States,* vol. 1 (Berkeley: University of California Press, 1930), 58.
40. "Says Flies Are Bad in This City," *The Oxnard Daily Courier,* October 15, 1919, front page.
41. Ibid.
42. Ibid.
43. Ibid.
44. Ibid.
45. Ibid.
46. Ibid.

and illness—inadequate medical care, exposure to raw sewage, and malnutrition."[47] In Oxnard, as in Los Angeles and elsewhere, such institutionalized neglect toward Mexicans did not go unchallenged.

About a week after Policewoman Webb's report, at an October 1919 meeting of the Monday Club, Charles H. Weaver, an ABSC representative, discussed newly built houses for "foreign laborers,"[48] and work to promote Americanization by developing "a better understanding between the laborer and the beet growers."[49] Weaver's remarks about the "industrial standpoint" echoed the ABSC directive from the previous July, which had instructed factory managers and supervisors to treat the Mexican sugar-beet workers well, so they would continue to stay "loyal employees."[50] His anecdotal observation of "the necessity of these foreigners being taught some idea of thrift"[51] exposed the paternalistic approach of the ABSC. At the same meeting, Father Gorman spoke on behalf of Father Ramirez, a priest working "among the people of his nationality here in Oxnard," to convey his colleague's concern for "the necessity of understanding these people before you could expect to help them to become good American citizens."[52] Ramirez's call foreshadowed collective efforts to improve living conditions by working "among" Mexicans. This contrasted with Weaver's call for understanding "between" the sugar-beet workers and their supervisors, which reified the unequal power dynamics between Mexicans and Whites. Such tensions of race and class, east and west, intensified as the Mexican population continued to grow in the city and schools.

Mexican labor indeed fueled tremendous growth and profit in the agricultural economy. Restrictions on Japanese and Chinese immigration and land ownership, and the revolution in Mexico, all contributed to higher numbers of Mexicans working in Ventura County fields, burgeoning packinghouses, and canneries.[53]

47. Molina, *Fit to Be Citizens?*, 2.

48. The Oxnard Monday Club appears to have been a group of women who met regularly on Mondays. In line with nationwide organized efforts to Americanize immigrants, their discussions, according to the newspaper, emphasized local and regional Americanization efforts. "Good Talk on Americanization," *The Oxnard Daily Courier*, October 21, 1919, "Society" page.

49. Ibid.

50. American Beet Sugar Company Agricultural Meeting Minutes, July 22, 1918; thank you to Frank P. Barajas for sharing this memo. Similarly, as Jeffrey Garcilazo explains in his study of Mexican railroad workers, companies such as Southern Pacific Railroad provided a "free-rent" housing incentive and encouraged men to bring their families to elicit a loyal, stable workforce. Jeffrey Garcilazo, "Traqueros: Mexican Railroad Workers in the United States, 1870–1930" (Ph.D. dissertation, University of California, Santa Barbara, 1995).

51. "Good Talk on Americanization," *The Oxnard Daily Courier*, October 21, 1919, "Society" page.

52. Ibid.

53. For further discussion of these laws, see Tomás Almaguer, *Racial Fault Lines: The Historical Origins of White Supremacy in California* (Berkeley: University of California Press, 1994); Molina, *Fit to Be Citizens?* The Chinese Exclusion Act of 1882 established a moratorium on immigration of Chinese workers, a ban that remained in effect until 1943; the 1907–8 Gentlemen's Agreement between the United States and Japan was a treaty wherein the Japanese government agreed to deny Japanese laborers passports to the United States and the latter agreed to end an anti-Asian school ordinance in San Francisco; the Alien Land Acts of 1913 and 1920 aimed to prohibit Asian immigrants from owning land, or leasing it longer than three years in the state of California. For more on the revolution in Mexico, see Devra Weber, *Dark Sweat, White Gold: California Farm Workers, Cotton, and the New Deal* (Berkeley: University of California Press, 1994). The number of Japanese residents in Ventura County decreased from 872 in 1910 to 675 in 1920. Similarly, the number of Chinese residents decreased from 235 in 1910 to 155 in 1920. Mexicans were not disaggregated from the Whites until the 1930 census, though the number of foreign-born from Mexico does provide some insight about immigration during these

U.S. Census records for Ventura County estimated that the population increased from 18,347 residents in 1910 to 28,724 in 1920.[54] During that same time, the city of Oxnard grew from a population of 2,555 to 4,417.[55] Historian Juan Gómez-Quiñones has noted that the peak in emigration from Mexico to the United States in the 1920s intensified anti-immigrant and "anti-Mexican rhetoric."[56]

In Oxnard, Whites employed anti-Mexican rhetoric when alluding to problematic social issues emanating from the east-side area, including hygiene and truancy. Without acknowledging the vested interest in maintaining the west side as exclusively White, these complaints about the Mexican community inadvertently exposed strategically constructed substandard housing east of the boulevard. The crescendo of voices blaming Mexicans as a problem in the 1920s enabled school officials to feverishly work toward complete segregation of Mexican children the following decade without any public rationalization.

Women of the Red Cross: "We Are Afraid of Nobody"

One notable challenge to the city trustees' refusal to understand and respond to the Mexican community's perspectives occurred during a "decidedly interesting and tense" half-hour meeting in 1920 between three women of the local Red Cross and the city trustees. Led by Mrs. Frank McCulloch, and including Miss Garrison, a nurse, and Mrs. Parker, an interpreter, these women had spoken with Mexican residents over a three-week period, as they had inspected each home and alley in the east-side area. They reported "terrible" housing conditions endured by Mexican laborers and their families.[57] The newspaper detailed, "Needless to say they found lots of vermin, lots of flies and intolerable sanitary conditions in many places. But the good of the trip was found in the willingness on the part of the Spanish speaking population to co-operate with the Red Cross ladies, when they were shown how."[58] Here the reporter assumed most readers knew of the poor

years. U.S. Bureau of the Census, *U.S. Census of the Population: 1930*, "Population, California, Table 17. Indians, Chinese and Japanese 1910 to 1930 and Mexicans, 1930 for Counties and for Cities of 25,000 or More" (Washington, DC: U.S. Government Printing Office, 1930), 266.

54. U.S. Bureau of the Census, *U.S. Census of the Population: 1930*, "Population, California, Table 4. Population of Counties by Minor Civil Divisions: 1930, 1920, and 1910" (Washington, DC: U.S. Government Printing Office, 1930), 140.

55. U.S. Bureau of the Census, *U.S. Census of the Population: 1950*, "California, Table 4. Population of Urban Places of 10,000 or More from the Earliest Census to 1950" (Washington, DC: U.S. Government Printing Office, 1950), 5–10.

56. Juan Gómez-Quiñones, *Mexican American Labor, 1790–1990* (Albuquerque: University of New Mexico Press, 1994), 104. The U.S. Census counted 33,444 foreign-born Mexicans living in California in 1910, and that number increased to 86,610 by 1920. U.S. Bureau of the Census, *U.S. Census of the Population: 1940*, "California, Table 15. Foreign-Born White, 1910–1940 and Total Foreign-Born, 1850–1900, by Country of Birth, for the State" (Washington, DC: U.S. Government Printing Office, 1940), 533.

57. "Red Cross Makes Move for Better Housing Conditions," *The Oxnard Daily Courier,* October 27, 1920, front page, 2. The city trustees recorded McCulloch's appearance at their meeting on September 21, 1920, with a note that she represented the local Red Cross with a "request for advice and assistance in combating the presence of vermin among some of the Mexican population." The minutes indicate McCulloch was referred to the health officer for action. City of Oxnard Board of Trustees Meeting Minutes, September 21, 1920, folder 07, file no. 00021135. An October presentation by the three women was not found in the city trustee minutes.

58. "Red Cross Makes Move for Better Housing Conditions," *The Oxnard Daily Courier,* October 27, 1920, front page, 2.

living conditions east of the boulevard (likely the Meta Street neighborhood) and presumed few would have considered the Mexican community's willingness to collaborate in forging a remedy.

The women described that a ditch on Eighth Street had become an open garbage dump, and that they gave instructions to the residents about how to cover the ditch and clean the area. They also instructed about sixty children how to dispose of the vermin in and around the dump. Considered in retrospect, this visceral detail exposed the city powerbrokers as "a threat and a menace" to Mexican schoolchildren, not the reverse, as Haydock had claimed a few years prior. As the Red Cross representatives expressed enthusiasm for the immediate, "gratifying results" of their visits, they framed the problem as one of inferior conditions, not inferior Mexican culture. McCulloch stated, "Recently we have been hearing lots about Americanization work among the foreigners ... but there is also lots to be done in Americanization with Americans, and that is where the work should start."[59] She went on to explain, "When the Mexicans were asked why they did not go to the landlord to have a window pane replaced, and sometimes all the window panes were found broken, and the holes nailed up but one, leaving the room dark and dismal, they were told that these tenants were afraid to ask for repairs, because when they did they often failed to get them, but the rent would be raised forthwith."[60] After confirming that she and the other women had the receipts of these higher rent bills in their possession, she continued: "All that these people want is to be shown how to be sanitary and to be treated like human beings. Treated in this way they respond, and it is up to the property owners to improve the conditions. We expect to notify the owners of the needed improvements, and will see to it that they make the places fit for human beings. We are no respecter of persons ... and we are afraid of nobody."[61]

Boldly asserting the human rights of Mexicans, McCulloch warned that she and her colleagues would not be intimidated in demanding safe, sanitary living conditions. The city trustees gave these women a few opportunities to demonstrate whether they indeed would back down. For instance, Nurse Garrison stated that within the adobe housing units of the ABSC, only three of the twenty-four toilets "were in good condition," and that during their visit they came across "a dead man, and the flies were bad."[62] City trustee Weaver, an ABSC supervisor, reportedly "arose a little hot under the collar" to challenge Garrison. He argued that the state inspectors "frequently commended the company for the way they looked after conditions there."[63] He suggested the responsibility for the nonworking toilets and the festering dead body lay with the residents, who, he reiterated, were provided housing without charge, exclaiming they lived "rent absolutely free."[64] The women of the Red Cross recognized that the ABSC intended to provide screens for the ABSC homes and that the city trustees planned for garbage removal, but they persisted in their critique, reiterating they would seek a remedy directly from the state housing commission if necessary.[65]

59. Ibid.
60. Ibid.
61. Ibid.
62. Ibid.
63. Ibid.
64. Ibid.
65. In contrast to trustee Charles Weaver and Mayor Herbert H. Eastwood, the city health officer, Dr. G. A. Boughton, offered "a word of praise" for the Red Cross women's efforts, noting he had convinced them to present to the city trustees first, before taking the case to the state housing commission. Ibid.

Mayor Herbert H. Eastwood positioned himself as unable to mitigate the situation, suggesting that the city trustees had no legal power to regulate housing conditions.[66] He also argued that landlords had their share of "troubles" attempting multiple times a month to collect rent on each residence. McCulloch countered, "Considering the investment made $3 a month on many of those shacks was big returns," and gave an example of "one small lot that brought the owner $25 a month in small rentals like that."[67] These interactions shed light on the city trustees' profit-driven paternalism, enabling overcrowded, "intolerable sanitary conditions" for Mexican residents. The city trustees, led by Mayor Eastwood, empathized with the landlords because they too were White landowners, real estate developers, growers, and representatives of the ABSC. They shared the perspective that Mexicans should be grateful for a job that provided them housing "rent absolutely free."[68] There is no record of Mayor Eastwood or the city trustees following through with their promise to review a list of offending landlords or to cooperate with the Red Cross efforts. A few months later, in February 1921, McCulloch resigned from "all committees of the local Red Cross and welfare work of the community on account of her [own] ill health."[69]

Haydock's "Future American"

Like Mayor Eastwood and the city trustees, Haydock exhibited a disregard for Mexicans. He reiterated these sentiments in a 1921 speech to the Oxnard Rotary Club.[70] Because his educational philosophy was not publicly recorded elsewhere, Haydock's 1921 remarks merit focused analysis. In line with the arguments of "scientific" racism and the eugenics movement,[71] he began with an assertion that the Puritans who landed on Plymouth Rock, Massachusetts, were "representative of the stock from which the pure American breed

---

66. Herbert H. Eastwood served as a city trustee from 1909 to 1920 and 1936–42. He served as mayor from 1920 to 1926 and 1942–44. *City of Oxnard Elected Officials History, 1903–2014*, Office of the City Clerk, Oxnard, CA.

67. "Red Cross Makes Move for Better Housing Conditions," *The Oxnard Daily Courier*, October 27, 1920, front page, 2.

68. Ibid.

69. "Mrs. McCulloch Quits Account Her Health," *The Oxnard Daily Courier*, February 2, 1921, front page.

70. "'Our Schools and the Future American': Principal R. B. Haydock Tells Rotary Club What He Thinks on This Subject," *The Oxnard Daily Courier*, December 29, 1921, 2. The Oxnard Rotary Club was founded in 1920 and met weekly for dinner.

71. Haydock's words here echoed those of then–Stanford professor Lewis Terman, who had been applying French psychologist Alfred Binet's intelligence tests to identify the mental age, or intelligence quotient, of school children. In his 1916 book Terman asserted: "Cases … which test at high-grade moronity or at border-line … represent the level of intelligence which is very, very common among Spanish-Indian and Mexican families of the Southwest and also among negroes. Their dullness seems to be racial, or at least inherent in the family stocks from which they come" (91). Haydock's efforts to segregate Mexicans ran consistent with his words, but he never publicly rationalized his actions explicitly. In contrast, Terman publicly advocated: "Children of this group should be segregated in special classes and be given instruction which is concrete and practical. They cannot master abstractions, but they can often be made efficient workers, able to look out for themselves. There is no possibility at the present of convincing society that they should not be allowed to reproduce, although from a eugenic point of view they constitute a grave problem because of their unusually prolific breeding" (92). Lewis M. Terman, *The Measurement of Intelligence: An Explanation of and a Complete Guide for the Use of the Standard Revision and Extension of the Binet-Simon Intelligence Scale* (Boston: Houghton Mifflin, 1916), 91–92.

has sprung."[72] He referenced previous Rotarian discussions to explain that creating and maintaining the "purest breed" of dairy calves with "unquestioned pedigree" required a significant financial investment and the collective will to do so. He then connected this idea to schooling, assuring the audience that while he would support each child's aspirations, he also recognized that "some of these kids are going to become valuable assets, and some are going to become mighty expensive liabilities."[73] To drive home his point about the public's will to pay for high-quality education as one of the many challenges facing schools, he asserted, "The better the breed, the bigger and better the returns in every aspect."[74]

Haydock then discussed a recent report indicating that New Bedford, Massachusetts, had the country's highest rate of illiteracy. Referring to U.S. census data for 1919 and recalling his own trip to Boston a few years prior, he attributed the illiteracy rate to the influx of "foreigners" who did not speak English. He worried about the future of schooling in the United States given these realities: "I tell you it brings a touch of sadness to the man who traces his American ancestry back to preRevolutionary days; and it must bring misgivings to every American, even by adoption, who looks forward with real interest into the future of his country and its institutions."[75]

After these comments, he transitioned from the eastern region to the South, reflecting on the legacy of African slavery for the southern states and for the nation. He argued that the struggle to end slavery represented a "glorious victory for human rights," but warned, "Unto the last generation the sins of our forefathers will rest upon our children." To further this point, he explained:

> More than fifty years have elapsed since the black man was freed; yet a full billion dollars of the cost are charged on the books of the government against you and me. But that sinks into insignificance when we think of the more than seventeen millions of sons and daughters of these former slaves who are still with us and whose children will be with us to the end. What would we not give if the whole horrible story could be wiped out! How gladly would we double of [sic] treble the cost of the civil war if we could but remove every trace of Ethiopian blood from out [sic] national life. Be it ever so slight, even as in the octoroon, the unfortunate is still a negro. Regrettable as this may be, it is nevertheless a fact. Few men will say that the American for which we hope and pray can ever be made out of such stock—that there can ever be a perfect fusion of black and white. And these few, if there can be any such, will not attempt to gainsay we have been set back generations in the development of our race and nation.[76]

While conveniently omitting the tremendous socioeconomic gains Whites and the country realized from slavery, he expressed fidelity to the concept of segregation, noting the futility of educating Blacks, or

---

72. "'Our Schools and the Future American': Principal R. B. Haydock Tells Rotary Club What He Thinks on This Subject," *The Oxnard Daily Courier,* December 29, 1921, 2.

73. Ibid.

74. Ibid.

75. Ibid., 3.

76. Ibid.

integrating them with Whites in the hopes of a "perfect fusion."[77] Why Haydock went into such detail about Blacks when there were only eight Black school-age children in the district at the time remains unclear. His racist remarks, however, expose the ideology undergirding his actions as a city and school official. Rather than make an explicit connection to Mexican children, he utilized these remarks to frame his subsequent discussion of "strictly local issues."[78]

Haydock asked his fellow Rotarians for their patience as he recounted figures of inconsistent attendance and low achievement, implying as a matter of fact that Mexicans were to blame for these patterns. He reported that he and the teachers had conducted a district-wide census of all the children ages three to seventeen in October 1920,[79] and found that of the 1,345 children counted, Whites comprised 53 percent and Blacks, Chinese, Japanese, and Mexicans made up 47 percent.[80] He further disaggregated these numbers to emphasize that Mexicans comprised 41 percent of the student population and that 60 percent of children ages three to seventeen had parents born outside the United States. "In other words," he explained, "the children whom it is our duty to prepare for American citizenship are preponderantly of foreign born parentage."[81] This highlighted the contrast between Haydock, who traced his "American ancestry back to preRevolutionary days," and the ostensibly foreign origins of most of the elementary schoolchildren in Oxnard.

Presenting anecdotal observations and "figures" as objective facts, Haydock noted cases of head lice, irregular attendance, and "retarded" promotion patterns—all problems supposedly attributed to Mexican children. Beyond this speech, public records fail to record any rationale for school segregation. Instead, Haydock and the other architects segregated Mexican children as a mundane practice. He concluded his speech by calling for Whites to pass on a hard work ethic to their boys: "We must teach the dignity of labor. We must do more than teach it: we must give it dignity; we must live it."[82] Haydock's "racially charged vision"[83] for education did not appear to extend dignity to Mexican laborers or their children.

77. Ibid.

78. Ibid.

79. As he described the difficult task of the teachers engaged in mapping out the district into twenty sections, he noted, "In many instances, parents could not speak English, they did not even know the ages of the children, and it was impossible to get absolutely accurate information." "'Our Schools and the Future American': Principal R. B. Haydock Tells Rotary Club What He Thinks on This Subject," *The Oxnard Daily Courier,* December 31, 1921, 6.

80. Ibid. He reported, "716 are classed as White, 8 are classed as Black, 23 are classed as Chinese, 42 are classed as Japanese, 551 are classed as Mexican."

81. Ibid. Of the children, he remarked, "1063 are native born, 282 are foreign born."

82. Ibid.

83. See Molina, *Fit to Be Citizens?,* where she explains that in Los Angeles, public health officials determined "who was healthy enough to work or attend public school ... [and] not only incorporated their racially charged visions into policies and ordinances that targeted ethnic communities but also helped shape the ways mainstream populations perceived ethnic peoples" (2–3).

The Mexican Community Takes Collective Action

About five months later, a group of thirty-three Colonia residents further exposed the institutionalized indifference toward Mexicans when they requested the city to move the dump away from their neighborhood. The newspaper reprint of their petition confirmed the Red Cross women's prior statement that when "treated like human beings" Mexicans would "respond."

> Oxnard, Calif., June 1, 1922.
>
> Members of the Oxnard City Council.
>
> Gentlemen—We, the undersigned, residents and taxpayers of the city of Oxnard, and living in that section known as Colonia Home Gardens, due west and north of the city dumping grounds, do hereby respectfully petition the city council of Oxnard to declare the present city dumping grounds a public nuisance, unsanitary, and menacing to the health of the inhabitants in its near vicinity, and menacing as well to our livestock and garden plants, both of which are vitally essential and necessary to our peaceful endeavor of earning our living and sustaining the health of ourselves, our wives, our children, and others who may abide with us.
>
> Not only has the city of Oxnard outgrown its present dumping facility, necessitating an immediate removal from its present location, but we declare said dumping ground unsightly, a breeder of disease, a menace to the health and to the moral stability of contentment to residents nearby. We therefore respectfully ask that the city council appoint a committee to investigate the truth of our grievance and to act upon our suggestion and the results of your committee's investigation with American fairness and Christian sympathy.
>
> *Signed, V. Zarate, C. Soutana, Juan Martinez, Jose Roduarte, Joes Martinez, Makule Chavez, Pedro Herrera, Cecilio Ybarro, Otancio Nilo, Jesus Morales, Fernando Jabalos, Jose Romero, Reyes Landon, Chas Martel, Pete Marrie, Y. Rubio, Josephine Andrade, Camile Herrera, Santiago Meredez, E. Rubio, A. Leon, Mrs. M. Silveria, Serapio Rivay, Pans Padille, Gil Razo, Jose Ramirez, Aurelio Moreno, John V. Sotelo, Amador Jimenez, Patricio Martinez, O. Cortez, Daniel Mendosa, Rito Gonzalez.*
>
> After note—the above signatures are only those who are not living on the aforesaid tract. There is almost double the number who have lots and who will all, in the very near future make their residence with the others who have signed.[84]

Inserting their voices into the public record about living conditions in La Colonia, these Mexican women and men strategically asserted themselves as a legitimate, financially contributing, and demographically

---

84. "Colonia Gardens Folk Petition City Dads to Change City Dump," *The Oxnard Daily Courier*, June 22, 1922, front page. Spelling errors in original (e.g., Joes Martinez was Jose Martinez).

significant part of Oxnard. While the newspaper condescendingly headlined their letter "Colonia Gardens Folk Petition City Dads to Change City Dump,"[85] they positioned themselves as taxpayers and residents who requested consideration as equal citizens pursuing the "peaceful endeavor of earning our living and sustaining the health of ourselves, our wives, our children." These women and men understood the racial hierarchy, which identified Mexicans as the source of the problems in La Colonia. Their petition posed a direct challenge to Haydock's 1917 call for a policewoman nurse because Mexicans, he claimed, would otherwise "become a threat and a menace to the welfare of the community."[86] They declared the dumping facility as the "menace" to their "health and moral stability" and proposed that an investigation would corroborate their claims. Whereas Haydock had referred to Mexicans as livestock, the petitioners asserted their humanity, describing the dump as a threat to their livestock and livelihood. They also appealed to the moral conscience of the city trustees, requesting timely consideration based on "American fairness and Christian sympathy."[87] To avoid dismissal of their request as a concern of a small minority, the petitioners noted that imminent population growth in the area necessitated urgent action.

While it remains unclear whether the petition successfully elicited enough "American fairness and Christian sympathy" from the city trustees to remove the city dump from La Colonia,[88] a few months later, in December 1922, the newspaper confirmed persistent substandard conditions east of the railroad tracks: "Residents of the Colonia Home Gardens on the east side of the railroad tracks north of the Oxnard Municipal water works will soon have water service.... The W. H. Lathrop piece, between the Colonia subdivision and the railroad tracks will also be piped for water ... the work of laying the pipes and putting in connections has just started.... The residents of that section are to pay for the installation of the pipe. They are still without electric service or sewerage."[89] The article offered no explanation for why the city trustees held east-side residents financially responsible, above and beyond their taxes, for infrastructure projects the city fully subsidized for west-side residents. Records confirm that developers such as Walter H. Lathrop, who also served as a city trustee,[90] extended basic amenities to La Colonia only when profitable. As the demand for labor and subsequent need for housing continued to increase, the geographic containment of Mexicans east of the tracks became more complicated.

Segregated Playgrounds

In addition to segregating Mexican families geographically, Whites sought ways to socially contain Mexican children through playground activities. In May 1923, the newspaper reported on plans for Oxnard Community

85. Ibid.
86. "Policewoman Graduate Nurse for City Health," *Oxnard Daily Courier*, January 31, 1917, front page.
87. "Colonia Gardens Folk Petition City Dads to Change City Dump," *The Oxnard Daily Courier*, June 22, 1922, front page.
88. The city trustees noted receipt of the petition from the Colonia Gardens residents and indicated deliberation would follow to plan mitigation of the problems identified from the dumping site, but a record of such action was not found. City of Oxnard Board of Trustees Meeting Minutes, June 20, 1922, folder 07, file no. 00021194.
89. "Colonia Home Gardens Being Piped for Water," *The Oxnard Daily Courier*, December 1, 1922, front page.
90. Walter Lathrop served on the city board of trustees from 1914 to 1916. *City of Oxnard Elected Officials History, 1903–2014*, Office of the City Clerk, Oxnard, CA.

Service to train "play leaders" from cities throughout Ventura County in "an all-round program of community recreation."[91] The wives of many city leaders, including Mrs. Matthew Lehmann, Mrs. Henry Levy, Mrs. Charles Donlon, and Mrs. Rudolph Beck, simultaneously announced that Community Service would initiate "recreation for women and girls."[92] These committees adapted regional programming that ensured leisure activities would be racially distinct for Whites and Mexicans.[93]

For example, a few months later, in July 1923, Mrs. Charles Weaver, who had previously led an ABSC Americanization committee, proclaimed that in response to a needs assessment survey of the Mexican community, and "in connection with the playground movement now underway in Oxnard," she would "organize a class in games and story-telling for Mexican children."[94] In 1924, Community Service established a dedicated recreational space on the corner of Saviers Road and Sixth Street, which reportedly attracted about two hundred children on an average day, even before the construction of a playground apparatus.[95] This was commonly known as the Mexican playground. Within three years, the ABSC donated land on Seventh Street to move and expand the space for inclusion of *rebote* (handball) courts, baseball stops, and a "play apparatus."[96]

For Mexicans, the playground became a site for community building and organizing.[97] The board of directors of Community Service elected Mexican men as playground directors, and Mexican residents volunteered for the tasks of building, maintaining, moving, and cleaning the playground.[98] They requested support to utilize the outdoor recreational areas for community musical endeavors, which led to the creation

91. (Oxnard) Community Service was sponsored by the city government and responsible for community affairs, including the city's parks and recreation activities. "Special Classes in Playground Activity to Be Started Here," *The Oxnard Daily Courier,* May 24, 1923, front page.

92. "Recreation for Women and Girls Is Plan of Community Ser. Here," *The Oxnard Daily Courier,* May 22, 1923, front page.

93. The article specified, "The Americanization group met again just days later to discuss the applicability of Santa Barbara's programming in domestic science and art ... cultivating artistic talent in basketry, pottery, clay modeling." "Americanization Group of Community Service to Meet This Evening," *The Oxnard Daily Courier,* May 29, 1923, front page.

94. "To Include Mexicans in Playground Work," *The Oxnard Daily Courier,* July 17, 1923, front page.

95. "Children Show Great Interest in Community Playground Activities," *The Oxnard Daily Courier,* June 27, 1924, front page. The article discussed A. Martinez's leadership in chairing "the committee for Mexican recreation," which indicates the site attracted Mexican youth and adults well beyond Oxnard as well. For example, the reporter noted plans to install bleachers in advance of a countywide *rebote* contest, from which winners would participate in a Los Angeles state championship. This even aimed to contribute to funds for a playground apparatus. The article also mentioned the formation of several boys' baseball teams, the scheduling of games for a junior playground championship, and the beginning of a class for "the study of community singing and harmony."

96. "City Guests Cleaning 7th Street Playground," *The Oxnard Daily Courier,* June 23, 1927, front page. The article detailed, "A. L. Sexton, caretaker of the community center, is supervising a committee of guests of the city jail in renovating the grounds."

97. See "Mexicans from Many Colonies Organize," *The Oxnard Daily Courier,* May 12, 1924, front page; "Mexicans Offer Aid in Making City Law Abiding Community," *The Oxnard Daily Courier,* May 15, 1924, front page. For more on Mexican participation in recreation and on Americanization for Mexican adults in Oxnard, see Frank P. Barajas, *Curious Unions: Mexican American Workers and Resistance in Oxnard, California, 1898–1961* (Lincoln: University of Nebraska Press, 2012), 111–30.

98. "A labor day for the Mexicans is to be established.... [W]ith the aid of the Spanish ladies' lodge they will be served with refreshment while they work." "New Saviers Road Playground Presents Busy Scene Today," *The Oxnard Daily Courier,* January 30, 1924, front page.

of a successful Mexican band, comprising men who labored in the sugar factory, and a Mexican girls' chorus.[99] Here men, women, and children cultivated their artistic talents and athletic skills and interacted in competitive and collaborative ways, beyond their roles as laborers.

For Whites, the space ensured the social separation of Mexican children from their own. Public writings about the Mexican playground suggest that Whites framed their efforts in supporting segregated recreational activities as altruistic contributions to pluralism. Tam Deering, a secretary of Oxnard Community Service, wrote in a nationally circulated magazine that the idea for the playground built on efforts "to overcome the indifference and more or less ill-feeling on the part of the Anglo-Americans toward the Mexicans."[100] He went on to critique "superficial methods of past Americanization work," noting that a more effective "means for fostering cooperation between the Anglo-Americans and Latin-Americans in Oxnard is to be found in the leisure time activities."[101] Six months later, in February 1924, the newspaper boasted that Oxnard Community Service had received national recognition by the Elks organization for playground activities, which ostensibly reduced crime:

> Oxnard, California, in the sugar beet section, has a bit of a problem in its Mexican inhabitants. Strangers in a land that was once theirs, they spent most of their leisure hours in poolrooms or the police court, until someone had the idea of building a court for their favorite game of rebote, the Mexican version of handball. Now the Mexican interpreters [*sic*] in the courts is on a permanent vacation and the beet growers go to the rebote courts instead of the employment agencies for extra men when harvest time comes around.[102]

Published as front-page news in *The Oxnard Daily Courier*, this article, touting recognition by a racially exclusive organization such as the Elks, exemplified the paternalistic ideology driving Haydock and the other White architects' efforts to contain and control the "Mexican problem."[103] Indeed, the playground reified racial segregation as a seemingly natural, everyday part of life in the city.

99. For example, A. Martinez was elected to the board of directors for Community Service and placed in charge of the Mexican playground. The article notes, "A. Martinez, chairman of the recently organized Mexican central committee was elected a member of the board in place of R. G. Beach ... Mr. Martinez is well known in Oxnard, particularly among the Mexicans and it is believed he will do good work." "Martinez Takes Place of Beach on Board of Directors Com. Service," *The Oxnard Daily Courier*, December 7, 1923, front page. Another article confirms his role as the "chairman of the central Mexican committee of Community Service." "New Saviers Road Playground, Present Busy Scene Today," *The Oxnard Daily Courier*, January 30, 1924, front page. In 1927, A. Bustamonte is noted as in charge of this playground. "City's Guests Cleaning 7th Street Playground," *The Oxnard Daily Courier*, June 23, 1927, front page.
100. "Former Secretary of Community Service Writes about Oxnard," *The Oxnard Daily Courier*, August 7, 1923, 4.
101. Ibid.
102. "Community Playground Development in Oxnard Received Publicity," *The Oxnard Daily Courier*, February 4, 1924, front page.
103. The local chapter of the Elks had just received its charter two years prior, approved by the national organization after demonstrating that five thousand Whites resided in the area. "It Took a Special Census to Get Elks Lodge Their Charter in 1922," *Oxnard Press-Courier*, September 24, 1948, front page. See also "Elks Liquor License Talks to Continue," *The Press-Courier*, May 22, 1972, 13; "Letters on Elks Liquor License Sent to ABC," *The Press-Courier*, May 24, 1972, 13.

Wanted As Laborers, But Not Students

By October 1923, the school trustees' minutes report "very badly crowded" conditions in schools requiring "immediate action."[104] In August of that year, the Oxnard Grammar School had burned down, and Theodore Roosevelt School was constructed on the same grounds, on Third Street between A and B streets.[105] In 1924, the school board oversaw the building of a third school, Woodrow Wilson School, on Palm Drive and C Street.[106] The board's minutes note ongoing concern about accommodating students within their three available facilities: Haydock, Wilson, and Roosevelt.

A January 1926 meeting of the Oxnard Parent-Teachers' Association (PTA) demonstrated that the White community shared this anxiety. *The Oxnard Daily Courier* reported on a meeting of approximately one hundred members of the PTA discussing the need to move forward on school segregation plans. A local minister, the Reverend Thomas Burden, led the meeting that night, and in his opening remarks explained: "Forty percent of Oxnard school children are of Spanish extraction, and the question here is an important one. Neighboring cities have dealt with the situation effectively by the separate school system. Santa Paula is a notable example."[107] For Burden and the PTA, the "question" of segregation appeared to be "an important one" simply based on demographics. The group understood that his reference to children of "Spanish extraction" meant Mexican.

In Santa Paula, an agricultural town about fifteen miles northeast of Oxnard, school officials and church leaders argued for segregating Mexicans based on supposed hygiene, language, and cultural needs. These unsubstantiated claims justified actions to segregate Mexicans within existing Santa Paula facilities, and complete segregation in the Canyon School, beginning in the 1925–26 academic year.[108] The main teacher of the Canyon School, Miss Dorothy Lewis, spoke to the Oxnard PTA about "her supervision of between 800 and 1000 Mexican pupils" in kindergarten through eighth grade in this facility, and "illustrated graphically with her talk what has been accomplished by separate schools."[109] Further inspired by the Santa Paula example

---

104. Oxnard School Board of Trustees meeting minutes, October 25, 1923.

105. Roosevelt School primarily enrolled children in kindergarten through sixth grade. See "Attendance Registers by Years," Oxnard School District Archives, date unknown.

106. Ibid. Wilson School initially enrolled children in upper elementary, fourth through eighth grades. After 1940, Wilson became a dedicated junior high school, enrolling only seventh and eighth grade students. The existing plaque demarcating the now-closed Woodrow Wilson School in Oxnard reads 1928–75. These opening and closing dates do not correspond with school district records.

107. "Parent-Teachers' Association," *The Oxnard Daily Courier*, January 29, 1926, "Society" page.

108. According to Martha Menchaca and Richard Valencia, prior to the opening of the separate facility, Mexican children were forced to take showers before entering school and were then placed into racially segregated classrooms that emphasized English and Americanization. The Canyon School was a schoolhouse of eight classrooms, two bathrooms, and an office for 950 Mexican students from kindergarten through eighth grade. In stark contrast, 667 White students attended the newly constructed Isabel School with twenty-one classrooms, a cafeteria, an auditorium, a training shop, and administrative offices. See Martha Menchaca and Richard R. Valencia, "Anglo-Saxon Ideologies in the 1920s–1930s: Their Impact on the Segregation of Mexican Students in California," *Anthropology and Education Quarterly* 21, no. 3 (1990): 222–49, 238–39; Martha Menchaca, *The Mexican Outsiders: A Community History of Marginalization and Discrimination in California* (Austin: University of Texas Press, 1995).

109. "Parent-Teachers' Association," *The Oxnard Daily Courier*, January 29, 1926, "Society" page.

and Burden's remarks, the PTA planned to assign a committee to "cooperate with the Oxnard school trustees in considering this matter as a constructive issue to be solved at once."[110]

Regional labor demands intensified "overcrowding" in schools and the pressure on the trustees to segregate Mexican children.[111] On Thursday, March 4, 1926, the Oxnard Chamber of Commerce adopted a resolution favoring "unrestricted immigration for Mexicans into this state, on the ground that the farmers would be crippled without Mexican labor."[112] Within the week, *The Oxnard Daily Courier* questioned the Chamber's position in relation to schools. Under the headline "Our Race Problem," the newspaper suggested that unrestricted Mexican immigration presented a greater threat than "the so-called Japanese menace," but "the danger ... is escaping our notice under the spur of present economic necessity."[113] The brief editorial continued, "It is quite probable that the Mexican birthrate is almost as large as the Japanese ... the adult population in Oxnard is probably two whites to one Mexican, and yet the ratio in grammar school enrollment is just reversed."[114] The newspaper editors urged resolute, concerted action from school officials: "For many years there has been a demand for segregation in our local schools, but conditions have not been such in the past as to justify the remark reported to have been made by Principal R. B. Haydock of the Oxnard grammar schools that he would be glad to provide separate schools for the white children providing the white people will furnish them."[115] This critique of Haydock articulated an expectation that city officials and school leaders would dedicate public resources to segregate Mexicans from Whites.

In November 1927, the PTA again met to talk about segregation, this time with the school board and Superintendent Haydock present. Together they discussed a ruling by the U.S. Supreme Court denying a Chinese American girl, Martha Lum, access to an all-White high school in Mississippi.[116] Oxnard's PTA president, Mrs. Sam Weill, explained that locally, "there is no objection to the Japanese or Chinese children, as they are cleanly and of a high standard of intellect. The school district does not have sufficient funds to completely segregate the Latin American children from the American children, but we have already accomplished separation in cases where particularly desirable."[117] This clarification established that the PTA and the district officials distinguished Mexicans as a separate and inferior class of children, and shared an understanding that complete segregation would be the goal, when funds became available. They extended the privilege of integration with Whites to Japanese and Chinese children, whom they perceived to be

---

110. Ibid.

111. Some school officials and scholars questioned the efficacy of segregating students during the 1930s, but such debates are not reflected in the actions of the Oxnard School Board of Trustees. In any case, Charles Wollenberg notes, "The doubts expressed about segregation in the thirties were transformed into new convictions during the forties." Charles M. Wollenberg, *All Deliberate Speed: Segregation and Exclusion in California Schools, 1855–1975* (Berkeley: University of California Press, 1976), 120.

112. "Farmers Here Need a Big Scare to Awaken Them," *The Oxnard Daily Courier,* March 5, 1926, front page.

113. "Our Race Problem," *The Oxnard Daily Courier,* March 10, 1926, 2.

114. Ibid.

115. Ibid.

116. "Supreme Court School Ruling Affects Oxnard," *The Oxnard Daily Courier,* November 22, 1927, front page. Case of *Martha Lum v. Rosedale Consolidated High School in Bolivar County, Mississippi; Gong Lum v. Rice,* 275 U.S. 78 (1927).

117. Ibid.

"cleanly and of a high standard of intellect."[118] Records show no evidence of how the district made these determinations, other than by race. Superintendent Haydock contributed to the conversation, noting that "states already have the power to decide the question of segregation, because each separate state has its own particular problems. The Supreme Court ruling does not change the situation in California."[119] Ventura County justice of the peace Judge C. J. Elliott also remarked that the current practice of separating Mexican children from Whites within the same facility represented the most feasible way to avoid integration. This pragmatic strategy delineated the racial hierarchy in schools, with Whites at the top and in the position to determine the racial order beneath them. Judge Elliott reassured the PTA: "It is the right thing to do, and it is to the advantage of both races to be separated up to about the eighth grade. Children of foreign parentage can be better educated when they have their own classes. It is not necessary to build separate buildings, having separate schoolrooms in the same school is sufficient."[120]

Taken together, Superintendent Haydock and Judge Elliott interpreted the school-within-a-school strategy as legally valid and within their authority. Knowing there were no provisions under California statutes to segregate Mexican children on the basis of simply being Mexican, Haydock, the PTA, and civic leaders such as Judge Elliott manufactured the myth that Mexican children posed an escalating racial threat in schools. Without substantiating repeated claims of lower intelligence and poor hygiene, they pursued a strategy of segregation that separated Mexican students as an ostensibly necessary, and even benevolent policy. Indeed, their sense of urgency to segregate increased in step with further growth of the city's Mexican population. U.S. Census records show that by 1930, Mexicans comprised at least 13,839 of Ventura County's 54,976 residents (approximately 25%).[121] By 1927, children of Mexican descent accounted for 34 percent of Ventura County's public and Catholic elementary school enrollments, while Japanese students represented a little over 1 percent.[122] Statewide, over 70 percent of Mexican elementary schoolchildren "were reported as born in the United States."[123] In Oxnard, the trustees recognized that Mexican students did indeed account for "about two-thirds" of the elementary school population, and that almost all of these children were U.S.

118. Ibid.
119. Ibid.
120. Ibid. The article goes on to reprint Section 3, Article 10 of the California educational code, establishing the right of school districts to "exclude children of filthy or vicious habits or children suffering from contagious or infectious disease, and to establish separate schools for Indian children and for children of Chinese, Japanese, or Mongolian parentage. When such separate schools are established, Indian children or children of Chinese, Japanese or Mongolian parentage must not be admitted into any other school." The article ends with an overview of the Supreme Court case itself.
121. U.S. Bureau of the Census, *U.S. Census of the Population: 1930*, "Population, California, Table 17. Indians, Chinese and Japanese 1910 to 1930 and Mexicans, 1930 for Counties and for Cities of 25,000 or More" (Washington, DC: U.S. Government Printing Office, 1930), 266.
122. The percentage of Mexican students in Ventura County elementary schools (34.2%) marked the second highest in the state of California, behind only Imperial County, which was 36.8 percent. Paul S. Taylor, *Mexican Labor in the United States,* vol. 6. (Berkeley: University of California Publications in Economics, 1930), 266, "Table 2. Mexican Children Enrolled in Public and Catholic Elementary Schools of California, February 1, 1927; Distribution by Divisions of the State, and by Counties."
123. Ibid., 264.

citizens.[124] Race apparently trumped citizenship status for the trustees, who in violation of the law worked to "completely segregate" Mexican children.[125]

In 1927, when the House Immigration Committee in Washington, DC, held hearings about whether to include Mexico in the Immigration Quota Act, California representatives again argued against restricting Mexican immigration.[126] The Los Angeles Chamber of Commerce also urged Oxnard Chamber of Commerce members to write to their senators and congressmen, "requesting that they use every effort to defeat enactment of any legislation which would disrupt the present status of immigration between the United States and Mexico."[127] These growers and Oxnard business owners held a vested interest in unrestricted Mexican immigrant labor.[128] Like other towns and cities across the Southwest, Mexicans were welcomed to the extent that they continued to enable the accumulation of wealth for the nation, but they were never quite considered "fit to be citizens,"[129] or students.

School officials also contributed to this problem with inconsistent and insufficient provisions for children of migrant farmworkers. One researcher, Wilbur K. Cobb, observed that for Ventura County children who worked alongside their parents harvesting walnuts prior to 1928, "there had been no concerted effort to provide schooling facilities. Some districts provided rooms for these migratory children with a half-hearted program. Others treated them as unwanted, while one school known to the writer [Cobb] put up a big sign, 'No Migratory Children Wanted Here.'"[130] *The Oxnard Daily Courier* reported that some Ventura County schools incorporated walnut and bean "holidays" into their academic year, stopping classes for up to four weeks during the harvests.[131]

124. See chapter 2 for further discussion of trustee J. H. Burfeind's written admission that U.S.-born Mexicans possessed the same legal rights as other U.S. citizens.

125. "Supreme Court School Ruling Affects Oxnard," *The Oxnard Daily Courier*, November 22, 1927, front page.

126. "Quota Bill under Fire in the House," *The Oxnard Daily Courier*, February 24, 1928, front page.

127. "Urge Action against Mexican Quota Bills," *The Oxnard Daily Courier*, January 24, 1930, front page.

128. Years prior, the ABSC had expressed a need for factory managers and supervisors to treat the Mexican beet sugar workers well, so they would continue to be "loyal employees." American Beet Sugar Company Agricultural Meeting Minutes, July 22, 1918.

129. Molina, *Fit to Be Citizens?*

130. Wilbur K. Cobb, "Retardation in Elementary Schools of Children of Migratory Laborers in Ventura County, California" (master's thesis, University of Southern California, Los Angeles, 1932), 14.

131. See "El Rio School Pupils to Work in Orchards," *The Oxnard Daily Courier*, September 19, 1922, front page; "Rio School Closes for Walnut Picking," *The Oxnard Daily Courier*, September 18, 1926, front page. Helen Heffernan of the State Department of Education conducted a survey in October 1929 and found that many children attended separate schools for a few hours a day in "cow barns and roadside tents," just a short distance away from "well-ventilated and properly lighted buildings," where "permanent children" received "all the advantages for which California is famous." She identified labor law violations in relation to the placement of children within these facilities; in early release policies, where children would attend school for a few hours and then be released to work in the fields; and in "crop vacations" timed to coincide with the harvest. "36,000 State Pupils Listed as Migratory: Survey Shows Many Have Poor Schooling Because of Parents' Moving," *Oakland Tribune*, January 1, 1929, B23.

"Little Bits of Mexicans"

In October 1927, Ventura County superintendent of schools Blanche T. Reynolds[132] warned growers and parents that the walnut harvest could no longer take priority over school.[133] She explained, "Hundreds of children are working in the walnut orchards, and this is plainly against the law."[134] In 1919, she asserted the need for Mexican children to attend school from an early age. Speaking to an audience of about seventy-five people at Oxnard Union High School, she introduced a keynote speaker by remarking that she had initially believed in prioritizing that "older Mexican children should be educated," and recounted examples of teenage Mexicans drawing pictures in a first-grade class.[135] Without explaining why these youth may not have previously attended school, she stated that the underenrollment of younger children in schools presented an even more pressing concern. She told the audience she had become "firmly convinced that the 'little bits of Mexicans' are of first importance, and a greater serious problem to the community."[136] Her demeaning reference to children as "little bits of Mexicans" typified Reynolds's mundane disregard for the Mexican community, evidenced in her words and deeds as the county's top education official.

Reynolds's invited lecturer, Dr. Frank Fielding Nalder from the University of California, further revealed the racist framework developing in Ventura County schools.[137] According to Nalder, "Norwegians and Danes were easily assimilated. They made our best citizens and many of our most prominent men are of this race. These people mix easily with Americans and quickly learn our language."[138] In contrast, he argued, southern European immigrants "do not assimilate so easily and have a tendency to keep in colonies."[139] He cited the 1910 census that "over five and a half million people over 10 years of age" did not speak, read, or write English, which he stated "constituted a real problem before this country."[140] He then applied his concerns to Oxnard, observing: "This morning in the grammar school I noticed one frail school teacher in charge of 45 Mexican children. As each Mexican child is as hard to teach as two Americans because the teacher has to first teach in Mexican and then in American, this was altogether a too hard job."[141] Titled "Education and Inheritance," Nalder's speech presented ideas that Haydock would affirm in his "Education and

132. Blanche T. Reynolds served as the first deputy school superintendent in Ventura County, from 1911 to 1917, under her husband James E. Reynolds's administration. When he left his position to serve with the Red Cross in World War I, she filled in for him, and he then asked in an open letter to voters that her name be written in to replace his on the ballot for Ventura County school superintendent. She served as superintendent from 1918 to 1935. Both she and her husband also served as councilmembers for the city of Ventura at different points in time. See John Allan Rogers, "A History of School Organization and Administration in Ventura County" (Ph.D. dissertation, University of Southern California, Los Angeles, 1961), 124–34.

133. "Education Is of Greater Value than Walnuts Says School Head," *Ventura Free Press,* October 22, 1927, front page.

134. Ibid.

135. "Lecture at School by Dr. Nalder," *The Oxnard Daily Courier,* April 3, 1919, 8.

136. Ibid.

137. See Frank Fielding Nalder, "The American State Reformatory; with Special Reference to Its Educational Aspects" (Ph.D. dissertation, University of California, Berkeley, 1917).

138. "Lecture at School by Dr. Nalder," *The Oxnard Daily Courier,* April 3, 1919, 8.

139. 139. Ibid.

140. Ibid.

141. Ibid.

the Future American" speech three years later. Both presented ideology as fact and framed their observations of Mexicans in schools as local problems connected to nation, race, and culture.

Reynolds contributed significantly to casting Mexicans as racial problems that must be contained. Eight years after talking about "little bits of Mexicans," she spoke about the enforcement of compulsory education laws and her duty to ensure that Mexican children of migrant farmworkers received an education. Still, she complained, financially "this presents a real problem to us, not only to get these children into school, but to provide the schools for them."[142] She explained, "In some instances the parents are to blame, but in other cases employers of these children will be cited to appear before the labor commissioner on the charge of violating the state labor laws."[143]

Reynolds's October 1927 resolve to follow the law did not last long. Three months after asserting, "The Mexican child as well as others must be given an opportunity to receive an education. They are as much entitled to it as any," she told the Oxnard Rotary Club that Mexican immigration should be restricted altogether because "Mexican costs are too high."[144] Her January 1928 remarks before the club and its president, Superintendent Haydock, began with a plea, "Give us a chance to make proper American citizens out of the Mexicans by not flooding our country with them."[145] Reynolds reported that in the 1926–27 academic year Mexican children comprised 4,886 (33%) of the 14,887 total county school enrollments. She noted that accounting for Mexicans presented a unique challenge because, she claimed, "they scattered like quail when the officer came to see them."[146] Reynolds's dehumanizing reference to Mexicans as quails echoed her previous public remarks and realigned her with Haydock, who had likened Mexicans to "livestock."[147]

Reynolds expressed frustration that Mexicans burdened public resources at the expense of "American taxpayers." She estimated that since they accounted for 33 percent of the student population, at least one-third of the county's schooling budget went to Mexican children. She lamented that these "American" tax dollars spent educating Mexicans had to be directed toward fixing Mexican children's "handicap" in English and compensating for the delays in the migrant students' promotion to the next grade. Clearly conscious that Rotarian members included local growers and businessmen, Reynolds avoided mention of her recent cooperation with state authorities in citing employers who violated labor and compulsory school attendance laws. Instead, she sought to convince the group that the benefits of open Mexican immigration policies could not be reconciled with the detrimental impacts Mexicans caused to "Americans" in schools and beyond. She characterized Spanish speaking as a disadvantage and generalized that "the average Mexican child" took two years to complete one grade, which "drags down the average for the American child."[148] She went on to present data on the disproportionate incarceration and mental health hospitalization rates of Mexicans. As she continued to position her ideological arguments as facts, she warned that increased Mexican immigration

142. "Education Is of Greater Value than Walnuts Says School Head," *Ventura Free Press,* October 22, 1927, front page.
143. Ibid.
144. "Mexican Costs Are Too High Says Co. Head," *The Oxnard Daily Courier,* January 31, 1928, front page.
145. Ibid.
146. Ibid.
147. "Policewoman Graduate Nurse for City Health," *Oxnard Daily Courier,* January 31, 1917, front page.
148. "Mexican Costs Are Too High Says Co. Head," *The Oxnard Daily Courier,* January 31, 1928, front page.

would exacerbate children's academic underachievement and adult incarceration, leading to an inevitable "lowering by the Mexicans of the moral and health tone of our children, and of the general community."[149]

While Reynolds's position against Mexican children seemed to contradict her previous calls for their receiving access to education, her condescending tone of racial superiority remained consistent. Her comments reverberated with Haydock's 1917 arguments to the city trustees, warning that Mexican children posed an urgent "threat and a menace" to schools with their "filth and contagion and disease."[150] Reynolds concluded with more of the same contemptuous remarks: "Mexicans are not immoral … they are merely unmoral. They don't know any better … they will lower and undermine our lives and standards eventually if floods of them are let in in the future as at present."[151] *The Oxnard Daily Courier* reported that Reynolds's talk elicited "lively discussion" among the Rotarians and that club president Haydock postponed full deliberations "til a future meeting can take care of the question."[152] The newspaper did not report on those deliberations, and after this article rarely published civic or school leaders making such blatant assertions of White racial superiority over Mexicans.[153]

Though their bigoted views were not so publicly expressed on the front page of the newspaper, by 1930 the White architects had embedded their racist ideologies into public policies within and beyond schools. They strategically implemented separate and unequal treatment for children of Mexican descent as mundane educational practice. Indeed, the ideologies of Haydock, Thornton, Reynolds, and leaders of the PTA were deeply felt in the everyday schooling experiences of Mexican children.

"Draw a Circle in the Dirt"

> So one day, I don't know what I said, anyways, it was a Spanish word, and oh God, you'd think I'd done away with the school or something. They put me on restriction. I had to get a rock, draw a circle in the dirt, and stand in the middle … until the bell rang, and I felt like a weird person because, you know, everybody would come by and look at me, like I was on display.… And I felt like the ugliest, the dirtiest little girl around, you know, really bad.… I could have forgotten Spanish right then and there, but I thought, "no." [Laughs]
> —Antonia Arguelles DiLiello[154]

Antonia Arguelles (DiLiello) was born in Winfield, Kansas, in 1925 and enrolled in the second grade at Roosevelt School in 1932, after her family moved to Oxnard. In addition to segregated classrooms, distinct recess/lunch play areas, and public punishment for speaking Spanish, Antonia and other Mexican children

---

149. Ibid.

150. "Policewoman Graduate Nurse for City Health," *Oxnard Daily Courier,* January 31, 1917, front page.

151. "Mexican Costs are Too High Says Co. Head," *The Oxnard Daily Courier,* January 31, 1928, front page.

152. Ibid.

153. A Ventura elementary school was named after Blanche T. Reynolds, and she attended the dedication ceremony on October 18, 1956. "Rededication Day Honors Blanche Reynolds Anew," *Ventura County Star–Free Press,* May 29, 1978, A4. This article also credits Reynolds with heading the first Parent Teacher Association in Ventura.

154. Antonia Arguelles DiLiello, interview by David G. García and Frank P. Barajas, June 1, 2010, Oxnard, CA.

who attended Oxnard schools in the 1930s were sent home at least ten minutes after White students each afternoon—to avoid potential interracial socializing.

Antonia remembered this scene over seventy years after it had occurred. She recognized that the punishment was intended to be memorable, to teach her a lesson about the error of speaking her language, even outside of class. She admittedly felt horrible, "like the ugliest, the dirtiest little girl around." Yet she also laughed, in retrospect, about the fact that she refused to forget Spanish. She went on to say that she and her friends learned to be "very careful" to avoid punishment. "By the time I got to Wilson School, I made sure if I spoke Spanish, it would be when none of the teachers were around."[155] Her narrative sheds much light on the ways Mexican American children confronted subtle and stunning racism in school.

Antonia's parents immigrated from Chihuahua, Mexico, to El Paso, Texas, in 1906. Her father, who had worked for a smelting company in Texas and as a railroad worker in Kansas, labored in the fields and in the street maintenance department for the city of Oxnard. In addition to being a homemaker, her mother worked seasonally pitting apricots and shelling walnuts. To financially contribute to the household, her two older brothers stopped attending school after junior high and started working full time. During the summers, the entire family camped in the nearby Conejo Valley Ranch to harvest and pit apricots.[156] Antonia remembered feeling conflicted about her family's social circumstances, which seemed to stand in stark contrast to what her teachers said made America great. She explained, "Going through school, we were made to believe that the country was beautiful and we had all of these things. Things that our parents couldn't afford."[157] To make sense of why her family was so poor in comparison to White families just across the tracks, she theorized that her father did not want to work hard enough. "I think that's when I decided my dad was lazy. 'Cause we didn't have the things they had. And so maybe because he's lazy we don't have the things they have, which is so sad."[158]

Years later, she realized that stereotypes about Mexicans likely reinforced what she learned at school, and contributed to her unsubstantiated belief that her dad was lazy. Eventually, as part of a family history project, she discovered evidence that her father had been commended for working in an "industrious and conscientious manner,"[159] and that he did so until personnel regulations necessitated his compulsory retirement at age seventy.[160] She expressed a sense of embarrassment that she did not fully appreciate this as a child. "I can remember my father going out clean, clean as a whistle, and coming back dirty from head to toe from working in the fields. I thought he was lazy, I really thought he was lazy! And I thought, my gosh,

155. Ibid.
156. "Community of 3000 Rises at Ranch for Apricot Work," *The Oxnard Daily Courier,* July 17, 1939. The article reported, "With a sprinkling of Americans the workers are mostly Mexican. They are paid 3 cents a box for picking and 12 1/2 cents a tray for pitting, at which jobs the entire family, children and all, may work.... Over 1,400 were registered for work there, the Courier was told, which with children and others unregistered formed a community of over 3,000 people." This statement indicates that children comprised at least half of the apricot "community."
157. Antonia Arguelles DiLiello, interview by David G. García, June 24, 2011, Oxnard, CA.
158. Antonia Arguelles DiLiello, interview by David G. García and Frank P. Barajas, June 1, 2010, Oxnard, CA.
159. Correspondence from Mrs. Ethel Dale, city clerk of the city of Oxnard regarding employee record of Mr. Antonio Arguelles for city of Oxnard, October 7, 1947. Personal collection of Antonia Arguelles.
160. Correspondence from Paul E. Wolven, city manager of the city of Oxnard, regarding reason for retirement of Antonio Arguelles from city of Oxnard, May 4, 1954. Personal collection of Antonia Arguelles.

it's so sad, because that's the picture they give you and that's what you think."[161] In hindsight, she regretted being unable to see her father as the hard worker he was. Being publicly humiliated at school and "shunned" in places around Oxnard further distorted the "picture" Antonia held in her head and the shame she felt about her family and herself. As a child, Antonia could not shake the feeling that she was dirty and ugly. Indeed, the daily disparate treatment of Mexican American children such as Antonia sent insidious messages about race, class, and gender, which reverberated well beyond the classroom.

Conclusion

In this chapter, I analyzed the ways the White architects embedded their racial ideologies into the very structures, practices, and discourses of schooling in Oxnard from the city's founding. They divided the city by residence and race and according to an understood racial hierarchy. They intentionally established separate, unequal schooling and housing conditions for Mexican families. Their school-within-a-school strategy of segregation normalized discrimination against Mexican American students and aimed to limit their social mobility.

Antonia's voice and other oral histories throughout this book help to reassert the human experiences of mundane racism. Their collective memories complicate mainstream accounts of Oxnard's history that almost completely ignore those laborers and their families who contributed in multiple pioneering ways to the developing city. The resilience of Antonia, her peers, and the generations that followed contested the White architects' attempts to frame them as a health menace, a tax burden, and a race problem. In the next chapter, I consider experiences of Mexican youth as they navigated Oxnard's east-west "color-line."[162] I document the White architects' strategic interconnection of school and residential segregation, examining how these school and civic leaders codified their racist words through their property deeds.

161. Antonia Arguelles DiLiello, interview by David G. García and Frank P. Barajas, June 1, 2010, Oxnard, CA.
162. W. E. B. DuBois, *The Souls of Black Folk: Essays and Sketches* [1903] (New York: Fawcett, 1961), v.

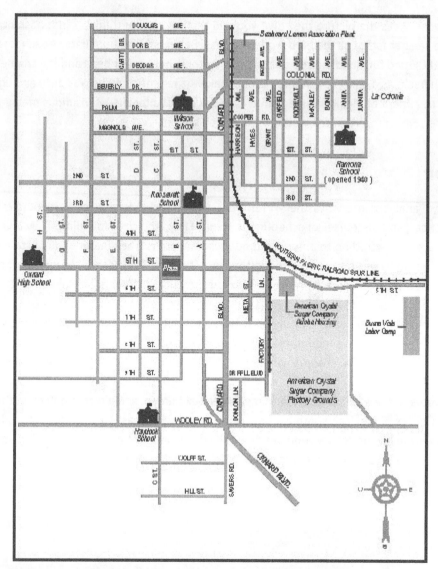

FIGURE 6.1.3   Oxnard, California, circa 1950. Adapted from original by George W. Y. Moller. Not to scale. Courtesy of the Museum of Ventura County and Oxnard School District.

The Foundation for a Critical Bicultural Pedagogy

Antonia Darder

Antonia Darder, "The Foundation for a Critical Bicultural Pedagogy," *Culture and Power in the Classroom: Educational Foundations for the Schooling of Bicultural Students*, pp. 79–102, 238–239, 241–256. Copyright © 2012 by Taylor & Francis Group. Reprinted with permission.

> The solution is not to integrate them into the structure of oppression, but to transform that structure so that they can become beings for themselves.
>
> Paulo Freire, *Pedagogy of the Oppressed,* 1970

Historically, bicultural education has been linked most directly to bilingual instructional theory. The powerful relationship between culture and language suggests the logic at work in this connection and the symbiotic manner in which these concepts are often discussed. As a consequence, the majority of early work in the field was extensively focused on educational assessment, curriculum content and teaching strategies related to cultural values, language, and cognition (Ramirez & Castañeda, 1974; Pialorsi, 1974; Valverde, 1978; Turner, 1982; Fishman & Keller, 1982; Ovando & Collier, 1985). Although these questions clearly represent primary areas of concern, the traditional manner in which these areas were often addressed in the classroom did not necessarily guarantee that bicultural students would participate in a process of social empowerment or that they would develop their voice or become critically discursive with respect to the economic and sociopolitical conditions that shape their lives.

A major reason for this phenomenon was the failure to change the structure of schools—a change required in order to alter the asymmetrical power relations that prevent the emancipatory development of both biculturalism and bilingualism. Despite the extensive work directed at altering the content and language of curriculum, bicultural educators were able to accomplish very little in transforming the traditional pedagogical structure of their classrooms. So although bilingual/bicultural students may have acquired a stronger sense of cultural

293

identity, self-esteem, and both language and cognitive proficiency, they were simultaneously socialized within the context of a technocratic and instrumental pedagogy that stifled the development of their critical cognitive skills and ignored important questions of human agency, voice, and empowerment.

Nevertheless, twenty years ago, when *Culture and Power in the Classroom* was first written, there still remained vital public avenues for strengthening and fortifying bilingual education in the United States. However, following a series of successful conservative initiatives across the country, beginning with Proposition 227 in California, the end of the millennium also brought with it an end to widespread support and resources for bilingual education in public schools. The consequence was an uneven provision of bilingual services for children whose first language is not English and schools increasingly returning to the sink-or-swim approach that characterized the education of bilingual/bicultural students before the civil rights era.

Hence, today it is more important than ever for teachers of children from working-class racialized communities to contend with issues of culture and power in more substantive ways. Yet seldom are issues of power seriously addressed with respect to the structure of classroom life. Even when educators do make some effort to address the issues in their classrooms, often it is done in a "banking education" mode (Freire, 1970), which in content may be theoretically emancipatory, but in practice is pedagogically oppressive (Bartolomé, 1994). Thus, what is missing is a critical educational foundation on which bicultural educators can build a liberatory practice of bicultural education.

In order for this need to be met, teachers must grapple with the basic structure of traditional American education that pushes toward an assimilative curriculum of standardized knowledge. The previous chapters have helped to illustrate the need for this structural change and to highlight specific issues that must be considered in generating such a transformation. In addition to confronting the different forms of cultural invasion through a commitment to a culturally democratic principle, there are specific theoretical constructs related to critical pedagogy that must also be incorporated in the process of establishing a critical foundation for bicultural education.

From the standpoint of critical theory, education must hold an emancipatory purpose and acknowledge schooling as a political process. A key to this perspective is the recognition of the contextual relationship that exists between the cultural politics and economic forces in society and the structure of schools. Hence, critical pedagogy espouses a view of knowledge that is both historical and dialectical in nature. True to its critical dimensions, it is built around a serious commitment to the union of theory and practice. Further, a theory of ideology and hegemony is closely linked to critical pedagogy's concern with the nature of student resistance and a view of education's counterhegemonic possibilities. And finally, critical pedagogy incorporates an understanding of critical discourse and the goal of conscientization as a consequence of the dialogical relationships that shape the structure of classroom life.

The following discussion outlines the basic principles that inform a critical pedagogy, which can effectively serve as an important philosophical foundation for bicultural education. It is a foundation that is clearly based on an understanding of the link between culture and power and is firmly rooted in a political construct of cultural democracy and the commitment to student empowerment. It represents, in theory and practice, the critical dimensions that have often remained absent from the foundational groundwork necessary for preparing teachers to teach children from racialized communities.

Principles of Critical Pedagogy

The theoretical foundation of any educational practice must be understood by educators in order to develop fully the ability to evaluate their practice, confront the contradictions, and transform their classrooms into democratic environments where they can genuinely address the actual needs of students, anchored in the conditions of their everyday life. Thus, to move toward a critical practice of bicultural education, it is most important to examine the fundamental theoretical dimensions of critical education and its merit with respect to the education of bicultural students.

In the spirit of a critical theory, it is important to begin by stating that there is no recipe for the universal implementation and application of any form of critical pedagogy. In fact, it is precisely this distinguishing characteristic that constitutes its genuinely critical nature and therefore its emancipatory and democratic function. This quality is consistent with the philosophical principles espoused by major critical theorists over the years. Those theorists who have most influenced the critical theory movement include members of the Frankfurt School, Italian Marxist Antonio Gramsci, and more recently Jurgen Habermas (1970). It goes without saying that much of the tenets espoused by early critical theorists emerged from the direct influence of the writings of Karl Marx and others writing within that tradition.

Paulo Freire's *Pedagogy of the Oppressed,* released in an English translation in 1970, proved to be a watershed in the evolution and coalescing of the field now loosely known as the critical pedagogy movement in the United States. Freire's writings, along the works of progressive educators, such as Herb Kohl (1967, 1969), Jonathan Kozol (1967, 1972), Maxine Greene (1967, 1973), Ivan Illich (1971), and Myles Horton (Adams & Horton, 1975), had an important influence on a number of up-and-coming education scholars whose radical pedagogical ideas would help to lay the groundwork for the field in the early 1980s. Seminal works by Henry Giroux, Peter McLaren, Michael Apple, Roger Simon, and others provided the contours for a theoretical reading of culture and power within U.S. public schooling.[1],[2] The following set of philosophical principles, based on the work of these scholars, provides a foundation for forging a critical bicultural pedagogy.

Cultural Politics

Above all things, a critical pedagogy encompasses an unwavering commitment to the empowerment of the powerless and the transformation of existing social inequities and injustices (McLaren, 1988). This commitment is clearly linked to a basic principle that we, as men and women, are called upon to struggle for: what Freire (1970), in concert with Marx, defines as our "vocation"—to be truly humanized social agents in the

---

1. For a more substantive introduction to critical pedagogy and its foundations, see *The Critical Pedagogy Reader* (Darder, Baldodano, & Torres 2002/2009); *Critical Pedagogy Primer* (Kincheloe, 2008a); *Life in Schools: An Introduction to the Foundations of Critical Pedagogy* (McLaren, 1989/1998); *Critical Pedagogy: Notes from the Real World* (Wink, 2010).
2. Over the last twenty years, there has been a third wave of critical pedagogy scholarship from theorists who branched out and brought diverse interpretations to contemporary notions of a critical pedagogy (Macedo, 1987; Shor, 1987, 1992; hooks, 1994, 2009; Weiler, 1985; Fine,1991; Luke & Gore, 1992; Daspit & Weaver, 2000; Denzin, 2003; Trifonas, 2002; Wink, 2010; Christensen, 2000; Leistyna, 1999; Grande, 2004; Kincheloe, 1995, 2008a, 2008b; Monchinski, 2008; Steinberg, 2009, 2010; Kanpol, 1999; Bigelow, 2006; Mayo, 2004; Kahn, 2010; Hinchey, 2006; Bartolomé, 2007; Duncan-Andrade & Morrell, 2008; Au, 2009; Carr, 2010).

world. This spirit of social justice moves the critical educator to an irrevocable commitment to the oppressed and to the liberation of all people. Moreover, it comprises a commitment to a democratic and participatory form of education, in which teachers struggle *with,* rather than *for* the oppressed.

Before continuing with this discussion of critical pedagogy, it seems useful to distinguish the concept of *pedagogy* from that of simply teaching. Roger Simon (1987) describes this distinction:

> Pedagogy is a more complex and extensive term than teaching, referring to the integration in practice of particular curriculum content and design, classroom strategies and techniques, a time and place for the practice of these ... and evaluation purpose and methods. All of these aspects of educational practice come together in the realities of what happens in classrooms. Together they organize a view of how teachers' work within an institutional context specifies a particular version of what knowledge is of most worth, what it means to know something, and how we might construct representations of ourselves, others, and our physical and social environment. In other words, talk about pedagogy is simultaneously talk about details of what students and others might do together and the cultural politics such practices support. To propose a pedagogy is to propose a political vision. In this perspective, we cannot talk about teaching practices without talking about politics. (p. 371)

In light of this definition, a major task of pedagogy is to expose and challenge the roles that schools play in the political and cultural life of students. Of particular importance is a critical analysis and investigation into the manner that traditional theories and practices of American schools thwart or support the participation of working-class racialized students. Hence, schools must be seen critically as both sorting mechanisms where select groups of students are entitled and privileged, while others are not, and as important public arenas for individual and community empowerment (McLaren, 1988).

Fundamental to critical pedagogy is the assumption that teachers comprehend the role schooling plays in uniting knowledge and power, and how these dynamics relate to the development of critical thought and socially active individuals. Unlike traditional educational perspectives that view schools as neutral and apolitical in nature, a critical theoretical perspective views power, politics, history, and culture as intimately and ideologically linked with any theory of education. McLaren (1988) writes in *Life in Schools*: "Schools have always functioned in ways that rationalize the knowledge industry into class-divided tiers; that reproduce inequality, racism, and sexism; and that fragment democratic social relations through an emphasis on competitiveness and ethnocentrism" (pp. 160–161).

Critical pedagogy incorporates Freire's (1970) assertion that the form and content of knowledge, as well as the social practices through which it is appropriated, have to be seen as an ongoing struggle over what counts as legitimate culture and forms of empowerment. In response, critical pedagogy seeks to address the concept of cultural politics by both legitimizing and challenging experiences and perceptions shaped by the histories and socioeconomic realities that give meaning to the everyday lives of students and their constructions of what is perceived as truth (Darder, Baltodano, & Torres 2002/2009).

Economics

Critical pedagogy fiercely challenges the prevalent assumption that American schools reflect a broad Western humanistic tradition for individual and social empowerment. In fact, it contends that, in truth, schools often work against the interests of those students who are most vulnerable and most in need of educational opportunities. Consequently, the issue of economics is considered vital to developing a critical understanding of how school curriculum, knowledge, and policy are organized around the inequity of competing interests within the social order—interests that are informed by the corporate marketplace and the ever-changing waves of the national economy.

Critical theorists maintain a view of schooling as a cultural and historical process in which select groups are positioned within asymmetrical relations of power on the basis of class, skin color, gender, sexuality, physical ability, and so on, rather than a process that is value free and neutral. Its political dimensions are sharply defined by and operate with the intent to reproduce the values and privileges of the dominant ruling class. McLaren (1988) speaks to this question: "Critical theorists challenge the often uncontested relationship between school and society, unmasking mainstream pedagogy's claim that it purveys equal opportunity and provides access to egalitarian democracy and critical thinking. Critical scholars reject the claim that schooling constitutes an apolitical and value-neutral process" (p. 163).

As discussed earlier, nowhere is this form of inequity so clearly evident as in the current system of meritocracy utilized in most American schools—a system that, in order to succeed, requires students to be versed in the dominant cultural versions of truth and knowledge. Those who succeed are considered to possess the individual merit that consequently also makes them privilege to the economic goods that success can bring in the United States. Those who fail are considered to lack the individual intelligence, maturity, or drive to succeed. Seldom acknowledged in this traditional analysis of student success or failure are the asymmetrical power relations at work, determined by cultural and economic forces that grant privilege and opportunities to students from the dominant class, thus reproducing the mainstream material and social arrangements that sustain capitalist accumulation. Those unable to fulfill their designated roles within this process of accumulation are marginalized and deemed disposable, within schools and society.

Historicity of Knowledge

Critical pedagogy is strongly influenced by the Frankfurt School's ideas tied to the *historicity of knowledge*. True to this underlying principle, the theory calls for the examination of schools within their social practices but also their historical realities. Herein lies a counterlogic to the positivist, ahistorical, and depoliticizing analysis of schooling that searches for *inner histories* within a narrow and limiting definition of history. In response, Giroux (1983) argues that

> [the] given social order is not simply found in modes of interpretation that view history as a natural evolving process or ideologies distributed through the culture industry. It is also found in the material reality of those needs and wants that bear the inscription of history. That is, history is to be found as "second nature" in those concepts and views of the world that make the most dominating aspect of the social order appear to be immune from historical sociopolitical development. Those aspects of reality that rest on an appeal to the universal and invariant often slip from historical consciousness and become embedded

within those historically specific needs and desires that link individuals to the logic of conformity and domination. (p. 38)

Critical educational theorists strongly support the view that the study of history, which has deteriorated at all levels of schooling, must be elevated to a position of critical influence. However, instead of orienting the curriculum to a patriotic purpose that stresses the role of great men in shaping our contemporary world, or featuring events whose meaning is usually lost to students, teachers should assist students in understanding history as a social process—a process that incorporates both the participation of social movements and the state, as well as the economic and cultural forces acting as significant determinants in the society. Further, since historical events often conceal more than they reveal, a critical historical understanding is also closely predicated on deconstructing events, texts, and images of the past. Within this context, the meaning of history is to be found not only in what is included in mainstream explanations, but also in what is excluded (Aronowitz & Giroux, 1985).

Important to this discussion is the manner in which the dominant school culture functions to support the interests and values of the dominant society while marginalizing and invalidating knowledge forms and experiences that are significant to oppressed groups. This function is best illustrated in the ways that curriculum often blatantly ignores the histories of women, people of color, and the working classes. Freire (1970) speaks to the impact of this historical neglect of oppressed groups: "There is no historical reality which is not human. There is no history without men [and women], and no history for men [and women]; there is only history of men [and women], made by men and [and women] ... in turn making them. It is when the majorities are denied their right to participate in history as subjects that they become dominated and alienated" (p. 125).

With this in mind, a critical pedagogical approach must integrate students' own histories by delving into their own biographies and systems of meaning. But this can only happen when conditions are created in the classroom for students' voices to be heard and where they can name and authenticate their own experiences. This is vital to the learning process, for not until students can "become aware of the dignity of their own perceptions and histories [can they] make a leap to the theoretical and begin to examine the truth value of their meanings and perceptions, particularly as they relate to the dominant rationality" (Giroux, 1983, p. 203).

Hence, unlike traditional discourses on education, a critical pedagogy opposes the positivist emphasis on historical continuities and linear development. In its place is found a mode of analysis that stresses the breaks, discontinuities, and tensions in history, all of which become valuable in that they highlight the centrality of human agency and struggle while revealing the gap between society as it presently exists and society as it might be (Giroux, 1983). Also significant to this understanding, as Marx and later Freire contended, is that part of the intent of an emancipatory education is for both teachers and students to embrace themselves as historical subjects, capable of beginning to transform themselves in the now rather than waiting for some illusive fixed historical moment in the future (Allman, 2007).

Dialectical Theory

Unlike traditional theories of education that seek certainty and the technical control of knowledge and power, critical education theory posits a dialectical notion of knowledge that seeks to uncover the connections between objective knowledge and the norms, values, and structural relationships of the wider society. As such, it provides students with a mode of engagement that permits them to examine the underlying political, social, and economic conditions which shape their lives and their communities.

A dialectical view[3] begins with the fact of human existence and the contradictions and disjunctions that, in part, shape it and make problematic its meaning in the world. It functions to assist students to analyze their world; to become aware of the limitations that prevent them from changing the world; and, finally, to help them collectively struggle to transform that world. McLaren (1988) describes this process:

> Critical [pedagogy] begin[s] with the premise that men and women are essentially unfree and inhabit a world rife with contradictions and asymmetries of power and privilege. The critical educator endorses theories that are, first and foremost, dialectical: that is, theories which recognize the problems of society as more than simply isolated events of individuals or deficiencies in the social structure. Rather, these problems are part of the interactive context between the individual and society. (p. 166)

Dialectical thought seeks out these social contradictions and sets up a process of open and thoughtful questioning that requires reflection to ensue back and forth between the parts and the whole, the object and the subject, knowledge and human action, process and product, so that further contradictions may be discovered. As these contradictions and their inherent tensions are revealed, new constructive forms of thinking and action are necessary to transcend the original state. The complement of elements is dynamic rather than absolute, fixed, or static, and results in a form of creative tension rather than a state of polarization. Thus, within a dialectic, the elements are regarded as mutually constitutive rather than separate and distinct (McLaren, 1988). Breaking free from smothering positivist dichotomies is epistemologically what is at the heart of dialectical thought. Harmony does not exist without discord; strength does not exist without weakness; subject does not exist without object; life does not exist without death. The meaning of seemingly opposites is enlivened and rich as long as the dialectical tension inherent in their opposition remains intact in our reading of the world.

Therefore, significant to a dialectical understanding of education is a view of schools as sites of both oppression and empowerment. Here, the traditional view of schools as neutral, value-free sites that provide students with the necessary skills and attitudes for becoming good and responsible citizens in society is rejected. Instead, this view argues for a partisan perspective that is fundamentally committed to a struggle for the transformation of society based on the principles of emancipatory education—principles that are realized only through nonexploitative relations and social justice. Within this context, the contradictions that result within undemocratic forms of relationships are perceived as a multitude of questions that must be explored with students to reveal how they are linked to class, gender, and racialized interests (McLaren, 1988).

In this way, dialectical thought reveals the power of human activity and human knowledge as both a product of and force in the shaping of social reality. Further, it argues that there are links among knowledge, power, and domination. Therefore, it recognizes that some knowledge is false and that the ultimate purpose of a dialectical critique is a critical mindfulness in the interest of social change. It is important to note that,

---

3. For an excellent introduction to the historical and philosophical roots of dialectical theory, see *The Emergence of Dialectical Theory* (Warren, 1984).

consequently, critical thought can be exercised without falling into the ideological trap of relativism, in which the notion of critique is negated by the assumption that all ideas should be considered equally. In contrast, Giroux (1981), in *Ideology, Culture, and the Process of Schooling*, argues that the dialectic must incorporate "an historical sensibility in the interest of liberating human beings not only from those traditions that legitimate oppressive institutional arrangements, but also from their own history, i.e., that which society has made of them. This is the critical point that links praxis and historical consciousness" (p. 118).

Critical theorists argue that a theory of *dialectical critique* is what is needed to unravel the source, mechanisms, and elements that constitute the fabric of school culture. Based on Adorno's (1973) notion of *negative dialectics,* drawn from Marx, dialectical critique begins with a rejection of traditional representations of reality. The underlying assumption is that critical reflection is formed out of the principles of negativity, contradiction, and mediation. This calls for a thorough interrogation of all universal "truths" and social practices that go unquestioned in schools because they are concealed in an absolute guise of objectivity and neutrality (Giroux, 1983).

An important emphasis here is that students are encouraged to engage the world within its complexity and fullness in order to reveal the possibilities of new ways of constructing thought and action beyond how they currently exist. Rooted in a dialectical view of knowledge, critical pedagogy supports dynamic interactive elements rather than participation in the formation of absolute dichotomies or rigid polarizations of thought or practice. By so doing, it supports a supple and fluid view of humans and nature that is relational; an objectivity and subjectivity that is interconnected and interactive; and a coexistent understanding of theory and practice. Most importantly, this perspective affirms the power of human activity and human knowledge as both a product and a force in the shaping of the world, whether it is in the interest of domination or the struggle for liberation.

Praxis: The Alliance of Theory and Practice

Critical educational theory, in the tradition of Marx's critical revolutionary praxis, encompasses a practical intent that is fundamentally centered on the transformation of the world. It is this basic interest in the human condition—never seen as separate from the development and liberation of self-consciousness in individuals actively involved with determining their own destiny—that is at the center of a critical pedagogy. Unlike the external determinism, pragmatism, and instrumental or technical application of theory so prevalent in traditional American educational discourses, *praxis* is conceived as self-creating and self-generating free human action. Freire (1970) makes reference to this notion of praxis: The difference between animals—who … cannot create products detached from themselves—and men [and women]—who through their action upon the world create the realm of culture and history—is that only the latter are beings of praxis…. It is as transforming and creating beings that men [and women], in their permanent relations with reality, produce (pp. 90–91).

Within this view of human beings, all human activity consists of action and reflection, or praxis. And as praxis, all human activity requires theory to illuminate it. This interface between theory and practice occurs, for example, at the point where oppressed groups come together and raise fundamental questions of how they might assist one another, and how—through such an exchange of views—an action might emerge in which all might benefit. But it is crucial to note, once again, that this does not suggest that all views are to be given equal weight, for such a view could easily degenerate into relativistic nonsense. Instead, what it suggests is that the human subject must be integrated into the process of theorizing, and that truth claims of specific theoretical perspectives must be analyzed and mediated through dialogue and democratic social relations. Central, then, to this interface of theory and practice is the fundamental notion of *critique* (Giroux, 1983).

From the standpoint of a critical pedagogical perspective, we can further examine the dialectical relationship between theory and practice with respect to concrete and theoretical contexts. In the *concrete* context, students can be perceived as subjects and objects in a dialectical relationship with the world. In the *theoretical* context, they play the role of cognitive subjects of the subject–object relationship that occurs in the concrete moment. In this way, they are able to return to a place where they can better react as subjects against an oppressive reality. This represents a vital point in the unity between theory and practice (Freire, 1985).

Further, it is only as *beings of praxis*—as students accept their concrete situation as a challenging condition—that they are able to change its meaning by their action. This is why Freire (1985) argues that a true praxis is impossible in the undialectical vacuum where we are driven by a subject–object dichotomy. For within the context of such a dichotomy, both theory and practice lose their power to transform reality. Cut off from practice, theory becomes simple verbalism. Separated from theory, practice is nothing but blind activism. Thus, authentic praxis can only occur where there exists a dialectical alliance between theory and practice.

However, it is important to note that whereas critical pedagogy incorporates an alliance between theory and practice in education, this does not mean theory and practice—although interconnected at the point of experience—are considered identical in character. Rather, to the contrary, they represent distinct analytical moments and should not collapse into each other (Horkheimer, 1972). Giroux (1983) explains:

> Theory must be celebrated for its truth content, not for the methodological refinements it employs.... Theory is informed by practice; but its real value lies in its ability to provide the reflexivity needed to interpret the concrete experience.... Theory can never be reduced to practice, because the specificity of practice has its own center of theoretical gravity, and cannot be reduced to a predefined formula. That is, the specificity of practice cannot be abstracted from the complex forces, struggles, and mediations that give each situation a unique defining quality. Theory can help us understand this quality, but cannot reduce it to the logic of a mathematical formula.... Experience and concrete studies do not speak for themselves, and ... will tell us very little if the theoretical framework we use to interpret them lacks depth and critical rigor. (pp. 99–100)

Ideology

Critical educational theorists conceive of ideology as the framework of thought that is used in society to give order and meaning to the social and political world (Hall, 1981). The notion of ideology cannot be ignored within the context of a critical pedagogy, for it defines for students the perceptual field from which to make sense of the world. As described earlier, ideology not only structures our perceptions but also gives meaning and direction to all we experience. McLaren (1988) defines ideology as the production and representation of ideas, values, and beliefs and the manner in which they are expressed and lived out by both individuals and groups.... Ideology refers to the production of sense and meaning. It can be described as a way of viewing the world, a complex of ideas, various types of social practices, rituals, and representations that are accepted as natural and as common sense. It is the result of the intersection of meaning and power in the social world. (p. 176)

Utilizing the Frankfurt School's notion of depth psychology, critical educational theorists see ideology as existing in the depth of the individual's psychological structure of needs. This supports the view that critical educators must take into account students' inner histories and experiences; for these are central to questions of subjectivity, as they are constructed by individual needs, drives, passions, and intelligence, as well as by the changing political, economic, and social landscapes of the wider society. But further, ideology also exists in the realm of common sense. Here, *common sense* refers to the level of everyday consciousness with its many forms of unexamined assumptions, moral codes, contradictions, and partial truths (Giroux, 1981).

Essential to a critical theory of education is the notion that ideology provides individuals with the means for critique. This occurs through its own structure of thought processes and practical activities. Hence, ideology becomes a critical pedagogical tool when it is used to interrogate the relationship between the dominant school culture and the contradictory lived experiences that mediate the reality of school life. Within this context, Giroux (1983) argues that three important distinctions provide the foundation for a theory of ideology and classroom practice:

> First, a distinction must be made between theoretical and practical ideologies.... Theoretical ideologies refer to the beliefs and values embedded in the categories that teachers and students use to shape and interpret the pedagogical process, while practical ideologies refer to the messages and norms embedded in classroom social relations and practices. Second, a distinction must be made between discourse and lived experience as instances of ideology and as the material grounding of ideology as they are embedded in school texts, films, and other cultural artifacts that make up visual and aural media. Third, these ideological elements gain part of their significance only as they are viewed in their articulation with the broader relations of society. (p. 67)

One implication for classroom practice, to be drawn from a theory of ideology, is that it provides teachers with a context to examine how their own views about knowledge, human nature, values, and society are mediated through the commonsense assumptions they use to structure classroom experiences. Here, the concept of ideology provides a starting point for asking questions about the social and political interests and values that inform many of the pedagogical assumptions teachers take for granted in their work. In their quest for democratic schooling, educators must evaluate critically their assumptions about learning, achievement, teacher-student relations, objectivity, and school authority.

Further, critical educational theorists contend that ideology as critique must also be used to investigate classroom relations that freeze the spirit of critical inquiry among students. These pedagogical practices must be measured against the potential to foster, rather than hamper, intellectual growth and social inquiry. This becomes particularly important for those students who experience daily humiliation and a sense of powerlessness due to the fact that their own lived experiences and cultural histories are in conflict with the dominant school culture (Giroux, 1983).

Ideology as critique is also an essential tool that can be used by teachers to understand how the dominant culture becomes embedded in the hidden curriculum. Understanding how curriculum materials and other artifacts produce meaning can assist teachers in decoding the messages inscribed in both form and content. This is particularly significant in light of the results garnered by content analysis studies (e.g., Pokewitz, 1978; Anyon, 1979, 1980) that consistently reveal the prominence of dominant cultural values reflected in the majority of textbooks and curricula utilized in American schools.

Another significant factor in producing self-awareness in teachers is the ability to decode and critique the ideologies inscribed in the form of structuring principles behind the presentation of images in curriculum materials. The significant silences of a text can be uncovered, as teachers learn to identify the ideological messages in texts that focus on individuals to the exclusion of collective action, that juxtapose high culture and structures that reproduce poverty and exploitation, or that use forms of discourse that do not promote critical engagement by students (Giroux, 1983).

Critical educational theorists, thus, argue for a view of the hidden curriculum that encompasses all the ideological instances of the schooling process that silence students and work, to both materially and relationally reproduce the dominant society's assumptions and practices. Such a focus is important because it shifts the emphasis away from a preoccupation with reproducing the status quo to a primary concern for cultural engagement and social action with and among those who are silenced and disenfranchised.

Hegemony

Critical pedagogy incorporates Gramsci's (1971) view that educators need to understand how the dominant worldview and its social practices are produced throughout society in order to shatter the mystification of the existing power relationships and social arrangements that sustain them. Through his theory of hegemony, Gramsci argues that there exists a powerful interconnection between politics, cultural ideology, and pedagogy.

Hegemony, as previously discussed, is systematically carried out through the moral and intellectual leadership of a dominant society over subordinate groups. This form of societal control is achieved not through physically coercive means nor arbitrary rules or regulations, but rather through winning the consent of the subordinated to the authority of the dominant class. The dominant society does not have to impose hegemony by force, because the oppressed actively subscribe to many of the values and objectives of the dominant class without being aware of the source of those values or the interests that inform them. Through hegemonic control, the dominant culture is able to exert domination over women, racialized populations, and members of the working class. This process occurs whenever relations of power established at the institutional level are systematically asymmetrical—that is, when they are unequal and therefore grant power and privilege to some groups over others.

Given this view, teachers practice hegemony when they fail to teach students how to question the prevailing social attitudes, values, and social practices of the dominant society in a sustained, critical manner. Thus, the concrete challenge for teachers is to recognize, critique, and attempt to transform those undemocratic and oppressive features of hegemonic control that shape classroom relationships in ways that may not be readily apparent (McLaren, 1985).

Critical educators recognize that hegemony, in whatever form it manifests in society, must be fought for constantly in order to maintain the status quo. This, however difficult, is most successfully accomplished through various forms of cooptational forces constantly at work in the classroom and the society at large. But despite this oppressive quality, Giroux (1981) points to another significant aspect for critical educators. He argues that a theory of hegemony can also serve as an important pedagogical tool for understanding both the prevailing modes of domination and the ensuing contradictions and tensions that exist within such modes of control. In this way, hegemony functions as a theoretical basis for helping teachers to understand how the seeds of domination are produced and also how they may be overcome through various forms of resistance, critique, and social action.

Resistance and Counterhegemony

Critical pedagogy incorporates a theory of resistance in order to understand better the complex reasons why many students from subordinate groups consistently fail in the educational system, and how this understanding may be used to restructure classroom practices and relationships as a form of *counterhegemony*: "an alternative public sphere that is clearly guided by emancipatory interests." (Giroux & McLaren, 1987, p. 64)

Critical educators adhere to the philosophical principle that all people have the capacity to make meaning of their lives and to resist oppression. But they also recognize that the capacity to resist and understand is limited and influenced by issues of class, race, gender, sexuality, and physical ability. People will use whatever means at hand or whatever power they can employ to meet their needs and assert their humanity. But, unfortunately, since the solutions they often select arise from the ascribed beliefs and values of the dominant society, they may in fact lead themselves and others deeper into forms of domination and oppression (Weiler, 1988; Willis, 1977).

Giroux (1983) has addressed extensively this notion of resistance by suggesting that a construct of resistance points to a number of assumptions and concerns generally unexamined by traditional views of schooling:

> First, it celebrates a dialectical notion of human agency that rightly portrays domination as neither a static process nor one that is ever complete.... [similarly] the oppressed are not viewed as being simply passive. [It] points to the need to understand more thoroughly [how] people mediate and respond to the interface between their own lived experiences and the structures of domination.... Secondly, resistance adds ... depth to Foucault's (1977) notion that power works so as to be exercised on and by people within different contexts that structure interacting relations of dominance and autonomy.... Power is never unidimensional.... Finally, inherent in the notion of resistance is an expressed hope, an element of transcendence, for radical transformation. (p. 108)

Central to a critical theory of resistance is the concern with uncovering the degree to which a student's oppositional act speaks to a form of refusal that expresses the need to struggle against elements of dehumanization. From this context, an understanding of resistance serves a critical function in analyzing behavior based on the specific historical and relational conditions from which it develops and the consequences that ensue. This is vital to the process of critical pedagogy, for without this process of critical inquiry resistance could easily be allowed to become a category indiscriminately assigned to all forms of student oppositional behavior. It is the notion of emancipatory interests that must be central to determining when oppositional behavior constitutes a moment of resistance.

The pedagogical value of resistance is clearly linked to notions of structure and human agency and the concept of culture and self-formation, which situates these in a new problematic for understanding the process of schooling. Giroux (1983) speaks to this aspect of resistance:

> It rejects a notion that schools are simply instructional sites, and in so doing, it not only politicizes the notion of culture [and ideology], but also points to the need to analyze school culture within the shifting terrain of struggle and contestation. Educational knowledge, values, and social relations are now placed within the context of lived antagonistic relations, and the need to be examined as they are played out within the dominant and subordinate cultures that characterize school life. (p. 111)

Hence, elements of resistance are emphasized within a critical educational perspective in an effort to construct different sets of lived experiences—experiences in which students can find a voice and maintain and extend the affirming aspects of their own social and historical realities. Freire and Macedo (1987) comment on the importance of this function of resistance for the critical educator:

> Understanding the oppressed's reality, as reflected in the various forms of cultural production—language, music, art—leads to a better comprehension of the cultural expression through which people articulate their rebelliousness against the dominant. These cultural expressions [of resistance] also represent the level of possible struggle against oppression ... Any radical educator must first understand fully the dynamics of resistance on the part of learners ... to better understand the discourse of resistance, to provide pedagogical structures that will enable students to emancipate themselves. (pp. 137–138)

At this point, it is necessary to recall again that, at times, despite the well-intentioned actions of critical educators, there are students whose oppositional behavior is directed toward holding firm to their hegemonic views of the world. Brian Fay (1987) explains that, having internalized the values, beliefs, and even worldview of the dominant class, these students resist seeing themselves as oppressed, and so they willingly cooperate with those who oppress them by maintaining social practices that perpetuate their subordinate position. Freire (1970) identifies this phenomenon as the initial stage of emancipation, where the oppressed, instead of striving for liberation, tend themselves to become oppressors.

> The very structure of their thought has been conditioned by the contradictions of the concrete, existential situation by which they were shaped.... This phenomenon derives from the fact that the oppressed, at a certain moment of their experience, adopt an attitude of adhesion to the oppressor.... Their perception of themselves as oppressed is

impaired by their submersion in the reality of oppression.... The oppressed find in the oppressor their model. (pp. 29–30)

Thus, in light of the forms that resistance takes in the lives of oppressed students, the starting point of any counterhegemonic pedagogy must be the world of these students, from the standpoint both of their oppression and their opposition. Essential to this process is the struggle for counterhegemony and a movement toward more democratic institutional relationships and alternative value systems that are based on a critical understanding of the world and an overriding commitment to the emancipatory nature of human beings.

Critical Discourse

An understanding of the power dynamics that embody the notion of discourse is essential to understanding the purpose that underlies critical pedagogy. For what critical pedagogy represents, in actuality, is an effort to develop a critical discourse in the face of a dominant discourse that has worked systematically to silence the voices of marginalized populations in the United States.

Discourse, here, is defined as a system of discursive practices that reflect the values, beliefs, ideology, language, and economic constraints found within a particular set of inscribed power relations. As such, discursive practices refer to the rules by which discourses are formed, and thus determine what can be spoken and what must remain unspoken; who can speak with authority and who must listen in silence. Thus, discourses and discursive practices influence how we live out our lives and how we interact with others. They shape our subjective experiences because it is primarily through language and discourse that social reality is given meaning (McLaren, 1988).

Critical educational theorists argue that, because knowledge is socially constructed, culturally mediated, and historically situated, dominant discourses function to determine what is relegated to arenas of truth and relevancy at any given moment in time. Thus, they hold a view of truth as relational, in that statements considered true are seen as arising within a particular context, based on the power relations that are at work in society, a discipline of study, or educational institution. This helps to explain why only those discourses that accommodate to the power relations prescribed by the dominant discourse are generally acknowledged, and how these are clearly linked to the question of what they produce and in whose interest they function (Freire, 1985).

Consequently, critical discourse must focus on those interests and assumptions that inform the generation of knowledge itself. But true to its emancipatory principles, it must also be self-critical and deconstructive of dominant discourses the moment they are ready to solidify into hegemonic knowledge. In this way, critical pedagogy can work to replace the "authoritarian discourse of imposition and recitation with a voice capable of speaking one's own terms, a voice capable of listening, retelling, and challenging the very grounds of knowledge and power" (Freire & Macedo, 1987, p. 20).

Critical pedagogy relegates to critical reason the possibility of establishing the conditions of discourse for the raising and reconciling of controversial claims tied to knowledge and power. Here, *critical reason* stands for liberation from all regulations of social intercourse and interactions that suppress the debatability of truth (Forester, 1987). Many critical theorists turn to Habermas's (1970) theory of *practical discourse* and the *ideal speech situation* for a rational standard by which to judge existing discourses. Such a standard suggests that a system of communication can only be free from both internal and external constraints when all participants to a discourse possess equal opportunity to select and use speech acts. John Forester (1987) describes the process as having the following four requirements for all potential participants:

1. the same chance to employ communication speech acts, that is, to initiate and perpetuate the discourse.
2. the same chance to employ representative speech acts to express attitudes, feelings, and intentions.
3. equal chance to use regulative speech acts; they must be equally able to command and oppose, permit, and forbid arguments. They must also have equal opportunity to both make and accept promises and provide and call for justifications....
4. equal opportunity to provide interpretations and explanations and also to problematize any validity claims so that in the long run no one view is exempt from consideration and criticism. (pp. 186–188)

What this concept suggests to critical educational theorists is that respecting different discourses and putting into practice a theory committed to the plurality of voices will require nothing short of political and social transformation. Given this reality, *critical discourse as a transformative act* must assume an active and decisive participation, relative to what is produced and for whom. Freire and Macedo (1987) address this idea through the *reinvention of power:*

> The reinvention of power that passes through the reinvention of production would entail the reinvention of culture within which environments would be created to incorporate, in a participatory way, all of those discourses that are presently suffocated by the dominant discourse. [This] legitimation of these different discourses would authenticate the plurality of voices in the reconstruction of a truly democratic society. (p. 55)

Critical pedagogy addresses this transformative requirement through a discourse that rigorously unites the language of critique with the language of possibility. Here, Giroux (1985) calls for a process of schooling in which educators as *transformative intellectuals* recognize their ability to transform critically the world. In so doing, educators can carry out a counterhegemonic project as they work to challenge economic, political, and social injustices, both within and outside schools. Teachers can work to create the conditions that give students an active voice in their learning and to support their development as social agents who have the knowledge and courage to struggle for a discourse of hope. At the same time, they must also struggle to overcome the discourse of despair that is so often found in the lives of both teachers and students from working-class bicultural communities.

Dialogue and Conscientization

Critical theorists unwaveringly support the Freirian notion of dialogue as an emancipatory educational process that is, above all, dedicated to the empowerment of students through disconfirming the dominant ideology of traditional educational discourses and illuminating the freedom of students to act on their world.

For critical educators, dialogue is never perceived as a mere technique to be utilized for appropriating students' affections or obedience. Instead, it is perceived as an educational strategy committed to the development of critical consciousness through a process of *conscientization*. In *A Pedagogy for Liberation* (Shor & Freire, 1987), Freire contends dialogue must be understood as something taking part in the historical nature of human beings. It is part of our historical process in becoming human beings.... Dialogue is a moment where human beings meet to reflect on their reality as they make and remake it.... Through dialogue, reflecting together on what we know and don't know, we can act critically to transform reality (pp. 98–99).

This dialogical emphasis represents the basis for a critical pedagogical structure in which dialogue and analysis serve as the foundation for reflection and action. It is an educational strategy that clearly supports the principles of what Freire (1970) calls a *problem-posing educational approach*: an approach in which the relationship of students and teachers is, without question, dialogical—students learn from teachers; teachers must also learn from students. The content of this form of education takes into account the concrete lived experiences of the students themselves, as the historical character of their experiences are explored through questions that often begin, "How did we come to be as we are?" and "How can we change?" In this way, critical educators encourage the free and uncoerced exchange of ideas and experiences. They demonstrate a caring for their students and provide them with emotional support to help them overcome their feelings of inadequacy and guilt as they become critics of the social world they inhabit (Fay, 1987).

What dialogue, then, represents is a human phenomenon in which students, with the guidance of the teacher, move into a discovery of themselves as social agents. It is through their encounter with reality that they are supported and yet challenged to assess their world critically and to unmask the central contradictions of their existence. And, in so doing, by way of praxis—the authentic union of their action and reflection—they enter into a process of conscientization.

For Freire (Shor & Freire, 1987), conscientization refers to the process by which students—not as recipients of knowledge, but as knowing subjects—achieve a deepening awareness of the sociopolitical and economic realities that shape their lives and their capacity to re-create them. This implies the critical insertion of a conscientized individual into a demythologized reality. It is this state of conscientization that assists students to transform their apathy—formerly nourished by their disempowerment—into the *denunciation* of the previous oppressive reality and their *annunciation* into a viable, transformed existence. Further, conscientization is conceived as a recurrent, regenerating process that is utilized for constant clarification of what remains hidden within, while students continue to move into the world and enter into dialogue anew.

It is also within the power of this collective dialogical process that the intimacy necessary for the establishment of solidarity and thus collective action can be generated. Within the emancipatory experience of dialogue, students can break the estrangements of their everyday world and enter into a solidarity that is rooted in what Freire calls an "armed love." In a similar vein, Kincheloe (2008b) contends that

> Critical pedagogy believes that nothing is impossible when we work in solidarity and with love, respect, and justice as our guiding lights. Indeed the great Brazilian critical educator, Paulo Freire, always maintained that education has as much to do with the teachable heart as it does the teachable mind. Love is the basis of an education that seeks justice, equality, and genius.... Critical pedagogy uses [dialogue] to increase our capacity to love,

to bring the power of love to our everyday lives and social institutions, to rethink reason in a humane and interconnected manner. (p. 9)

Epistemological Concerns

Darder, Baltodano, and Torres (2002/2009), in *The Critical Pedagogy Reader,* argue that although the critical principles posited by critical education scholars offer a strong foundation for liberatory education, there are several other contemporary epistemological questions that must be incorporated into the discussion. This is particularly salient to establishing a foundation for a critical bicultural pedagogy if it is to sustain its emancipatory potential for all students, particularly working-class students who enter the classroom with a long historical legacy of gendered and racialized inequalities. The following is a brief discussion of these questions, which a number of prominent scholars have addressed in their work over the last twenty years.

Decolonizing Sexual Politics

Significant critiques of critical pedagogy were initially issued by such notable feminist scholars in education as Elizabeth Ellsworth (1989), Carmen Luke & Jennifer Gore (1992), Patti Lather (1991), and Magda Lewis (1992, 1993). These feminist critical scholars and educators called for the interrogation of the missing discourse of power and privilege associated with deep patriarchal tenets of Western philosophical thought that undergirds critical theory. Namely, feminist views challenged masculine notions of technocratic rationality, instrumentalism, efficiency, objectivity, and a privileging of the cognitive domain in the production of knowledge—values considered to permeate the hierarchical structures and pedagogical relationships within schools and society.

Feminist educators argue that in order to create a genuinely emancipatory classroom environment, the specific conditions and struggles that give rise to educational issues tied to gender and sexuality have to be integrated into the curriculum and anchored upon the lived experiences and knowledge forms of female and queer students. As such, critical educators are called to challenge the ideologies, structures, and practices of patriarchy and homophobia that are reenacted daily within traditional public school education.

Additionally, in an effort to challenge what some believe is the privileging of reason as the ultimate sphere upon which knowledge is constructed, critical feminist educators passionately argue for the inclusion of personal biography, narratives, a rethinking of authority, and an explicit engagement with the historical and political location of the knowing subject. These are all epistemological aspects that can support critical educators in both questioning patriarchy and reconstructing the gender politics that obstruct the participation of working-class female students, as full and equal contributing members within the classroom and society.

In the education of bicultural students, these issues are just as important as they are for Euroamerican students (hooks, 2000a). As is witnessed in the works of Black, Chicana, and Asian feminists and other feminists of color, the terrain of gender and sexuality can take similar and divergent cultural twists within different racialized communities (Moraga & Anzaldua, 1981; hooks 1981, 2000b; Minhha, 1989; Mohanty, Russo, & Torres, 1991; Anzaldua, 1995) This requires the willingness of teachers to culturally expand their critical lens when working to make sense of questions of gender and sexuality that arise in their practice with students, their parents, and their community.

Colonizing values, attitudes, and practices associated with ethnocentric perceptions of skin color, gender, the body, and sexuality can easily betray well-meaning educators, in their pedagogical perceptions of female and queer students of color. This is particularly the case when teachers essentialize the needs of bicultural students and inadvertently objectify them in the name of "helping." Again one of the primary issues here is the manner in which the teacher can employ the principles of ideology critique, resistance, and dialogue to critically affirm, question, and challenge bicultural students' perceptions of the world, of themselves, and one another, as they give voice to these areas of their lives that have typically been systematically silenced in public schools.

Teaching in the Borderlands

Similarly, deep concerns related to culture and power were raised among scholars of color intimately involved in the struggle against racialized inequalities within schools and society. Here, one of the "obvious" concerns was the fact that most of the early critical education scholars in the field were "white." At moments in the early history of critical pedagogy, this factor became a source of much contention. In an effort to recenter the discourse, critical education scholars of color, in time, built both metaphorically and concretely on the well-grooved concept of *the borderlands* asserted by Gloria Anzaldua (1999). These scholars insisted that questions of class/race/gender/sexuality be given equal weight in critical analysis of schooling in the United States.

Hence, questions were raised about the failure of critical pedagogy to explicitly treat those questions important to *teaching in the borderlands,* namely issues of race, culture, and indigeneity as central themes. Moreover, there were conflicts about the lack of opportunities to contribute cultural knowledge and new epistemological possibilities that were anchored within specific historical experiences of racialized and colonized populations themselves. When such concerns were raised, there was the danger of being silenced by accusations of "essentialism," particularly when the concerns voiced brushed against the views of leading figures in the field.

As an outcome, critical educators from the borderlands called for ongoing critical engagement with those tensions associated with the expression of voice, agency, and cultural and linguistics differences, when working with students across dominant–subordinate cultural communities. Over the last twenty years, critical educators have begun to theorize more substantively the inextricable relationships among power, culture, and language and their impact on the schooling of bilingual/bicultural students (Darder, 1991; Walsh, 1991; Freire & Macedo, 1995; Foster, 1995; Delpit, 1995; Frederickson, 1995; Diaz-Soto, 1997; Nieto, 2002/2010). The emphasis of this scholarship was not only placed on the production of different readings of culture, history, and society, but also on the political empowerment of those racialized populations who existed historically at the margins of U.S. mainstream life.

The result was the emergence of a variety of culturally and racially defined strands of critical pedagogy. Prominent discourses emerged in the field that included, for example, a *critical race theory* (CRT) of education (Ladson-Billings & Tate, 1995; Tate, 1966; Parker, Deyhle, & Villenas, 1999; Yosso, 2005; Leonardo, 2005; Dixson & Rousseau, 2006) that made central the issue of race in pedagogical discussions, as well as indigenous examinations of schooling, culture, and language (Cajete, 1994; Hornberger, 1997; Klug &

Whitfield, 2002; McCarty, 2002; Gallegos, Villenas, & Braybo, 2003; Grande, 2004); and ecopedagogical reinterpretations of emancipatory schooling and society (Ahlberg, 1998; Bowers, 2001, 2003; Andrzejewski, Baltodano, & Symcox, 2009; Kahn, 2010; Miller, Vandome, & McBrewster, 2010).

These important contributions to the field serve as significant examples of organic resistance to the universalizing of critical pedagogy in ways that could potentially reproduce racism and cultural invasion. Hence, critical scholars from a variety of cultural traditions have challenged the Western predispositions toward orthodoxy in the field, reinforcing Freire's persistent assertion that critical pedagogical principles must always remain open to reinvention. As such, teachers of bicultural students must remain ever conscious of the multidimensionality of oppression at work in the lives of working-class racialized students, who bring knowledge and wisdom centered in their own ways of knowing and being. Through a commitment to be vigilant and to engage social exclusions predicated on ethnocentrism and xenophobia, teachers can enact the principles of a critical pedagogy in ways that can genuinely add, rather than subtract, from the cultural knowledge that bicultural children already possess (Valenzuela, 1999).

Ecological Commitment

The ecological concerns briefly referred to previously represent the more recent generation of decentering efforts to a critical pedagogy. Concerns registered from an ecopedagogical stance question the Western modernizing legacy of progress that anchors the early theoretical underpinnings of critical pedagogy. Here, concerns are connected to how critical theory structures assumptions and meanings associated with notions of humanity, freedom, and empowerment. At issue is the manner in which a critical pedagogy could potentially intensify or reinscribe dominant values, particularly within contexts where nonwestern traditions or indigenous knowledge challenges critical pedagogical definitions of the world. As such, critical principles tied to knowledge production and dialogical relations are interrogated for the potential to essentialize and absolutize knowledge, despite their dialogical intent.

C. A. Bowers (2003, 2001), one of the most strident critics, claims, for example, that the drawback with Freire's perspective of dialogue is not its emphasis on critical reflection, but the manner in which individual reflection is privileged—in the name of empowerment. At issue here are concerns related to the tension of differential power, which can surface between the privileging of traditional forms of communal knowledge and the privileging of individual knowledge, when these two views conflict in the praxis of dialogue. Hence, from an ecological standpoint, there is concern that critical pedagogy, albeit unintentionally, fractures knowledge and supports the further alienation of human beings from nature.

However, in light of such critiques, it is significant to note that, more recently, critical education scholars have begun to seriously engage these questions (Andrzejewski, Baltodano, & Symcox, 2009; Kahn, 2010; Miller, Vandome, & McBrewster, 2010) in an effort to explore the manner in which critical educators can assist students in facing the ecological dimensions so vital to community sustainability. This is particularly important within working-class racialized communities, where the impact of environmental racism heavily impacts the lives of children who reside there.

As such, teachers with a clear eco-pedagogical commitment recognize that a strong, healthy relationship between the environment and communities must serve an integral component of classroom life. This commitment is most important with working-class bicultural children who find in their education the opportunities to reclaim their right to exist and to flourish with a planet that can sustain life for today and the future. Rooted in a deep sense of ecological awareness, a critical ecopedagogy supports critical educators as they cultivate approaches to teaching and learning that go beyond mastery and manipulation, encouraging students to develop a sense of kinship with all life, through an integrated commitment to the ecological welfare of the planet (Darder, Baltodano, & Torres, 2002/2009).

A Critical Bicultural Pedagogy

From this lengthy but useful discussion of critical pedagogy, it should be apparent that the theoretical foundations that constitute a contemporary critical perspective of education are also highly conducive to the educational needs of bicultural students. Coupled with a political theory of cultural democracy, critical pedagogical principles in their reinvention can surely provide the foundation for a liberatory practice of bicultural education—one that can genuinely prepare Black, Latino, Asian, Native American, Muslim, and other racialized students to become transformative agents in their world, on behalf of themselves as individuals and collectively for their communities.

A critical bicultural pedagogy holds the possibility for a discourse of hope in light of the tensions, conflicts, and contradictions that students must face in the process of their bicultural development. A teaching practice based on a framework of critical bicultural education can well prepare teachers to offer their students opportunities to explore their world as they seek also to understand how the dominant culture affects their lives and their view of themselves as human beings. From this educational vantage point, students can undergo an intellectual formation that is both humanizing and integral in preparing them to embrace life within an intimate collective vision rather than an isolating and alienating nightmare.

Through their political awareness of hegemony and cultural invasion, critical bicultural educators can create culturally democratic environments where they can assist students to identify the different ways that domination and oppression have an impact on their lives each day. As participants of dialogue, students can examine and compare together the contents of curricular texts against their own personal and cultural stories of survival, and thus come to understand their role as social agents of change. In this way, bicultural students can experience democratic participation as part of a lived history, as they develop knowledge together, in the spirit of solidarity and a critical understanding of the common good.

A critical bicultural pedagogy can also create the conditions for bicultural students to develop the courage to question the structures of domination that control their lives. In this way, they awaken their bicultural voice as they participate in moments of reflection, critique, and action together with other racialized students who are also experiencing the same process of discovery. In this way, these students are provided with curricular content that is considered culturally relevant and often also language instruction in their native tongues. They are also actively involved in considering critically all curricular content, texts, and classroom experiences, including their own relationships, for the emancipatory as well as oppressive and contradictory values that might inform their thoughts, attitudes, and behaviors. Through this process, bicultural students can develop their abilities to understand critically their lives as cultural and political beings, as well as how to engage actively as full cultural citizens of the world.

If bicultural students are to succeed in American schools, their teachers must enter the classroom with an emancipatory commitment to work toward transforming the traditional oppressive structures and relationships of American public schools. Such a commitment of mind, body, heart and spirit also dictates the willingness to struggle with bicultural students, their parents, and communities, to create decolonizing conditions within the classroom so that students feel welcomed and at home, and also truly find the space and support to become *beings for themselves*.

In summary, if teachers are going to enact a classroom environment that can genuinely meet the needs of working-class racialized students, this will require a critical bicultural pedagogy that uncompromisingly embraces an emancipatory philosophy of teaching and learning. As such, this entails that it

1. be built on a theory of cultural democracy;
2. support a dialectical, contextual view of the world, particularly as it relates to the notion of culture within the bicultural experience;
3. recognize those forms of cultural invasion that negatively impact the lives of bicultural students and their families;
4. utilize a dialogical model of communication that can create the conditions for students of color to find their voice through opportunities to reflect, critique, and act on their world to transform it;
5. acknowledge the issue of power in society and the political nature of schooling; and
6. above all, be committed to the empowerment and liberation of all people and all living sentient beings, including the planet.

The foundational discussion in this book, thus far, has been presented to more clearly inform a theory of cultural democracy and a foundation for a critical bicultural pedagogy. The task remains, however, to consider how teachers can create the conditions for cultural democracy in the classroom and to explore some of the ways that these principles for a critical bicultural pedagogy manifest in the work of educators in the field. Needless to say, the previous discussions have served as the theoretical anchor for the last two chapters of the book, wherein we move steadily to better understand how these theoretical concepts translate into a living praxis—both within the classroom and within teachers' lives.

Bibliography

Adams, F., & Horton, M. (1975). *Unearthing Seeds of Fire: The Idea of Highlander.* Winston-Salem, NC: John F. Blair.

Adorno, T. (1973). *Prisms.* London: Neville Spearman.

Ahlberg, M. (1998). "Ecopedagogy and Ecodidactics: Education for Sustainable Development, Good Environment and Good Life." *Bulletins of the Faculty of Education* 69. Joensuu, Finland: University of Joensuu.

Allman, P. (2007). *On Marx: An Introduction to the Revolutionary Intellect of Karl Marx. Key Critical Thinkers in Education* Series, eds., M. A. Peters & T. Besley. Rotterdam: Sense Publishers.

Andrzejewski, J., Baltodano, M., & Symcox, L., eds. (2009). *Social Justice, Peace, and Environmental Education.* New York, NY: Routledge.

Anyon J. (1979). "United States History Textbooks and Ideology: A Study of Curriculum Content and Social Interests." *Harvard Educational Review* 46: 49–59.

–––. (1980). "Social Class and the Hidden Curriculum of Work." *Journal of Education* 162: 67–92.

Anzaldua, A. (1995). *Making Face, Making Soul/Haciendo Caras: Creative and Critical Perspectives by Feminist of Color.* San Francisco: Aunt Lute Books.

–––. (1999). *Borderlands/La Frontera: The New Mestiza.* San Francisco: Aunt Lute Books.

Aronowitz, S., & Giroux, H., eds. (1985). *Education under Siege: The Conservative, the Liberal, and Radical Debate over Schooling* (pp. 139–162.) South Hadley, MA: Bergin & Garvey.

Au, Wayne. (2009). *Unequal by Design: High Stakes Testing and the Standardization of Inequality.* New York, NY: Routledge.

Bartolomé, L. (1994). "Beyond the Methods Fetish: Toward a Humanizing Pedagogy." *Harvard Educational Review* 64(2): 173–194.

–––. (2007). *Ideologies in Education: Unmasking the Trap of Teacher Neutrality.* Bel Air, MD: Peter Lang.

Bigelow, B. (2006). *The Line Between Us: Teaching about the Border and Mexican Immigration.* Portland, OR: Rethinking Schools.

Bowers, C. A. (2001). *Educating for Eco-Justice and Community.* Athens: University of Georgia Press.

– – –. (2003). "Can Critical Pedagogy be Greened?" *Educational Studies* 34: 11–21.

Cajete, G. (1994). *Look to the Mountain: An Ecology of Indigenous Education.* Skyland, NC: Kivaki Press.

Carr, P. (2010). *Does Your Vote Count? Critical Pedagogy and Democracy.* New York, NY: Peter Lang.

Christensen, L. (2000). *Reading, Writing, and Rising Up*: Teaching about Social Justice and the Power of the Written Word. Portland, OR: Rethinking Schools.

Darder, A. (1991). *Culture and Power in the Classroom.* Westport, CT: Bergin & Garvey.

Darder, A., Baltodano, M., & Torres, R. D. (2002/2009). *The Critical Pedagogy Reader.* New York, NY: Routledge.

Daspit, T., & Weaver, J. A., eds. (2000). *Popular Culture and Critical Pedagogy: Reading, Constructing, Connecting.* New York, NY: Garland.

Delpit, L. (1995). "The Silenced Dialogue." *Harvard Educational Review* 58(3): 280–299.

Denzin, N. (2003). *Performance Ethnography: Critical Pedagogy and Politics of Culture.* Thousand Oaks, CA: Sage Publications.

Diaz-Soto, L. (1997). *Language, Culture and Power: Bilingual Families and the Struggle for Quality Education.* Albany, NY: State University of New York Press.

Dixson, A. D., & Rousseau, C. K., eds. (2006) *Critical Race Theory in Education: All God's Children Got A Song.* New York, NY: Routledge.

Duncan-Andrade, J., & Morell, E. (2008). *The Art of Critical Pedagogy: Possibilities for Moving from Theory to Practice in Urban Schools.* New York, NY: Peter Lang.

Ellsworth, E. (1989). "Why Doesn't This Feel Empowering? Working through the Repressive Myths of Critical Pedagogy." *Harvard Education Review* 59(3): 297–324.

Fay, B. (1987). *Critical Social Science.* London: Cornell University Press.

Fine, M. (1991), *Framing Dropouts: Notes on the Politics of an Urban High School.* Albany, NY: State University of New York Press.

Fishman, J., & Keller, G., eds. (1982). *Bilingual Education for Hispanic Students in the United States.* New York, NY: Teacher's College Press, Columbia University.

Forester, J. (1987). *Critical Theory and Public Life.* Cambridge, MA: MIT Press.

Foster, M. (1995). "Talking That Talk: The Language of Control, Curriculum and Critique." *Linguistics and Education: An International Journal* 7: 129–150.

Foucault, M. (1977). *Power/Knowledge: Selected Interviews and Other Writings 1972–1977.* Ed. C. Gordon. Trans. C. Gordon, L. Marshal, J. Mepham, and K. Sober. New York, NY: Pantheon Books.

Frederickson, J. (1995). *Reclaiming Our Voices: Bilingual Education, Critical Pedagogy and Praxis.* Ontario, CA: California Association for Bilingual Education.

Freire, P. (1970). *Pedagogy of the Oppressed.* New York, NY: Seabury Press.

– – –. (1985). *The Politics of Education: Culture, Power, and Liberation.* South Hadley, MA: Bergin & Garvey.

Freire, P., & Macedo, D. (1987). *Literacy: Reading the Word and the World.* South Hadley, MA: Bergin & Garvey.

– – –. (1995). "A Dialogue: Culture, Language and Race." *Harvard Educational Review* 65: 377–402.

Gallegos, B., Villenas, S., & Braybo, B. (2003). *Indigenous Education in the Americas. A Special Issue of Educational Studies.* Mahwah, NJ: Lawrence Erlbaum.

Giroux, H. (1981). *Ideology, Culture, and the Process of Schooling.* Philadelphia: Temple University Press.

– – –. (1983). *Theory and Resistance in Education.* New York, NY: Bergin & Garvey.

– – –. (1985). "Teachers as Transformative Intellectuals." *Social Education* 2: 376–379.

Giroux, H., & McLaren, P. (1987). "Teacher Education as a Counter Public Sphere: Radical Pedagogy as a Form of Cultural Politics." *Philosophy and Social Criticism* 12: 51–69.

Gramsci, A. (1971). *Selections from Prison Notebooks.* New York, NY: International Publications.

Grande, S. (2004). *Red Pedagogy: Native American Social and Political Thought.* New York, NY: Rowman and Littlefield.

Greene, M. (1967). *Existential Encounters for Teachers.* New York, NY: Random House.

– – –. (1973). *Teacher as Stranger: Educational Philosophy for the Modern Age.* Belmont, CA: Wadsworth Publishing.

Habermas, J. (1970). "Toward a Theory of Communicative Competence." In H. P. Dreitzel, ed., *Recent Sociology.* New York, NY: Macmillan.

Hall, S. (1981). "Cultural Studies: Two Paradigms." In T. Bennett et al., eds., *Culture, Ideology, and Social Process.* London: Batsford Academic & Educational.

Hinchey, P. (2006). *Becoming a Critical Educator: Defining a Classroom Identity, Designing a Critical Pedagogy.* New York, NY: Peter Lang.

hooks, b. (1981). *Ain't I a Woman? Black Women and Feminism.* Boston, MA: South End Press.

– – –. (1994). *Teaching to Transgress: Education as the Practice of Freedom.* New York, NY: Routledge.

– – –. (2000a). *Feminism Is for Everybody: Passionate Politics.* Boston, MA: South End Press.

– – –. (2000b). *Feminist Theory from Margin to Center.* Boston, MA: South End Press.

– – –. (2009). *Teaching Critical Thinking: Practical Wisdom.* New York, NY: Routledge.

Horkheimer, M. (1972). *Critical Theory: Selected Essays.* New York, NY: Herder & Herder.

Hornberger, N. (1997). *Indigenous Literacies in the Americas: Language Planning from the Bottom Up.* Berlin, Germany: de Gruyter Mouto.

Illich, I. (1971). *Deschooling Society.* New York, NY: Harper & Row.

Kahn, R. (2010). *Critical Pedagogy, Ecoliteracy, and Planetary Crisis: The Ecopedagogy Movement.* New York, NY: Peter Lang.

Kanpol, B. (1999). *Critical Pedagogy,* 2nd ed. Santa Barbara, CA: Praeger.

Kincheloe, J. (1995). *Toil and Trouble. Good Work, Smart Workers, and the Integration of Academic and Vocational Education.* Boulder, CO: Westview.

– – –. (2008a). *Critical Pedagogy Primer,* 2nd ed. New York, NY: Peter Lang.

– – –. (2008b). *Knowledge and Critical Pedagogy: An Introduction.* New York, NY: Springer.

Klug, B., & Whitfield, P. (2002). *Widening the Circle: Culturally Relevant Pedagogy for American Indian Children*. New York, NY: Routledge.

Kohl, H. (1967). *Teaching the "Unteachable": The Story of an Experiment in Children's Writing*. New York, NY: New York Review of Books.

———. (1969). *The Open Classroom*. New York, NY: A New York Review Book.

Kozol, J. (1967). *Death at an Early Age: The Destruction of the Hearts and Minds of Negro Children in the Boston Public Schools*. Boston, MA: Houghton Mifflin.

———. (1972). *Free Schools*. Boston, MA: Houghton Mifflin.

Ladson-Billings, G., & Tate, W. F. (1995). "Toward a Critical Race Theory of Education." *Teachers Record* 97(1): 47–68.

Lather, P. A. (1991). *Getting Smart: Feminist Research and Pedagogy with/in the Postmodern*. New York, NY: Routledge.

Leistyna. P. (1999). *Presence of Mind: Education and the Politics of Deception*. Boulder, CO: Westview.

Leonardo, Z., ed. (2005). *Critical Pedagogy and Race*. Boston, MA: Wiley-Blackwell.

Lewis, M. (1992). "Interrupting Patriarchy: Politics, Resistance and Transformation in the Feminist Classroom." In C. Luke and J. Gore, eds., *Feminisms and Critical Pedagogy*. New York, NY: Routledge.

———. (1993). *Without a Word: Teaching Beyond Women's Silences*. New York, NY: Routledge.

Luke, C., & Gore, J. (1992). *Feminisms and Critical Pedagogy*. New York, NY: Routledge.

Mayo, C. (2007). *Disputing the Subject of Sex: Sexuality and Public School Controversies*. Lanham, MD: Roman & Littlefield.

McCarty, T. L. (2002). *A Place to Be Navajo: Rough Rock and the Struggle for Self-Determination in Indigenous Schooling*. Mahwah, NJ: Lawrence Erlbaum Associates.

McLaren, P. (1989/1998). *Life in Schools: An Introduction to Critical Pedagogy in the Foundations of Education*. New York, NY: Longman.

Miller, F., Vandome, A., & McBrewster, J. (2010). *Ecopedaogy*. Mauritius: Alphascript Publishing.

Minh-ha, T. (1989). *Woman, Native, Other: Writing Postcoloniality and Feminism*. Bloomington: Indiana University Press.

Mohanty, C., Russo, A., & Torres, L., eds. (1991). *Third World Women and the Politics of Feminism*. Bloomington: Indiana University Press.

Monchinski, (2008). *Critical Pedagogy and the Everyday Classroom*. Dordrecht, Netherlands: Springer.

Moraga, C., & Anzaldua G. (1981). *This Bridge Called My Back: Writings by Radical Women of Color*. Watertown, MA: Persephone Press.

Nieto, S. (2002/2010). *Language, Culture, and Teaching: Critical Perspectives*, vol. 2. New York, NY: Routledge.

Ovando C., & Collier V. (1985). *Bilingual and ESL Classrooms: Teaching in Multicultural Contexts*. New York, NY: McGraw-Hill.

Parker, L., Deyhle, D., & Villenas, S. (1999). *Race Is … Race Isn't: Critical Race Theory and Qualitative Studies in Education*. Boulder, CO: Westview Press.

Pialorsi, F. (1974). *Teaching the Bilingual*. Flagstaff, AZ: University of Arizona Press.

Pokewitz, T. S. (1978). "Educational Research: Values and Visions of Social Order." *Theory and Research in Social Education* 6(4): 20–39.

Ramirez, M., & Castañeda, A. (1974). *Cultural Democracy: Bicognitive Development and Education*. New York, NY: Academic Press.

Shor, I. (1987). *Critical Teaching and Everyday Life*. Chicago, IL: University of Chicago Press.

———. (1992). *Empowering Education: Critical Teaching for Social Change*. Chicago, IL. University of Chicago Press.

Shor, I., & Freire, P. (1987). *A Pedagogy for Liberation: Dialogues on Transforming Education*. South Hadley, MA: Bergin & Garvey.

Simon, R. (1987). "Empowerment as a Pedagogy of Possibility." *Language Arts* 64(4): 370–382.

Steinberg, S. (2009). *Diversity and Multiculturalism*. New York, NY: Peter Lang.

———. (2010). *19 Urban Questions: Teaching in the City*. New York, NY: Peter Lang.

Tate, W. (1996). "Critical Race Theory and Education: History, Theory, and Implications." *Review of Research in Education* 22(1): 195–247.

Trifonas, P. (2002). *Pedagogies of Difference: Rethinking Education for Social Change*. New York, NY: Routledge,

Turner, P. (1982). *Bilingualism in the Southwest,* 2nd ed. Flagstaff, AZ: University of Arizona Press.

Valenzuela, A. (1999). *Subtractive Schooling: U.S.-Mexican Youth and the Politics of Caring*. Albany, NY: State University of New York Press.

Valverde, L. (1978). *Bilingual Education for Latinos*. Washington, DC: Association for Supervision and Curriculum Development.

Walsh, C. (1991). *Pedagogy and the Struggle for Voice: Issues of Language, Power and Schooling for Puerto Ricans*. New York, NY: Bergin & Garvey.

Warren, S. (1984). *The Emergence of Dialectical Theory*. Chicago: University of Chicago Press.

Weiler, K. (1988). *Women Teaching for Change: Gender, Class, and Power*. New York, NY: Bergin & Garvey.

Willis, P. (1977). *Learning to Labor*. New York, NY: Columbia University Press.

Wink, J. (2010). *Critical Pedagogy: Notes from the Real World*. Upper Saddle River, NJ: Pearson Education.

Yosso, T. J. (2005). *Critical Race Counterstories along the Chicana/Chicano Educational Pipeline*. New York, NY: Routledge.

A Comparative Study of the History and Educational Systems of Australian Aborigines and American Aborigines

Marjorie L. Kopacsi

Marjorie L. Kopacsi, "A Comparative Study of the History and Educational Systems of Australian Aborigines and American Aborigines," *NAAAS Conference Proceedings* (2010), pp. 1137–1151. Copyright © 2010 by National Association of African American Studies. Reprinted with permission.

Introduction/Thesis

The thesis of this paper is that there is a comparison between the American Aborigines and the Australian Aborigines in their histories as related to their educational and political systems. They have suffered and are still suffering from similar levels of marginalization. Marginalization is defined by The American Heritage College Dictionary (Houghton Mifflin, 2002) to mean to relegate to an unimportant or powerless position within a society or group. Both cultures continue to live as underrepresented citizens in their countries of origin.

Aborigine is defined by The American Heritage College Dictionary (Houghton Mifflin, 2002) as a member of the indigenous or the earliest known population of a region. However, the term is often used solely to describe a member of any of the indigenous peoples of Australia and, not necessarily, used to describe the Native American Indians.

A synopsis of one of the legendary myths from one of the aboriginal tribes in the United States is explaining why the snake has no legs. The legend speaks volumes and allows this paper to illustrate the analogy between the historical treatment of the American Indian Nations by the United States government and the Australian Aborigines by the Australian government. The author of the myth alludes to the fact that a snake was walking along the Painted Desert and an eagle flew over the snake and as the snake ran under a rock the eagle swooped down and ate the snake's legs. Are the United States and Australian governments the eagles and did they actually take the American and Australian Aborigine's lands (legs) out from under them thereby marginalizing them? Are the American and Australian governments waging a power struggle with their Aborigines?

Many philosophers have strong opinions about empowered peoples versus powerless peoples. It is often suggested that power is the ability to influence what people say and do. When and where determines who controls or manages. Power is a ubiquitous force that makes some people obedient to others. This may be conscious or unconscious by some (the dominant) but is an effort to exercise control over another person or persons (the dominated). Power reflects back to the powerful and how they have their own values, beliefs, and behavior sets and interests that set them apart from the powerless.

This paper will attempt to examine the realities of some of the areas of historical significance contributing to the marginalization and thus provide support that the marginal or under educating of the indigenous peoples of American and Australia (i.e., the powerless) by their particular governments (i.e., the powerful) is historically significant. The indigenous peoples of the United States will be referred to as Indians and the indigenous peoples of Australia as Aborigines. This issue of marginalization has created significant impact on the lives of all individuals in both countries (i.e., the powerful vs. the powerless).

Literature Review

The Literature Review will provide a historical perspective of the lives of the American Aborigines and Australian Aborigines. To focus only on the comparisons of their educational histories would create a disconnection between their histories and their educational historical backgrounds. As related to the Indians historical background the following thought from Cheyfitz (2001) is significant:

> The Bureau of Indian Affairs in the United States was established by President James Madison in 1824, as part of the Department of War. In 1832, Congress authorized the President to appoint a Commissioner of Indian Affairs, and, in 1834, enacted a bill to organize a Department of Indian Affairs. In 1849, the Bureau of Indian Affairs was transferred to the newly created Interior Department. "By the 1850s, overseeing Indian reservations had become its principal arena of activity. In this context, the term colonialism has a precise meaning: the control by the federal government over what the federal law terms Indian country, which, in broadest terms, includes all federal reservation land; all Indian allotments; and all dependent Indian communities, whether they are residing within a reservation or not. In Indian country, reservation land is land used by federally recognized tribes, but titled to the federal government, which thus has legal ownership of it, keeping the lands in trust for the tribes, of which there are 300 today in the lower 48 states (Cheyfitz, 2001)."

The definition of reservation gives one an inclination and a compulsion to question what was the original intent by the United States government in establishing reservations. "In the United States, an Indian reservation is land managed by a Native American tribe under the United States Department of the Interior's Bureau of Indian Affairs. Reservations were established when Americans began to forcibly take land from the Indians who lived there for thousands of years. The land is federal territory and Native Americans have limited National sovereignty meaning limited independence (or an interdependence) and self-government (Wikipedia, 2007, see Indian Reservation)."

The question is why is it use and not ownership? The word reservation is an opportunity to occupy a venue temporarily and not to own it. If there are about 300 Indian reservations in the United States, why do not all of the country's 550 plus recognized tribes have a reservation? Some tribes have more than one reservation while others have none. Each piece of tribal trust and privately held land is a separate enclave. It seems that this distortion of contiguous lands creates a great deal of ambiguity and fragmentation. In comparison, the Australian Aborigines were forced to assimilate. "By the late 1800's most aborigines had joined white rural and urban communities. Aboriginal people became economically marginalized and were exposed to new diseases. The consequence was massive depopulation and extinction of some Aboriginal tribes" (Siasoco, 2007). While American Indians also faced a history of forced assimilation, then-problems differed from other groups because they were owners of land and resources. A central focus of their activism was on gaining enforcement of treaty rights, not civil rights (Winfrey, 1986)." President Ulysses S. Grant suggested a Peace Policy as a possible solution to conflicts between western settlers and Natives. The policy included a reorganization of the Indian Service, with the goal of relocating various tribes from their ancestral homes to parcels of lands established specifically for their inhabitation.

It took 54 years after the 15th amendment that gave all citizens the right to vote, for the American Indians to gain their citizenship and their right to vote. President Lyndon B. Johnson signed into law in 1965 the Voting Rights Act. This act is scheduled to expire in 2007. In the past Indian's voting blocs have determined the results of some national elections. The threat of this bloc has prompted continued attempts to disenfranchise the American Indian. For example, "the Arizona Apartheid Act in the early 1980's was an attempt to create an all-Indian county and it was implied that this was an attempt to discriminate against the rights of the Indian population to elect representatives of their choice to their county and school board offices (Jackson, 2004)."

In some regard the Australian Commonwealth legislation can be compared to the Indian's voting bloc. In 1962 the Commonwealth gave Aborigines the right to vote in Commonwealth elections in Australia. The 1967 referendum allowed the Commonwealth to make laws with respect to Aboriginal people and for them to be included when the country needed to be counted to determine electoral representation. "In a controversial 1971 land rights case it was ruled that Australia had been terra nullis (having no land) before British settlement and that no concept of native title existed in Australian law. In 1992 this previous legal concept was found to be invalid. Under Section 41 of the Australian Constitution, Aboriginals always had a legal right to vote in Australian Commonwealth elections if their State granted them the right. This meant that all Aborigines outside Queensland and Western Australia had a legal right to vote, but the question is did Indigenous Australians already have the unqualified right to vote in Federal elections in 1962 (Klar, 2009)?"

An important aspect of both of the aboriginal cultures and, therefore, their history is their spiritual beliefs. "The native people of the Southwest and Southeast had full-time religious leaders with shrines or temple buildings. Most Native Americans believe that in the universe there exists an Almighty, a spiritual force that is a source of all life. Is this description unlike all cultural beliefs in a higher power? The Almighty belief is not pictured as a man in the sky, but is believed to be formless and exist in the universe. The sun is viewed as the power of the Almighty. Without the sun, where are we? They are not worshipping the sun, but praying to the Almighty, and the sun is a sign and symbol for that. They assume the souls of the dead go to another part of the universe where they have a new existence carrying on everyday activities like they were still alive. They are just in a different world. (Eck, 1998)"

"In the traditional Australian Aboriginal belief systems there exists a phenomenon know as Dreamtime. This idea goes back into a remote time in their history when the creator ancestors known as the First Peoples traveled across the land, creating and naming as they traveled. Indigenous Australian's oral tradition and religious values are based upon reverence for the land and a belief in this Dreamtime. The dreaming is both the ancient time of creation and present-day reality of dreaming. These cultures overlapped to a greater or lesser extent and evolved overtime. The dream catcher is a result of this belief system as is the ancestral spirits including the Rainbow Serpent and others (Klar, 1993)." These beliefs are very often seen as non-Christian.

United States President U.S. Grant's plan provided and called for the replacement of government officials by religious men, nominated by churches to oversee the Indian agencies on reservations in order to teach Christianity to the native tribes. The civilization policy was aimed at eventually preparing the tribes for citizenship. In many cases, the lands were not ideal for agricultural cultivation or for any other productive purpose. When the Indian Reorganization Act terminated the policy, the American Indians continued to live under the policy. "Today many Native Americans who live on reservations have a quality of life that is among the poorest to be found in the United States. Life qualities in reservations are sometimes so poor that they are easily comparable to the quality of life in the developing countries (Langston, 2007)."

Do the governments of the two countries keep aborigines in poverty? Of all the ethnic groups in this country, Native Americans who live on reservations are the most impoverished. "The Indian land that is privately owned and not controlled by the Bureau of Indian Affairs is far more productive than the land allotted to individual Indians but held in trust by the Bureau of Indian Affairs (individual trust land) or the land belonging to some tribes (tribal trust land) but, also, is held in trust by the Bureau of Indian Affairs (Anderson, 1995)."

American Aborigines and Australian Aborigines remain at the bottom in almost every measurable economic category. They earn only a little more than half as much money as the average citizens of their countries. "Indians are four times more likely to succumb to alcoholism, three times as likely to die of tuberculosis, and nearly twice as likely to die of diabetes (Carlson, 1997)."

The indigenous Australian population is a mostly urbanized demographic with 27% living in remote settlements often located on the site of former church missions. The health and economic difficulties facing the groups are substantial. The remote urban populations have an adverse rating on a number of social indicators including health, education, unemployment, poverty and crime. "This is analogous to the Natives of America where "a steady flow of supplicants coming into the tribal offices at Pine Ridge, which is in Shannon County, South Dakota, the poorest county in America, a place where unemployment hovers around 80 percent, where the per capita income is $3,417 a year, the lowest in the nation, where two out of three live below the federal poverty level. One example of the level of living conditions is eleven people living in a house without electricity on a reservation with a population of about 23,000, where there are 1,200 families on the 10-year-long waiting list for subsidized federal housing. Half a millennium after Columbus misnamed them; American Indians are the poorest people in the United States. This is a 'National Disgrace' (Carlson, 1997, p. W06)."

Education is a large factor in the search for equality for both nations. Education is basically a process that entails strategies and materials meant to influence our thinking and behaviors. This education can be unpredictable and individualized and most often, experiential. It has been concluded by some educators that there are three types of education, formal (schooling), non-formal (training and capacity building), and informal (lived and daily experiences). Education can also be a product or a consequence of the process. The Indian and the Aborigine is truly a student of all three of the types of education, but suffers most often from the consequences of their educational history. The Stolen Generations is a term used for the children of Australian Aboriginal descent who were removed from their families by the government and church missions. The removals occurred between 1869 and 1970.

The government further confused the system by forcing children away from the evil influence of their parents and into schools to gain proper education. Many Aborigines wanted education as a means to adapt, whereas the churches gave education as a means to convert. Most Aborigines were hampered legally because they were not Christian, or legally recognized as British subjects. They could not be tried or give evidence, so they were simply declared to be in a state of war. "This meant there was no need for justice and Aborigines could be dealt with under articles of war. Australian Governor Grey accepted violence against Aborigines for the purpose of order and settler confidence. The British had brought their cultural baggage with them, including the class system, which placed Aborigines in the lowest class of non-citizen. An 1860 report acknowledges the lack of equity and justice toward the original inhabitants. In comparison to the Aborigines, the American government instituted The Boarding School Experience for the Indians (Klar, 2009)."

In August 2005, the U.S. Senate Democrats conferred with more than 150 tribal leaders for nearly six months working on recommendations on Indian country issues. A recommendation was made to amend the No Child Left behind Act to address problems unique to Indians. Amendments were recommended to take into consideration the cultural factors affecting the lack of success of the NCLB Act on the reservations. Senator John McCain, as the chair of the Senate Committee on Indian Affairs, said that "our treatment of Native Americans is a national disgrace (Carlson 1997, p. W06)". In the past, educators believed that the job of schools was to help individuals assimilate into the predominate culture. This was often referred to as cultural genocide. "Historically, education was used as a method of indoctrinating Native American children and undermining their own language, religion, and culture; thus, silencing the Native American culture. In the typical educational institution, Native American students become invisible because of the lingering assimilationist attitudes. The pressure to pull away from their culture has driven Native American students away from education and who they are. They were all forced to disassociate from traditional communities if they chose higher education (Eshelman, 1997)."

"One part of the U.S. Termination policy was the Relocation Program begun in 1952. This program offered one-way bus fare and the promise of assistance in finding jobs and housing in urban areas for reservation Indians, usually younger tribal members with more employable skills (Baylor, 1994; Ziegelman, 1985)." "In 1940, 13 percent of Indians lived in urban areas, but by 1980 more than half were urban (Olson, 1984)." "The Bureau of Indian Affairs estimated that 200,000 Indians were relocated under this program, while the Indian Removal Act of 1830 had forced less than half this number, 89,000 to relocate (Winton, 1999)." "The high point of the termination policy occurred during the period from 1952 to 1962 (Winfrey, 1986)." With the election of President John F. Kennedy the policy went into remission and was formally overturned in 1972.

The "trust" relationship between the tribes and the federal government is at best a double-edged sword. Ostensibly guaranteeing federal protection of Indian assets, it also casts Indians in the role of perpetual minors, a barely veiled version of the classic European stereotype of the childlike "savage". Indians, by definition legally are incompetent to manage their own resources, find these resources placed in the hands of a federal bureaucracy, overseen by Congress, which has historically grossly mismanaged them. The Bureau of Indian Affairs currently finds itself embroiled in an almost five-year-old class action lawsuit filed by the Native American Rights Fund against the Bureau and the Department of Interior for the mismanagement of an estimated ten billion dollars in Indian trust funds since the end of the nineteenth century. In February 1999, as reported in the Washington Post of August 17, 2000, Govern (a Comanche tribal member and outgoing head of the Bureau of Indian Affairs) himself was held in contempt of court for not turning over records in this case, records he claimed "no longer exist" (Cheyfitz, 2001).

Do the United States government and the Australian government have a special relationship with their indigenous peoples?

This special relationship has seldom worked out well for the Indians. Over the last 150 years, the government has tried a series of conflicting ways of dealing with the natives of this continent—making war on them, making treaties with them, breaking treaties with them, sending them to Oklahoma (**The Trail of Tears**), forcing them onto reservations, forcing them off reservations, permitting them to own land collectively, forcing them to divide the land into individual plots, dispatching their children to boarding schools hundreds miles from home, closing the schools and sending the children home, outlawing practice of their religions, legalizing practice of those religions, discriminating against them in employment at the Bureau of Indian Affairs, discriminating in favor of them in employment with the Bureau of Indian Affairs, permitting them to run gambling operations under certain circumstances, increasing funding for the Bureau of Indian Affairs, and in fiscal 1996, cutting funding for Bureau of Indian Affairs by $160 million, or 9 percent (Carlson 1997).

"The South Australian Company lied about not taking land that had not been ceded, and its commitment to a 10% land sales levy for the welfare of the native peoples was quickly abandoned. Neither was its promise to respect the rights of Aborigines and provide adequate welfare upheld. This was due in large part because of the common feeling by 1860 that the Aboriginal race was, 'doomed to become extinct'. Yet before settlement it was thought that even if no one else benefited from colonization, the Aborigines would. Initial relations were encouraging. The government displayed the best of intentions but also the pervading ethnocentricity of the time. Some thought was given to the native welfare but this largely ignored basic Aboriginal life systems and customs (Klar, 2007)."

There were few meaningful employment opportunities for Aborigines and even fewer chances of moving beyond menial tasks. During the gold rush period Aborigines ably filled positions vacated by those who had left for the goldfields. By 1854 there were upwards of 200,000 sheep being cared for by native shepherds in the South-East alone. Yet they were just as quickly replaced when new labor became available.

Later in the early 1900s Aborigines would be refused loans and land grants for no substantive reason. Aborigines, despite their honest intentions and best endeavors to adapt, were exploited by those who employed them. Aborigines for the most part were refused health care and immunization against European diseases. This, along with a poorer diet, reaped drastic consequences. The only time whites paid any real attention to Aboriginal health was when it threatened white society.

Those trying to survive in a traditional manner gathered around degraded waterholes as their lands were fenced in and traditional food sources destroyed. Although Crown leases supposedly guaranteed Aborigines access to and through rights on traditional lands, there was little way of enforcing this. Some aborigines adapted by taking sheep and cattle instead of the declining native fauna and camping in places that whites found difficult to access. With drought problems the Aborigines were forced to accept rations and blankets, or steal, which most often brought strong reprisal from local settlers. This had the effect of pushing Aborigines into centralized food ration depots and destroyed the entire base of their economic systems.

Preliminary Results of Initial Investigation and Findings

UNESCO provides historical and current information from the world data updated for the 6 edition. Their information was updated in November of 2006. The site provided basic information about Australia and specific statistical information about education regarding laws and basic regulations, administration and management of the education system, structure and organization, and specifics of the various levels within the educational paradigm. The site was used for some information, but seemed to be outside the realm of the research specific to the thesis at this time.

There are many areas that the American Indians and the Australian Aborigines have been marginalized and, thereby, underrepresented. Underrepresented groups are inclusive and contextualized concepts. Its essence lies in the fact that it is not static and predetermined as the term minority denotes. In the end, each and everyone is underrepresented in one situation or the other. This concept compels one to explore and to further research the information supporting or dispelling the precepts related to the many areas concerning the history of the American and Australian Aborigine. The historical relationships of disenfranchisement, treaties and land ownership, education and poverty are complex areas deserving more contemporary evaluation and research. "Although the freedom of their ancient way of life has been lost, the religion, culture, legends, and spirit of the American Indian will always endure (Louisiana Office of Indian Affairs, 2007)."

"No serious study of American Indian people can be undertaken without references to the historical, ethnological, anthropological, and artistic work of Charles Bird King, George Catlin and Karl Bodner (Moore, 2008)". These three men were working independently of one another and under differing circumstances, yet they collectively had a unique vision. They were dedicated to preserving the various cultures of American Indian people through their art work and their writings.

Vine Deloria wrote a short essay in 1978 and presented it at a White House pre-Conference on Indian Library and Information Services or Near Reservations, held in Denver, Colorado. It was filed under "Doctrines of Discovery". The essay focused on education, the field that initially launched Deloria's career in indigenous activism. In the first part, he traced the early history of intercultural relations between Native nations and colonial Americans and described the contrasting cultural paradigms of the two peoples. "The English settlers conceived education to be that of memorizing established truths which had passed down from generation to generation by their forebears, while Native peoples sought the maturity of the human personality rather than the transmission of a body of factual knowledge and doctrinal beliefs and [Indian education's] pragmatic approach encouraged individual development and an attitude of intelligent subsistence in the world (Wilkins, 2009)."

Methodology

This dissertation will be written in a qualitative paradigm using a narrative and/or an interview methodology in a theoretical lens will be based on research sources including conversations with Native American Aborigines and Australian Aborigines. Two specific sources will be Brother Charles Schilling at the St. Michael's Navajo School in St. Michaels, New Mexico and Sabina and Keith Evans in Sydney, Australia. The author's personal experiences through research and some experiential activities at St. Michaels Navajo School in St. Michael's, New Mexico have also been a source of information.

References

Anderson, T.L. (1995). How the Government Keeps Indians in Poverty. Wall Street Journal. Retrieved May 31, 2007, from http://www.perc.org/printer.php?id=170 & http://www.indybay.org.

Carlson, P. (1997). In the Year of the Dances with Wolves', Everybody wanted to be on the Senate Indian Affairs Committee. Nearly a decade later, it can hardly get a quorum. The Washington Post. Retrieved May 30, 2007, from http://www.emayzine.com/lectures/indian

Cheyfitz, E. (2001). Doctrines of Discovery. Retrieved July 25, 2007, from www.common-place.org.

Eck, P. (1998). Southwest Food and Religion. Retrieved May 30, 2007, from http://inkido.indiana.edu/w310work/romac/sw

Eshelman, M. (1997). Issues in Native-American Education. Arizona State University. Retrieved June 23, 2007, from http://seamonkey.ed.asu.edu/~mcisaac/emc

Foucault, M.

Jackson, D.R. (2004). Effect of the Voters Rights Act on Indians. Race, Racism and the Law. Retrieved May 31, 2007, from http://academic.udayton.edu/Race/04needs/voting.

Klar, N. (1993) "How did European settlement of South Australia proves to be so destructive of Aboriginal society? "Retrieved July 31, 2009 from www.klarbooks.com/academic/aborig.html.

Langston, D.H. (2006). American Indian Women's Activism in the 1960's and 1970's. Retrieved July 25, 2007 from http://www.indybay.org

Louisiana Governor's Office of Indian Affairs. Indian Affairs. Retrieved May 30, 2007, from http://www.thewildwest.org/native_american & http://www.thewildwest.org/interface/index.php

McMaster, G. & Trafzer, C. (Eds.). Native Universe: Voice of Indian America. National Museum of American Indian, Smithsonian in association with National Geographic, Washington, DC.

Moore, R.J. (2008). The Art and Travels of Charles Bird King, George Catlin and Karl Bodner. VMB Publishers, Vercelli, Italy. National Park Service (2007). History and Culture. Retrieved July 25, 2007 from http://www.nps.gov/trte/historyculture/index.htm.

Principals and general objectives of education. Retrieved June 6, 2009 from www.ibe.unesco.org/Countries/WDE/2006/ASIA

Siasoco, R.V. (2007). Pearson Education, Inc. Retrieved May 22, 2009 from www.infoplease.com/spot/aboriginal1.

The American Heritage College Dictionary (Fourth Ed.). (2002). New York: Houghton Mifflin Company.

Wikipedia, the free encyclopedia. Retrieved June 20, 2007, from http://en.wikipedia.org/wiki/Indian_reservation

Wilkins, D.E. (2009). The right to know: Another Deloria suggestion. Indian Country Today. Four Directions Media, Inc. Canastota, New York.

Winfrey, R.H. (1986). Civil Rights and the American Indian: Through the 1960's. Retrieved from Langston (Ed.), (2006). American Indian Women's Activism in the 1960's and 1970's. http://www.indybay.org

Winton, B. (1999). Alcatraz changed everything. Retrieved from Langston (Ed.), 2006. American Indian Women's Activism in the 1960's and 1970's. http://www.indybay.org.

Ziegelman, K. (1985). Generational politics and American Indian youth movements of the 1960's and 1970's. Retrieved from Langston (Ed.), (2006). American Indian Women's Activism in the 1960's and 1970's, http://www.indybay.org.

A Brief History of Indian Education

Douglas L. Medin and Megan Bang

> As such, self-identification may or may not reject the "sign" Indian—or that which signifies what a "real Indian" is or looks like (often an ecology-loving, bead-wearing, feather-having, long-haired, tall dark man or woman)—and its meanings to others. Brayboy (2005, 434)

Choosing when to begin the history of Indian education necessarily has political implications. The "beginning" of Indian educational history often is assumed to coincide with "European contact." This, of course, is *not* the beginning. Indigenous people had been educating their children to become successful adult members of their communities for millennia. Perhaps the post-contact marker as the beginning can be thought of as the recognition of a significant shift in Indian education. We worry, though, that this practice has the effect of erasing or suppressing the reality of education in indigenous communities in favor of facilitating a short view and the colonial timeline. An even more serious reading of this move is that it reflects the actual stance toward Indian education—as if education only *began* with contact. We begin our narrative of Indian education with post-contact not because it is the beginning, but because it marks a significant shift in the purposes and implementation of education and because our current situations in Indian education are born of this era.

Post-contact Indian education has been an effort to assimilate Indian people into the American mainstream. Some indigenous scholars have called out these efforts as part of the ongoing intellectual genocide of indigenous peoples (Warrior 1994). More generally education imposed in a variety of forms—e.g., through the narratives or histories that are told or not told—has been a central place in which whites have sought, implicitly and often explicitly, to define Native peoples in ways that benefited whites. The narratives and images of Indians produced by the mainstream have shifted from time to time for different (non-Indian) purposes.

For some purposes of environmental education, the constructed image is that of an ecology-loving, feather-having, longhaired, tall dark man like "Iron-Eyes Cody," featured in a Keep America Beautiful television campaign in the early 1970s, with a single tear running down his cheek, whose purpose has been to remind whites of their environmental shortcomings. (Ironically enough, Iron-Eyes Cody was not an Indian but rather an Italian actor.)

For other purposes such as undermining treaty rights, whites argue that Indians should be treated just like them. For example, although the U.S. Constitution is a living document, the U.S.-Indian treaties established much later are seen as "out of date," often because they are perceived to "give" Indians "special privileges" rather than being seen as binding agreements that enabled the creation of the United States. In still other circumstances blatant racial slurs and other forms of racism (e.g., mascots) are seen as socially acceptable when targeted at Native peoples and in some minds are seen as "honoring" Native Americans. While the forms and purposes for white-produced images of Indians shift, they all fundamentally work to erode and assault, intentionally or unintentionally, indigenous sovereignty and self-determination. We'll take up some of the issues associated with these views at the end of this chapter. For now, we want to focus on schools.

Before going into details on schools and schooling, we want to provide a frank overview of a history that often carries over to the present. You may have heard that Indian children are "just not competitive," that an Indian school student would rather get a C and be like other students than get an A and excel over classmates. Some scholars ascribe this tendency to the importance of community over the individual. Although this idea may have merit, it implicitly treats schools as innocent and, if anything, as victimized by this collectivist bias.

But let's try an analogy. Change the setting to World War II and Nazi Germany and suppose that Jewish children were being sent to special schools to be educated with the explicit and implicit message that the Aryan way of life was superior in every way to that of other races. (For the record, we're not endorsing this objectifying construct of race. Race is a social construct, not a biological one, and what may seem to be obvious racial boundaries in one country are interpreted differently in other countries. In the same way there may be historical changes within a country—for example, at one point in the United States, people from southern Europe were not considered to be "white.") You can elaborate this analogy in various ways, but you can see that it's far from obvious that Jewish children in this scenario would identify with the school system or that their parents would push them to get superior grades, even if there were some benefits from doing so.

Is this a bad or inappropriate analogy? Maybe. Maybe not. Arguably, the United States has engaged in actions (e.g., the Sand Creek massacre; mass removals like the Trail of Tears or Longest Walk; or sterilization of Native women without their knowledge or consent) that resulted in genocidal outcomes for Native peoples. There are many instances of events, policies, and whites' attitudes across the United States that encouraged the killing of Native Americans. For example, in 1853 the state of California created a bounty on Indian scalps, a policy that continued up to the beginning of the twentieth century. The school system can be seen as an extension of this policy, focusing on, as some scholars put it, "colonizing" children's minds. One could argue that the United States, until the self-determination era, fluctuated between policies set on terminating Indian peoples' sovereign status, for example through termination and relocation policies which included educational opportunity as a feature of relocation, and policies set on assimilating Native Americans into the mainstream, for example through boarding schools or through mass removal of children (sometimes referred to as the "Lost Bird era"). This removal sent Native youth into predominantly white foster homes in the 1960s and 1970s based on accusations of child abuse. This so-called "abuse" was often defined by claims of cultural differences in childrearing practices or not complying with compulsory attendance laws for schooling. The Indian child welfare act (ICWA) was eventually created to prevent this form of forced assimilation. The school systems characteristically have been positioned as tools in both policy stances. In fact, much of education focused on Indians was defined by Captain Pratt's infamous statement, "Kill the Indian, save the man." The boarding school era of the twentieth century was intended to do just that by engaging in the forced removal of children from their families and communities under the guise of educating them.

A great deal of scholarly work has explored the brutalities of the boarding school era, in which Indian children died in great numbers and severe physical, emotional, psychological, and sexual abuses were inflicted on Indian children in the schools (e.g., Lomawaima 1995, 2000). Depriving children of their families, community, culture, religion, values, and language was the explicit aim of these efforts. There have been substantial changes in education policies directed at Native children, but serious problems remain. Atrocities are often seen as something from the distant past. Well, they just aren't. For many people this is the experience of their grandparents or even later during the "Lost Bird era" mentioned above.[1] Many of the Indian parents of children in K–12 education today experienced this trauma, along with associated educational, physical, and emotional abuse.

There are also enduring, significant issues that are ongoing and not confined to the past. Language is perhaps the most obvious example; most Indian children go to schools or have access to learning environments that are taught in English only. Further, most schools serving Indian children, whether they are tribally controlled schools or not, abide by national rather than Native American standards. Given that we are in the era of "tribal self-determination," there is something amiss with this. Imagine if China or any other country determined the U.S. public education system, its learning goals, assessments, language of instruction, and more. Neither the U.S. government nor the general population would be happy with it.

If this were your collective history and experience with education, would you be single-mindedly focused on having your children do well in school? Perhaps not. Remarkably, many Native nations and communities have demonstrated extraordinary resiliency and a balancing of goals such that success in mainstream education and the vitality and engagement in their own ways of knowing remain focal aspirations. Despite the historical justification for disengagement from public education, academic achievement remains a central goal for many Native peoples and a high funding priority for tribes. Education is often framed as important to improving lives and protecting and maintaining community. Although we're going to talk about science education from Native perspectives, much of what we will have to say likely holds for or is relevant to indigenous education in general.

1. For the story of Lost Bird, see Flood (1995).

Education from Native Perspectives

The story of science education from Native perspectives necessarily comes from a distinct frame of reference. Understanding the history of science education from Native perspectives means understanding the evolution of formalized schooling, with its changes or impositions of new forms of knowledge construction and new (and often alien) frameworks for understanding the natural world. There is much to say about this and we will continue to elaborate on these issues later. Here we provide a brief survey of the larger shifts occurring in indigenous education.

As mentioned in the beginning of this chapter, pre-contact (pre-contact with Europeans, that is) education in indigenous communities is rarely considered in the history of Indian education. Many lives' work could be made detailing the educational practices of indigenous communities from a historical perspective. For our purposes, we first point out that education in indigenous communities did not start with missionaries or the U.S government. There were sound models of education that had worked for tribes for thousands of years to ensure economic, social, and political vitality.

Although many of these models of education may not have been formalized in the way we think about them now, some were. For example the Choctaw had formal school systems for their children pre-contact (Szasz 1977). Post-contact, the federal government would look to these schools as models of success. Many people shared the role of teacher within a tribe. At the same time, there also were individuals who had proven themselves expert in certain areas or who undertook specialized training, and they would be charged with educating all children within a band or tribe (Szasz 1977).

Although there was great diversity across tribes in the practices that needed to be mastered by youth, many Nations shared the practice of using apprenticeship models for teaching. It was standard in Native communities for young people to observe tasks for long periods of time before attempting the tasks themselves. Interestingly, there are contemporary educational researchers who are exploring and documenting this learning and developmental dynamic in various settings (e.g., Rogoff 2003). Most communities had elaborate developmental pathways for their children and clear markers for, and recognition of, accomplishment.

The insertion of religious and federal education into Native education marked a dramatic change in the learning process for Native children. It sought to terminate, devalue, and delegitimize the use of indigenous knowledge in all of its forms (Noel 2002). Within communities, Native people have always had highly developed knowledge of natural phenomena as well as sophisticated technology that improved the quality of life for tribes (Deloria and Wildcat 2001). This wisdom, as we noted earlier, sometimes labeled as "traditional ecological knowledge," is continually being reevaluated, accepted, and, perhaps more importantly, sometimes recognized for its accuracy and efficacy by the "mainstream" American culture. (As an aside, this recognition in itself demands reflection.)[2] But we're getting ahead of ourselves—let's turn to post-contact "education," starting with mission schools.

From at least the seventeenth through the nineteenth century, the goal of Christian missionaries and the U.S. government was to displace indigenous knowledge and values in all forms by "educating and Christianizing the Indian." The major components of this education included speaking, reading, and writing English, with a primary focus on speaking so that Indians could participate in church services (Provenzo and McCloskey 1981). The intent of destroying indigenous knowledge has been termed intellectual genocide and is arguably one of the most destructive forces that Native communities have endured (Warrior 2000).

The establishment of the United States changed these Christianizing educational efforts in important ways. By the early 1800s, with the appearance of the Monroe Doctrine, "promoting civilization among the aborigines" became a central focus of the U.S. government. The thrust of the associated curricula included reading, writing, and arithmetic, as well as a focus on agricultural techniques and Christian religion (Sharpes 1979). The federal government also tried to change hunting and gathering communities into farming communities, conveniently forgetting that they very often had forced tribes onto land not suited for agriculture. During this time the federal government was also subsidizing mission schools to continue the Christianization process. These goals dominated education efforts until after the Civil War.

Perhaps the most well-known counterexample to federal education efforts is the story of literacy within the Cherokee Nation lead by Sequoyah (Foreman 1938; Bender 2002). The impact of written text on the unfolding of the history of the Americas is extraordinarily complex. Sequoyah, respecting the ingenuity of written systems, was convinced that written text was something that all people could master and that it could be useful to his own people. Quite remarkably, he developed an eighty-six-symbol system (now eighty-five) for the Cherokee language, and this Cherokee written language spread very rapidly in the Cherokee Nation. Within just four years the majority of Cherokees were reading and writing. In short, the Cherokee very likely had the most effective educational system for literacy development this continent had ever seen. Literacy rates among the Cherokee were substantially higher than among the surrounding "settlers." However, the introduction of U.S.-run schools led to the demise of Cherokee literacy and academic success, replicating a pattern of failure of U.S. efforts throughout Native nations.

Following the Civil War a further shift occurred, marking a new era of Indian education. Previously the federal government had not forced Indians to attend schools, but rather assumed that Indian people would voluntarily attend them, change their beliefs and practices, and easily assimilate into the American mainstream. As land increasingly became a sought-after commodity, the government's desire to reduce allotted lands increased, as did its impatience with the lack of Indian participation in the mainstream. By the 1880s the government had decided to force education and a specific model of culture on all Indians (Stahl 1979). The creation of boarding schools became the answer to the problem of "educating the Indian."

---

2. There are indigenous scholars who do not see any reason for optimism, and they argue that indigenous knowledge or practices should be left in communities and not brought into schools or other arenas. Though we agree in part, we also think that there are legal developments and institutional changes (e.g., the U.N. Declaration of the Rights of Indigenous Peoples [2007] or increasing sovereignty in our own schools) that invite a more nuanced navigation through this space. Further, we resist the idea that Native children will just have to continue to survive an alien education system rather than having one that reflects their values.

The boarding school era was devastating to Indian communities. Many children were forcibly removed from their families and communities and transported great distances to intertribal boarding schools (Peshkin 1997). The conditions in these schools were horrific—conditions that would ultimately cause the federal government to close them down. The precise death toll of Indian children during this time is still unclear (Heart and DeBruyn 1998).

Boarding schools continued the goals of teaching reading, writing, and arithmetic, but also placed great value on Native children learning European cultural norms and practices. Boarding schools also introduced trades based on gender identity to Indian youth; for example, girls were predominantly instructed in housework and sewing (Szasz 1977). Here's an example that will make things concrete. A Menominee elder once shared stories with Medin about how the wife of the (white) School Superintendent tried to get Menominee girls to become "proper ladies." She described being brought to a tennis court where the girls were supposed to play tennis in long dresses, as was the custom in that day. The elder told Medin, "I just climbed a tree to watch and laugh." But of course the intent behind the goal of creating proper ladies was not at all funny.

The Meriam report (1928) marked another new stage in Indian education, one that is still very active. The Meriam report denounced boarding schools and called for dramatic improvement in Indian education. By 1934, legislation had been passed to petition states and territories to partner with the federal government for the education, medical care, and social welfare of Indian children (Stahl 1979). Essentially this legislation permitted Native American children to attend public schools; it is still what permits reservation children to attend public schools off reservation, as well as allowing for the creation of public schools on reservations. By the 1930s, the curriculum delivered to Indian children was theoretically not different from other children's; however, some Indian historians have argued that assimilating Indian children into mainstream American ideals was still at the heart of education.[3] This legislation also provided for penalties to parents who did not send their children to school (Sharpes 1979) and contributed to the mass removals of children in future decades.

Over the next forty years the requirement that Indian children attend school would remove more Indian children from their families than any other factor. In many ways this legislation allowed for a new form of boarding school. The U.S. Department of Child and Family Services (DCFS) removed Indian children from their homes and placed them with white families because Indian parents were not forcing their children to attend school (Peshkin 1997).

There are several generations of Indian adults alive today that spent at least several years living with white families and attending public schools away from their homelands. Eventually Indian activists and lobbyists called enough attention to these practices that a new law, the Indian Child Welfare Act of 1978, was created to stop the massive removal of Indian children from Indian communities. This law provides guidelines and appropriate procedures for DCFS that ensures that even if an Indian child is removed from his

3. Medin remembers one particular article in the *Weekly Reader* that was commonly circulated in Iowa grade schools when he was a boy. The article was about Indians and the question in focus was whether they should be assimilated or allowed to be different. No one, and certainly not the *Weekly Reader*, questioned the premise that this was a decision to be made by non-Indians.

or her parents, that child will usually be placed with either relatives or other Indian people. Only in very rare instances will Indian foster children be placed in non-Indian homes (see www.nicwa.org).

Of course it is one thing to pass a law and quite another to enforce it. As we write, there continue to be stories of the widespread practice of placing Indian children in orphanages rather than placing them in foster care in Native families. (See for example Sullivan and Walters 2011.)

The American civil rights movement would mark another era in Indian education. Two major pieces of legislation started to change the educational landscape for American Indians. The first, the Indian Education Act of 1972, part of the Elementary and Secondary Schools Act, appropriated monies for remedial programs, bilingual programs, and teacher training for teachers of American Indians, and training monies for graduate and professional studies and facilities improvement. This was important because it provided funds for state-run schools to specifically serve American Indian needs.

The second piece of legislation, the Indian Self-Determination and Education Assistance Act of 1975, led to the emergence of contract schools. Contract schools involved independent Indian school boards contracting with the Bureau of Indian Affairs (BIA) to run their own schools (Noel 2002). This was the first time that there was any form of local control of the educational process. The 1994–1995 school year was the first time that there were more tribally controlled schools than BIA-controlled schools (Tippeconnic 1995). However, given the facts that (1) there are 565 federally recognized tribes and only about one hundred tribally controlled schools, and (2) almost two-thirds of the American Indian population does not live on reservations, non-Indian entities and institutions are still primarily in control of educating Indian youth.

Culture in the Classroom

Over the past thirty to forty years of Indian education, scholars and practitioners have been struggling with the best ways to think about and see culture in the classroom. Demmert and Towner (2003) wrote an extensive review about the ways in which culture has been taken up in educational research.

From their literature review Demmert and Towner propose six critical elements of culturally based education: "(1) recognition and use of indigenous languages, (2) pedagogy that stresses traditional cultural characteristics and adult-child interactions, (3) teachers' pedagogy congruent with traditional culture as well as contemporary ways of knowing and learning, (4) curriculum based on traditional culture that places children in a contemporary context, (5) strong community participation, and (6) knowledge and use of the social and political mores of the community" (Demmert and Towner 2003, 10). Other scholars have argued for a seventh proposed component: incorporation of relationship to place and values associated with land (e.g., Cajete 2000; Kawagley 1995; Ledward, Takayama, and Kahumoku 2008).

There is a growing literature examining these issues in depth and exploring the negative consequences of ignoring them. For example, Philips (1988) did remarkable work focusing on the ways in which gesture, response time, and functions and relationships to silence (among other dimensions) impact education for Native children. She demonstrated that educators' privileging of particular culture norms for gesture, response time, and verbal performance had significant effects on the educators' perceptions of children's learning, engagement, and ability, and conversely had negative consequences for children's perceptions of classrooms, learning, and engagement.

There are three case studies and contexts we will highlight that have demonstrated the power of developing culturally based education, including efforts by Native Alaskans, Native Hawaiians, and the Navajo Nation. These three have been well studied and have had a longevity that is particularly noteworthy. In each of these cases, education systems have been rebuilt from community-based perspectives and have intentionally rooted themselves in the culture and language of communities, but also simultaneously worked to engage contemporary contexts.

Perhaps the most developed model, though, has emerged from Maori communities in New Zealand. Three entire school systems have been developed and implemented at the national level: a normative system in which Western culture and content was the foundation, a language-based system in which students learned the same basic content but in a Maori medium, and a third system based in Maori language and culture (Reid 2000).

In all of these cases the development of culturally based education has been aligned with the increasing assertion of sovereignty and school improvement. These efforts are indicators that we are witnessing the emergence of a new era in indigenous education, one in which self-determination is the leading paradigm (Tippeconnic 2000).

If the history of Indian education seems like a sad history, it is. This chapter has described the history of (assimilative) education of Native children in the United States; we have difficulty seeing why anyone would expect Native children to do well in a system that is so opposed to Native values and orientations. Before moving on, however, there's one elephant in the room that bears some attention. Oddly enough the elephant is often well camouflaged and it is easy to miss. It concerns race and culture.

Tribal Critical Race Theory

In what follows we're going to rely on the scholarship of Bryan Brayboy (2005) and we're going to state the central issue and conclusion right off the bat. "Native American" is treated as a racial entity for many purposes, but Native Americans also comprise many sovereign nations (as we mentioned, there are 565 federally recognized tribes and numerous other state-recognized tribes) with treaty-based relationships with the U.S. government spelling out rights and responsibilities for all parties. Often people wittingly or unwittingly subvert the latter relationships by focusing on race. Racism is an endemic and ongoing issue, but for Native peoples it commonly gets interwoven with the denial of sovereignty in a pernicious way.

Critical race theory focuses on racism and the ways in which the constructions of race and racism are structurally embedded in our legal, political, social, and moral systems. These systems function in ways to keep racism a normative feature of American society and to support white privilege. Numerous education scholars have suggested that these issues play out in education contexts, where issues of racism and inequality are reproduced through the explicit and implicit privileging of whiteness. In addition, the reproduction of narratives of nondominant communities are often damaging at best. Tribal critical race theory (TCRT) makes a number of complementary claims and we focus on four of them (see Brayboy 2005).

TCRT asserts that:

1. Colonization is endemic to society.
2. U.S. policies toward indigenous peoples are rooted in imperialism, white supremacy, and a desire

for material gain.

3. Governmental policies and educational policies toward indigenous people are intimately linked around the problematic goal of assimilation.

4. Tribal philosophies, beliefs, customs, traditions, and visions for the future are central for understanding the lived realities of indigenous peoples.

Brayboy goes on to analyze how the U.S. imperialist mindset led to policies like "Manifest Destiny," the idea that individuals have a right and moral obligation to use lands considered "vacant" because these were not being "improved." This policy was blind to Native peoples' relationships with land (e.g., the idea that land wasn't the sort of thing one could own any more than your grandmother is) and blind or opposed to Native peoples' land management practices. Even modern practices may be so entrenched that their role in preserving the status quo goes unnoticed. For example, although "white supremacy" nowadays is seen as radically racist and condemned, status quo policies such as "legacy admissions" to college[4] continue to be seen as natural and legitimate at the same time as affirmative action policies are being attacked and dismantled.

TCRT argues that Native peoples face the challenge of being both racialized and having a status as legal/political beings. Neither works to the advantage of Native Americans; the former is associated with racism and the latter, as we have noted, typically gets conceptualized as a guardian/ward relationship between the U.S. government and Native nations when trustee/beneficiary may be more appropriate. And perhaps most ironically, these two wrongs make a third wrong—obfuscating Native American legal rights under a trustee/beneficiary relationship by shifting the discourse to one of race, implicitly demolishing the legal/political dimension.

We cannot hope to do more than touch the surface of TCRT. It is multidimensional and far-reaching in its consequences—for example, when participation as a member of a legal/political entity is based on "blood quantum," a racialized marker. But we do *not* see this discussion as a diversion—the intermixing of race and culture is a complex issue for all peoples of color, but its particular historical association with the legal status of the relationship of Native nations with the U.S. government adds another layer of complexity. As we will see in the next chapter, the efforts of Native entities to reclaim sovereignty play out in the domains of education in general and science education in particular.

References

Bender, M. 2002. *Signs of Cherokee culture: Sequoyah's syllabary in Eastern Cherokee life.* Chapel Hill: University of North Carolina Press.

Brayboy, B. M. K. J. 2005. Toward a tribal critical race theory in education. *Urban Review, 37*(5), 425–446.

Cajete, G. 2000. Indigenous knowledge: The Pueblo metaphor of Indigenous education. In M. Battiste (Ed.), *Reclaiming Indigenous voice and vision*, 181–191.Vancouver: University of British Columbia Press.

Deloria, V., and Wildcat, D. 2001. *Power and place.* Golden, CO: Fulcrum Resources.

4. This is the policy adopted by many universities such that if your parent attended the school, you are all but certain of being admitted yourself. Where a school has a history of excluding minorities, as almost all do, this policy perpetuates exclusion and arguably it implicitly perpetuates the associated white supremacy that accompanies it.

Demmert, W. G., Jr., and Towner. J. C. 2003. A review of the research literature on the influences of culturally based education on the academic performance of Native American students. Portland, OR, Northwest Regional Educational Laboratory. Retrieved from http://educationnorthwest.org/resource/561 on May 30, 2013.

Flood, R. S. 1995. *Lost bird of Wounded Knee: Spirit of the Lakota*. New York: Perseus Books.

Foreman, G. 1938. *Sequoyah*. Norman: University of Oklahoma Press.

Heart, M. Y. H. B., and DeBruyn, L. M. 1998. The American Indian holocaust: Healing historical unresolved grief. *American Indian and Alaska Native Mental Health Research*, 8(2), 60–82.

Kawagley, A. O. 1995. *A Yupiaq worldview: A pathway to ecology and spirit*. Prospect Heights, IL: Waveland Press.

Ledward, B., Takayama, B., and Kahumoku, W. III. 2008. *Kiki Na Wai: Swiftly flowing streams. Examples of 'Ohana and community integration in culture-based education*. Honolulu: Kamehameha Schools, Research and Evaluation Division.

Lomawaima, K. T. 1995. *They called it prairie light: The story of Chilocco Indian school*. Lincoln: University of Nebraska Press.

Lomawaima, K. T. 2000. Tribal sovereigns: Reframing research in American Indian education. *Harvard Educational Review*, 70(1), 1–23.

Meriam, L. 1928. The problem of Indian administration. Report of a survey made at the request of Honorable Hubert Work, Secretary of the Interior, and submitted to him, February 21, 1928, Washington, DC: Brookings Institution.

Noel, J. R. 2002. Education toward cultural shame: A century of Native American education. *Educational Foundations*, 16(1), 19–32.

Peshkin, A. 1997. *Places of memory: Whiteman's schools and Native American communities*. Mahwah, NJ: Lawrence Erlbaum Associates.

Philips, S. 1988. Similarities in North American Indian groups non-verbal behavior and their relation to early child development. In R. Darnell and M. K. Foster (Eds.), *Native North American interaction patterns*, 150–167. Quebec: National Museums of Canada.

Provenzo, E. F., and McCloskey, G. N. 1981. Catholic and federal Indian education in the late 19th century: Opposed colonial models. *Journal of American Indian Education*, 21(1), 10–18.

Reid, M. S. 2000. Toward effective technology education in New Zealand. *Journal of Technology Education*, 11(2).

Rogoff, B. 2003. *The cultural nature of human development*. New York: Oxford University Press.

Sharpes, D. K. 1979. Federal education for the American Indian. *Journal of American Indian Education*, 19(1), 19–22.

Stahl, W. K. 1979. The US and Native American education: A survey of federal legislation. *Journal of American Indian Education*, 18(3), 28–32.

Sullivan, L., and Walters, A. 2011. Native foster care: Lost children, shattered families. *All Things Considered*. Retrieved from http://www.npr.org/2011/10/25/141672992/native-foster-care-lost-children-shattered-families on June 3, 2013.

Szasz, M. 1977. *Education and the American Indian: The road to self-determination since 1928*. Albuquerque: University of New Mexico Press.

Tippeconnic, J. W. 1995. Editorial … on BIA education. *Journal of American Indian Education*, 35(1), 1–5.

Tippeconnic, J. 2000. Towards educational self-determination: The challenge for Indian control of Indian schools. *Native Americas: Hemispheric Journal of Indigenous Issues*, 17(4), 42–49.

United Nations. 2007. Declaration on the Rights of Indigenous Peoples. Retrieved from http://social.un.org/index/IndigenousPeoples/DeclarationontheRightsofIndigenousPeoples.aspx on June 3, 2013.

Warrior, R. A. 1994. *Tribal secrets: Recovering American Indian intellectual traditions*. Minneapolis: University of Minnesota Press.